ENGENDERING CITIES

Engendering Cities examines the contemporary research, policy, and practice of designing for gender in urban spaces. Gender matters in city design, yet despite legislative mandates across the globe to provide equal access to services for men and women alike, these issues are still often overlooked or inadequately addressed. This book looks at critical aspects of contemporary cities regarding gender, including topics such as transport, housing, public health, education, caring, and infrastructure, as well as issues which are rarely addressed in planning, design, and policy, such as the importance of toilets for education and clothes washing machines for freeing-up time. In the first section, a number of chapters in the book assess past, current, and projected conditions in cities vis-à-vis gender issues and needs. In the second section, the book assesses existing policy, planning, and design efforts to improve women's and men's concerns in urban living. Finally, the book proposes changes to existing policies and practices in urban planning and design, including its thinking (theory) and norms (ethics).

The book applies the current scholarship on theory and practice related to gender in a planning context, elaborating upon some critical community-focused reflections on gender and design. It will be key reading for scholars and students of planning, architecture, design, gender studies, sociology, anthropology, geography, and political science. It will also be of interest to practitioners and policy makers, providing discussion of emerging topics in the field.

Inés Sánchez de Madariaga is UNESCO Chair on Gender Equality Policies in Science, Technology and Innovation, and Professor of Urban Planning at Universidad Politécnica de Madrid. She is a leading international expert on gender in city planning, architecture, and STEM with extensive experience in both public policy and research. She is a member of the Leadership Advisory Council of the Spanish UN-Sustainable Solutions Development Network and an Advisor to the Executive Director of UN-Habitat.

Michael Neuman is Professor of Sustainable Urbanism at the University of Westminster. He is the author of numerous articles, reports, and plans translated into ten languages. His research and practice span urbanism, planning, design, engineering, sustainability, infrastructure, and governance. He has advised the mayors of Barcelona, San Francisco, Oakland, and Wroclaw; the Regional Plan Association of New York; the Barcelona Metropolitan Plan; and governments and private clients around the world.

ENGENDERING CITIES

Designing Sustainable Urban Spaces for All

Edited by Inés Sánchez de Madariaga and Michael Neuman

Routledge
Taylor & Francis Group

NEW YORK AND LONDON

First published 2020
by Routledge
52 Vanderbilt Avenue, New York, NY 10017

and by Routledge
2 Park Square, Milton Park, Abingdon, Oxon, OX14 4RN

Routledge is an imprint of the Taylor & Francis Group, an informa business

© 2020 Taylor & Francis

The right of Inés Sánchez de Madariaga and Michael Neuman to be
identified as the authors of the editorial material, and of the authors for
their individual chapters, has been asserted in accordance with sections
77 and 78 of the Copyright, Designs and Patents Act 1988.

Trademark notice: Product or corporate names may be trademarks or
registered trademarks, and are used only for identification and
explanation without intent to infringe.

Library of Congress Cataloging-in-Publication Data
Names: Sánchez de Madariaga, Inés, editor. | Neuman, Michael, editor.
Title: Engendering cities : designing sustainable urban spaces for all /
edited by Inés Sánchez de Madariaga and Michael Neuman.
Identifiers: LCCN 2019055669 | ISBN 9780815391739 (hbk) |
ISBN 9780815391746 (pbk) | ISBN 9781351200912 (ebk)
Subjects: LCSH: City planning–Social aspects–Case studies. |
Sustainable urban development–Case studies. | Sustainable living–Case
studies. | Sex discrimination against women–Case studies. | Women in
development–Case studies. | Community life–Case studies.
Classification: LCC HT166 .E534 2020 | DDC 307.1/216–dc23 LC
record available at https://lccn.loc.gov/2019055669

ISBN: 978-0-815-39173-9 (hbk)
ISBN: 978-0-815-39174-6 (pbk)
ISBN: 978-1-351-20091-2 (ebk)

Typeset in Bembo
by Swales & Willis, Exeter, Devon, UK

CONTENTS

FIGURES AND TABLES

Figures

Tables

CONTRIBUTORS

Tobias Berg is a former research associate of the research group "Gender and Diversity in Engineering" (GDE), RWTH Aachen University.

Lucile Biarrotte is a PhD Candidate at the Lab'Urba, Université Paris-Est, France. Her research focuses on the gendered organization and culture of French urban planning spheres, with a research-action approach. She created collaborative tools on her topic: the French-speaking mailing list Urba.Genre (500+ subscribers), and Zotero public libraries on "Genre et urbanisme", "Gender and planning", and "Género y urbanismo". She co-founded the young researchers group GenrEspace, and is a member of UN-Habitat Gender Hub.

Evelyn Blumenberg is a Professor of Urban Planning and Director of the Lewis Center for Regional Policy Studies in UCLA's Luskin School of Public Affairs, USA. Her research examines the effects of urban structure – the spatial location of residents, employment, and services – on economic outcomes for low-wage workers, and on the role of planning and policy in shaping the spatial structure of cities.

Charis Christodoulou has worked as a professional architect/urban designer, a consultant to local authorities for almost 20 years. She is Assistant Professor at the School of Architecture, Aristotle University of Thessaloniki, Greece. She has published numerous articles on housing issues and social exclusion, gender in urban design and public space, urban planning, and socio-spatial transformations. Her current research focuses on studying, planning, and repairing landscapes of sprawl.

Sonia De Gregorio Hurtado is a Lecturer at the Department of Urban and Regional Planning at the School of Architecture of Universidad Politécnica de Madrid, Spain. Her research examines urban regeneration programs and policies addressing downgraded neighborhoods from an institutional viewpoint. She has participated in various national and international research projects and been on short term scientific missions in a number of European universities.

Julie Fairey is a local government politician married to a central government politician and has served on the Puketāpapa Local Board since 2010, as Chair from 2013 to 2016 and as Deputy Chair since then. She hosts one radio show a month on Red Alert Radio. Julie helped establish and grow New Zealand's first feminist group blog, The Hand Mirror.

Clara Greed is Emerita Professor of Inclusive Urban Planning at the University of the West of England, Bristol, UK. She is a chartered town planner and received an MBE for services to urban design. Her research interests include designing for equality, accessibility, gender and the social aspects of planning, and especially drawing attention to those issues that are below the radar of the planners" but are of great concern to ordinary people, such as toilet provision.

Claire Hancock is Professor of Social Geography at Université Paris-Est Créteil, France, and a member of the Lab'Urba. She has a long-standing interest in the gendered dimensions of space and spatial justice, and has published extensively on these issues, with an emphasis on large cities in Europe and the Americas. She strives to bring intersectional perspectives to bear on urban gender main-streaming policies, and work with local authorities to make their public spaces more truly inclusive.

Jade Kake (Ngāpuhi, Ngāti Whakaue, Te Whakatōhea) is an architectural designer, writer, and housing advocate. Her practice is focused on working with Māori organizations on their marae, papakāinga and civic projects, and in working with mana whenua groups to express their cultural values and narratives through urban design. She has written for a variety of housing and architecture magazines and contributed chapters to several books on architecture and urbanism. She lives and works in Whangārei.

Sibylle Kelp-Siekmann (Dipl.-Ing.) is a graduate of the TU Dortmund University, Faculty of Spatial Planning. She worked from 1983 to 2014 at the Regionalverband Ruhr, Essen (Regional Association Ruhr) in different fields of town planning as well as in issues of regional development – including the gender perspective. Currently she is a speaker of the Woman's Network Ruhr Area in connection with other regional and European networks.

Gudrun Kemmler-Lehr is Equal Opportunities Officer at the Regionalverband Ruhr in Essen, Germany. Her responsibilities include classical equality work and cross-sectional tasks in the areas of action of the RVR, with a focus on fields of spatial planning. She is managing director and spokeswoman of the Women's Network Ruhrgebiet and chairperson of the Commission Women in the City at the German Association of Cities.

Bente Knoll holds a Master's in Landscape Planning and Architecture, and a PhD in Transport and Traffic Planning. She is managing director of B-NK GmbH Büro für nachhaltige Kompetenz (Consultancy for Sustainable Competence) – an SME specializing in integrating gender and diversity perspectives in research and consulting processes in the STEM field, urban and transport planning, mobility research, and sustainable development. She is also a Lecturer at the Technical University in Vienna.

Carmen Leicht-Scholten is Head of the research group Gender and Diversity in Engineering, Faculty of Civil Engineering, RWTH Aachen University, Germany. A political scientist, she has worked in science and technology studies for many years, building bridges between engineering and social sciences. Her research areas are the social embeddedness of technology, sustainability with focus on social responsibility, engineering education, and social innovation. She is rector's delegate for socially responsible education.

Anastasia Loukaitou-Sideris is Professor of Urban Planning at UCLA and Associate Dean of the UCLA Luskin School of Public Affairs, USA. She is the co-author of *Urban Design Downtown* (1998), *Sidewalks* (2009), *Transit-Oriented Displacement or Community Dividends?* (2019), and the co-editor of *Jobs and Economic Development in Minority Communities* (2006), *Companion to Urban Design* (2011), *Informal American City* (2014) and *The New Companion to Urban Design* (2019).

Nuno Marques da Costa has a PhD in Human Geography. He is an Auxiliary Professor at the Institute of Geography and Spatial Planning (IGOT) and a researcher at the Centre for Geographical Studies (CEG) of the University of Lisbon. Research interests include transport and mobility, urban modeling, quantitative methods, regional planning, and public policies evaluation.

Emma McInnes is the Co-founder and Chair of Women in Urbanism, Aotearoa New Zealand and Designer for MRCagney Pty Ltd., New Zealand. Emma is a walking and cycling advocate and is currently studying to be a planner and urban designer. She has experience in design, branding, communications, illustration, research, campaigns, and event management.

Yamini Narayanan is Senior Lecturer in International and Community Development at Deakin University, Melbourne, Australia. She is the author of *Religion, Heritage and the Sustainable City: Hinduism and Urbanisation in Jaipur* and editor of *Religion and Urbanism: Reconceptualising Sustainable Cities for South Asia.* Her research is supported by two Australian Research Council grants.

Michael Neuman is Professor of Sustainable Urbanism at the University of Westminster, UK. He is the author of numerous books, articles, reports and plans, translated into ten languages. His research and practice span urbanism, planning, design, engineering, sustainability, infrastructure, and governance. He has advised the mayors of Barcelona, San Francisco, Oakland, and Wroclaw; the Regional Plan Association of New York; the Barcelona Metropolitan Plan; and governments and private clients around the world.

Inés Novella Abril holds a Master's in Architecture and a Master's in Equal Opportunities. She is a member of the UNESCO Chair on Gender Equality Policies in Science, Technology, and Innovation of the Universidad Politécnica de Madrid, Spain. Her research focuses on gender-sensitive architecture and urban planning, and on gender policies in STEM. She has coordinated a number of national and international projects on gender in STEM, with a focus on spatial planning and design.

Camilla Perrone holds a PhD in Urban, Regional, and Environmental Design. She is associate professor of Urban and Regional Planning at the University of Florence, Italy. She is founding Director of the Research Laboratory of Critical Planning and Design and Coordinator of the PhD Program on Urban and Regional Planning and Design. She has served in numerous academic roles at UniFi, University of Tübingen, City Futures Research Centre, UNSW in Sydney, York University in Toronto and other European universities.

Margarida Queirós holds a PhD in Human Geography from the University of Lisbon, Portugal. She is an Associate Professor at the Institute of Geography and Spatial Planning (IGOT) and a researcher at the Centre for Geographical Studies (CEG), of the University of Lisbon. Research interests include gender mainstreaming in urban and spatial planning, mobility, and work–life arrangements, gender equality in research and teaching institutions.

Dory Reeves is a PhD and the Principal of Reeves and Associates. She lives in Aotearoa New Zealand; an urban planner and Fellow of the Royal Town Planning Institute specializing in planning for equality and diversity and cities for all. She has written the books *Management Skills for Effective Planners* (2016), *Planning for Diversity* (2005), *Gender and Urban Planning, for UN-Habitat* (2010), and *Te Whaihanga*, bit.ly/tewhaihanga.

Inés Sánchez de Madariaga is UNESCO Chair on Gender Equality Policies in Science, Technology and Innovation, and Professor of Urban Planning at Universidad Politécnica de Madrid, Spain. She is a leading international expert on gender in city planning, architecture, and STEM with extensive experience in both public policy and research. She is a member of the Leadership Advisory Council of the Spanish UN-Sustainable Solutions Development Network and an Advisor to the Executive Director of UN-Habitat.

Teresa Schwaninger holds a Master's Degree in Spatial Planning and a Bachelor Degree in Geography. Between 2013 and 2016 she worked as a project coordinator and junior researcher at B-NK GmbH Büro für nachhaltige Kompetenz (Consultancy for Sustainable Competence), located in Vienna/Austria.

Jeanette Sebrantke is a Spatial and Urban Planner and works at the Ruhr Regional Association, the municipal association for the Ruhr Metropolis. As part of regional development, she is a specialist planner with a special focus on gender issues in regional planning. Sebrantke leads a working group, Metropolis Ruhr fair plan, with the claim of integrating the possibilities and necessities of a gender-equitable planning into the planning of the Ruhr Regional Association.

Linda Steuer-Dankert is Research Associate at the research groups, Gender and Diversity in Engineering (GDE) and the Technology and Innovation Management Group (TIM) at RWTH Aachen University, Germany. As a graduate business psychologist, her research fields cover the context between innovation and diversity, diversity management, change management, innovation management, as well as labor research. In this frame she is integrated in the Cluster of Excellence "Internet of Production".

Mechtild Stiewe is a Spatial Planning Engineer from the University of Dortmund, currently working at ILS, Research Institute for Regional and Urban Development in Dortmund, Germany. Her research interests focus on mobility management, sustainable transportation development and traffic planning, gender mainstreaming and evaluation methods and impact measurements of traffic.

Roja Tafaroji is a PhD student at the University of Auckland, New Zealand. In her PhD research, Roja developed a theoretical and methodological framework to approach "difference" in the society of differences by applying place attachment as well as incorporating a feminist postcolonial approach into both the practice and theory of planning. Roja is interested in applying a mix of methods and techniques in bottom-up planning approaches, informing policies in order to promote equitable outcomes.

Elena von den Driesch is Research Associate at the research group, Gender and Diversity in Engineering (GDE) at RWTH Aachen University, Germany. She studied Sociology, Psychology, and English Literature at RWTH Aachen University. Her research focuses on educational equality and diversity, the evaluation of talent development programs as well as gender and diversity in the engineering sciences.

Eva Zombori is a full member of the New Zealand Planning Institute and she is currently working as a Principal Urban Designer for the Strategy Unit of the Auckland Design Office at Auckland Council. Eva's professional interest is in how to achieve gender equality through urban design policymaking.

ACKNOWLEDGMENTS

A good number of the contributions to this book have been produced as a result of activities carried out within the framework of the policy-driven network Gender, Science, Technology and Environment (genderSTE). The editors would like to acknowledge the European COST Association for the funding of the activities of genderSTE during the years 2012–2016, along with the editors of *Town Planning Review*, in which a number of these chapters were originally published in a special issue titled "Planning the Gendered City", volume 87, number 5.

Inés Sánchez de Madariaga and Michael Neuman
Editors

Sonia De Gregorio Hurtado
Assistant Editor

1

PLANNING THE GENDERED CITY

Inés Sánchez de Madariaga and Michael Neuman

Women and gender became more prominent issues in city planning and architecture in the 1970s, propelled by activists and scholars whose ideas seeped into practice, even as they were fueled from practice in the feminist movements of the era. Prior to this, initial forays were made by pioneers in the US including Catherine Bauer Wurster (Bauer 1934; Wurster 1963), Jane Addams (Knight 2005), Jaqueline Tyrwhitt (Shoshkes 2013). In Europe, collaborative efforts uniting female patrons, architects, social reformers and designers contributed to the building of a great number of women's spaces in Berlin from the German unification in 1871 to the end of World War I (Stratigakos 2008). These included housing, restaurants, schools, and exhibitions halls. Women have long played important roles in urban development as patrons and social reformers (Durning & Wrigley 2000).

However, conventional histories of planning and architecture do not always acknowledge these roles, or, more importantly, their impact on the built environment. A case in point is the key role played by Henrietta Barnett in the building of Hampstead Garden Suburb (Hall 1988). While the roles of Ebenezer Howard and Raymond Unwin in the development and design of this most important example of 20th-century urbanism is taught in planning courses around the world, the role played by Barnett in securing actual development and buying the land goes mostly unnoticed. Yet without it, Hampstead as a model garden suburb would not have been built. Histories have also typically missed the pioneering housing complexes designed for professional women who did not have time to devote to overseeing that domestic chores were properly carried out by service personnel.

Women were also active in those earlier times in countries not well represented in the mainstream planning literature, such as Spain. There, the accomplishments of women such as Concepción Arenal, founder of Spanish feminism, who established a company devoted to building cheap homes for workers, reformed the prison system, and was the first woman to attend university in 1841 (Martínez et al. 2000) often go unnoticed. Of course there are many other less well-known women pioneers, in Spain and many other countries, who need to be found in local and national historical research sources and archives, and brought into the light of planning and its history. This would serve to give a fairer and more balanced representation of the role women played individually, as professionals, patrons, or social reformers, and through collective action, in shaping urban environments, and how they addressed gender or women's issues as they would have been called at the time, during the 19th and early-to-mid-20th centuries.

These activist-professionals practiced primarily, and some came to the academy on the strength of their accomplishments. Since the beginning of the 1970s, a more academic outlook prevailed in the US with the work of pioneering academics such as Dolores Hayden, Susana Torre, Karen Franck, Mary McLeod, Joan Ockman, Daphne Spain, Diana Agrest, Sandra Rosenbloom, and many others. Although significant research was also produced in Europe from the 1980s by Clara Greed, Marion Roberts, Chris Booth, Jos Boys, Dory Reeves, Teresa Boccia, Sasa Lada, Liisa Horelli, Inés Sánchez de Madariaga, and others, the European approach was overall more practically oriented. Matrix, the Women Design Service in the UK (Matrix 1984; Berglund & Wallace 2013), or the Eurofem network in Scandinavia (Horelli, Booth, & Gilroy 2000) are good examples of this, as well as specific initiatives developed both by public administration in many countries, such as in Oslo (Ministry of Environment 1993), by professional associations, such as the British Royal Town Planning Institute (RTPI) (Reeves 1989) and more recently by academic entities such as the UNESCO Chair on Gender in Science Technology and Innovation based at Universidad Politécnica de Madrid, in Spain (Sánchez de Madariaga 2020). In Latin America, women architects and planners have approached the issue from a mostly activist position, even if sometimes grounded in the academy. A case in point is the network Mujer y Habitat de América Latina.[1]

The development of these experiences was supported by insights resulting from those early gendered approaches to the city and its living practices, tracing the differences in experiencing urban space by the two genders. Moreover, the gender-sensitive approach to cities and their planning and design was abetted by a European-wide legal framework developed since 1998, when the Treaty of Amsterdam included a requirement for gender mainstreaming in all spheres of public policy (Council of Europe 1998; Sánchez de Madariaga 2003). Today, although the practical experience of gender planning is uneven across countries in Europe, fragile in many cases, and generally far from real institutionalization, it is true that specific experiences are widespread and gender is finally becoming embedded in the city-building agenda (Sánchez de Madariaga & Roberts 2013).

The current context is quite different from the one in which earlier, pioneering work on women and gender in cities, planning, and architecture took place. While the situation of women has greatly improved in terms of access to employment, full integration, and equal recognition is still far into the future. It is worth mentioning that an increasing number of women among students in the professions of the built environment translates very unevenly into their actual participation in the work-force and in decision-making in those professions, which in most countries has remained heavily male dominated (De Graft-Johnson, Manley, & Greed 2005; Sán-chez de Madariaga 2010). At the same time, care of the home and of dependents continues to be basically women's work, as the statistics produced by Eurostat demonstrate.[2]

Thus, built environments need to better respond to gender-specific needs aris-ing from new societal challenges, which imply profound social and economic changes. Such changes include evolving and less-predictable life cycles for both men and women, the reduction in birthrates, the diversification of household structures, including the increase of single-person and female-headed households with children, the aging of the population with mostly female higher quintiles, a mostly female population of care givers, whether at home or in public or pri-vate services, and the increasing racial and ethnic diversification of societies.

"Intersectionality", a new concept referring to the ways in which discrimin-ation affects groups and individuals in whom more than one potential trait of discrimination coalesce – because of gender, race, ethnicity, age, socio-economic status, etc. – and are for this reason in positions of greater vulnerability, is an increasingly important focus of attention for both research and policy.

While economic growth in the developing world is substantially improving the quality of life of many, increasing economic disparities within countries and reduction of safety nets in Europe and elsewhere at the aftermath of the crisis, provide for more unstable contexts for many in the developed world. Greece is a case in point, but significant sections of the population in Southern European, as well as Northern European countries, live in situations of greater precarious-ness than became the norm in the last half of the 20th century, as the "jobs for life" typical of the Fordist period have all but disappeared and the safety nets provided by welfare state provisions are trimmed across the continent. Women and children in Europe are over-represented among those living in precarious conditions.

Factoring in gender-specific concerns allows planners and designers to provide and enable a physical environment where daily life is better supported than it is today. Additionally, as new urban issues arise in relation to environmental chal-lenges, technological developments, globalization, and the aspiration of reaching the UN Sustainable Development Goals by improving the quality of life of people around the globe, means that research and action need to address these issues while at the same time properly integrating gender considerations.

We expect that the key contribution of this book will be to assert that it is time once again to bring women and gender to the forefront of the research agenda in planning. It is an important moment from the point of view of urban policy, with major ongoing international developments: the New Urban

Agenda, the Agenda 2030 for Sustainable Development, the Paris COP Agreement on Climate Change, the Sendai Agreements, and others.

Within this context, as existing European and national legislation on gender mainstreaming in city building is further implemented, we need to inform these developments with gender-aware theoretical and conceptual frameworks and with the necessary empirical data fitted to present and especially future contexts. This potentially positions planners as leaders in setting the urban research, policy, and design agendas. This book addresses a number of relevant topics for this advancement of gender into contemporary planning agendas.

The chapters in this book cover key topics that are central to gendered approaches to planning, authored by mostly European and North American scholars whose focus goes in a number of cases beyond these geographical areas to also include other parts of the world.

The persistent disparities that women face in cities and in rural areas are pertinent to planners and policymakers. In those parts of the world that international organizations refer to as "emerging economies" or "the developing world", wealth and other disparities are more pronounced. In the developing world women still face massive material needs and suffer explicit legal discrimination in terms of gender equality, for instance in access to property and inheritance rights (Giovarelli & Wamalwa 2011). In countries where water, energy, or sanitation is not widely accessible, women spend endless hours fetching for water and biomass because they cook without a steady source of energy and many still wash by hand. Lack of access to water, sanitation, and toilets in homes and schools is a major cause of girls not getting educated, resulting in reduced employment opportunities for adult women, and of sexual violence against them.

Clara Greed looks at global sanitation issues with particular reference to the needs of girls and women in respect of toilet provision in her chapter, "Public Toilets: The Missing Component in Designing Sustainable Urban Spaces for Women". Over two billion people lack adequate toilet provision and women are particularly badly affected. Fifty percent of schoolgirls in Africa leave school when menstruation starts because of lack of school toilets, thus undermining education and development goals. Greed's chapter also addresses the public toilet situation in the West with particular reference to inadequate provision in the United Kingdom. Historically, women have been given fewer facilities than men, but arguably their need is greater. Lack of toilets has implications for health and wellbeing by restricting the mobility of the elderly, those with disabilities and children, undermining, as a result, sustainability, transportation, inclusive urban design, and regeneration policies. Ways of integrating toilet provision into city-wide strategic planning policy and into local urban design are discussed in this chapter as crucial elements to creating sustainable, efficient, accessible, and equitable cities.

For the many millions in the next higher income bracket, who do have access to electricity and energy for cooking, among whom there are many who do not have access to washing machines, not even shared ones, washing by hand is a major obstacle to freeing time for education and gainful employment. In Europe, the widespread access to washing machines during the middle of the 20th century has been a major factor allowing women the time to educate themselves and enter the labor force in big numbers. One co-author of this chapter has argued elsewhere, in an op-ed written for UN-Habitat, that access to washing machines could be a good indicator to measure progress in three concurrent agendas – i.e. the New Urban Agenda of Habitat III, the Sustainable Development Goals, and the Climate Change Agreements – that would simultaneously take into consideration their gender equality implications (Sánchez de Madariaga 2015).

According to Rosling[3] only two billion people today have access to private washing machines, while washing linen and clothing for many from among the remaining five billion people in the world is done by women who spend many hours every day washing by hand. Following Rosling's estimations, when the two billion people today under the poverty line and the additional two billion impoverished persons expected to gain access to electricity in the coming years do so, it is imperative that we look at the gender dimensions of how this happens. Ensuring access to washing for these wide sections of the population in the so-called developing world will have very significant implications in terms of urban infrastructure and planning, use of energy, and emissions into the atmosphere. A significant increase in the number of women in the segment of those who have access to *both* electricity *and* washing machines will prove a key leap forward for gender equality in the world. But this cannot happen in an environmentally sustainable way without a very significant change in energy production and in consumption patterns by people in the upper-income bracket. Again, according to Rosling, given current trends, this group will consume more than half of the world's energy, which consumption itself is projected to almost double. This unsustainable pattern needs to be cut by half or more, through more efficient use of energy and increased use of green energy.

The transportation sector, which has significant gender implications as shown in the chapters by Loukaitou-Sideris and Blumenberg, is one sector in which important changes need to occur in order to reduce environmental impacts and energy consumption. The potential negative implications for gender equality in urban policies that prioritize environmental objectives are illustrated within a First-World context by Evelyn Blumenberg in her chapter, "Why Low-Income Women Need Cars in the U.S.". Drawing on a diverse body of literature and data, she shows why low-income women need automobiles. Their demand for cars emerges from the shifting geographic location of employment and homes, the characteristics of women's work and the labor market, and women's household responsibilities. A growing body of scholarship on the role of automobiles in shaping outcomes for low-income women shows how those who are able to access automobiles experience a host of benefits including better employment opportunities, access to healthier food, and greater health-care use. In spite of this evidence, there are relatively few efforts to increase automobile use among low-income households in the US, likely due to the costs and the negative environmental externalities associated with driving. Programs and policies that have proven to be effective are discussed. Blumenberg argues that if automobiles are essential to women's livelihoods, policies ought to balance the need for automobiles with efforts to reduce their negative environmental impact.

While today in many of the OECD countries basic material needs are mostly covered, women still tend to face greater constraints than men in their daily lives. These constraints relate to: (i) unequal access to employment, including the gender pay gap and greater part time employment for women; (ii) greater home and caring responsibilities; (iii) and scarce free time for leisure and self-care. Urban structures and transportation systems put constraints on the movements of persons who have to juggle care responsibilities and paid employment, including the lack of sufficient and adequately located and accessible support services for caring for the young and the old, as is explained below. Factors contributing to this state of affairs include gender stereotypes, gender bias, which can sometimes be unconscious, and discrimination – both direct and indirect – even in Europe despite it technically being illegal (Sánchez de Madariaga et al. 2011).

Contemporary labor markets across the world show both vertical and horizontal gender segregation, both of which contribute to women's greater economic fragility. Horizontal segregation occurs when women are concentrated in jobs traditionally considered feminine jobs, mostly in the health, the educational, and the service sectors. These are often less well paid compared with jobs in male-dominated professions such as engineering. Vertical segregation happens when women concentrate on the lower rungs of any profession, which happens independently of the degree of feminization of professional fields, and is sometimes explained in terms of the "glass ceiling". Contrary to what some might expect, horizontal segregation is greater in the Scandinavian countries, which also have the greatest participation of women in the workforce.[4] This is explained by how Scandinavian countries have transferred care activities into paid employment, mainly in the form of public services. Yet for the most part, women perform the same caring functions as before.

As a result of gender roles and sexual divisions of labor, women face what has been called a "double workload", in paid employment and in the home. The Harmonized European Time Use Statistics (HETUS) – the European survey on the use of time – and the United States Bureau of Labor Statistics both still show very significant gender differences in the time allocated to work, to household tasks, and to leisure. Within Europe there remain great variations between countries, but these are slowly converging over time. While women have joined the labor force in great numbers, the mirroring movement of men engaging in household chores is advancing at a much slower pace. Women take responsibility for the greater share of care work in the home, including both personal and household chores. With the aging of the population, the care of elderly persons implies even greater demands on time for care givers than the childcare requirement of previous generations. Because women live longer, the majority of the elderly population are women, and most of the people who care for them are also women.[5] The issue of care and its urban implications are crucial for women.

In her chapter "A Gendered View of Mobility and Transport", Loukaitou-Sideris addresses the implications of gender roles and differences in employment and care activities in urban environments through the lens of transportation. She argues that women's mobility in cities is not only challenged by physical, economic, cultural, and psychological constraints but also inadequate transportation policies that often neglect or disregard women's needs. Women have distinct mobility needs and travel patterns while, at the same time, important differences exist among women based on socio-demographic characteristics and geographic contexts. Such differences and nuances are not always understood and much less addressed by policymakers. Gender distinctions in travel patterns hold true for both the Global North and the Global South.

It is important to note that we need to look at these categories of "Global North" or "Global South", or First World, and developing world, cautiously.[6] We use them as useful metaphors, but we must be clear that the boundaries between rich and poor at a global level are not geographically clear any longer and they are rapidly evolving, with countries under the developing tag increasingly dissimilar. Statistician Hans Rosling has argued that what most people think of as the divisions between the "developed" and "developing world" no longer exist, that using the term "developing world" is intellectually lazy, and that we should classify countries more precisely.[7] Moreover, many wealthy countries have rural areas, towns, and urban neighborhoods that resemble emerging economy countries. Conversely, many emerging nations have areas that resemble advanced nations.

Where do we stand with respect to gender mainstreaming in the planning arena? Some chapters address this topic and provide forward-looking suggestions. Camilla Perrone analyses the international debates on the New Urban Agendas to reflect on the need to reconceptualize gender as a constitutive versus a nominal essence. Inés Novella provides evidence of how practical tools such as Gender Impact Assessments can be used for engendering the planning and design phases of important urban regeneration projects. Dory Reeves contributes a New Zealand perspective on gender and planning, showing a gender-neutral approach resulting from the subordination of the feminist discourse to the discourse on culture and ethnicity, which is a feature of the country.

What We Have Learned, Where We Need to Go

What should feminists and gender-sensitive planners and scholars be thinking about and doing now so that future conditions for women will be better in both developed and developing countries? We first posit the obvious, that women in the so-called developing world need to have basic material needs equivalent to those in OECD countries, which we take for granted. Yet given this, we hasten to add that the same profligacy and impacts on the environment that First-World acquisition of material wealth by expropriation of the natural environment and exploitation of the cultural environments at home and elsewhere should not be replicated. Developing countries should adapt existing methods and create new methods and materials that are appropriate to their contexts. This is already occurring in some places. In many of these countries, particularly the poorest in Africa, scarcity is leading to innovation and new models in consumption and production.

Examples of material improvements abound. A signal improvement is something as seemingly innocuous as access to washing machines, which is a key household implement for women's quality of life, requiring previous development of significant urban infrastructure, including electricity, water, sewerage, and a sufficient level of household income. While this can make qualitative enhancements in the non-OECD nations, we go further and ask planners and scholars: what are the equivalents of washing machines in OECD countries? What innovations would provide a significant leap forward for women in wealthy nations now and into the future? We argue, for various reasons, that the answer to this question is not necessarily a material thing or an artifact.

First, when considering *in combination*, and at a global level, the natural environment, gender inequality, other aspects of inequality, and urban development agendas, it is obvious that in order to provide basic material goods to the growing world population – especially the rapidly increasing urban population – consumption by the upper-income brackets need to be significantly curtailed.

We argue that women can play a key role in advancing an agenda for reduced consumption and more efficient use of natural and other resources in the developing world. This is because of women's roles as carers of persons, homes, and environments. Gendered divisions of labor have led men into the public domain of the formal economy and political power, often leading to unnecessary accumulation and fierce competition, including violence – among individuals, organizations, and countries – as well as exploitation of natural resources.

While men have fought for power and resources, women have been and still are mostly providers of care. They are the ones who provide the essential "soft activities" necessary to protect and sustain life at its most fragile: to babies and infants as well as the elderly, the dying, the infirm, and those with forms of physical inability. They continue to do so even as they enter the workforce in increasingly diverse positions.

The values necessary and inherent to protect, support, and care for the life of those who cannot take care of themselves, so beautifully described by the philosopher and Saint Edith Stein (Stein 1996), patron of Europe, in her many essays on women, are the values that could underlie a global shift to a world less predatory with nature, more voluntarily frugal, and more sensitive to the needs of all human beings irrespective of age, gender, race, ethnicity, physical ability, or any other individual or group characteristic that sets persons in positions of vulnerability. Taking care of others sometimes means putting their needs ahead of one's own.

We further argue for a reconsideration of the use-value of things rather than their exchange value, and the huge urban implications of these ideas. One example of this is the emerging sharing economy, something women worldwide pioneered generations ago, without giving it a name, so ingrained was it to the women's way of living. The current resurgence of the sharing economy is a consequence, among other things, of the current economic crisis and the new expression of sustainability consciousness. In this process, we can learn from the experience of collaborative survival strategies developed by women in the developing world (Moser 2009).

Another example of a more austere lifestyle that is being developed in the rich parts of the world is one based more deeply on caring values in which responsibility for the wellbeing of self and others overpowers the pressures of competition for "having more than the neighbor", whether this "having more" refers to material things, prestige, or power. This is another instance in which traditionally feminine perspectives of caring for others can contribute to shifting priorities from material wealth to the personal growth of all.

We posit that these traditionally feminine values, developed in the domestic sphere of the home, have the potential to transform the public sphere of professional activity and decision-making as they become more widely embraced by all, irrespective of gender.

These factors and facts – the rise of the caring and the sharing economies, the increasing participation of women in the workplace and positions of leadership, and the increasing proportion of women as societies age – converge to place a greater emphasis on the role of women and the leadership nature of those roles in directing societies in the future. As these societies become more urban – up to 70 percent of the global population by the year 2050 – they also point to the need for urban planning to change its foci to adapt to these realities, and for gender-aware women and men to lead these changes in the planning professions and their scholarship.

Structure of the Book

This book is the third of a group of recently edited collections focusing on gender in urban planning and development. Sánchez de Madariaga and Roberts (2013) provided a state-of-the-art analysis of gender in planning practice, looking at different experiences and conceptual approaches across eight European countries. Zibell, Damyanovic, and Sturm (2018), on the other hand, provide an interesting comparative outlook at gender in planning, again in Europe, by considering topics, practices, and approaches, through the joint work within individual chapters of contributors from different countries, in combination with a mapping and comparative analysis of planning systems and gender measures.

The contributions we present in this book open the geographical focus beyond Europe to include two North American studies, two from New Zealand, and one from India. In addition, compared to the greater focus on central and Northern European countries in the other collections, this book provides a substantive coverage of examples from five Mediterranean countries, including Portugal, Spain, Italy, France, and Greece.

Following this introduction, the sequence of the chapters and a summary of each of their contents is as follows. First is a section on mobility and accessibility issues, fundamental to the prospects for women in cities. Anastasia Loukaitou-Sideris provides an overview of the literature from both the Global North and the Global South to discuss the issues and challenges affecting women's unobstructed movement around the city, both historically and at present. It also draws from feminist theory to discuss why mobility patterns are characterized as "gendered" and discusses how women's transport needs are different from those of men, because of safety concerns, sociocultural norms, and differential access to private means of transport. Additionally, the chapter examines how transport needs may vary among different women, due to age, class, or race/ethnicity. Lastly, her contribution assesses the extent to which policy and practice in the Global North and Global South has responded to women's needs and concerns, outlining some next steps and future directions.

Bente Knoll and Teresa Schwaninger follow Blumenberg, using data from Austrian travel surveys. Their gender analysis shows that the interpretations of the data, along with the questionnaires themselves, reveal biases and simplifications. These biases and simplifications obscure crucial aspects in human behavior concerning mobility, particularly the behavior of carers in their everyday lives. Therefore, gender-sensitive qualitative methods have been developed and applied in order to better reveal mobility patterns and needs of people accompanying dependents on their day-to-day trips.

Yamini Narayanan takes to India, where women in Indian cities have experienced high rates of rape, molestation, and even murder on moving public and private transportation. Since the liberalization of the Indian economy in the 1990s, the rate of rape on moving transport has increased substantially, illustrating tensions at the intersections of class, gender, and urban spaces. The main gendered policy response that planning authorities in some large Indian cities like Mumbai and Delhi have instituted is to have a few "Ladies-only" coaches or seats for women in trains and metros. This chapter argues that in order to adequately respond to current Indian urban gendered realities, transport policies aimed at the elimination of violence in India cannot be divorced from engagement with social change.

Margarida Queirós and Nuno Marques da Costa investigate gender inequality in mobility in Portugal. They examine the role that transport services play in the everyday experiences of men and women with respect to trip-chaining, using statistical data. The research methodology is grounded in literature review and in statistics on mobility concerning commuting displacement. Findings demonstrate that women's daily lives are more complex than men's. Yet these differences, increasingly shaped by the use of the car, are diminishing, setting up new needs for policy making and planning.

Von den Driesch and her colleagues look at the implementation of gender and diversity perspectives in Transport Development Plans (TDPs) in Germany. As mobility should ensure access to and participation in society, transport planning has to deal with a variety of gender and diversity categories affecting users' mobility needs and patterns. Exemplified by an analysis of an instrument of transport development processes – TDPs – the chapter investigates to what extent diverse target groups and their mobility requirements are implemented in transport strategy papers. Research results illustrate a still-prevalent neglect of several relevant gender and diversity categories while prioritizing and focusing on eco-friendly topics. But, the authors ask, how sustainable can transport be without facing the diversification of life circumstances?

Closing this section, Evelyn Blumenberg details her empirical analysis of automobile ownership in the US. She finds that low-income households remain less likely to have access to automobiles than higher income households. Today, given the continued dispersion of US metropolitan areas and the growing number of jobs, as well as low-income families living in the suburbs, the evidence suggests that low-income women who do not have access to automobiles are increasingly disadvantaged. To engender greater economic and social sustainability, the evidence suggests that low-income women would benefit from policies to increase their access to automobiles.

The next section takes on a number of specific cases from countries around the globe in which the authors describe and analyse concerns relating to policy, planning, and design of cities from a gender perspective, addressing issues ranging from safety to toilets and many others besides. This section covers scales ranging from neighborhoods and cities, through regions and continental unions (the EU), and begins with an article on the important issue of safety in urban space.

In asking whether safe cities are just cities, Claire Hancock and Lucille Biarrotte shed light on recent attempts to put gender issues on the agendas of municipalities and urban planning actors in France. Their case studies in Greater Paris and Lyon raise important questions: how to construct a "right to the gendered city" that does not overrule other rights; and how to acknowledge difference in a way that does not define some publics and neighborhoods as needing help, and others as needing to be made more secure? They suggest that thinking in terms of "spatial justice" can help frame the discussion of inclusiveness using an intersectional perspective.

Clara Greed addresses an often overlooked yet critical aspect of the daily life of women in cities by analyzing public toilets. They are essential to creating accessible and sustainable urban spaces for all sorts of men and women. Yet women endure unequal and inadequate toilet provision that limits their mobility. Although this is a human-rights issue, successive governments have done little for women's toilet needs. In contrast, progress has been rapid to provide gender-neutral toilets and to desegregate public toilets. While gender may now be seen as a continuum, women's biological differences and reasons for needing the toilet have remained the same, including menstruation, pregnancy, and menopause.

Roja Tafaroji highlights how globalization shapes and affects contemporary cities. National and international immigration has led to increases in ethnic and cultural diversity. Accordingly, groups from different ethnicities, religions, languages, and cultures have come to live in the same spatial context. Gender and ethnic minority groups are considered to be the subjects of exclusion by the mainstream cultures in culturally diverse societies. Amongst them are immigrant women from non-Western countries living in Western countries whose everyday life experience are considered as a "struggle to survive" in their "places of resistance". Based on extensive fieldwork, this chapter discusses the conflictive life experiences of eight immigrant women from Afghanistan who live in the global city of Auckland in New Zealand.

Jeanette Sebrantke and her colleagues follow with their analysis of regional discourse about the future of the Ruhr region in Germany. In 2009, the Ruhr Regional Association regained charge of regional planning for the Ruhr Metropolitan Area with its 53 municipalities and more than 5 million inhabitants. To enhance its legitimization and involve the general public, a regional discourse was initiated. Under the slogan "the regional discourse ... on the road to the future of the Ruhr Metropolitan Area", citizens, scientists, politicians, institutions, and municipalities were encouraged to participate in the discourse over the current challenges along the regional development topics. Gender mainstreaming was an essential part of this process.

Taking the perspective up a scale, Sonia De Gregorio Hurtado addresses the question: has the urban dimension of the EU policy integrated the gender perspective vision embraced by the Treaty of Amsterdam? The study undertakes the analysis of the policy discourse adopted in the period 1997–2013 in order to understand whether the gender perspective has been mainstreamed into the urban policy of the EU. The results show that the gender dimension has been excluded from the definition of the policy problem. This illuminates the current situation, in which the Urban Agenda for the European Union is being constructed and the Member States are implementing the Integrated Sustainable Urban Development Strategies.

To close this section, and turning our attention to Greece, Charis Christodoulou builds a hypothesis of gender mainstreaming in urban planning and design. It reviews critical attempts, both direct and indirect, of gender-awareness activities in recent years. Specifics of the statutory regimes and the actual practices in Greek cities are set forward in order to advance a context-specific framework of focused action. Finally, she argues that the issues at stake are not only contextually institutional and knowledge-based, but depend on the creative mobilization of all agents involved so as to formulate an updated conceptualization of inclusive urban environments.

In the concluding section of the book, Dory Reeves and colleagues' assessment of the progress made while marking the 125th anniversary of the vote for most (albeit not all) women in Aotearoa New Zealand was marked in July 2018 by an important exhibition in the Auckland War Memorial Museum on women's equality entitled "Are we there yet?" The chapter shows how far Aotearoa has come and how far it still has to go. The key conclusion is that Aotearoa, New Zealand, is at a potential tipping point when it comes to gendering cities. Women's activism, the work of mana wāhine, politics, research, education, and practice are highlighting the importance of gender perspectives.

Inés Novella looks at practical tools that are already being used for the implementation of the New Urban Agenda and the Agenda for Sustainable Development. In particular, she looks at Gender Impact Assessments (GIAs) of urban development plans as useful tools for integrating gender aspects in urban plans. GIAs are one main tool proposed by the First Quadrennial Report for the Implementation of the New Urban Agenda published by the United Nations in 2018. They have been introduced in European Union directives and in some European national legislations, as well as applied in practice at several urban development plans of various scales. One such experience is Madrid Nuevo Norte, an extensive regeneration project in the north of the city involving the construction of over 10,000 housing units, a new Central Business District, and many new facilities and infrastructures. This chapter discusses the possibilities and conditions for the effective application of GIAs.

Camilla Perrone takes the international debates of the UN and the EU regarding a New Urban Agenda as its starting point for reconceptualizing a gendered urban agenda for the 21st century. While recalling the controversial debate on the implementation of a "gender mainstreaming strategy", the chapter reflects on the need to reconceptualize gender as a constitutive versus nominal essence to advance the debate. Theoretical criteria are suggested that mirror the complexity of gendered practices and create the conditions for their flourishing. These are further explicated for their policy relevance. Gender-sensitive policies, inspired by an analysis of an urban life experiment of food production in Mondeggi, Italy, are suggested.

Closing the book is a reflective essay by Inés Sánchez de Madariaga. In it she lays out an argument supporting the need to rebalance and find common ground from which to build and transcend current debates between supporters of a feminism of difference that stresses women's issues, with supporters of a feminism of equality that stresses equality between men and women in the workplace and the public sphere. Rather than looking at the problem from the extremes of each side, which leads to a confrontational framework of equality versus difference, a more nuanced outlook should allow to set the conceptual discussion in terms of complementarity, that is, of equality and difference as two interrelated, equally important, and inextricable sides of the same coin.

Notes

1   www.redmujer.org.ar/.
2   The Harmonized European Time Use Statistics, HETUS, offers opportunities to calculate user defined, comparable statistical tables on the organisation and activities of everyday life in fifteen European countries. www.h5.scb.se/tus/tus/
3   www.gapminder.org/.
4   www.gender.no/Facts_figures/1322.
5   http://unstats.un.org/unsd/gender/default.html.
6   The World Bank classifies countries into low, lower-middle, upper-middle and high-income groups, each associated with an annually updated threshold level of Gross National Income per capita, and the low- and middle-income groups taken together referred to as the "developing world". The IMF classifies 37 countries as "Advanced Economies" and considers all others as "Emerging Market and Developing Economies". The UNDP's Human Development Index groups countries into: very high, high, medium and low levels of human development. This index draws on various indicators including those related to income, education and health. The United Nations has no formal definition of developing countries but still uses the term "developing world" for monitoring purposes and classifies as many as 159 countries as such.
7   http://live.worldbank.org/hans-rosling-beyond-open-data.

References

Bauer, Catherine (1934). *Modern Housing*. Boston, MA: Houghton Mifflin.
Berglund, Eeva with Barbra Wallace (2013). "Women's Design Service as Counter-Expertise", in Inés Sánchez de Madariaga & Marion Roberts (eds.) *Fair Share Cities: The Impact of Gender Planning in Europe*. Aldershot, UK and New York: Ashgate.
Council of Europe (1998). *Gender Mainstreaming, Conceptual Framework, Methodology and Presentation of Good Practices*. Strasbourg: Council of Europe.
De Graft-Johnson, Ann, Sandra Manley & Clara Greed (2005). "Diversity or the Lack of it in the Architectural Profession", *Construction Management and Economics*, Vol. 23, pp. 1035–1043.
Durning, Louise & Richard Wrigley (2000). *Gender and Architecture*. New York: Wiley.
Giovarelli, Renee & Beatrice Wamalwa (2011). *Land Tenure, Property Rights, and Gender: Challenges and Approaches for Strengthening Women's Land Tenure and Property Rights (USAID Issue Brief – Property Rights and Resource Governance Briefing Paper #7)*. New York: United States Agency International Development (USAID).
Hall, Peter (1988). *Cities of Tomorrow*. Cambridge, MA: Basil Blackwell.
Horelli, Liisa, Christine Booth & Rose Gilroy (2000). *The EuroFEM Toolkit for Mobilising Women Into Local and Regional Development*, Revised version. Helsinki: Helsinki University of Technology.

Knight, Louise W. (2005). *Citizen: Jane Addams and the Struggle for Democracy*. Chicago, IL: University of Chicago Press.

Martínez, Cándida, et al. (2000). *Mujeres en la Historia de España. Enciclopedia biográfica*. Barcelona: Planeta.

Matrix (1984). *Making Space: Women and the Man Made Environment*. London: Pluto.

Michaud, Anne, et al. (eds.) (1997). *Une ville à la mesure des femmes, le rôle des municipalités dans l'atteinte de l'objectif d'égalité entre hommes et femmes*. Montreal: Ville de Montreal.

Ministry of Environment (1993). *A Cookbook for Grass-Roots Planning*. Oslo and Norway: Ministry of Environment.

Moser, Caroline (2009). *Ordinary Families: Extraordinary Lives: Assets and Poverty Reduction in Guayaquil, 1978–2004*. Washington, DC: Brookings Press.

Reeves, Dory (1989). "Planning for Choice and Opportunity", *Papers by the Women and Planning Working Party for a Conference on Managing Equality*. London: RTPI.

Sánchez de Madariaga, Inés (2003). "Configurar el espacio intermedio. Urbanismo y conciliación entre vida familiar y vida laboral", in Tomás Font (coord.) *Los nuevos retos del urbanismo*. Barcelona: Marcial Pons, pp. 145–168.

Sánchez de Madariaga, Inés (2010). "Women in Architecture. The Spanish Case", *Urban Research and Practice*, Vol. 3, 2, pp. 203–218.

Sánchez de Madariaga, Inés, et al. (2011). *Structural Change of Research Institutions: Enhancing Excellence, Gender Equality and Efficiency in Research and Innovation*. Brussels: European Commission.

Sánchez de Madariaga, Inés (2015). *Access to Washing Machines: An Indicator for Measuring Advance in the Global Agendas on Gender, Sustainability and Urban Quality*. UN-Habitat. http://unhabitat.org/washing-machines-indicator-for-measuring-advances/ accessed April 7th 2016.

Sánchez de Madariaga, Inés (2020). "Género y urbanismo en España: tres décadas de investigación 1990-2020", in Elsa Guerra (ed.) *Reflexiones sobre Género, Arquitectura y Ciudad*. Las Palmas: Universidad de Las Palmas de Gran Canaria.

Sánchez de Madariaga, Inés & Marion Roberts (eds.) (2013). *Fair Share Cities: The Impact of Gender Planning in Europe*. Aldershot, UK and New York: Ashgate.

Shoshkes, Ellen (2013). *Jaqueline Tyrwhitt: A Transnational Life in Urban Planning and Design*. Aldershot, UK: Ashgate.

Stein, Edith (1996). *Essays on Woman*, translated by Freda Mary Oben. Washington, DC: ICS Publications.

Stratigakos, Despina (2008). *A Women's Berlin: Building the Modern City*. Minneapolis, MN: University of Minnesota Press.

Wurster, Catherine Bauer (1963). *Cities and Space*. Baltimore, MD: Johns Hopkins University Press.

Zibell, Barbara, Doris Damyanovic & Ulrike Sturm (2018). *Gendered Approaches to Spatial Development in Europe – Perspectives, Similarities and Differences*. New York: Routledge.

PART I

Engendering Urban Transportation

2

A GENDERED VIEW OF MOBILITY AND TRANSPORT

Next Steps and Future Directions

Anastasia Loukaitou-Sideris

Introduction

Physical mobility – the ability to move from one place to another smoothly, quickly and without impediment – has been the epitome of modernity. Mobility has been greatly valued in a modern society constantly on the move (Urry, 2000); it has often been associated with privilege, power and freedom. Mobility often enhances accessibility – the ability to access and take advantage of physical amenities (e.g. parks, supermarkets, schools) and economic opportunities (e.g. jobs). For this reason, physical mobility is often linked to opportunities for achievement and enjoyment of a better life and more material resources (Wachs, 2009). At the same time, the way that transport is designed and delivered impacts mobility patterns.

However, both historically and at present, social groups have not all enjoyed equal levels of mobility. Women, in particular, have often faced important mobility hurdles, lessening their accessibility to city resources and opportunities. Feminist scholars agree that 'how people move (where, how fast, how often) is demonstrably gendered and continues to reproduce gendered power hierarchies' (Cresswell and Uteng, 2008, 2). Indeed, gender distinctions in travel patterns hold true for both the Global North and the Global South (Law, 1999; Tanzarn, 2008).

This paper argues that women's mobility in cities is challenged by physical, economic, cultural and psychological constraints, but also inadequate transportation policies that often neglect or disregard women's needs. Women have distinct mobility needs and travel patterns, while, at the same time, important differences exist among women, based on socio-demographic characteristics and geographic contexts. Such differences and nuances are not always understood and much less addressed by policymakers.

The paper will first set its arguments within the larger theoretical context of feminist theory. It will follow with an overview of historic and contemporary challenges to women's mobility in the Global North and Global South. It will draw from the literature to examine why travel patterns are characterised as 'gendered' and examine how transport needs vary among different women, due to factors such as age, class, race/ethnicity and geographic context. Lastly, it will assess the extent to which policy and practice in the US, Canada and Europe have responded to women's needs and concerns and outline next steps and future directions in research, design, transport policy and technology.

Gender, Mobility and Transport: The Feminist Perspective

Over the last three decades, feminist theorists have problematised the triad of gender, mobility and transport, emphasising that they intersect and influence one another in deep and complex ways (Cresswell and Uteng, 2008). Their interest stems from the understanding that one's ability to move in the city without obstruction denotes freedom (Hanson, 2010).[1] In contrast, restriction of movement (because of rules, social norms or lack of resources) signifies exclusion, oppression and subordination for those excluded. Women have been more affected than men by restrictions to their mobility, and this control over women's movement and presence in public spaces reflects and reinforces patterns of inequality between genders (Massey, 1994); what Valentine (1992) calls 'spatial expressions of patriarchy'. As argued by:

> spaces and places are not only themselves gendered but, in their being so, also reflect and affect the ways in which gender is understood. The limitation of women's mobility in both identity and space has been in some cultural contexts a crucial means of subordination.
>
> *Massey (1994, 177)*

Control over mobility can be explicit, implicit or indirect. For example, religious rules or cultural norms that explicitly forbid women to drive vehicles or ride transit unescorted diminish their mobility and tie them to their homes. Societal perceptions depicting women as vulnerable and in need of protection implicitly reduce their freedom to be present in public spaces during certain times (McDowell, 1999). Lack of resources preventing the purchase of private automobiles indirectly results in 'captive riders', with diminished mobility and less access to jobs (Rutherford and Wekerke, 1988; Blumenberg and Ong, 2001). Of course, gender is only one, albeit prominent, aspect that determines differentiated mobilities and the scale and extent of inequalities. As will be discussed later, race/ethnicity, class and geographic and cultural context represent additional important modifiers.

As Hanson (2010) explains, feminist interest in gender and mobility relates to two important aspects. The first examines how mobility/immobility impacts the power relations and dynamics embedded in gender. The second examines how gender affects mobility and transport, differentiating travel patterns and behaviour. She argues that these two concerns have led to two 'disparate strands of thinking that have remained badly disconnected from each other' and calls for greater attention to the wider geographic and sociocultural context (2010, 5). Similarly, in an earlier article, Law (1999, 568) asks for a more nuanced theoretical approach that encompasses the 'social and cultural geographies of mobility', in order to understand the differentiated relationships between gender, mobility and transport.

Historic and Contemporary Challenges to Women's Mobility

Feminist theorists have been concerned about the historic and contemporary injustices that women have faced in moving freely around the city. While men could easily navigate the public sphere, and their 'mobile subjectivities' as explorers, adventurers or frontiersmen were highly celebrated in the nineteenth-century cities of the Global North (Sheller, 2008), middle- and upper-class women were confined to the private edifices of their homes (Loukaitou-Sideris and Ehrenfeucht, 2009). It was considered highly inappropriate for women to venture out into city streets on their own. During the daytime, only working-class women peddlers could be found on the streets of US cities, while at night women 'street-walkers' were considered prostitutes (Wolff, 1990). Harassment and violence greeted women on the streets. Men cast them 'lecherous gazes' and followed or insulted them with sexual comments (Ryan, 1990, 69). Thus, women who acted 'improperly' by walking in public were intimidated, stigmatised and even assaulted at times.

While men's wandering and visual explorations of the city were romanticised as examples of the flâneur (Benjamin, 1999), women's movement or presence in public spaces was a source of anxiety. As explained:

> In streets, the threat to social order posed by a mixing of classes and genders was cause for middle- and upper-class angst. So too was the worry that female forms of male property (mothers, wives, daughters) would be visually and sexually available for other men.
>
> *(Rendell, 1998, 88)*

As public transit started crisscrossing the early twentieth-century American and European cities, a few women appeared as riders. The proximity of bodies in the enclosed spaces of streetcars and train wagons generated uncomfortable circumstances for women. Referring to the experiences of female riders on New York's Interborough Rapid Transit, *Outlook* magazine complained in 1912 that: '[A] crowding at best is almost intolerable, and at its worst is deliberately insulting ... Males were often not chivalrous, and sometimes coarse-grained, vulgar or licentious' (Outlook, 1912). *New York Times* articles at the time referred to sexual harassment and fondling of women riders on the subway as 'the Subway problem' (*New York Times*, 10 March 1905, in Hood, 1996).

These social anxieties about women's safety in transit environments subsided after the 1920s and until the 1950s in the US, as many middle- and upper-class women moved with their families to the suburbs and were largely confined to the realms of home, shopping mall, neighbourhood school and church. As women started entering the labour force in large numbers in the 1960s, and the civil rights and feminist movements in the US were in full swing, social expectations about unescorted women in public settings, streets and transit began to change. Still, half a century later, women's mobility in the Global North remains more restricted than men's. As shown in Table 2.1, four types of barriers affect it: cultural, economic, physical and psychological.

TABLE 2.1 Barriers affecting women's travel

Barriers	Type of barrier	Impact on women's travel patterns	Group affected
Cultural	Religious norms/ practices	Banning women from public settings, public transit, bicycles	Women in some Muslim countries
	Women as primary caregivers for children & parents	Shorter trips	Women in Global North and Global South
	Women primarily responsible for domestic chores	Accompanied by others in travel	Women in Global North
		Trip chaining/ hypermobility	Women in Global North and Global South
		Carrying large items during travel	
Economic	Lack of economic resources for private automobile	Transit dependency	Poor men and women in the Global North and Global South
		Lack of access to public transportation	
	Having to live in peripheral shanty towns/ colonias	Localized mobility patterns; many foot trips	Poor men and women in the Global South
			Poor men and women in the Global South
Physical	Automobile-oriented urban form/ sprawl	Overreliance on private automobiles	Women in the Global North
	Lack of adequate infrastructure for walking	Long time spent on transportation	Women in the Global North and Global South
	Limited transit networks	Unsafe and uncomfortable travel	Women in the Global South
Psychological	Fear of harassment and victimization	Avoidance of public transit, bicycles	Women in the Global North and Global South
	Parental fear of stranger-danger	Avoidance of particular transit routes	
		Travelling only during daytime	
		Travelling only accompanied by others	

Women have been and remain the primary caregivers for children and elderly parents and are mostly responsible for domestic chores. In the UK, even fully employed women spend significantly more time on childcare and household chores than men (ONS, 2004). Similarly, in the US, women reported allocating twice more time than men to such chores and elderly care (Coltrane, 2000). Such responsibilities affect women's mobility, as they reduce the amount of time for discretionary activities, increase trip-chaining (short trips for household errands) and can impact upon women's access to well-paid jobs far from home (Women's Planning Network Inc., 1995). Empirical studies of women's travel find that it typically involves more people than that of men's (young children, elderly relatives) and is often associated with domestic chores (Franck and Paxson, 1989). Surveys of women transit riders in the UK have noted the hurdles they encounter when carrying large items, such as strollers, packages and shopping bags on buses and trains (Hamilton et al., 1991).

Ironically, while mobility may be empowering for most individuals, a sort of 'hypermobility' can be constraining to women (Hanson, 2010). Murray (2008) discusses the plight of suburban mothers in the Global North, who are constantly behind the wheels of their cars, transporting their children to various destinations. Sánchez de Madariaga (2013) calls these service trips 'the mobility of care', arguing that they should become more visible and accounted for in transport policies. If hypermobility is encountered in the Global North, some women in the Global South face extremely constrained mobility, because of religious/cultural norms preventing them from driving, cycling or using transit.

Economic hurdles, such as lack of adequate resources, also affect mobility. Globally, the proportion of women below the poverty level is higher than men. Although the number of women who own and drive cars has increased consistently over the years in the Global North, more underprivileged and immigrant women are carless and transit-dependent than men (Cox, 2007; Currie et al., 2009; Rosenbloom and Plessis-Fraissard, 2009). When only one car exists in the family, men are more likely to use it for work, even if both spouses are employed (European Commission, 2014).

Physical barriers to women's mobility are embedded in the design of urban form (especially in suburban and exurban areas) that separates land uses, has limited and disconnected transit networks, lacks sidewalks and other environmental amenities to encourage walkability and dictates an over-reliance on private automobiles for the accomplishment of household chores. Since women are disproportionately carrying out such chores, these physical barriers affect them more than men.

Perceptual/psychological barriers also play a role in constraining women's mobility. Parents are more likely to give their sons greater latitude for movement across city spaces than their daughters, who are perceived as more susceptible to the threat of 'stranger danger' (Loukaitou-Sideris and Sideris, 2010). As a result, girls tend to be more confined to a circumscribed use of spaces (Young, 1990).

Such social attitudes transcend childhood and remain in adulthood, resulting in women's under-representation in public spaces and their more limited use of cycling in comparison to men (Rosenbloom and Plessis-Fraissard, 2009).

Studies have shown that a hurdle to women's unobstructed mobility in the Global North is their fear and anxiety over possible victimisation in public spaces and transit environments. The situation is particularly aggravating for low-income and minority women, who live in high-crime neighbourhoods, may return home from work in the late evening hours and have less private transportation options than more affluent women. For women with more transportation options, the fear of victimisation may affect their mode choice and time of travel, leading them to prefer private automobiles or taxis (Loukaitou-Sideris, 2014).

Thus, a variety of cultural, economic, physical and perceptual hurdles are still making women's mobility inferior to men's. This situation is more acute in the Global South. While the context of cities there is widely varied, women in the Global South have less access to motorised transportation than women in the Global North. The inequalities that impede their mobility are magnified, because of inferior access to power, economic and educational resources compared to men (Uteng, 2009). This is particularly true in Africa, where only a small fraction of women are in the labour force (World Bank, 2009). Even though some Global South countries have witnessed progress since the establishment of the Millennium Development Goals (MDGs) by the United Nations in 2000, in 2012 only 18 per cent of women were employed in Northern Africa compared to 68 per cent of men and 49 per cent of women were employed in Latin America and the Caribbean compared to 75 per cent of men (UN, 2013).

Women of the Global South also serve as the primary caregivers for their children. Reporting on women's travel in urban Uganda, Tanzarn (2008, 161–62) observes that:

> [W]omen are largely responsible for taking children to school or hospital. … While the majority of women sometimes travel with their children or younger dependents, most men never travel with them. Uganda's transport services do not cater to passengers travelling with children, which affects women disproportionately, restricting their ability to move freely.

Fear of victimisation and harassment is a serious concern for women in the Global South and this constrains their mobility. The possibility of tripping and falling is also a concern, because of inadequate pedestrian infrastructure and the loads that women often have to carry, which can affect their balance (Rosenbloom and Plessis-Fraissard, 2009). In many countries, the governments have been unable or unwilling to respond to these concerns. Thus, Roy (2009) identifies a major transportation policy disconnect in some countries of the Global

South, where governments allocate resources for the construction or expansion of highway or railway networks, but fail to improve local routes and means of transport, primarily used by women, or to address their safety concerns. Additional mobility obstacles are faced by the poor, who are disproportionately women and who often live in squatter settlements and shanty towns at the edges of metropolitan areas, largely cut off from public transit networks. This leads Roy (2009, 52) to identify a significant 'gender-transportation-poverty nexus' in countries of the Global South, where transportation policies fail poor women and thus deepen their poverty.

Gendered Travel Patterns

The aforementioned challenges impact some women's travel patterns. Analysing travel between home and work, feminist geographers observed twenty years ago that travel patterns are gendered and noted significant differences between the longer distance, single-destination travel of men in the Global North and the shorter distance, multiple-destination travel of women who try to accomplish household chores on their way to/from work (Hanson and Pratt, 1995; Law, 1999). As shown in Table 2.2, women and men in both the Global North and Global South make trips for different purposes, use different modes and display different travel behaviours and patterns (see Table 2.2).

More specifically, women in both the Global North and Global South tend to commute shorter distances for work, even after controlling for socio-demographic differences. This likely happens because many women seek jobs closer to home. As a result of the shorter commuting trips, the average time that women spend commuting to/from work in the US (23.4 minutes in 2009) is somewhat shorter than men's (26.7 minutes in 2009), but these numbers are converging rapidly, and gender differences in travel time of commuting trips are less pronounced than decades ago (American Community Survey Reports, 2011). Travel patterns vary significantly among the countries of the Global South, but in some countries women, on average, spend longer time travelling than men. Rosenbloom and Plessis-Fraissard (2009, 67) attribute this to 'the nature of their jobs, their need to combine household and childcare duties with their commutes, and their use of slower modes'.

Women in the Global North tend to take more trips than men, and many of these trips are related to parental and household obligations, such as taking children to school and extracurricular activities, accompanying parents to medical appointments or shopping for groceries. Scholars, however, have noted differences associated with marital status, race/ethnicity and urban/suburban/rural settings (Wachs, 2009).

In the urban areas of the Global North and Global South, women tend to use public transportation more than men (Cresswell and Uteng, 2008; Khan, 2013). This is primarily true for poor women, who are captive riders and lack other

TABLE 2.2 Gender differences in travel patterns

Differences	Global North	Global South
Commute trip length	• Women commute shorter distances (but variations exist based on socio-demographic characteristics)	• Women commute shorter distances
Number of trips	• Women make more total trips	• In some (but not all) countries women make more trips
Travel time	• Women's average commute trip time is less than men's (but numbers are converging)	• Varies by country
Travel mode	• More women use public transportation than men	• Women use more public transportation
	• More women use carpools and vanpools than men	• Women are more dependent on non-motorized modes; make more trips by foot
	• Fewer women bike than men	
	• Women use the family car less	• Women are more likely to use informal transportation modes
Car ownership/ Driver's license	• Women are less likely to own a car	• Women are less likely to own a car
	• Women are less likely to have a driver's license*	• Women are less likely to have a driver's license
Type of trips	• Women have more complicated trips (with multiple destinations)	• Women make more trips for household and children-related errands
	• Women make more trips for household and children-related errands	

* However, in the US, by 2006 more licensed drivers were women (FHWA, 2010).

transportation alternatives. But the use of public transportation is challenging when women have to combine different trips and carry parcels (European Commission, 2014). More women than men in the Global North use carpools and vanpools for their work trip (Wachs, 2009), while more women than men in the Global South undertake work and non-work trips on foot, especially in rural areas (Shrinivasan, 2008; Roy, 2009; Rosenbloom and Plessis-Fraissard, 2009). Overall, significantly fewer women than men use bicycles (Greed, 2008), because of fear of victimisation, falling or harassment or due to cultural norms (Goddard and Dill, 2013), although in the Netherlands and Scandinavia the gender gap in cycling has largely closed (Emond, 2009). In some of the poorest countries of the Global South, the vast majority of women's trips are on foot along local trails and paths. As has been argued: '[T]he most common means of transport in Africa are the legs, heads, and backs of African women' (Malmberg-Calvo, in Porter, 2008, 89).

Significantly fewer women than men in the Global South own cars or have a driver's licence (Rosenbloom and Plessis-Fraissard, 2009). The same is true in the Global North, especially among low-income women. Scholars have indicated that lack of automobile ownership hurts social mobility, because it presents a significant obstacle for job prospects (Blumenberg and Ong, 2001). Nevertheless, as cultural attitudes about women's roles change, and more women become educated and enter the labour force, the 'gender gap' in travel patterns is closing. This is more pronounced in countries of the Global North and among higher-income and educated women (European Commission, 2014), for whom the gap in auto mobility is closing. For example, in the US by 2007, over 90 per cent of women of driving age had acquired a driver's licence (FHWA, 2010). Similarly, the number of women drivers has steadily increased by 3.5 per cent over the last ten years (European Commission, 2014). This increased access to a private automobile allows women to acquire jobs that are farther from home. As a result, the gender gap in the length of commute is also narrowing in the Global North.

An emerging literature evaluates the evolving travel pattern convergence among men and women of the Global North (Rosenbloom, 2004; Crane, 2007). Rosenbloom (2004) identifies three trends: (1) increasing numbers of women in the paid labour force; (2) changing household roles, with more men assuming domestic and childcare responsibilities; and (3) changing household composition, with more single-person and single-parent households. She concludes, however, that the aggregate travel behaviour between men and women is still unequal, even in the Global North. However, scholars also highlight the significant differences in travel patterns among different groups of women (Rosenbloom, 2004; Hanson, 2010).

Differentiation among Women

A common misconception equalises all women under a broad and uniform category, ignoring important differentiations that exist among them. Conditions vary widely for women in different countries, because of different sociocultural norms, available economic resources and varied policies. Importantly, differentiations also exist among women within the same country, due to race/ethnicity, age, income, cultural and educational background, sexual orientation and disability status, as well as more personal characteristics, such as personality traits and lifecycle stages. Such differences affect mobility and travel patterns, and the gender gap is more pronounced for some groups.

Examining gender-age differences in European countries, a recent report by the European Commission (2014, 9) found that:

While there is a clear-cut gender gap in mobility patterns in the age group 35–54 years, the gap narrows in older age groups and also in the younger age group ... which has adopted new behavior in mobility and transport (decreased overall driving). Women over 54 ... [have] more access than their mothers to the family car and to car driving. As they grow older, the habit of personal mobility is not so easily abandoned and comes closer to that of men in the same age group. Similarly, young men and women ... are coming closer together in their mobility patterns.

In the countries of the Global North, the gender gap in travel patterns is more or less pronounced, depending on the racial/ethnic group. For example, in the US, researchers have found that while white women have typically shorter commuting trips than men, African American and Latina women have longer commutes than men, because of racially segmented labour and housing markets (McLafferty and Preston, 1991). Income and education (which often correlate) also play an important differentiating role among women, with high-income and well-educated women having higher levels of mobility and automobility and travelling more (Dobbs, 2005).

Fear and anxiety affect the way in which women travel and where they choose to go, but also where they consciously or unconsciously avoid going, thus limiting mobility and life options. Studies have uncovered a significant differentiation among women in their fear regarding possible victimisation in public settings, typically finding, for example, that older women feel less safe than younger women (St. John, 1995). Low-income women and women of ethnic backgrounds often experience higher levels of fear walking around their neighbourhoods than white women (Madriz, 1997; Ross, 2000). Similarly, women with physical or mental disabilities and lesbian women are more fearful of assault in public spaces (Morrell, 1996; Valentine, 1996). Such differences lead to different levels of mobility and accessibility.

Responding to Women's Transport Needs through Policy

As the previous discussion clearly shows, women's mobility, accessibility and travel behaviours are different from men's, which also leads to different transportation needs. Nevertheless, as Hamilton and Jenkins (2000, 1794) observe:

As consumers of transport, women have too often been assumed to have identical needs to men's. However, it is clear that women have travel needs as significant as those of men and in many respects distinct from them. We do not believe or assume that all women are the same or feel the same about public transport ... However, there are sufficiently significant differences between women's transport demands and experience as opposed to men's ... to justify treating women separately.

Policy responses around the world addressing women's mobility needs have been uneven. Thus, it can be argued that the persistence of hurdles that impede women's mobility in the city have their root not only in sociocultural norms and physical or economic obstacles, but also in the inability of policymakers to comprehend and respond effectively to women's mobility needs. As an example, transit agencies in the US have by-and-large not developed particular programmes targeting the safety or comfort of women transit riders. A survey of 131 US transit agencies found that only about one-third of them identified the need for specific women-friendly transit services, and only three had instigated such relevant programmes (Loukaitou-Sideris and Fink, 2009).[2]

In many countries of the Global South, policy-initiated imbalances are quite severe. Scholars have argued that transportation policies in countries of the Global South often tend to favour mobility over accessibility (Roy, 2009). In other words, emphasis is placed on promoting intercity transportation networks and reducing travel time on highways and railway networks. This is the case in China and India, where high-speed rail projects have been constructed (China) or proposed (India), in addition to highways and roadway overpasses (Shrinivasan, 2008). Such projects privilege automobility and rapid intercity transit, but fail to improve intra-city, non-motorised means of transport that are critical to many women, such as local roads, buses and bus stops (Roy, 2009). In some cities of the Global South, the frequent failure to respond effectively to women's safety concerns on buses and trains results, at best, in uncomfortable and stressful settings for women riders and, at worst, in intimidation, sexual harassment and rape.

Arguably, the most promising policy initiative is the 'gender mainstreaming' mandate included in the Treaty of Amsterdam in 1997, amending the Treaty of the European Union. This led to the adoption of gender mainstreaming initiatives by some Western countries (e.g. UK, Sweden, Ireland, Austria, Germany) seeking 'the integration of the gender perspective into every stage of the policy processes – design, implementation, monitoring, and evaluation – with a view to promoting equality between women and men' (Transgen, 2007, 16). Such initiatives use gender analyses in transportation activities, settings and projects to evaluate and measure their impact on women and men; they also seek to involve women in decision-making processes. A number of gender mainstreaming tools are used, such as gender disaggregated statistics, gender impact assessments and equality indicators (Transgen, 2007).

In 2007, the British Government issued the Gender Equality Duty, mandating all public agencies to promote gender equality. As will be discussed later, this led to a series of important initiatives on the part of transit operators. Elsewhere, the number of gender mainstreaming strategies and projects is limited, and researchers have complained that their implementation presents a greater challenge than their formulation (Polk, 2004; Greed, 2005; Transgen, 2007). Assessing the Swedish transport policy, Polk (2008) observed that it had not been very successful in achieving equality goals. She attributed this to the inefficient use of gender as an analytical tool, a lack of basic knowledge regarding gender inequality, a lack of a systematic strategy dealing with gender inequality and a lack of resources needed to accomplish it. As some researchers have noted, the over-representation of men in the transportation sector and the use of universalistic language about transportation services helps to deflate the issue and leads to gender imbalance in decision-making (Transgen, 2007; Sheller, 2008; Loukaitou-Sideris and Fink, 2009).

Lastly, of special note are 'women-only' transportation services that now operate in Japan and some countries of the Global South (Mexico, Brazil, India, Egypt, Belarus, Philippines) to tackle the harassment and victimisation of women passengers. Such services range from railway cars or buses on which men are not allowed to taxi cabs driven by women that only accept women passengers. Women-only transportation services vary depending on the city and transit company; some operate only during rush hours, and some are limited to specific lines and types of trains. They have generated considerable debate between supporters and critics, who either find them less stressful and more comfortable for women or paternalistic to women and discriminatory to men (Feministing, 2006; Valenti, 2007; Dunckel-Graglia, 2013).

Future Directions: What Needs to Happen?

How can women's mobility increase? How can the hurdles that many women face in their everyday movement lessen? There are no easy fixes or single responses to a phenomenon that is persistent and resulting from deeply engrained sociocultural norms, economic and perceptual factors. Rather, the scale and nature of changes should be structural, tailored to particular socio-spatial contexts and have at least four prongs: research, design, transport policy and technology.

Research

Inclusion of gender issues in research about mobility is essential to the development of gender-sensitive and gender-proof policies. In the last few decades, women's mobility has attracted the attention of scholars, with a resulting significant increase in scholarly articles, books, reports and conferences. Still more progress is necessary in identifying how particular contexts affect the interplay between gender and mobility, developing appropriate methodologies for data collection, casting light on unexplored issues and geographic settings, understanding the varying needs of different groups and disseminating the findings beyond academic communities.

Hanson (2010, 17) argues that the social, cultural and geographic context is 'absolutely central' to understanding the relationship between gender and mobility. Gender mainstreaming policies ask for the collection and analysis of gender disaggregated data. Such data will be more useful if it is further disaggregated to take into account social–cultural categories, such as age, class, race/ethnicity, age, disability status, lifecycle stage and sexual orientation. At the same time, researchers can develop appropriate metrics to measure the extent of inequalities in mobility among different groups in particular geographic contexts, as well as tailoring already existing tools, such as Safety Audits and Gender Impact Assessments, to better fit these contexts.

Research is more developed for particular geographic contexts and topics than others. We have significantly more research on the Global North than the Global South, even if gender inequalities are often more pronounced in the latter. Most scholarly work on the topic of gendered mobility has focused on travel patterns – in particular, the journey to work for urban women (Law, 1999). As Sánchez de Madariaga (2013) observes, a whole array of trips related to the 'mobility of care' is currently understudied. There is considerably less research available on issues relating to social mobility, and less knowledge about the mobility patterns of people in rural areas (Wachs, 2009). Filling in the gaps of these 'blind' research spots should be a priority for scholars.

Design

Appropriate urban design can enhance access to neighbourhood amenities, shorten trip lengths and make travel more comfortable and enjoyable. Mixed-land uses, concentration of amenities at nodal points (thus not requiring multiple trips to reach them), childcare services close to home or work, good public transportation connections, pedestrian-friendly local routes with sidewalks and good lighting enhance the mobility of men and women and reduce the need for trip-chaining.

As noted earlier, pedestrian accessibility is particularly important for women in many cities of the Global South. This not only involves the provision of good-quality footpaths, but also road drainage, shade, street lighting, garbage collection and disposal and even the provision of public toilets (Badami, 2009).

Additionally, the design of transit vehicles, transit stops and transit systems can contribute to comfort and feelings of safety for all riders, particularly women. The placement of bus stops at settings that facilitate natural surveillance by bystanders, as well as good lighting, makes the wait for the bus less stressful. The design of buses with low floors makes it easier for disabled and elderly passengers and also riders pushing strollers to alight them. Having a designated space on the bus for the storage of strollers or shopping bags makes the ride comfortable for those carrying them.

It should be noted that women-friendly neighbourhood design is synergistic with the interest in 'barrier-free' and 'universal design' concepts, which seek to increase accessibility to neighbourhood amenities for all, including elders and the disabled. One such example is the 'Lifelong Communities Initiative' in the Atlanta region, which seeks to enhance neighbourhood connectivity, walkability and easy access to neighbourhood services and amenities to all residents, including seniors

(Keyes et al., 2011). Some German cities (Vauban, Rieselfeld, Freiburg) have actively sought to reduce car penetration in residential neighbourhoods by strategically placing parking structures away from main pedestrian thoroughfares to create traffic-free streets. Such designs are credited for creating a friendly urban form for seniors and families with young children (Hamiduddin, 2015). In addition to this, they are also women-friendly, as they enable a level of independent mobility among children, thus reducing the need for them to be driven everywhere by their mothers.

Transport Policy

Women-friendly transport policies should be enacted at both the federal and municipal (local) levels. As discussed previously, federal mandates for gender mainstreaming policies that were initiated in some countries of the Global North represent a promising trend. Such mandates of gender equality in mobility should be developed by all governments, but should be also accompanied by concrete plans for action, protocols for evaluation and systematic gender impact assessments of different interventions and policies.

A good example is provided by Transport for London (TfL), London's transport authority, which produced a series of initiatives in recent years in response to Britain's gender mainstreaming mandate. These initiatives were informed by extensive consultation with multiple women's groups in London and included: (1) a Transport Policing Initiative, hiring additional uniformed transit officers to oversee safety in transit settings; (2) a Safer Travel at Night Initiative, providing personalised night travel information at college campuses and the designation of safe waiting areas along night bus routes; (3) a Real-Time Information Initiative, posting electronic displays at stations and bus stops; and (4) a Secure Stations Scheme, offering security enhancements for transit stations and stops (TfL, 2004, 2007).

Incorporating women's voices in policy development is important, because women are often the real experts of their neighbourhoods and are best placed to articulate their own needs and identify mobility barriers. One earlier such effort was in Canada, where the Toronto Transit Commission joined forces with the nonprofit Metropolitan Action Committee on Violence against Women and Children (METRAC) to conduct safety audits of Toronto's transportation settings and define ways to make them safer for women. The tool was used extensively by the city of Toronto, where, between the years 2000 and 2004, community groups audited more than 150 neighbourhoods (METRAC, 2006). Subsequently, safety audits have been used by various groups in different countries, providing a method to evaluate space from the perspective of those who feel threatened (UN-Habitat and Huairou Commission, 2007). Such safety and gender impact audits should be tailored to the particularities and needs of local contexts. Community, grassroots and non-profit groups and local NGOs can partner with local government and transit operators to use such tools, which seek to promote women's mobility.

Transport Technology

New mechanical and digital technologies (e.g. high-speed trains, smartphones) have significant influence on mobility patterns, as they impact how we move around, communicate and access others. They can improve inequalities or further aggravate them. However, we need more research on the differential impact of these new technologies on different groups, so that we can understand how to better employ them to reduce inequalities, rather than sharpen them.

New technologies are more readily available in the cities of the Global North. As discussed previously, new technologies can help increase mobility and make travel safer and easier for women. For example, real-time information that transit riders can access through their smartphones or at information displays at bus stops can help them better plan their trip. Studies have shown that women riders, in particular, are leery of long waits at bus stops and afraid of possible victimisation (Loukaitou-Sideris, 2014). On the other hand, the use of closed circuit television technologies (CCTV) for the surveillance of transportation settings over the last two decades has not put the fears of victimisation of women riders at ease (Trench et al., 1992; Wallace et al., 1999).

For women of the Global North whose travel patterns are often characterised by a series of short trips for household tasks, a fleet of neighbourhood electric vehicles for rent may provide a more affordable alternative to having a second car in the household. Neighbourhood bike-sharing programmes may also be appropriate for some cities of the Global North and the Global South.

The above suggestions incorporate a gender perspective as a deliberate response to the gendered patterns of mobility in cities. Mobility and accessibility should be viewed as important rights of all citizens, but these rights are at times compromised for women who face physical, economic, cultural and psychological constraints. Being able to access desired destinations safely and comfortably enhances the quality of life in cities and may also relate to economic and physical wellbeing. More context-specific research is necessary to identify and prioritise appropriate design and policy elements that can support mobility and accessibility for both men and women in different contexts. It is clear, however, that design and policy responses and technological advances that seek to close the gender gap in mobility would not only enhance women's access to city resources, but will also improve their lives and those of their families.

Notes

1   The literature distinguishes between mobility (geographical movement) and motility (potential for undertaking movement) (Cresswell and Uteng, 2008). Motility has always been considered as a positive; on the other hand, some scholars have argued that mobility may not always be positive, if it leads to rootedness and the lack of social networks (Hanson, 2010).
2   One programme is a night-stop service that allows passengers to alight the bus at locations other than bus stops. A second programme is a partnership between a transit agency and a domestic violence prevention agency. If a victim boards a bus and

requests help from the driver, the agency has a protocol in place to transfer the person to the domestic violence facility. A third programme involves teaching drivers to encourage female passengers to sit at the front of the bus and notify operators if some-one is causing them to feel uncomfortable.

References

American Community Survey Reports. (2011). 'Commuting in the United States: 2009', US Census, www.census.gov/prod/2011pubs/acs-15.pdf (accessed 11 May 2015).

Badami, M. G. (2009). 'Urban transport policy as if people and the environment mattered: pedestrian accessibility the first step', *Economic and Political Weekly*, XLIV, 43–51.

Benjamin, W. (1999). *The Arcades Project*, Cambridge, Harvard University Press.

Blumenberg, E. and Ong, P. (2001). 'Cars, buses, and jobs: welfare participants and employment access in Los Angeles', *Transportation Research Record*, 1756, 22–31.

Coltrane, S. (2000). 'Research on household labor: modeling and measuring the social embeddedness of routine family work', *Journal of Marriage and the Family*, 62, 1208–33.

Cox, J. B. (2007). 'Public transport trends: efficiency and equity considerations', *Road and Transport Research (A Journal of Australian and New Zealand Research)*, 16, 41–55.

Crane, R. (2007). 'Is there a quiet revolution in women's travel? Revisiting the gender gap in transportation', *Journal of the American Planning Association*, 73, 298–316.

Cresswell, T. and Uteng, T. P. (2008). 'Gendered mobilities: towards a holistic under-standing', in T. P. Uteng and T. Cresswell (eds), *Gendered Mobilities*, London, Ash-gate, 1–14.

Currie, G., Richardson, T., Smyth, P., Vella-brodrick, D., Hine, J., Lucas, K., Stanley, J., Morris, J., Kinnear, R. and Stanley, J. (2009). 'Investigating links between transport dis-advantage, social exclusion and wellbeing in Melbourne: preliminary results', *Transport Policy*, 16, 97–105.

Dobbs, L. (2005). 'Wedded to the car: home, employment and the importance of private transport', *Transport Policy*, 12, 266–78.

Dunckel-Graglia, A. (2013). 'Women-only transportation: how "pink" public transporta-tion changes public perception of women's mobility', *Journal of Public Transportation*, 16, 85–106.

Emond, C. R. (2009). 'Gender considerations in performance measures for bicycle infrastructure', in *Conference Proceedings 46: Women's Issues in Transportation: report of the 4th International Conference; Volume 2: technical Papers*, Washington, Transportation Research Board of the National Academies, 254–63.

European Commission Directorate-General for Mobility and Transport. (2014). *She Moves: Women's Issues in Transportation*, Belgium, European Commission.

Federal Highway Administration (FHWA). (2010). *Highway Statistics 2008*, Washington, US Department of Transportation, www.fhwa.dot.gov/policyinformation/statistics/2008/index.cfm#d1 (accessed 21 June 2016).

Feministing. (2006). 'Women-Only Cars in Brazil', www.feministing.com/archives/004937.html (accessed 21 June 2016).

Franck, K. and Paxson, L. (1989). 'Women and urban public space', in I. Altman and E. Zube (eds), *Public Places and Spaces*, New York, Plenum Press, 121–46.

Goddard, T. and Dill, J. (2013). 'Gender differences in adolescent attitudes about active travel', conference paper delivered to the 93rd Annual Meeting of the Transportation Research Board. Washington, 12–16 January.

Greed, C. (2005). 'An investigation of the effectiveness of gender mainstreaming as a means of integrating the needs of women and men into spatial planning in the United Kingdom', *Progress in Planning*, 64, 239–321.

Greed, C. (2008). 'Are we there yet? Women and transport revisited', in T. Cresswell and T. P. Uteng (eds), *Gendered Mobilities*, London, Ashgate, 243–56.

Hamiduddin, I. (2015). 'Social sustainability, residential design and demographic balance: neighborhood planning strategies in Freiburg, Germany', *Town Planning Review*, 86, 29–52.

Hamilton, K. and Jenkins, L. (2000). 'A gender audit for public transport: a new policy tool in the tackling of social exclusion', *Urban Studies*, 37, 1793–800.

Hamilton, K., Jenkins, L. and Gregory, A. (1991). *Women and Transport: Bus Deregulation in West Yorkshire*, Bradford, Bradford University.

Hanson, S. (2010). 'Gender and mobility: new approaches for informing sustainability', *gender, place, and Culture*, 17, 5–23.

Hanson, S. and Pratt, G. (1995). *Gender, Work, and Space*, New York, Routledge.

Hood, C. (1996). 'Changing perceptions of public space on the New York rapid transit system', *Journal of Urban History*, 22, 308–31.

John, C. (1995). 'Fear of black strangers', *Social Science Research*, 24, 262–80.

Keyes, L., Rader, C. and Berger, C. (2011). 'Creating communities: Atlanta's lifelong community initiative', *Physical and Occupational Therapy in Geriatrics*, 29, 59–74.

Khan, Y. (2013). 'Making transport safer for women', *The City Fix*, http://thecityfix.com/blog/women-public-safety-demands-yasmin-khan/ (accessed 21 June 2016).

Law, R. (1999). 'Beyond "women and transport": towards new geographies of gender and daily mobility', *Progress in Human Geography*, 23, 567–88.

Loukaitou-Sideris, A. (2014). 'Fear and safety in transit environments from the women's perspective', *Security Journal*, 27, 242–56.

Loukaitou-Sideris, A. and Ehrenfeucht, R. (2009). *Sidewalks: Conflict and Negotiation over Public Space*, Cambridge, MIT Press.

Loukaitou-Sideris, A. and Fink, C. (2009). 'Addressing women's fear of victimization in transportation environments: a survey of US transit agencies', *Urban Affairs Review*, 44, 554–87.

Loukaitou-Sideris, A. and Sideris, A. (2010). 'What brings children to the park? Analysis and measurement of the variables affecting children's use and physical activity', *Journal of the American Planning Association*, 76, 89–107.

Madriz, E. (1997). 'Latina teenagers: victimization, identity, and fear of crime', *Social Justice*, 24, 30–46.

Massey, D. (1994). *space, place, and Gender*, Minneapolis, University of Minnesota Press.

McDowell, L. (1999). *gender, identity, and Place*, Minneapolis, University of Minnesota Press.

McLafferty, S. and Preston, V. (1991). 'Gender, race, and commuting among service sector workers', *Professional Geographer*, 43, 1–15.

Metropolitan Action Committee on Violence Agianst Women and Children (METRAC). (2006). 'Why women's safety?', www.metrac.org/programs/safe/why.htm (accessed 21 June 2016).

Morrell, H. (1996). 'Women's safety', in C. Booth, J. Darke and S. Yeandle (eds), *Changing Places: Women's Lives in the City*, London, Paul Chapman Publishing, 100–01.

Murray, L. (2008). 'Motherhood, risk, and everyday mobilities', in T. Cresswell and T. P. Uteng (eds), *Gendered Mobilities*, London, Ashgate, 47–64.

Office for National Statistics (ONS). (2004). *Focus on Gender*, London, Office for National Statistics.

Outlook. (1912). 'New York's subway problem: a review', *Outlook*, 101, 384–88.

Polk, M. (2004). 'Gender mainstreaming in transport policy in Sweden', *Kvinnor Kön Och Forskning*, 13, 43–54.

Polk, M. (2008). 'Gender mainstreaming in Swedish transport policy', in T. Cresswell and T. P. Uteng (eds), *Gendered Mobilities*, London, Ashgate, 229–42.

Porter, G. (2008). 'Transport planning in sub-Saharan Africa II: putting gender into mobility and transport planning in Africa', *Progress in Development Studies*, 8, 281–89.

Rendell, J. (1998). 'Displaying sexuality: gender identities and the early 19th century street', in N. Fyfe (ed.), *Images of the Street: Planning, Identity, and Control in Public Space*, London, Routledge, 75–91.

Rosenbloom, S. (2004). 'Understanding women's and men's travel patterns: the research challenge', in *Research on Women's Issues in Transportation*, Conference Proceedings 35, Volume 1, Washington, Transportation Research Board, 7–28.

Rosenbloom, S. and Plessis-Fraissard, M. (2009). 'Women's travel in developed and developing countries: two versions of the same story?', in *Women's Issues in Transportation*, Conference Proceedings 46, Volume 1, Washington, Transportation Research Board, 63–77.

Ross, C. E. (2000). 'Walking, exercising, and smoking: does neighborhood matter?', *Social Science and Medicine*, 51, 265–74.

Roy, A. (2009). 'Gender, poverty, and transportation in the developing world', in *Women's Issues in Transportation*, Conference Proceedings 46, Volume 1, Washington, Transportation Research Board, 50–62.

Rutherford, B. M. and Wekerke, G. R. (1988). 'Captive rider, captive labor: spatial constraints on women's employment', *Urban Geography*, 15, 116–35.

Ryan, M. (1990). *Women in Public: Between Banners and Ballots, 1825–1880*, Baltimore, John Hopkins University Press.

Sánchez de Madariaga, I. (2013). 'From women in transport to gender in transport: challenging conceptual frameworks for improved policymaking', *Journal of International Affairs*, 67, 1–29.

Sheller, M. (2008). 'Gendered mobilities: Epilogue', in T. Cresswell and T. P. Uteng (eds), *Gendered Mobilities*, London, Ashgate, 257–66.

Shrinivasan, S. (2008). 'A spatial exploration of the accessibility of low-income women: Chengdu, China and Chennai, India', T. Cresswell and T. P. Uteng (eds), *Gendered Mobilities*, London, Ashgate, 143–58.

Tanzarn, N. (2008). 'Gendered mobilities in developing countries: the case of (urban) Uganda', in T. Cresswell and T. P. Uteng (eds), *Gendered Mobilities*, London, Ashgate, 159–72.

Transgen. (2007). *Gender Mainstreaming European Transport Research and Policies*, Copenhagen, University of Copenhagen, Coordination for Gender Studies.

Transport for London (TfL). (2004). *Expanding Horizons: Transport for London's Women's Action Plan*, London, TfL.

Transport for London (TfL). (2007). *Gender Equality Scheme 2007–2010*, London, TfL.

Trench, S., Oc, T. and Tiesdell, S. (1992). 'Safer cities for women: perceived risks and planning measures', *Town Planning Review*, 63, 279–93.

UN (United Nations). (2013). *The Millennium Development Goals Report*, New York, United Nations.

UN-Habitat and Huairou Commission. (2007). 'Global assessment on women's safety', (Draft Working Document). Nairobi, UN-Habitat and Huairou Commission.

Urry, J. (2000). *Sociology beyond Societies: Mobilities for the Twenty-first Century*, London, Routledge.

Uteng, T. P. (2009). 'Gender, ethnicity, and constrained mobility: insights into the resultant social exclusion', *Environment and Planning A*, 41, 1055–71.

Valenti, J. (2007). 'Is segregation the only answer to sexual harassment?', *The Guardian*, www.guardian.co.uk/lifeandstyle/2007/aug/03healthandwellbeing.gender/   (accessed 22 June 2016).

Valentine, G. (1992). 'Images of danger: women's sources of information about the spatial distribution of male violence', *Area*, 24, 22–29.

Valentine, G. (1996). '(Re)negotiating the "heterosexual street": Lesbian production of space', in N. Duncan (ed.), *BodySpace: Destabilizing Geographies of Gender and Sexuality*, London, Routledge, 146–55.

Wachs, M. (2009). 'Women's travel issues: creating knowledge, improving policy, and making change', in *Women's Issues in Transportation*, Conference Proceedings 46, Volume 1, Washington, Transportation Research Board, 41–49.

Wallace, R. R., Rodriguez, D., White, C. and Levine, J. (1999). 'Who noticed, who cares? Passenger reaction to transit safety measures', *Transportation Research Record*, 1666, 133–38.

Wolff, J. (1990). 'The invisible flâneuse: women and the literature of modernity', in J. Wolff (ed.), *Feminine Sentences: Essays on Women and Culture*, Cambridge, Polity Press, 34–50.

Women's Planning Network Inc. (1995). *Women's Transport Needs*, Victoria, Women's Planning Network.

World Bank. (2009). *World Development Report: Reshaping Economic Geography*, Washington, World Bank.

Young, I. M. (1990). *Throwing like a Girl and Other Essays in Feminist Philosophy and Social Theory*, Bloomington, Indiana University Press.

3

GENDERED MOBILITY PATTERNS OF CARERS IN AUSTRIA

Bente Knoll and Teresa Schwaninger

Introduction

Within transport planning and mobility research different parameters such as distance, vehicle ownership and availability, means of travel and trip purposes are all used to describe people's mobility behaviour. These parameters are also used when political decisions related to transport planning are being made. To obtain data, public administrators as well as public transport providers carry out standardised household travel surveys (Stopher, Wilmot, Stecher and Alsnih 2006). Questioning is carried out by means of PAPI (paper-and-pencil interviews), CATI (computer-aided telephone interviews) or CAWI (computer-aided web interviews). Using the examples of completed travel surveys, this chapter provides insight into these procedures in Austria. Our gender analysis shows that not only the interpretation of the data but also the questionnaires themselves reveal biases and simplifications, which conceal crucial aspects within mobility behaviour, particularly the behaviour of carers in their everyday lives. More robust data that could otherwise be obtained in transport planning and mobility research is therefore lacking. The findings suggest that more emphasis needs to be placed on the design of research methods as well as on the data collection process itself. Both quantitative and qualitative research approaches are important components of a mixed-methods approach that could more effectively yield and communicate more accurate results.

Quantitative Travel Survey Methods Analysed from a Gender Perspective

Using the examples of completed travel surveys, such as the Austrian-wide survey from 1995, the Lower Austrian survey from 2008, the Tyrolean survey from 2011 and the Austrian-wide survey of 2013/14, the authors provide insight into these procedures as they were carried out in Austria. These travel surveys collected information about an individual (socio-economic, demographic information), as well as their household circumstances (number of people living in the household, possession of vehicles etc.), and in-depth information concerning the trips and journeys that an individual has undertaken on a given day (number of trips, starting point, modes of transport, travel purpose, destination etc.).

All questionnaires from the Austrian travel surveys mentioned above used pre-defined weekdays to document the trips undertaken by household members older than the age of six. The travel surveys define 'trip' as every stationary change for an unequivocal purpose which takes place within the public sphere regardless of the modes of transportation used. A journey starts at a certain place, at a certain time and has a certain travel purpose. A trip can also be taken by several means of transportation. A trip ends when the person has achieved their purpose and/or the place reached at which an activity occurs. Within the questionnaire people provide information concerning their start and end location, the start and end time, mode(s) of travel and purpose of travel. Similar travel survey methodologies such as these are employed not only in Austria, but also in other countries, regions, or cities (Stopher, Wilmot, Stecher and Alsnih 2006).

Results from travel surveys taken in Austria provide empirical evidence of differences in mobility behavioural patterns between women and men. Appropriate literature and data evaluations repeatedly have indicated the following results (Knoll and Szalai 2005):

- Although the number of trips made by women and men per day is nearly equal (3.3 resp. 3.4 trips per day in Lower Austria), the average distance travelled on roads by women is shorter than for men: Trips with a length under 0.5 kilometres – which are mostly walkable distances – are undertaken by 15% of all interviewed women and just by 9% of all men. Trips with a length between 20 and 50 kilometres are undertaken by 11% of women, but by 16% of men.
- Regarding the duration of the trips, results indicate that trips taken by women lasted on average 23.4 minutes while trips taken by men lasted 28.4 minutes.
- Women use public means of transportation more often and walk more often than men. The average trip length for women is 29 kilometres per day, of which they travel 12 kilometres by car. Men's trip-length average is 46 kilometres per day, of which they travel 30 kilometres by car.
- Women tend to connect their activities during a single journey which results in their complex trip chains. (Knoll and Szalai 2005).

Concerning these four points above, it is crucial to point out the shortcoming of conclusions and figures stemming from limited or biased questionnaires. The analysis points out that, for everyday trips, the complex and differentiated trip chains with different purposes undertaken by people with child care duties or care responsibilities for the elderly still remain unaccounted for. In Austria, it is women who mostly bear the burden of unpaid work and childcare and therefore tend to work in paid jobs with shorter hours. They also generally work in sectors and occupations where jobs are compatible with their family responsibilities. As a result, women are more likely to work part-time, are employed in low-paid jobs and do not take on management positions. In 2014, 4,112,800 individuals (based on the international definition of the labour force concept) at the age of 15 years and older were employed in Austria. Of this figure, 2,966,300 individuals (1,029,000 women and 1,937,300 men) had full-time employment while 1,146,500 individuals (908,500 women and 238,000 men) worked part-time. However, the ratio of women to men is 35:65 for full-time employment and 79:21 for part-time employment (Stockinger and Schestak 2016: 32). For all employed women in 2016, 47.7% worked part-time while in 2006, 40.4% of women did so (Statistik Austria 2017). According to the gender pay gap published by Eurostat for 2015, women in Austria earned 21.7% less than men while the average pay gap for women across the 28 states of the EU was 16.3%. Lower incomes and the differences in employment opportunities for women and men ultimately result in women having lower pensions and a higher risk of poverty (Statistik Austria 2017). An analysis of the 200 top-selling companies in Austria shows that, at the management level, 7.2% of all positions are held by women. Among Austrian CEOs, only 3.6% are women (Spitzer and Wieser 2017). When it comes to gender roles in society within Austria, the unpaid housework and care responsibilities for children and the elderly are still mainly assumed by women. With the aid of a time-use survey it is possible to see how much time is spent by different groups in society on different activities each day. It is also possible to obtain information about the time of day the surveyed activities are performed. According to Statistik Austria, the 9.7 billion hours a year invested in housework such as childcare, caring for sick and elderly, or in voluntary work in Austria were accomplished primarily by women rather than men by a ratio of 2:1. On average, 92% of women and 74% of men carried out domestic work. Although the proportion of men, since the 1980s, who are engaged in housework has increased from less than 25% to now 75%, the time spent by men on such chores has, nevertheless, remained constant. Today women dedicate about 4 hours a day in doing the cooking, washing, cleaning and shopping while men spend, on average, 1.5 fewer hours working on such domestic chores (Ghassemi and Kronsteiner-Mann 2009).

Focussing on Travel Purposes

An in-depth look at travel surveys shows that trips related to purposes such as unpaid housework and care responsibilities for children and the elderly, remain invisible due to the fact that survey questions asking about such activities are not even raised.

Therefore, basic information on trips related to domestic care and housework is lacking in data used by decision makers in transport and urban planning.

Typical questions related to travel purpose usually provide answer-fields such as 'work', 'work-related', 'education', 'bringing and picking-up people', 'shopping', 'personal business (e.g., doctor's visit)', 'leisure activity' and 'home-related'. Moreover, a free field is usually provided for other purposes using a field marked as 'other, namely'. Only one out of these possibilities is to be marked ('Please pick only one trip activity' or 'You may tick one travel purpose'). This limitation causes a bias in favour of single-purposes trips being made.

From a gender perspective, such stated categories reflect current gender stereotypes and clichés (Knoll 2008). Purposes that are related to activities such as domestic work or care-providing are not questioned in their entire dimension and kept obscure within travel surveys and their results. Accompanying journeys or questions on trip chaining are also not provided. However, travel purposes that are related to paid work and the economic spheres have at least two answer-fields ('work' and 'work-related').

Within the questionnaires used in Austria, trip purposes are mainly seen as activities relating to a particular destination. Being on the move as an activity, e.g. going for a walk with the dog, strolling, walking – apparently without purpose or 'stopping along the way' trips, such as a trip chain from home to the bakery that continues on to the bus stop and to work, are not accounted for.

Thus, the common methods of mobility surveys do not adequately examine short trips or account for trips taken to accompany others or complex combinations of several destinations. The categories available under so-called 'travel purposes' reflect patriarchal living concepts. Trips made in connection with domestic work and care-giving are, therefore, either under-represented or fully hidden. This analysis shows that crucial information on people's mobility behaviour cannot be surveyed, analysed, or interpreted by employing the usual travel survey methods.

The separation of travel purposes and subsequently the planners' categorical interpretation of 'rush-hour traffic' and 'shopping traffic and leisure traffic' correspond to assumed patriarchal travel patterns of work and hence under-represent travel purposes related to childcare and other family or reproductive issues (Bauhardt 1995, 1997).

Day-to-day Trip Chains Remain Under-reported

In support of the argument that travel surveys reinforce bias principles that favour typical patriarchal travel patterns, we can portray the case of a 32-year-old man: He is a father on part-time paternity leave who carries out several activities and purposes, always in the company of his 2-year-old son and his 6 month-old daughter, which takes them to stops at the playground, the pharmacy and, further on, to the chemist's shop, bakery and grocery store. When filling out the travel survey, what options should be provided for describing such travel purposes?

- **Work** (?) As a father on part-time paternity leave he spends the working day at home. Can his current flat be considered to be his workplace? Also, with his work at home he must cover the expenses to care for his children.
- **Bringing and picking-up people** (?) On the one hand, this purpose should be ruled out because the son was not brought to a childcare facility. However, perhaps this could still be considered an option because the father has brought his son to the playground and has looked after him?
- **Shopping** (?) Yes, partly, but what about time spent at the playground?
- **Personal business** (?) No, not by any means! The father did not carry out any personal business; not at the playground, or at the chemist's shop (where he had to buy medicine for his son), or at the bakery (where bought a snack for his hungry child). However, maybe the trip to the grocery store can be considered as 'personal business' since the father also bought a newspaper for his pleasure?
- **Leisure activity** (?) Yes, this is the last but only possibility to be marked. The very last possibility to be marked ('back home') is used for the next trip.

Furthermore, the father will not mention person XX whom he had met along his way back home from the playground because the purpose of this trip was not to meet person XX. Additionally, the fact that his journey back home lasted longer due to his chat with person XX and because his children were playing along the way for half an hour, or longer than normal, are all issues that transport and urban planners should be more focused on in order to provide target-group-specific facilities in public spaces and infrastructure. Also, as it is not indicated 'with WHOM' the father undertook the trip, the vital aspect that he undertook an accompanying trip remains invisible.

Another example can be given as well: A person with care duties accompanies his/her children to their regular sports training and waits at the gym for an hour until the training is over. Which trip purpose should s/he mark?

- **Bringing and picking-up people** (?) What to do, then, with the hour-long waiting period?
- **Leisure activity** (?) This leisure time is related only to the children; however, the waiting period is, from the adult's perspective, without recreational value and recreational assets.

These examples show that possibilities to state that trips are for the purpose of care-taking are limited or missing in travel surveys.

Short Pedestrian Trips are Under-represented

Although more recent versions of travel surveys specify that all means of transport used for at least one trip are to be included, short pedestrian trips are not always considered by respondents.

One example: A person with care duties accompanies his/her children from the front door of their residential building to a public transport stop, which they reach by a three-minute walk. The trip continues by bus and ends with another short walking stage from the bus stop (which is 250 metres away from the building) to the entrance of the cinema. What modes should be stated by the respondent?

The correct indications would be:

- The first mode used is 'walking'.
- The second mode used is 'by bus'.
- And the third mode used is 'walking' again.

It is likely that the respondents will not include all modes, but reduce their statements to one mode, which is considered by them to be the 'main mode'. In this case, it will probably be the bus which will be chosen as the most important mode (Stopher, Wilmot, Stecher and Alsnih 2006).

Another example: People who commute by car and public transport and park their car in a Park-and-Ride facility at their final destination of an underground line are making – as part of their routine – a multimodal trip. Also, it is likely in this case that the respondents will not indicate walking as a mode of travel necessary to reach their final destination(s) in the inner districts. The result is an under-representation of pedestrian trips in travel surveys, which may lead to wrong priority setting in further planning activities.

A Gender-Sensitive Approach Is Needed

As the gender analysis above shows, not only the interpretation of the data, but also the travel surveys themselves reveal bias and simplifications, which veil crucial aspects of the mobility patterns of carers. It is obvious that a gender-sensitive approach is needed. A way to make up for this deficiency is to develop new surveying methods.

In order to respond to these issues, gender-sensitive, qualitative methods have been developed and applied by B-NK GmbH Consultancy for Sustainable Competence. This is to illustrate mobility patterns and needs of people accompanying other people or children during their day-to-day trip-making to a more satisfactory extent from a gender perspective. This work is based on the following hypothesis: Due to common quantitative mobility survey methods, travel habits and mobility patterns of those providing childcare and care for the elderly are underestimated.

The following section presents research that illustrates how to incorporate gender and diversity aspects into applied mobility research. It is important to keep in mind that from a mobility researcher's perspective, quantitative and qualitative methods are not to be regarded as diametrically opposed approaches. Rather, inclusiveness and multi-dimensioned perspectives are needed.

Women's Trips – Men's Trips

Based on results of the project 'Women's trips – men's trips' (commissioned by the Austrian Federal Ministry of Transport, Innovation and Technology, 2006–2007) (Knoll and Szalai 2008) as well as the gender analysis of Austrian common travel survey methods (Knoll 2008), a new gender-sensitive quantitative based travel survey was developed. The innovations of these surveys included the provision of categories to capture data covering more diverse family living arrangements of those being questioned, including response options for those persons not living in a household on a permanent basis. Since it has now become possible to focus on the mobility behaviour of adults according to such living arrangements, evidence can better reflect the mobility patterns of patchwork families. Questions for individuals with regular care-taking responsibilities became more revealing of mobility patterns for those escorting children, the elderly, or people with disabilities. One main change on the survey was the question concerning travel purpose, which was provided as an open question. Respondents were asked to write down, in their own words, the answer to the question, 'Why or for which purpose have you undertaken this trip?' To make accompanying trips visible, an additional question concerning 'other people with whom the trip was undertaken and the number of the children and/or number of the adults accompanied' was asked. For testing and validation purposes, the gender-sensitive travel survey was compared with a 'traditional' travel survey, both of which contain similar samples in terms of socio-economic and regional variables. An equal number of the traditional and gender-sensitive surveys were distributed to various sample groups.

Regarding the trip purposes, the results reveal the importance of each open question, to which each response given was recorded. Using two steps, the clustering of 21 different categories were arranged. Besides the well-known pre-defined categories of trips made for the purposes of work, work-related, education, school, shopping, pick up/drop off other people, home, the other pre-defined trip categories were collected in more detail: doctor's, health care, visiting friends, visiting relatives, meeting someone, going out for sports, going for a walk, further lessons e.g. music, dance, further training, honorary office, theatre, cinema and church-related trips.

Tyrolean Quantitative Travel Survey – Secondary Analysis from a Gender Perspective

In order to fill the gap of information that was lacking on gender-specific trip-related data, the Tyrolean Regional Government commissioned the report to provide a profound statistical working basis for the field of 'gender, traffic and mobility' (Knoll, Posch, Schwaninger and Spreitzer 2013). Within the survey itself, data on 21,145 trips from 5,092 participants was gathered. The secondary analysis from a gender perspective of the data provided had focused on the key indicators relevant for mobility: number of trips, duration of trips, distance of trips, purpose of trips, car availability and choice of transportation. A descriptive evaluation of the data was processed by means of a cluster analysis. In order to achieve an integral view from a gender perspective, in addition to the variable 'gender', further aspects were included like age, care-giving duties and scope of work. The Tyrolean travel survey (see Figure 3.1) was the one first one in Austria that reflected the previous formulated critique from a gender perspective. Within the written survey a question concerning care responsibilities was included.

Due to an in-depth gender analysis having taken gender roles into account, the following results could provide more revealing information in more detail:

- Number of trips: In comparison, men pursue fewer trips than women. Women older than 25 years tend to travel more.
- Duration of trips: Women's trips tend to take less time than men's. Women who work or are studying mainly take up to 5 minutes while men's trips respectively take 11 to 20 minutes.
- Distance of trips: Trips of both women and men predominantly have distances of between 2 to 5 kilometres. More than half of the trips up to ten kilometres are pursued by women while most of the trips longer than ten kilometres are pursued by men.
- Purpose of trips: All age groups older than 18 years display gender-stereotypical roles concerning the purpose of their trips. This is especially striking between the ages of 25 to 49 years.
- Car availability: Men have proportionally more frequent availability of cars at their disposal. Accordingly, women have less car availability or none at all. Statistically, part-time employees often don't have a car at their disposal to the extent that full-time employees do.
- Means of transportation: Proportionally, men travel more frequently by car or motorbike than women do. However, women are more often car passengers rather than driving on their own. They also travel more often by means of public transport or go by bike or foot.
- Regional differences: The shortest duration of trips for both women and men appears in central urban areas and in areas where the highest level of tourist activity take place. Remarkably, many trips are made by women in areas with high levels of tourism and in rural areas in order to retrieve or bring someone to their destination (accompanying trips).
- Teenagers: The average teenager only pursues two trips a day. This refers to both sexes. The duration of trips differs between girls and boys, especially

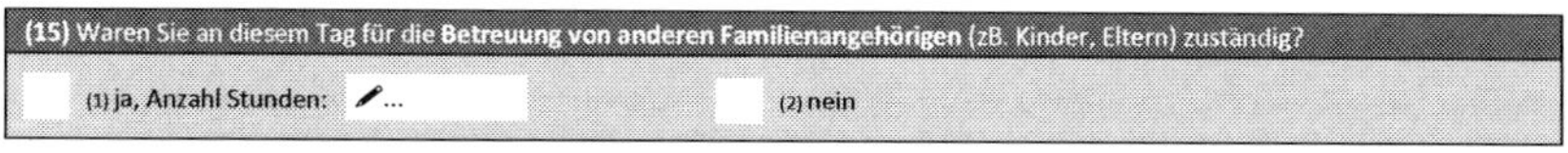

(15) Waren Sie an diesem Tag für die **Betreuung von anderen Familienangehörigen** (zB. Kinder, Eltern) zuständig?

(1) ja, Anzahl Stunden: ✎ ...   (2) nein

FIGURE 3.1   Detail from the written questionnaire

Source: Tyrolean Travel Survey 2011

at younger ages. For trips taken by young people up to 24 years of age, the predominant duration of women's trips ranged between 11 and 20 minutes while men's trips usually averaged up to 5 minutes in duration.

Case Study 1: 'Mobility4job'

This case study analyses the project 'Mobility4Job – Gender-appropriate mobility solutions for better working opportunities in rural areas', commissioned by the Austrian Research Agency and the Federal Ministry of Transport, Innovation and Technology (Unbehaun, Favry, Gerike, Hader, Knoll, Schwaninger and Uhlmann 2014). The goal of the project, which was conducted from 2012 to 2014, was to identify obstacles within the mobility system which hindered people from obtaining gainful employment. Furthermore, preconditions and mobility services in rural areas were defined in order to enable women and men who are responsible for the care of family members as well as their own households to have fair opportunities to participate in the workforce.

Part of the project was the work package 'qualitative mobility survey', which was conducted by the authors. It entailed conducting 15 in-depth interviews in rural areas (Triestingtal and Schneebergland, both located in the south-west region of Lower Austria). The central questions of the interviews focused on the respondent's personal attitude towards family, household, employment and the division of paid and unpaid work among family members. In addition, information concerning the day-to-day mobility patterns and travel purposes was also gathered.

Analysing Trips the 'Day Before'

During the research, special attention was given to those reported trips taken by participants the 'day before'. These trips were mapped to visualise the trip chains and their relations as well as their regional interrelations with the help of the method 'mapping everyday trips' (Knoll 2008), a gender-sensitive qualitative method for surveying people's everyday mobility that combines elements of surveying spatial structures of the built environment. 'Mapping everyday trips' is carried out, on the one hand, by conducting a face-to-face interview and, on the other hand, by mapping a person's everyday travel habits, trip patterns and the relevant everyday places on a city map that the respondent is familiar with. Thus, the everyday trips and the modes of transportation used could be visualised using various colours schemes on a map.

At the start of the interview process, the following questions were the first to be given focus: Where does a person typically start when setting out on a trip? Which trips are to be undertaken to help that person cope with her/his daily needs? What kinds of modes of transportation are used? What kind of activities take place within a residential area? What kind of activities take place farther away? This method is applicable for surveying people's everyday mobility that combines elements of surveying spatial structures of the built environment AND the day-to-day mobility modes and travel purposes of women and men. Using visual representations, as Figure 3.2 shows, mobility patterns and trip combinations of women, men and youth can be mapped out.

The example provides highlights of the various destinations and numerous trips that were undertaken (the dashed lines symbolise accompanied trips). During the interview, the respondent stated:

> And then, at about half past eight, or a quarter to nine, I went by car with my two boys to bring them to the kindergarten. They got out and I continued my travel and met my friend [x]. Afterwards, I drove that way to my grandmother's house, like I usually do on Tuesday. I am assisting my grandmother, which means I work there without charge.

This example shows, therefore, that trips used in everyday life require flexibility and innovative solutions in order to achieve a decrease in car use and consequently in car dependency.

Requirements Catalogue 'Adequate Mobility – Without Car Dependency: Gender-Sensitive Mobility in Rural Areas'

Based on the research, the 'Mobility4Job'-project team developed a 'Requirements catalogue' that depicts the action fields in spatial planning as well as measures in

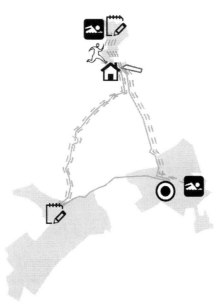

FIGURE 3.2 Visualisation of everyday trips
Source: B-NK GmbH.

transport and mobility for caregivers and the persons they care for. Relevant action fields are:

- Support of active mobility by foot and bike.
- Networking and interfaces in public transport.
- Quality of stations and means of transportation with regard to security and barrier-free access.
- Awareness-raising for active and environmentally friendly forms of mobility and their communication in public.
- Shared vehicles.
- Participation and targeted group-oriented spatial planning.

These relevant action fields show that gender-sensitive mobility planning does not necessarily include 'brand-new' solutions. In fact, gender-sensitive approaches are always in-line with the guiding principles of sustainable mobility planning and user-centred perspectives. Focus has been placed on encouraging students as well as elderly people and people with impaired mobility to attain more independence in terms of their travel behaviour. More independence for the care-takers means, consequently, more independence and extra time for caregivers.

The project results are outlined in the study 'On the move between job and family labour' as well as on the website www.regionale-mobilitaet.at – both of which are available in German only. The website presents solutions to improve regional mobility adapted to the requirements and resources of the particular municipality. Furthermore, it presents a compilation of resources for educators and parents to help implement projects that promote children's independent mobility. Methods on how to implement mobility strategies for children in schools as well as practical advice are comprehensively described.

Case Study 2: 'Gender Module'

The project 'Gender Module' was commissioned by the Federal Ministry of Transport, Innovation and Technology as an addition to the recent Austria-wide representative quantitative mobility survey conducted in 2013–2014 (Knoll, Fitz, Schwaninger, Spreitzer and Deimel 2016). In this piece of research, five areas with various (public) transportation and geographic characteristics in Austria were defined. In each area, face-to-face in-depth interviews were carried out with individuals who were responsible for (unpaid) day-to-day care of (their own) children, parents, in-laws etc. The five selected regions were:

- The inner-city districts of Vienna with a dense public transportation system and major infrastructure facilities.
- The City of Graz, the second largest city in Austria, with its inner districts as well as the outskirts, all of which have access to a relatively good public transportation system.

- The City of Eisenstadt which, as the regional state capital of Burgenland, serves as an example for mid-sized cities in Austria with a lower level of public transportation service that, nevertheless, supports a high-level of public service infrastructure, such as public authorities, secondary schools etc.
- The region of Waldviertel as a peripheral rural area with widespread villages and smaller cities that contain a limited supply of public transportation.
- The region of Defereggental as a peripheral alpine rural narrow valley with three municipalities with approximately 500 metres' distance of altitude from the lowest to the highest point of developed areas, and a limited supply of public transportation.

In addition to these five regions, another peripheral rural region with a limited supply of public transportation in the southern region of Burgenland was investigated (commissioned by the Office of the Provincial Government of Burgenland).

Up to now, little knowledge has been made available about unpaid carers and their mobility patterns or daily trips. For this research project, 143 in-depth interviews were carried out by the authors and their team between March 2013 and January 2014. A duration of 1 to 2 hours for each interview allowed for the team to conduct a personal conversation beyond the objective level and facilitated reflections by the interview partners. Detailed backgrounds and information concerning mobility patterns and related decisions of carers were generated and understood. The following questions arose: How does mobility behaviour differ between rural and urban areas in Austria? Which strategies do people apply to organise their mobility in everyday life and what kind of trip chains and mobility patterns occur? Which solutions were found for day-to-day mobility issues? What are the backgrounds for their mobility decisions concerning their work life, carer's life and leisure time altogether? Finally, what are the differences between travelling alone compared to accompanying others?

A trip is defined as a 'change of location for a specific purpose' (Fellendorf, Karmasin, Klementschitz, Kohla, Meschik and Rehrl 2011). If a trip involves the use of different means of transport (multimodal transport), it can be divided into several 'stages'. However, a trip chain can be described as a sequence of several trips with several purposes. The difficulty with trip chains is to define when a trip chain starts and when it ends, as there are no consistent definitions. One approach, however, can be taken towards defining a trip chain by asking the question: 'At which point of the journey does a new trip chain start and respectively end?'

- Time-wise (final destination is an activity that claims a certain timeframe).
- Problem – extent of the timeframe: For example, when I go to the bakery and afterwards go to the library for the rest of the day, is the way home from the library part of the same trip chain?
- Special activities ('a trip chain ends when the person arrives home or at the workplace').

- One problem posed is that of short 'side trips' to get home. An alternative definition of the final destination of a trip chain is to put focus on certain activities during which one could assume a certain 'mental' end of a trip chain, for example when getting home. However, this definition is also not really sufficient, since, a person might also make a short side trip to go back home to retrieve his or her umbrella when it rains.

Accompanying Trips

Trips pursued for and with people in need of company – i.e. children, elderly people, or persons with disabilities – are defined as accompanying trips. The term 'accompanying trips' can have a broad range of meanings. Accompanying trips can be obligatory, voluntary, necessary or a combination of these. Small children depend on the company and transport provided by care-giving persons. Sometimes even older children and grown-ups or persons with disabilities need someone to accompany and support them on their way. The crucial difference between voluntary and necessary accompanying trips depends on the level of dependency of the person to be accompanied. It is less a matter of age, but rather of restrictions, such as with safety and security issues, when determining the extent to which a person has a certain level of independent mobility. Reasons for restricted mobility can be due to factors such as illnesses, physical or mental disabilities, as well as insufficient availability of transportation.

Accompanying trips signify special challenges to care-giving persons. Requirements, wishes and the demands of the person to be accompanied, plus further factors like time, everyday life organisation, weather-related impediments, etc. influence the carer's mobility decisions in essential ways. The more people, with their individual requirements, that are involved in a trip chain, the more complex the choice of means of transportation gets. A multitude of questions – even if they might seem plain and simple – need to be clarified before starting. Dependents of the persons to be accompanied, their requirements, the chosen transport(s), as well as various external factors all create different sets of priorities. For example, the security and quality of chosen paths are the first priority for accompanying trips by foot or bike or with children and babies. Besides security considerations, short and barrier-free paths are definitely decisive when making accompanying trips with persons who have needs associated with reduced mobility.

General Characteristics of Carer's Mobility Patterns

Characteristics of crucial distinctions between solo travel and accompanying trips for or with others emerged from the survey results. Accompanying someone means taking over responsibility not only for oneself but also for the accompanied person. The accompanied person's requirements, wishes and demands become central for the carer and influence routes and means of transportation. Time management gets more complex because accompanying someone influences everyday life organisation on distinct levels which makes time a determining characteristic. Carers have to balance a schedule that accommodates several chores, trips and (perhaps) the opening hours of childcare facilities or schools together with their own work schedules, routes and available forms of transport. It is understandable that an area of tension could develop between precise organisation and flexibility. On the one hand, care-giving duties demand a thoroughly planned everyday life and selection of routes to fulfil necessary tasks punctually and efficient use of a timeframe. On the other hand, a certain degree of flexibility is required. Furthermore, the focus shifts from simply reaching the arrival point, when travelling alone, to 'spending time together' when travelling with someone else. The social aspect of travelling together and adapting to the requirements of accompanied persons leads to a change of perspective.

The following statements given to the interviewers demonstrate the issues that characterise the mobility patterns of carers:

- **Responsibility**: 'As long as the kids sit in the baby carriage, you can handle the situation. But when they start walking on their own, approximately at the age of three, you bear a great responsibility. You have to keep your eyes on the kids and look after them, so that nothing happens. For me, that is the big difference'.
- **Steadiness and flexibility**: 'These are two counterparts. On one hand, we have got a well-structured agenda of the week and well-organised workdays. But on the other hand, you have to keep flexible. There are so many odds and ends that force you to change your plans'.
- **Time as a determining factor**: 'One has to schedule more time for everything when accompanying kids. There are no just-for-fun-trips. And that does not change even when the children get older'.
- **Needs of accompanied people get more important**: 'When accompanying my walking-impaired father, I have to look out for a parking lot with enough space at the passenger's side for him to get out of the vehicle. I have to help him out of the vehicle. Everything goes very slowly'.

Care-giving Responsibilities Cause Complex Trip Chains

Day-to-day trips of care-giving people are not only influenced by specific challenges coming up in particular situations, but are also characterised by complex trip chains. Within the framework of the project 'Gender Module' various complexity factors could be identified, which appeared in the daily routine of the study participants. Figure 3.3 illustrates the factors that influence the complexity of trip chains:

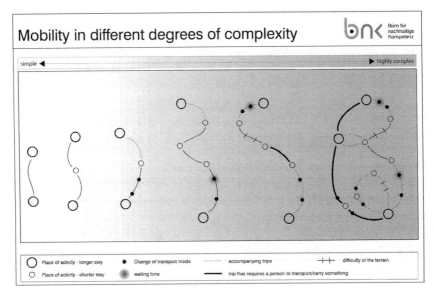

FIGURE 3.3   The complexity of trip chains and their influencing factors
Source: B-NK GmbH.

- Many activities during one trip chain: Accompanying trips are characterised by a high number of activities which need to be accomplished during trip chains. In addition to personal activities, additional activities for the persons under care have to be undertaken. For example: An adult leaves home to go on a short business trip accompanied by a child. Afterwards, they continue their trip chain to visit the doctor since the child needs to receive some medication.
- After the doctor's visit, the person has to do some shopping for the family. The child naturally has to come with the person. The question should then be asked: Who is accompanying whom?
- Many stages during one trip chain: Another complexity factor is the division of one trip into many stages. This is often necessary to meet the needs of the person under care as well as to accommodate the accompanying trip. One interviewee, for example, told us that he or she wanted his or her child to get to school by foot. So, he or she first accompanies the child to the school and then gets to work by car, even though it is the same direction. Another example: as a small child is not yet able to ride a bike, the carer does not choose for her/his trip their own bike, as she/he otherwise would have, but rather chooses walking (to the bus station) and riding the bus while accompanying the child.
- Further influences like carrying heavy or bulky loads and having, along the way, the 'necessary stuff' (such as buggy, shopping goods, drinks, medicines, etc.) and choosing the proper form of transport (depending on availability

and personal attitude towards means of transportation) all increase the complexity of the trip. This 'necessary stuff', which always needs to be available, is typical of a carer's trip chains.

- Barriers and the need of accessibility: In the context of heavy loads, possible barriers need to be considered as well. Having barrier-free accessibility is understood as a crucial precondition.
- Moreover, trip chains are characterised by a high degree of planning and coordinating that is often facilitated only through the help of others. Trip chains are the result of detailed planning and communication processes as well as assistance from other people (e.g. a privately organised transport service for children, operated by their parents). Often, carers must plan extensively in order to carry out their trip chains. This planning requires a good deal of communication and often involves other persons. In our qualitative research, for example, we learned about parents who organised a private transport service for their children.
- Need for awareness and safety: The special needs and the potential inappropriate behaviour of the persons under care require strategies from carers to handle difficult situations in everyday mobility. They therefore developed certain strategies to ensure the safety along the trip chain. Some interviewees, for example, choose different routes when they are with children.
- Unforeseeable situations and the time-sensitive variability of procedures are common elements of everyday life and of mobility patterns.
- Lack of flexibility: Flexibility is especially important for carers. Because the responsibility of care can bring with it unforeseeable situations, a certain variability concerning the duration of activities is needed. However, this flexibility is not always possible, especially in connection with paid working life.

With all aspects taken into consideration, trip chains present different degrees and variations of complexity. Nevertheless, in most cases, trip chains consist of a simple trip pattern (e.g. walking the child to kindergarten and continuing to a paid job) or a single trip (e.g. walking alone to the bakery).

Manifold Needs and Obstacles of Carers Regarding Their Modes of Transportation

Although there are various challenges that carers have to face on their daily journeys, especially in rural areas, one particular problem is that of **the last mile problem**, as made evident by the following carer testimony:

> A few years ago we moved two kilometres further away and now everything is a bit more difficult. Those two kilometres mean that the next bus stop is further away but despite this we still use public transport and bikes.

Another testimony emphasises the lack of necessary flexibility that carers face in rural areas:

> Let's say, I know that I have to be at a certain location at 3 pm. For a bus trip that is half an hour long, I would actually have to leave my home one hour earlier. Therefore, I have to allow twice the travel time as a buffer, since my child may not walk fast enough, or the traffic light suddenly turns red, or the bus leaves a minute or two early to stay on schedule, or in case there is any breakdown or disruption in service – any of these scenarios could conceivably happen. All in all, using public transport means I attend fewer appointments in a day than I would have attended if I had a car.

Additional problems for carers on **public transport** include issues such as a lack of connections between modes of transport, mismatching timetables, lack of barrier-free access, rude or inattentive passengers and weather-related impediments. In certain cases, time pressure discourage carers from choosing public transport over other mobility options. 'Just like I said, public transport isn't an option for us, because of the limitations of a fixed-route service. It's out of question since it takes over one and a half hours – and that's a long time'.

Concerning mobility by **car** (motorised private transport) different factors were noted such as high costs, bad weather conditions, lack of parking spaces, heavy traffic and jammed roads, especially during rush hour in urban areas. It became obvious that carers preferred to travel mostly by car, if available, for practical reasons, or even considered cars as their only choice when travelling with children or elderly persons.

In consideration of the **bicycle** as an alternative form of travel, several negative factors, most notably poor cycling infrastructure, discourage this. Besides dangerous traffic situations, physical effort, little comfort, problems in transporting other persons, or weather-related impediments are all significant problems when travelling by bicycle. Infrastructural deficits like fragmentary or non-existing networks of cycle paths and lack of lighting complicate day-to-day trips by bike and make them more dangerous.

Interviewees stated that **walking** also entails infrastructural problems like inadequate conditions for pedestrians and paths lacking barrier-free access (e.g. few crossing options, narrow pavements, plus barriers like traffic signs or post boxes, etc.) Further problems such as conflicts with other traffic participants and the dangers they posed were mentioned. Furthermore, long distances that are difficult to overcome by foot, as well as the need for transporting goods, were described as hindering factors.

> Unfortunately, there are still existing pavements with widths of 1 to 1.5 metres, and the public garbage cans which are located on the pavements

have a width of 55 centimetres, meaning that you can't pass them. On the way to our kindergarten when I was going with the baby carriage, I actually had to stop sometimes, putting the garbage cans on the parking lane, deliberately.

To conclude, this study surveyed the mobility needs of those people who are responsible for family members' care as well as their existing mobility obstacles. In accordance with the qualitative paradigm, this study provided a detailed understanding of those processes, mobility patterns and travel purposes, as well as their connections with a care-giver's daily life and care duties. This qualitative approach enables a multiple perspective on the mobility of people who are active carers. As a result of this study, it became apparent that far more information about everyday mobility patterns and trip chains can be generated than by simply focussing on the 5 to 7 pre-defined categories of 'travel purposes' (i.e. 'work', 'work-related', 'education', 'bringing and picking-up people', 'shopping', 'personal business (e.g., doctor's, authority)', 'leisure activity' and 'home-related') that are found in typical survey instruments (Knoll and Szalai 2005, 2008; Stopher, Wilmot, Stecher and Alsnih 2006). However, qualitative interviews reveal more hidden aspects that exist in the rigours of a carer's daily programme, such as complex trip chains with stops and multi-purpose destinations as well as those supporting and hindering factors when choosing a particular mode of transport over another.

This aspect of "travelling alone" means that I can act on an impulse. If something spontaneous occurs to me, I can simply shift my plan completely and act spontaneously – because I don't have to care. [...] But when I have my child with me, I am obliged to stick to a pre-defined plan or agenda – more or less.

Conclusions and Outlook

In general, our findings suggest that compared to quantitative mobility surveys with standardised questionnaires, the qualitative and gender-sensitive approach provides several benefits. Firstly, due to the face-to-face setting of the interviews within the case studies mentioned above, the respondents are actively encouraged to reflect upon their actions and habits in consideration of their own personal mobility patterns. Secondly, during the interviews, attempts were made to recall with each individual respondent the trip chain of their entire journey, including those stops made between trips that cannot be compiled in an accurate way using current quantitative methods. Thirdly, it is conceivable that there might be instances in which a respondent will not be able to accurately recollect certain segments of a trip. Using qualitative methods, such missing elements are registered. Fourthly, researchers using qualitative approaches are also able to enquire and determine why a respondent decided in favour of or against a particular mode of transportation. With the qualitative approach, the respondent's actions and habits can therefore be better 'understood' in the way of a 'general understanding' rather than just simply 'explained' with the help of pre-defined categories (Lamnek 2005: 182).

As life and also mobility patterns are getting more and more diverse, a qualitative survey should always accompany a quantitative survey in future. Mobility patterns and people's needs concerning mobility and transportation should no longer be understood based on typical socio-economic attributes such as age OR gender OR regional allocation. With the help of a gender and diversity perspective the multifaceted relationship between gender AND age AND care responsibility AND regional allocation can be tackled and taken into account. A mixture of methods is important in order to gain a more holistic view on the mobility patterns of people (Knoll 2016).

Acknowledgement

We want to thank all the interview partners and the staff of B-NK GmbH who supported and provided helpful comments on previous versions of this paper. The authors also gratefully acknowledge the grant from FFG (Austrian Research Promotion Agency), BMVIT (Austrian Federal Ministry of Transport, Innovation and Technology), Amt der Burgenländischen Landesregierung (Office of the Provincial Government of Burgenland) and Amt der Tiroler Landesregierung (Office of the Provincial Government of Tyrol). Special thanks additionally goes out to our partners within the project 'Mobility4Job': Wiebke Unbehaun, Tina Uhlmann (BOKU, University of Natural Resources and Life Sciences, Vienna) Eva Favry (Rosinak und Partner, Vienna) and Thomas Hader (Chamber of Labour, Vienna).

References

Bauhardt, Christine (1995). *Stadtentwicklung und Verkehrspolitik. Eine Analyse aus feministischer Sicht.* Berlin: Birkhäuser Verlag.
Bauhardt, Christine (1997). Mobilität und Raumstruktur. Feministische Verkehrspolitik in der Kommune. In: Becker, Ruth and Bauhardt, Christine (Eds.). *Durch die Wand! Feministische Konzepte zur Raumentwicklung.* Pfaffenweiler: Centaurus Verlagsgesellschaft, pp. 159–177.
Fellendorf, Martin, Karmasin, Helene, Klementschitz, Roman, Kohla, Birgit, Meschik, Michael and Rehrl, Karl (2011). KOMOD – Konzeptstudie Mobilitätsdaten Österreichs. Gesamtbericht. Edited by Bundesministerium für Verkehr, Innovation und Technologie (BMVIT). Available online at https://online.tugraz.at/tug_online/voe_main2.getVollText?pDocumentNr=287638&pCurrPk=69314, checked on 3/18/2014.
Ghassemi, Sonja and Kronsteiner-Mann, Christa (2009). Zeitverwendung 2008/09. Ein Überblick über geschlechtsspezifische Unterschiede. Endbericht der Bundesanstalt Statistik Österreich an die Bundesministerin für Frauen und Öffentlichen Dienst. Edited by Statistik

Austria. Wien. Available online at www.bka.gv.at/DocView.axd?CobId=40387, checked on 9/15/2013.

Knoll, Bente (2008). *Gender Planning. Grundlagen für Verkehrs- und Mobilitätserhebungen.* Saarbrücken: vdm Verlag Dr. Müller.

Knoll, Bente (2016). Gender & Mobilität. Herausforderungen und Grenzen beim Messen des Unterwegs-Seins von Menschen aus einer Gender-Perspektive. In: Wroblewski, Angela, Kelle, Udo and Reith, Florian (Eds.). *Gleichstellung messbar machen. Grundlagen und Anwendungen von Gender- und Gleichstellungsindikatoren.* Wiesbaden: Springer VS, pp. 129–148.

Knoll, Bente, Fitz, Bernadette, Schwaninger, Teresa, Spreitzer, Georg and Deimel, Andrea (2016). Mobilität von Personen mit Betreuungsaufgaben. Qualitative Studie (Gender Modul) zur österreichweiten Mobilitätserhebung "Österreich unterwegs 2013/2014". Available online at www.bmvit.gv.at/verkehr/gesamtverkehr/statistik/oesterreich_un terwegs/downloads/Mobilitaet_von_Personen_mit_Betreuungsaufgaben.pdf, checked on 12/ 17/2016.

Knoll, Bente, Posch, Patrick, Schwaninger, Teresa and Spreitzer, Georg (2013). Auswertung der Tiroler Mobilitätserhebung nach gender- und gesellschaftsrelevanten Fragestellungen. Available online at www.b-nk.at/wp-content/uploads/2015/07/B-NK-2013-Bericht_Mobilitaet_in_Tirol_B-NK_finale_gesamt.pdf, checked on 7/21/2015.

Knoll, Bente and Szalai, Elke (2005). Gender Mainstreaming und Mobilität in Niederösterreich. Edited by Amt der NÖ Landesregierung, Abteilung für Gesamtverkehrsangelegenheiten. Schriftenreihe Niederösterreichisches Landesverkehrskonzept, Vol. 22.

Knoll, Bente and Szalai, Elke (2008). Frauenwege – Männerwege. Entwicklung von Methoden zur gendersensiblen Mobilitätserhebung. Edited by Bundesministerium für Verkehr, Innovation und Technologie (BMVIT). Forschungsarbeiten aus dem Verkehrswesen, Vol. 175.

Lamnek, Siegfried (2005). *Qualitative Sozialforschung: Lehrbuch.* Weinheim and Basel: Beltz Verlag.

Spitzer, Sonja and Wieser, Christina (2017). Frauen Management Report 2017. Aufsichtsrat, Geschäftsführung und Prokura neu. Edited by Arbeiterkammer Wien. Available online at https://media.arbeiterkammer.at/wien/PDF/studien/AK_Frauen_Manage ment_Report_2017.pdf, checked on 7/8/2017.

Statistik Austria (Ed.) (2017). Gender Statistics. Available online at www.statistik.at/web_en/statistics/PeopleSociety/social_statistics/gender_statistics/index.html, checked on 7/8/2017.

Stockinger, Sieglinde and Schestak, Sandra (2016). Frauen und Männer in Österreich: Gender Index 2015. Geschlechterspezifische Statistiken. Edited by Bundesministerium für Bildung und Frauen (BMBF). Available online at www.bmb.gv.at/frauen/gender/gender_index_2015.pdf?5lidom, checked on 7/8/2017.

Stopher, Peter, Wilmot, Chester G., Stecher, Cheryl and Alsnih, Rahaf (2006). Household Travel Surveys: Proposed Standards and Guidelines. In: Stopher, Peter and Stecher, Cheryl (Eds.). *Travel Survey Methods. Quality and Future Directions.* Oxford and Amsterdam: Elsevier Ltd, pp. 19–74.

Unbehaun, Wiebke, Favry, Eva, Gerike, Regine, Hader, Thomas, Knoll, Bente, Schwaninger, Teresa and Uhlmann, Tina (2014). Unterwegs zwischen Erwerbs- und Familienarbeit. Eine Analyse in den niederösterreichischen Regionen Triestingtal und Schneebergland. Edited by AK Wien. Available online at www.regionale-mobilitaet.at/images/Unterwegs_zwischen_Erwerbs-und_Familienarbeit_2014.pdf, checked on 7/24/2015.

4

VIOLENCE AGAINST WOMEN IN MOVING TRANSPORTATION IN INDIAN CITIES

Reconceptualising Gendered Transport Policy

Yamini Narayanan

Introduction

The brutal gang rape and murder of a 23-year-old female student on a moving private bus in Delhi in December 2012 drew an unprecedented public outpouring of outrage and resistance in the capital and several Indian cities. Rapes, beatings and murders of women on moving transportation have been a fairly routine occurrence since the liberalisation of the Indian economy in the 1990s, when women started to emerge into the public in larger numbers to pursue education and employment opportunities (Amrute 2015). Among other things, this also led to the expansion of the Indian middle classes in India and, indeed, across South Asia. Gendered violence in public spaces – especially in transportation, a key site of growth and expansion – acquires specific class dimensions, and can be located at the unstable intersections of class, gender and urban spaces (Amrute 2015).

However, the gruesome nature of the widely publicised Delhi gang rape was the breaking point of decades. Notably, the December 2012 protests were not limited to rape, gang rape, and murder alone. The language of feminists following the Delhi gang rape/murder went beyond the limits of anti-rape discourse to encompass total freedom of movement, expression, desire and agency (Amrute 2015). The Delhi gang rape was also a profound reminder to seriously address the structural inequities in public policies and institutions – particularly urban planning and transportation policies – that allow women to be vulnerable to violence in the public spaces of the city. The fast pace of neoliberal growth, and the scale and speed of urbanisation in developing countries such as India necessitate swift corresponding changes in urban and transportation policies to meet the needs of a rapidly growing urban population. However, it is the economic and increasingly environmental aspects of transportation that constitute mainstream debates and discussions of sustainable transport planning, leaving the vulnerabilities of identity politics to be relegated to the less considered "social" planning (Jones & Lucas 2012; Levy 2013). Leinbach (2000: 2) says:

> The theory linking transport influences to social and economic change has not really been refined much beyond the general and aggregative levels … Few studies have addressed the matter of the distributional consequences of change nor derived comprehensive explanation to deal with this set of issues.

The gendered dimensions of equitable transport policies are crucial to all dimensions of development; freedom and ease of mobility are intimately linked with the alleviation of poverty, gender equality and empowerment (Uteng & Cresswell 2008). The routine violence against women that occurs in public and private transportation in Indian cities is a serious planning issue that is entrenched in deep social inequities. Much of transport planning in India is not only gender-insensitive, it is not even gender-neutral. Without addressing entrenched, deep-rooted patriarchies that sustain women's vulnerabilities in the private and public spheres of life, the foundations that sustain neoliberalism – such as urban infrastructures – have taken on similarly gendered biases. As Vasconcellos (2001: 5) writes, in most developing cities, "transport systems … propagate an unfair distribution of accessibility and reproduce safety and environmental inequities."

Since the liberalisation of the Indian economy in the 1990s, the opportunities of neoliberalism for women – without accompanying social change in patriarchal perceptions of women's traditional roles and statuses – have come with a violent backlash against their increased mobility and visibility in public. A key site of this contestation has been public and private transport in cities. However, in India the research funding and time allocated to prioritising and closely understanding gendered vulnerabilities in public transport has been almost entirely ignored (Levy 2013), even in the aftermath of the Delhi gang rape.

This chapter highlights the urgent need for planners in India to take on social change and engagement in order to deliver gender-sensitive, socially equitable transport policies. It argues that without deeply engaging with social issues, transport planning in India will not only remain gender-insensitive but in fact be complicit in reproducing, co-producing, and intensifying existing gendered inequalities. The chapter engages with two issues in particular. One, it shows how liberalisation has foregrounded the necessity for planning to participate in the project of engendering social change. Two, it addresses the only gender-conscious strategy that *some* planning authorities have conceptualised, in *some* transport networks, such as selected trains or buses, namely gender-segregated spaces on public transportation. Without getting involved in destabilising the patriarchy that has called for such an approach in the first place, urban planning can in fact intensify existing social inequities. The policy space, which is the most creative space for the encounter of the public space with the private, offers the opportunity for reflective planning wherein real change can be conceptualised. This requires planning – and planners – to take on hitherto radically different roles and engage with more knowledge and cultural systems than they have previously done.

VAW Urban Policy and Social Change

Globally, sexual violence against women (VAW) on urban transportation is surprisingly pervasive, though it rarely receives the attention that a problem of such magnitude deserves. In Japan, nearly 50 per cent of women over 20 years of age report at least one experience of being molested on trains (Horii & Burgess 2012). Consistent with such crimes around the world, studies across South Asian cities reveal that younger women such as university students are especially targeted for sexual abuse and violence in moving transport (Neupane & Chesney-Lind 2014). *Pakistan Today* (2011) reports that an overwhelming 92 per cent of women prefer to travel in women-only coaches on public transport. Further, transport workers themselves are regarded by women with fear and mistrust. Nepalese women report that bus conductors are among the highest perpetrators of sexual and gendered abuse as they work in maximum physical proximity to women (Action Aid 2013). The police are viewed with deep suspicion by women themselves.

In India, a study in 2008 found that nearly two-thirds of the women surveyed reported facing sexual abuse on public transport which ranges from groping, fondling, pinching of private parts, obscene language, deliberate leaning and touching, and intimidation (Chockalingam & Vijaya 2008). More than 25,000 rapes were noted by the National Crimes Record Bureau of India in 2012, of which about half occurred in different types of moving public transportation such as buses, taxis and auto-rickshaw three-wheelers. (Paul 2014). Anand and Tiwari (2006: 78) write:

> Women are the targets of sexual harassment while travelling to work and practically every woman interviewed had anecdotal evidence of suffering from the same. Harassment while walking down the street or travelling on a bus is a common occurrence for working women and is exacerbated by the absence of adequate lighting on streets and subways and by the small, lonely paths connecting the slum with the bus stops.

The 1993 United Nations Declaration on the Elimination of Violence against Women defines such violence as:

> any act of gender-based violence that results in, or is likely to result in, physical, sexual, or psychological harm or suffering to women, including threats of such acts, coercion or arbitrary deprivation of liberty, whether occurring in public or private life.

The vulnerabilities include not only physical assault and battery, and abduction, and murder, but also verbal abuse and "passive" violence (such as suggestive and intimidating staring, gesturing, indicating, and touching, among other acts). The objectification of women by regarding their physical bodies as targets to be abused and violated makes them vulnerable as well as consciously/unconsciously perpetuates their status as men's property to do with as they wish.

In India, women interviewed by a joint Jagori/UN project report that they believe their gender status to be their key vulnerability in urban public spaces, especially on public transport, putting it well above religion, ethnicity or age (Jagori and UN Women 2011). Freedom and autonomy in a public space is constituted by the capacity to maintain a measure of interpersonal distance, which can only be changed with mutual consent (Bowman 1993). When this freedom is violated without permission or consent, a woman's safety may be said to be compromised or in danger.

I previously suggested that VAW in public spaces needs to be mainstreamed in urban policy as a "sustainability problem" as it fundamentally compromises gender equality (Narayanan 2012). I now extend this further to argue that the social dimensions of urban sustainability in particular, in this case transport planning, need to be closely understood in order to deliver gender-equitable outcomes. On moving transport, the environmental factors that contribute to women's safety and freedom are comprised not only of design elements, but vitally, the socio-political-cultural factors and interchanges that also frame the urban landscape. Indeed, "urban transport" may be collectively understood as the sum aggregate of "the interrelationship between transport and urban processes, and the practices of transport planning – which together could be understood as a transport system" (Levy 2013: 48).

Without addressing the transport system in this entirety, it would be impossible to institute forward-thinking norms for addressing gender imbalances that currently obstruct equitable gendered access to mobilities. However, currently, modern transport planning, certainly in India, does not recognise:

> at least three critical issues central to transport and transport planning, namely the different social positions and multiple identities of transport users; the social construction of space, public and private; and the politics of transport in the context of social relations.
>
> *(Levy 2013: 49)*

Liberalisation, Mobility and Its Gendered Discontents

The liberalisation of the Indian economy in the early 1990s was heralded, among other things, by an unprecedented emergence of women into the public as professionals, and educational opportunities opened up rapidly. The sudden and widespread visibility of women in the public space, hitherto largely confined to the private, domestic sphere, has been accompanied by violence. Since liberalisation, studies have noted an escalated rate of violent crimes in public spaces of India's cities that involve a literal or a metaphorical collision of class and gender. Prominent among these crimes are the hit-and-run cases of middle/upper-class owners of luxury cars mowing down the homeless urban poor on sidewalks and pavements, and the moving vehicle as a site for physical – usually sexual – crime against women. This pattern is consistent with rapidly liberalising economies elsewhere. Twenty years ago, China reported that more than 88 per cent of women experienced sexual harassment on public transport, which included groping and obscene language, and was a notable escalation of such crimes from previous years (Can 1994). This period coincides with the start of the liberalisation of the Chinese economy, and the ensuing visibility of women into the public spaces as workers and professionals. Chesney-Lind (2013) explains the swift backlash against women's public visibility during rapid development and change that is yet to permeate or change old social norms:

> Especially in fast-growing developing economies like India, educational and occupational opportunities are expanding. Yet to take advantage of these opportunities, women must leave spaces defined as "private" – spaces controlled by family members or familiar neighbors – and move around in the public domain. In public areas they can seem "out of place" and fair game. They become vulnerable to threatening attacks or harassment. Women in developing nations certainly enjoy greater mobility, but their freedom to move and claim new opportunities comes at a cost ...

As women become more visible in public spaces, they become more exposed to "micro-inequalities" which typically manifest in different types of sexual harassment and assault that can range from "leering looks, winking, and gestures – to offensive acts such as unnecessary touching, unnecessary leaning or pressing against the woman, unexpected touching of the breast, brushing of thighs and bottoms, pinching of the bottoms, and pinching of the hips" (Chesney-Lind 2013). The pervasive extent of such violence in public spaces indicates that this is supported and reinforced by governance institutional systems to covertly deter women from accessing the opportunities of public spaces and services. As Eh Nahry (2012) notes from her work on cities of the Middle East:

> harassment is ... an institutionalized system of violence that functions to police women's participation, freedom of movement and behaviour in public spaces. It is not how women behave in the public sphere that makes them vulnerable to street harassment; it is that they have chosen to enter the public sphere at all.

These concerns echo strongly across Indian cities where the reconfigurations of power in gendered relations have been wrought by neoliberalism, not deeper social change and reflection. As such, women bear the brunt of the anxieties and outrage that accompany such one-dimensional change and as Agrawal and Sharma (2015: 423–24) note, the consequences for women frequently manifest in the highest criminal offences:

> The presence of women in public spaces is bound to be a source of unease in a society where their presence is not accepted unconditionally across the social spectrum. Very serious instances of gang rapes and even murder of women travelling in public and semi-public transport systems have already surfaced in the city of Delhi, making this an issue of significant social and political concern.

Mobility also does not occur in a social vacuum; rather, it takes place in a socio-cultural space whose political history shapes the infrastructure that allows or discourages feminised presence and movement in the public spaces of the city. "Being mobile is not just about geographical space but also, and probably above all, about social space" (Cattan 2008: 86). The particular socio-political tensions that rape in moving transport epitomises are fraught with class-based concerns that mark gendered relations in a changing political economy – but without accompanying socio-cultural changes. The embedded social codes, perceptions and relations of men and women in any society, and gendered identities, extend on to gendered interchanges in the public; the unstable space of moving transport, and freedoms located therein are determined by these gendered socio-cultural norms. Beyond the normative markers of social identity such as race, culture, age, and religion, among others, Levy (2013: 47) writes:

> The social identities of transport "users" are deeply embedded in social relations and urban practices, the latter ranging from the everyday lives of people to urban policies and planning. Furthermore, in transport, these social relations are played out in public space, with implications for how diverse women and men, girls and boys are able to exercise individual and collective "travel choice" and negotiate access to essential activities in the city.

Transportation is a highly critical and uneasy terrain that connects rapid change and postliberal modernity in the public sphere to older traditional gendered codes in the private realm. Rape in a moving vehicle has come to illustrate the rapid social changes wrought by liberalism in a socio-cultural context which has not had the time to evolve to accommodate these without upheaval. Public transport is currently geared towards male users based on a traditional model of division of labour; however, it is also not equipped to address and contain the violence that is caused by the social disruption of these traditional models (Levy 2013). Amrute (2015) analyses rape by locating it at the intersection of class, gender, mobility in urban spaces.

In this case, moving transportation, particularly private or semi-private vehicles like cars or privately owned buses become sites where class and gender can intersect, and both class and gender vulnerabilities can be exploited. Typically, reported crimes are of higher-class men in luxury cars raping vulnerable lower-class women, or working-class men working as employees/drivers or in buses, raping higher-class women. Rich men also take advantage of the vulnerability of poorer women such as maids. The lack of adequate public transportation and the consequent proliferation of private buses operating to supplement the state transport services, interestingly, serves to bring together an encounter of the classes.

Private buses such as the ones in which the Delhi physiotherapy student was raped and murdered now run on Indian cities by the hundred to supplement the highly inadequate numbers of public transportation. These buses rely on the large numbers of unemployed youth (Amrute 2015). Moving public and private transportation exposes women to similar vulnerabilities. Key among these is the invisibility of the perpetrator of violence, and a considerably diminished risk of being caught. Neupane and Chesney-Lind (2014: 23) write that "It appears that public transport offers males both proximity and anonymity, which, in turn, results in high levels of abuse with very little risk of social or legal consequences." The moving vehicle is a site for gendered class battles where the poor transport the middle classes to and from sites of their class consumption and pleasures. Amrute writes:

> The car is a site in which gender, class, and space come together. A new social and economic relationship is at work in cars that depends on lower-class men as dangerous subjects even while it makes their labor invisible … Violence against women in cars reveals the limits of the vehicle as a space protective of privatized economies and private middle-class pleasures … the violence of the moving rape should be understood within the contradictions of a postliberalization movement.
>
> *(Amrute 2015: 332)*

The policy responses to the sexual and other physical assault on public transport have far from rigorously addressed the heart of the problem. After the Delhi gang rape of December 2012, a judicial committee was established to investigate policies to address violence against women in moving transport. In January 2014, the Indian government set forth to implement some of these recommendations, which included chiefly the installation of CCTV cameras, GPS tracking facilities and emergency phone services in all public transport (Paul 2014). As per the Cabinet Committee on Economic Affairs (CCEA), the centre will "establish a unified system at the national level and state level in 32 cities of the country with a population of one million or more, over a period of two years." Information technology is the cornerstone of the policy which has been "formulated with the purpose of improving safety and protection of women from violence by using information technology."

However this approach has been regarded with suspicion as to whether the policy is seen as an opportunity to extend the Indian government's ambitious plan of designing a hundred "smart cities" that will extensively utilise real-time data, rather than genuinely address VAW. Further, this "smart" response has only been implemented in 32 cities that have a population of a million-plus. As Paul (2014) writes, "Defunct surveillance gadgets and poor police vigilance has always been a security concern in India – one reason why some women's rights activists are sceptical about the road safety scheme." Rapid growth in the size of the cities as well as the populations contained within them makes crime detection and surveillance that much more of a challenge.

Also, these strategies do not directly address real issue of violence against women, which is embedded in deeply internalised gendered social norms in men and women. As Chockalingam and Vijaya (2008: 178) note in their studies on gender and the cities of Tamil Nadu, "cultural traditions and societal values governing the day to day life of the women … have conditioned them to accept victimization … (and) accept discrimination and unequal treatment." Without interrogating ways of subverting these norms, any gendered response that planning institutes – such as gender-segregated spaces on public transport – can in fact serve to reinforce patriarchal norms. Moreover, they are incapable of eliminating VAW in private transportation.

Gendered Segregation/Women-Only Transportation

Recognising that the alleviation of poverty requires the facilitation of accessible mobility for travelling to access opportunities, transport policymakers in developing countries have been concerned with the building and maintenance of road infrastructure. However, the politics and logistics of transportation is not gender-neutral; women also having the right to unhindered mobility is imperative for their enhanced earning capabilities (Uteng & Cresswell 2008) and expanded agency and participation in determining the planning and future of their cities. When this right is compromised, it directly impacts women's capacity to exercise the full extent of their capabilities and gifts, which are vital for the maximal experience of their freedoms (Dunckel-Graglia 2013).

To address this, urban planning authorities in several cities have resorted to gendered segregation of spaces, wherein a certain number of seats, or an entire coach of a train compartment might be reserved for the exclusive use of women. Since 2010, the Delhi Metro Rail Service has allocated an entire coach to the exclusive use of women, in addition to the four seats that are women-only in most public transport across India. Women are not prohibited from using general seats/coaches; however, gender-segregated transportation does "not address societal attitudes and norms that permit harassment" (Action Aid 2011: 56); indeed, these continue to flourish outside of these ostensibly safe spaces which ironically reinforce the skewed sexism of patriarchy.

Gendered segregation on public transport is frequently proposed and enacted by municipal corporations but feminists find this worrying as it does not address gender inequalities; rather it seeks to paper over them by addressing only the symptoms of gendered violence Dunckel-Graglia (2013). Gendered segregation on public transport is "protection"-focussed which is a viable approach only in the short term as it does not directly address the root cause of violence which needs pervasive social change (Harrison 2012).

Gendered segregation in a public space can open up new freedoms for women (Agrawal & Sharma 2015) but also transfer a *zenana* culture – a culture which is enacted in the design planning of the private spaces of the home in traditional cultures where a separate ladies section/wing would be incorporated – from the private into the public. The freedom of movement, access and opportunity that is in conflict in private/public spaces can re-emerge in a public space. Tara (2011) refers to this practice as perpetuating "portable purdah." In a society where the underlying patriarchies are not addressed, the misogynistic practices merely take on a new form.

In a social context where private spaces are regarded as the most morally acceptable spaces for women, the reservation of feminised space on public transport can actually re-introduce and reinforce the restrictive moral norms of the private into the public (Agrawal and Sharma 2015). Segregation of women in public spaces increases their isolation, feelings of victimhood, and also the sense that they are responsible for their safety by avoiding certain spaces, times, and the way they dress, in addition to other fettering of their freedoms.

Logistical concerns also make gender-segregated transportation a compromised strategy. Women typically tend to travel more during off-peak hours, when public transport options are fewer (Levy 2013). But across several countries it has been noted that women-only transport, where it exists, arrives only every 20 minutes instead of every 2–3 minutes like mainstream (albeit masculinised) transport, making this an unreliable option for women.

Where gender-segregated spaces exist, they often function as an easy target that attracts harassment. Men often enter women-only spaces with the explicit purpose of harassing and abusing women who are captive in a confined space. Women worry about the stigma associated with publicising such behaviour and the erosion of hard-won freedom to be out, often unchaperoned, in public spaces. Violent and even "passive" crimes against women are invoked as a way of intensifying the severe existing gender imbalances pervasive in a patriarchal society – by marginalising women spatially it is possible to further disempower women socially (Hsu 2009). It forces women to continue to be dependent on men (Raju 2011). It can also perpetuate a culture of exclusion – their women interviewees reported that they often feel intimated or unwelcome in general coaches (where they are allowed), or sometimes disabled people or old men also choose to travel in women's coaches, perpetuating another stigma that needs to addressed – an undesirable social hierarchy. From their analysis of blogs where women reported extreme sexual harassment for daring to wander into men's spaces, and again, for inviting trouble by how they dressed:

> My station arrived and I pushed my way to make it to the door before it could close and during this struggle my top was pulled by a man to expose my breasts for 15 good seconds while at the same time somebody grabbed my behind. I somehow got onto the platform and they were laughing at me … I am not playing victim here and not trying to grab eyeballs.
>
> *(Ritika Popli 2012)*

If modern planning's objective is to allow public transportation to be accessed by all citizens without restrictions, then it becomes necessary for municipal corporations in India to recognise and respond to deep social inequities that would obstruct an equal claim on public infrastructure. Harrison (2012: 5) concludes:

> In order to alter perceptions of women on public transport, a strategy that priorities women's right to space must be pursued, but consequently there must also be an accessible support network in place to allow for suitable action when their right to space is questioned. Ultimately, no strategy will succeed without also tackling the wider cultural, political and religious gender inequalities that pervade South Asian societies.

While laws can only lay down rules, they can't change mindsets; as Paul (2014) notes, "To achieve the latter should be a matter of immediate concern for our thinkers." Dunckel-Graglia (2013) presents an analysis of "Pink transportation" in Mexico City where gender segregation was implemented, but along with strong support for vulnerable women and victims of violence, as well the mobilisation of the media to present and reinforce messages of strong women, and gender equality. The sides of buses are painted with key female historical figures, emphasising that women have played a key role in founding, revolutionising and establishing Mexico (Dunckel-Graglia 2013: 270), which has contributed to the "heavy hand in changing the image of women."

Planners' engagement with pervasive and restrictive social norms must go even deeper to contribute in fundamental ways to challenging sexism in public transport design, access, and rights. In this regard, even the notion of risk is mired in gender-bias, perpetuating a belief that only women are at risk, and hence their freedom of mobility must be curtailed. Phadke, Khan and Ranade (2011: 60) challenge the idea that even risk is gendered, and notes that men too experience vulnerability and bodily harm in public spaces. Rather, they say, what is vital is for women to be able to access "a citizen's right to redress" when their fundamental freedoms are violated in any manner. If planning explicitly acknowledged and responded to women's particular vulnerabilities in public spaces, it would serve a huge role in addressing an institutional weakness in increasing women's vulnerability.

Conclusions

Since the 2012 Delhi gang rape and murder of a young woman on a moving private bus, the issue of violence against women in moving transportation in India has gained traction in activist and academic literature. This chapter has argued that in order to comprehensively address the issue of widespread violence against women on moving public and private transportation, transport planning in India has to be much more closely attentive to the social dimensions of gendered violence. Urban planning in India has taken on sustainable development as a priority planning goal. However, without a rigorous engagement with the social dimension of sustainability, Indian urban planning's stated claim to adhere to the principles and practices of sustainable development stands compromised. Indeed, planning can even become complicit in perpetuating gendered inequalities and violence against women, hindering their capacity to access mobilities, urban spaces, and infrastructure.

To this end, Indian urban planning across the large cities as well as smaller towns must begin the process of actively taking on approaches such as community engagement, deliberative democratic strategies and other types of inclusive planning. Creative, sensitive and transparent engagement that is attentive to the wideranging social differentiation in India is vital to the creation of sustainable, safe, and gender-equitable cities. Without a radical social reform agenda in Indian planning, particularly transport policies, the cities may portend to be ever grimmer sites of all kinds of violence including and not limited to gendered assault.

References

Action Aid. 2011. *Women and the City: Examining the Gender Impact of Violence and Urbanisation*. Retrieved from: https://actionaid.org/sites/default/files/actionaid_2011_wome n_and_the_city.pdf.

Action Aid. 2013. *Women and the City II: Combating Violence against Women and Girls in Urban Public Spaces – The Role of Public Services*. Retrieved 1st August, 2017, from http://reliefweb.int/sites/reliefweb.int/files/resources/women_and_the_city_ii.pdf.

Agrawal, Anuja, & Sharma, Aarushi. 2015. Gender contests in the Delhi Metro: Implications of a reservation of a coach for women. *Indian Journal of Gender Studies, 22*(3), 421–36.

Amrute, Sareeta. 2015. Moving rape: Trafficking in the violence of postliberalization. *Public Culture, 27*(2), 331–59.

Anand, Anvit, & Tiwari, Geetam. 2006. A gendered perspective of the shelter–transport–livelihood link: The case of poor women in Delhi. *Transport Reviews, 26*(1), 63–80.

Bowman, Cynthia Grant 1993. Street harassment and the informal ghettoization of women. *Harvard Law Review, 106*, 517–80.

Can, Tang. 1994. Sexual harassment in China. *Chinese Education and Society*, 27, 39–46.

Cattan, Nadine. 2008. Gendering mobilities: Insights into the construction of spatial concepts. In Tanu Priya Uteng, & Tim Cresswell (Eds.), *Gendered Mobilities*, pp. 83–98. Aldershot: Ashgate.

Chesney-Lind, Meda. 2013. Violence against women riding public transport is a global issue – especially in developing countries. Retrieved 9th August, 2017, from www.scho larsstrategynetwork.org/sites/default/files/ssn_key_findings_chesney-lind_on_public_ transport_and_violence_against_women_1.pdf.

Chockalingam, Kumaravelu, & Vijaya, Annie. 2008. Sexual harassment of women in public transport in Chennai city: A Victimology Perspective. *The Indian Journal of Criminology and Criminalistics*, 29(3), 167–84.

Dunckel-Graglia, Amy. 2013. "Pink transportation" in Mexico City: Reclaiming urban space through collective action against gender-based violence. *Gender & Development*, 21(2), 265–76.

El Nahry, Fatma. 2012. She's not asking for it: Street harassment and women in public spaces. *Gender across Borders: A Global Voice for Gender Justice*. Retrieved 23rd November, 2015, from www.genderacrossborders.com/2012/03/20/shes-not-asking-for-it-streetharassment-and-women-in-public-spaces/.

Harrison, Jennifer. 2012. *Gender Segregation on Public Transport in South Asia: A Critical Evaluation of Approaches for Addressing Harassment against Women*. M.Sc. Dissertation. SOAS University of London.

Horii, Mitsutoshi, & Burgess, Adam. 2012. Constructing sexual risk: "chikan," collapsing male authority and the emergence of women-only train carriages in Japan. *Health Risk and Society*, 14, 41–55.

Hsu, Hsin-Ping 2009. *How does fear of sexual harassment on transit affect women's use of transit?* Women's Issues in Transportation, Summary of the 4th International Conference, Volume 2: Technical Papers, October 27–30, 2009, Irvine, CA, pp. 74–84.

Jagori and UN Women. 2011. *Safe Cities Free of Violence against Women and Girls Initiative: Report of the Baseline Survey Delhi 2010*. Jagori and UN Women.

Jones, Peter, & Lucas, Karen. 2012. The social consequences of transport decision-making: Clarifying concepts, synthesizing knowledge and assessing implications. *Journal of Transport Geography*, 21, 4–16.

Leinbach, Thomas R. 2000. Mobility in development context: Changing perspectives, new interpretations and the real issues. *Journal of Transport Geography*, 8(1), 1–9.

Levy, Caren. 2013. Travel choice reframed: "deep distribution" and gender in urban transport. *Environment and Urbanization*, 25(1), 47–63.

Narayanan, Yamini. 2012. Violence against women in Delhi: A sustainability problematic. *Journal of South Asian Development*, 7(1), 1–22.

Neupane, Gita, & Chesney-Lind, Meda. 2014. Violence against women on public transport in Nepal: Sexual harassment and the spatial expression of male privilege. *International Journal of Comparative and Applied Criminal Justice*, 38(1), 23–38.

Phadke, Shilpa, Khan, Sameera, & Ranade, Shilpa. 2011. *Why Loiter? Women and Risk on Mumbai Streets*. New Delhi: Penguin Books India.

Paul, Stella. 2014. Women on the move, and in danger. Retrieved 22nd August, 2015, from www.ipsnews.net/2014/02/women-move-danger/.

Popli, Ritika. 2012. I was molested, and the onlookers stared and laughed. Retrieved 9th August, 2017, from http://scrutinybykhimaanshu.blogspot.com.au/2012/09/i-was-molested-ritika-popli.html.

Raju, Saraswati. 2011. Introduction: Conceptualising gender, space and place. In Saraswati Raju (Ed.), *Gendered Geographies: Space and Place in South Asia*, pp. 1–28. New Delhi: Oxford University Press.

Tara, Shelly. 2011. Private space in public transport: Locating gender in the Delhi metro. *Economic and Political Weekly*, *66*(51), 71–74.

Uteng, Tanu Priya, & Cresswell, Tim (Eds.). 2008. *Gendered Mobilities*. Aldershot: Ashgate.

Vasconcellos, Eduardo Alcantara 2001. *Urban Transport: Environment and Equity: The Case for Developing Countries*. London and Sterling, VA: Earthscan.

5

PLANNING MOBILITY IN PORTUGAL WITH A GENDER PERSPECTIVE

Margarida Queirós and Nuno Marques da Costa

Introduction

According to Greed (2012), historical developments of the urban planning policy resulted in cities being based upon land-use zoning, separating home from work, thus extended commuting time, and enclosed housing estates mostly for women. Therefore, a dispersed land-use was developed, based on the rational planning paradigm supported by the use of the car. Consequently, daily tasks are allocated between motorised displacements, on traffic-jammed roads. Normally, it is women who are most likely responsible for daily home routines, childcare and shopping but, at the same time, with a professional activity outside the home, their mobility patterns are differentiated from men's. Normally, women combine home and work tasks in a more complex trip-chain than the traditional home-to-work pattern. When residential places are separated from working areas, as a result of a spatial functionality idea created by the modern movement during the twentieth century, women need a greater amount of public transport services, with transverse inter-area bus routes and off-peak services. As an outcome, transport planning policies have paid little attention to gender transport pattern differences, assuming that transport interventions are gender neutral.

Statistical systems do not differentiate between the transport behaviour of men and women. As a result, it is difficult to isolate gender differences with regard to the purpose of trips, trip frequency, distances travelled, mobility-related problems in gaining access to health services, employment and other related issues. Nevertheless, a growing number of studies over the last few years have addressed issues of gender and transportation. They all agree that men and women differ in terms of the types of trip-chains undertaken (Rivera, 2007; Primerano et al., 2008; Queirós and Marques da Costa, 2012; Sánchez de Madariaga, 2013; Scheiner, 2014), reflecting the different distribution of responsibilities (Polk,

2005; Kunieda and Gauthier, 2007). These differences are closely related to gender inequality in private life and the labour market, age, urban structures, socialisation and education processes (Hasson and Polevoy, 2011; Pitombo and Gomes, 2014; Queirós et al., 2016).

Women and men have substantially different patterns of transport demand. Women are more vulnerable users of transport; they frequently choose public transport and make several trips a day, often on foot. Ignoring the various roles of women, especially in the domestic economy and social reproduction, or in the formal economy, reduces the productivity of the entire economic system and impairs women's access to public services, social and political participation and household efficiency (Queirós and Marques da Costa, 2012; EIGE, 2013, 2015; Queirós et al., 2016). The reproductive responsibilities of women, such as home and family care, lead to different travel patterns and sometimes are a restriction to their full integration into the labour market.

Some studies have pointed to the integration of the gender perspective in transport in developed economies, which necessarily takes critical aspects into consideration (Mashiri et al., 2006); that is, public transport services should reflect women's domestic responsibilities which often result in different needs relating to journey times and destinations. Fewer women, particularly older women, drive their own cars, and are therefore more likely than men to rely on public transport. Women are more likely than men to be engaged in part-time employment, and this has implications with regard to transport needs and patterns (Polk, 2005; EOC, 2007; Economic Commission for Europe, 2009).

Research into women's travel patterns and needs has been undertaken, following in part from the identification and increased awareness of the divergent social and economic roles performed by men and women, and consequently the gendered nature of travel and mobility needs and constraints (Mashiri et al., 2006; Queirós et al., 2016). This knowledge can be used to inform transport operators of the consequences and impacts of their decisions, to outline public policies to improve women's access to public or private transport, and also to contribute to the rethinking of mobility aiming to reflect both men and women's lives and responsibilities. These specific features are both a challenge and an opportunity to bring transport operators in line with the demand by women and position them in a context of reducing poverty and boosting economic activity (Gaspar et al., 2009). Also, it reveals that transport policy can be more responsive to the needs of women and requires a structured approach to be developed to address those needs, identifying instruments and analysing their costs and benefits, and establishing an appropriate policy framework.

Unequal Mobility Patterns in Europe: A Gender Perspective

Until the 1950s, women were limited to traditionally female occupations, whereas today they can be found in almost any job. Gender roles in society have changed. Previously, men were the breadwinners and women quit their jobs as soon as becoming mothers – that is, if they worked away from home. Since that time women have known some progress in the labour market, management ranks and pay equity; the overarching trend is toward more equal gender roles (Queirós and Marques da Costa, 2012).

Although, throughout the world, during the last few decades, there have been significant variations and changes in terms of women's roles and household composition, women in general make shorter, more frequent trips dispersed throughout the day; they care for children as well as elderly relatives, and perform other reproductive and productive tasks (Eurostat, 2004; Gaspar et al., 2009; Queirós and Marques da Costa, 2012; Queirós et al., 2016). This means that major differences in the basic mobility needs of women and men are grounded in the gender-based division of labour within the family and community.

In developing countries, research developed under the auspices of global institutions, particularly the World Bank and the United Nations, show that the major differences in the basic mobility needs of women and men have their roots in the division of labour according to gender, within both family and community. In addition, the World Bank Group (2010: 15), states that transport planning models have not considered women's specific travel patterns, particularly differences in relation to trip purposes, frequency and distance of travel, mode of transportation used, and mobility constraints to access other services such as health. But even for developed economies, such as countries within the European Union, those differences were not entirely erased. The first compendium of European statistics on how Europeans spent their time (Eurostat, 2004) shows that, on average, men consume more time on gainful work than on unpaid domestic tasks while the situation is the opposite with women. Around two-thirds of all work done by women is unpaid, while the majority of the work done by men is paid work; women aged twenty to seventy-four spend on average more time on domestic than on gainful work.

The compendium also reveals that people aged twenty to seventy-four spend, on average, one hour and ninety minutes per day on travel. Men spend more time on daily travel than women and, when comparing women and men, travel related to gainful work is more evident among men, while women's trips are more connected with domestic tasks. To some extent, women and men use different transport modes for travel: men use the private car more than women do and this is true for both the amount of time spent and the share of total travel time. Women and men spend about the same amount of time on public transport. When looking at the share of total travel time, however, women tend to spend more of their time on a bus, train or tram, and compared with men, a larger share of women's travel time is done on foot or by bicycle (Eurostat, 2004).

Even in Europe, where the availability of public transport is denser, the systems rarely provide an adequate service to the everyday needs of women. Public transport is, in most cases, set up to meet the transportation needs of those who work outside the home in paid professions – usually men – who need transportation in concentrated and well-marked periods throughout the day. For example, a national survey conducted in Scotland in the early 2000s showed that women travel less frequently for work and more frequently for reasons associated with maternity care and visits to friends' homes. Women in Scotland travelled on average 10.3 km, and men 13.4 km. The study also stated that the women went out on foot, used collective public transport, travelled by train more often, and travelled shorter routes (Transport Scotland, 2017). In 2013, 64.3% of men still drive to work compared to 56.8% of women and 13.6% of women travel to work by bus compared to 9% of men (www.gov.scot/Topics/People/Equality/Equalities/TransportTravel). A similar study in Ireland identified the income and family responsibilities and boundaries of women's transport choices. These in turn limited the entry of women into the labour market and also limited women's leisure activities and opportunities for education and training (EOC, 2007).

Duchène (2011) reports significant differences between men and women in the transport modes used by both in all European countries. In Sweden, fewer women than men use cars, as men own 70% of cars on the road. In France, 60% of men living outside the Paris region only travel by car. French men only use public transport for 10% of their trips, while two-thirds of passengers on public transport networks are women. In Sweden, the same proportion of women uses public transport.

Access to individual motorized transport is determined by the economic and cultural context, resulting in gender differences regarding the use of individual transport. Despite the negative consequences of automobile use, well-documented and known, it remains a symbol of economic prosperity, at both the individual and the community level. The ownership and use of cars is associated with success, power and social status (Polk, 2005; Queirós and Marques da Costa, 2012).

Some interesting conclusions emerged from a large-scale survey amongst Oslo inhabitants regarding the cultural perceptions that men and women have of public and private modes of transport, showing that men and women had different cultural values directed toward different types of transport. Women seemed to be more positive than men towards public transport and believed that public transport gave them access when and where they wanted to travel. In contrast, men saw the car as enabling freedom in time and space; men's work on and maintenance of the car can be seen as an important arena for their identities. In contrast, women saw the car in purely functional terms (Transgen, 2007).

Interestingly, the Netherlands Institute for Transport Policy Analysis reports a clear discrepancy in car ownership among men and women (Van der Waard et al., 2012). Men are more likely to own a car than women and that is the case particularly for the group aged fifty and over; however, women are rapidly increasing their car ownership. In fact, women use the car more often for work-related activities. Each extra working woman not only results in two extra trips per working day, but also in journeys by car for other trip purposes. The combination of work, running a household and taking care of children, calls for flexible mobility for which the car is an ideal mode. As a result, the mobility patterns of these women have started to resemble more and more the mobility patterns of men. The so-called "gender gap" seems to have almost closed (Van der Waard et al., 2012: 18). Similarly, in the late 1980s, Swedish men were three times more likely to own a car than were women, whereas, twenty years later, men are only one and a half times more likely to be car owners (Kalter et al., 2011).

Gender Mobility Differences in Portugal: Destinations (Travel Purposes) and Modes (Means of Travel Used)

Research for the incorporation of gender equality in the transport sector is a very recent phenomenon in Portugal (Gaspar et al., 2009; Queirós and Marques da Costa, 2012; Queirós et al., 2016). Thus, the analysis of gender in the Portuguese transport system is constrained by limited information disaggregated by sex, both with regard to information provided by the National Statistical System, or in relation to information collected by different institutions and by the transport operators (Queirós and Marques da Costa, 2012). Neither policymakers nor regulators, such as transport operators themselves, have shown particular sensitivity to the integration of this issue in their practices. For operators, the principles of gender equality have been applied primarily at the level of ensuring equal opportunities via access to different functions within companies, thus following the general guidelines of labour law (Queirós and Marques da Costa, 2012). In relation to customers, there has been a particular emphasis on gender by operators, defining these services and addressing the demands of women and men, in aggregate, unlike the efforts that have developed in relation to other groups of customers, namely those with reduced mobility.

While the number of scientific papers on the subject is limited (Beirão and Cabral, 2007), the first study to instigate an analysis of gender differences in transport was carried out in Portugal in 2009 by the Portuguese Commission for Citizenship and Gender Equality (CIG). Framed by the policy goals defined in the "Third National Plan for Gender Equality" (III PNI), the acknowledgement by the Portuguese government of links between transport and gender issues established the need to promote research to support the integration of a gender perspective into urban and land-use planning, and to improve the accessibility, quality and adaptation of public transport to the needs of men and women, ensuring routes that facilitate the reconciliation of professional, personal and family life (Queirós and Marques da Costa, 2012; Queirós et al., 2016). Following the "Third National Plan" guidelines, a study was undertaken, followed by a "Guide to Gender Mainstreaming" (Gaspar et al., 2009). The methodological approach of the study was divided into three stages using both qualitative and quantitative approaches. These were: (i) theoretical literature from transport policy science, reports and studies of the processes of transport decision-making in the world and Portuguese context; (ii) interviews in urban and national transport authorities; and (iii) statistical data compiled in 2001 from official sources such as Statistics Portugal (INE).

The conclusions of that study (Gaspar et al., 2009; Queirós and Marques da Costa, 2012) reported that in Portugal, gender equality issues in transport do not differ significantly from other European countries. As regards mobility patterns, Portuguese women travel shorter distances for work-related reasons than do men; they walk more, spend less time commuting and use public transport more often. In more peripheral urban areas with a lower transport supply away from the fast public lanes designed for commuting, women depend to a lesser degree on the public transport service for shopping and social activities. Their daily household tasks demand multiple trips and multiple stops, which result in the use of many transport services and the additional costs of any subsequent tickets. For the group of people who do not use private transport, the combination of multiple tasks and reduced public transport services consume much of their time, limiting the tasks that can be undertaken throughout the day (Marques da Costa, 2007; Gaspar et al., 2009; Queirós and Marques da Costa, 2012).

According to Gaspar et al. (2009) and Queirós and Marques da Costa (2012), Portuguese 2001 statistics on gendered patterns of transport indicate that modal splits are more diverse in urban spaces than in rural areas; urban travellers tend to use a variety of modes during one single trip and also range greatly across geographical, social, cultural and economic levels, which allows for only cautious generalisations.

Concerning the mobility of the population in Portugal, the data used for the analysis of gender differences in relation to labour-study-home mobility is taken from the 2001 and 2011 national censuses. The information in the censuses of 2001 and 2011 identifies the destination of travel due to work or study in three domains, being movements whose objective lies: (i) in the parish of residence, (ii) in another parish in the county of residence, and (iii) in a place outside the county of residence.[1]

Mobility patterns are closely related to the definition of local labour markets and mainland Portugal employment basins of configuration are quite differentiating. For this reason, the authors have chosen the sub-regions NUTS 3 of Greater Lisbon, Alto Trás-os-Montes, Ave and Algarve to analyse the mobility gender gap in Portugal (NUTS: Nomenclature of Territorial Units developed by Eurostat, and employed in Portugal for statistical purposes; to know more see http://ec.europa.eu/eurostat/web/nuts/overview). The different values of main destinations and transport modes in these regions reveal gender differences. These differentiations result from the distinctive contexts of territorial relationships, where demographic structure, the presence of women in the labour market, income, education levels, proletarianisation level, or the provision of public transportation services, among others, certainly contribute to explaining the differences in mobility between men and women.

In regions where interaction between people across the region is greater, men travel outside their municipality (county) of residence more often than women. This is associated with the use of individual transport and the relative increase in travel times. In metropolitan areas, however, the differences between men and women are fewer in terms of travel, for reasons of employment or education, outside the municipality. In these areas women use public transport more often. The larger difference between men and women in public transport use can be seen in the NUTS 3 region of Grande Lisboa, with a percentage difference of 12% in 2001 and 10.5% in 2011.

In 2011, on mainland Portugal, seven in ten travel journeys either to work or study have as their destination the county of residence (71.8%, 74.0% in 2001), and four out of ten journeys are performed in the parish of residence (36.9%, 41.9% in 2001). Although the average difference between men and women is approximately 2% (2.2% in 2011, 2.6% in 2001), women live closer to the workplace. For 38.0% (43.3% in 2001) of women, their work or study place is located in the parish of residence and for 35.5% (32.6% in 2001) they are elsewhere in the county of residence, while values for men are 35.8% (40.7% in 2001) and 34.4% (31.7% in 2001), respectively. Work or study trips outside the resident municipality represent about 27% (24% in 2001), for women and 30% for men, 28% in 2011 (Figure 5.1).

In 2011, there was an enlargement of the labour market area for both men and women, so there is a decrease in the number of journeys taken to the same parish and increased travel to another place in the home parish and to another municipality. But the difference between men and women does not contain any significant changes. The differences between men and women in 2001 and 2011 are more pronounced with regard to the modes of transport (Figure 5.2).

The use of public transport is a behaviour associated with women, while car-use is associated with men. Therefore, more women than men depend on public transport modes. The most evident changes from 2001 to 2011 is that the use of private transport increases significantly: from 46.2% in 2001 to 61.6% in 2011, walking diminishes (24.9% to 16.4%) as does the use of public transport (20.7% to 17.1%), showing a period of high income, availability and access to cheaper credit for automobiles (and other consumer goods) as the opportunities for new jobs farther from home and more spatially dispersed led to increased use of cars for commuting. Nevertheless, the gap between men and women using different transport modes was reduced by nearly 3%: with regard to the use of cars, the difference between men and women was 10.2% in 2001 and 7.3% in 2011; in the use of

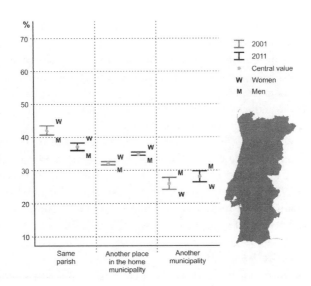

FIGURE 5.1 Portugal (mainland) – Commuting trip destination by sex
Source: Own elaboration.

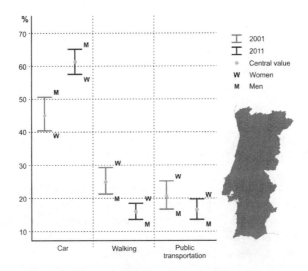

FIGURE 5.2 Portugal (mainland) – Transport mode used for commuting by sex
Source: Own elaboration.

public transport the difference was 8.6% in 2001 and 6.0% in 2011, and the differences in walking shifted from 7.7% in 2001 to 4.8% in 2011.

The NUTS 3 Alto Trás-os-Montes is a rural sub-region constituted of fifteen municipalities covering an area of 8,465 km^2 in the interior northeast of mainland Portugal, near Spain.It has a population of about 227,000 inhabitants, representing 40% of the Northern Region area holding only 6.1% of the population, evidencing low density, and regressive dynamics of the demographic behaviour (a decrease). It is a geographical unit framed in a rural area, with a territory suffering a process of population loss, with agro-forestry activities in a transitional situation, and where the urban centres are seeking to sustain their social and economic base.

Furthermore, Trás-os-Montes has the lowest differentiation destination (the trips are more diverse) for commuting (journey purpose) between men and women (Figure 5.3), not exceeding the difference of, on average, one per cent, verifying that the values are equal, 7.7% for both men and women in 2001, and not exceeding 0.5% in 2011, commuting outside of the county of residence. The national commuting pattern change can also be observed in this rural area. The evolution of displacements due to reasons of labour follows the national trend: a decrease of displacements in the parish of residence and an increase of displacements to other parishes in the municipal residence or a different municipality. For all that, it is important to note that movements to other municipalities, rather than the one of residence is quite low: around 10% in 2011 for both sexes, due to the incipient regional labour market in this marginal area.

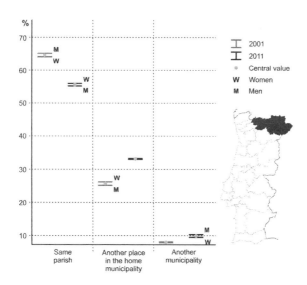

FIGURE 5.3   NUTS 3 Alto Trás-os-montes – Commuting trip destination by sex
Source: Own elaboration.

Following a national trend, the modal split in Alto Trás-os-Montes had a pronounced change. The use of the car increased by more than 20%, from 42.2% in 2001 to 62.7% in 2011, but maintaining the same differentiation between men and women (4.2% in 2001 and 4.3% in 2011). As car-use augmented, walking and public transport decreased, with convergence on the behaviour of men and women. Gender differences decreased, from 5.9% to 4.5% for walking and 2.3% to 1.9% for the use of public transport (Figure 5.4).

The NUTS 3 Vale do Ave is located in the northwest of Portugal between the cities of Braga and Porto. The territory of Ave is densely populated (about 421.4 inhabitants per square kilometre) and covers an area of about 1,250 Km^2, representing 6% of the surface of the North and 1.4% of the country's surface, with a population of about 500,000 inhabitants. The Vale do Ave has a dispersed urban model characterised by diffuse urbanisation and industrialisation patterns, where the multiple functionality of land-use interconnects, supported by good accessibility conditions. It is increasingly becoming an integral part of a vast urban–industrial space that transcends the municipality limits of NUTS 3, integrated in the Porto Metropolitan Area.

In Vale do Ave, the variation of journey purpose (Figure 5.5) in the same parish follows the same pattern as the other sub-regions (a decrease of 7.6%). In the Vale do Ave, the travel distances are augmented, due to the polycentric urban structure of the region as well as a lack of public transportation services. Figure 5.6, endorses the information of the previous example, as it shows that in the Vale do Ave the use of public transportation and walking were particularly reduced, whereas car usage increased hugely in the decade (an increment of

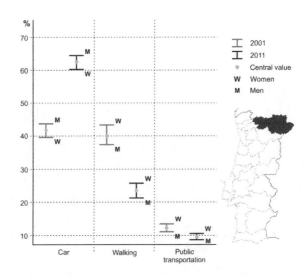

FIGURE 5.4 NUTS 3 Alto Trás-os-montes – Transport mode used for commuting by sex

Source: Own elaboration.

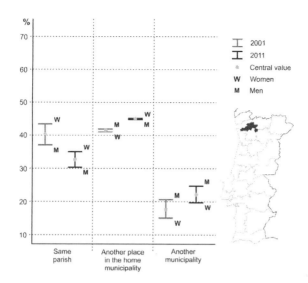

FIGURE 5.5 NUTS 3 Vale do Ave – Commuting trip destination by sex
Source: Own elaboration.

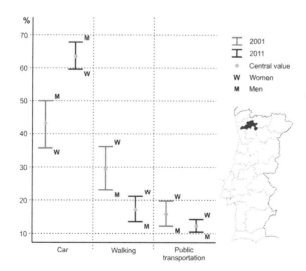

FIGURE 5.6 NUTS 3 Vale do Ave – Transport mode used for commuting by sex
Source: Own elaboration.

20.4%). However, discrepancies between men and women diminished, showing a gender convergence in behaviour (differences decrease from 14.1% to 8.1% in the use of the car, 7.5% to 3.7% in the use of public transport and 12.5% to 7.7% for walking). The concentration of residents; the urban sprawl and the mono-specialising structure of the industry; the deep working-class feminisation and the lack of public transportation services largely explain the development of these patterns during the decade.

In southern mainland Portugal, NUTS 2 Algarve is home to about 400,000 inhabitants: approximately 4% of the total population of Portugal, with a population density of about eighty-three inhabitants per km^2. This region has a population ratio of foreign residents which is approximately 6% of the total population. It is one of the regions with lower rates of female activity in the country and there are high proportions of persons working in services (mostly in tourism related to seasonal employment).

In Figure 5.7, the pattern repeats itself as in the decade the employment basins augmented slightly. Thus, journeys to the same parish diminished and, at the same time, journeys to a destination within the home municipality and in another municipality increased, mostly for men. In fact, in the Algarve, the differences between men and women increased with respect to commuting destination, namely in local displacements (1.4% in 2001 and 2.9% in 2011) and for outside the municipality of residence (1.8% and 2.6% for 2001 and 2011). Compared with other NUTS, the lower integration level of women in the labour market and the spread of the seasonal labour market, especially for female workers contributes to explain the differences in the Algarve compared to the national level.

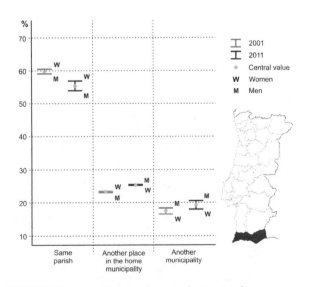

FIGURE 5.7 NUTS 2 Algarve – Commuting trip destination by sex
Source: Own elaboration.

In the Algarve, contemporary with the rest of Portugal, the car is by far the most used mode of transportation; mostly by men. Women walk more and use public transport more (Figure 5.8). Public transportation services in the Algarve have a local importance, albeit not so much for connecting the different munici- palities, as in other Portuguese regions where train services facilitate not only metropolitan areas but also the urban western coast areas. It is undoubtedly rele- vant that the modal split of the Algarve has not changed over the last decade, revealing stability in the local labour market, based on a consolidated service economy linked to tourism, real estate activities and personal services.

Grande Lisboa NUTS 3 is part of Lisbon's Metropolitan Area (LMA) with a little over two million inhabitants, representing one-fifth of the Portuguese population. On the northern bank of the LMA, the population density is 1,484 inhabitants per km^2. Despite population stabilisation over the last decade due to economic restructuring favouring suburban/metropolitan locations, a deep trans- formation of residential and work locations has led to a relative reduction in commuting to Lisbon and to an increase of commuting (mainly supported by the use of private cars) between the other municipalities of LMA.

As a metropolitan area, commuting movements to a municipality other than that of one's residence is quite relevant: almost 40% in 2011 and 2001. More- over, displacement within the residence parish decreased, particularly among women (Figure 5.9). The main observation is that differences between men and women decline in relation to movements within the parish of residence (4.1% to 1.7%) and to movements outside it (4.4% to 2.7%).

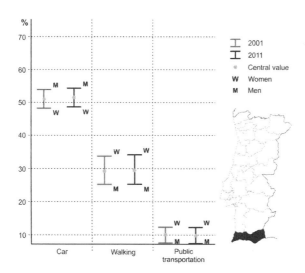

FIGURE 5.8   NUTS 2 Algarve – Transport mode used for commuting by sex
Source: Own elaboration.

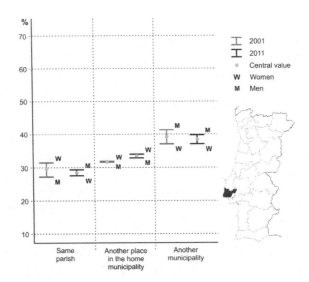

FIGURE 5.9 NUTS 3 Greater Lisboa – Commuting trip destination by sex
Source: Own elaboration.

Over the decade, NUTS 3 Grande Lisboa reveals the increase of car-use for commuting, from 42.9% in 2001 to 54.2% in 2011 (Figure 5.10). The use of public transport is much higher than in other NUTS, as a result of a denser network and high levels of service, namely along rail lines serving Lisbon. Nevertheless, the use of public transport declined due to the increase of displacements unrelated to Lisbon and the urban growth promoted by road network development based on car-use.

Differences between men and women also decreased in Grande Lisboa, in car-use (14.4% to 10.6%) and in walking (5.1% to 2.3%). On the other hand, differences in the use of public transport do not diminish to the same affect (12.0% to 10.5%).

Conclusion: Challenges for National Transport Policies

From the various NUTS (Nomenclature of Territorial Units), it is noticeable that gender differences in mobility manifest where there is local employment access for women and more access to employment outside the municipality of residence, compared to men. There are many factors that contribute to explain the differences in mobility patterns between sexes: the circumstances in which territorial and economic relations are developed; the demographic structure; the rate of feminisation of work, income, aspirations and perceptions; education levels; or the provision/availability of public transport. This is strongly related to the amplitude of travelling and the labour basins, which are different for men and women.

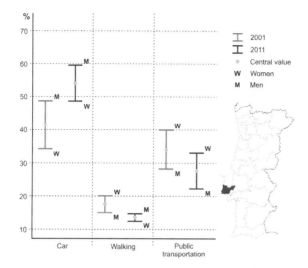

FIGURE 5.10   NUTS 3 Greater Lisbon – Transport mode used for commuting by sex
Source: Own elaboration.

We can conclude that in Portugal, national and regional mobility patterns are closely connected to the definition and enlargement of local labour markets and the rise of families' income, which also affects the needs and perceptions of the alternatives. In regions where interaction is greater, men travel outside their municipality of residence more often than women; this behaviour is related to the use of individual transport but it is clear from the evidence between 2001 and 2011 that this difference is decreasing.

Between 2011 and 2011 in northern Portugal, there were major disparities in regional standards with regard to modes of transport. In the Vale do Ave, the effects of "metropolisation", industrialization and a lack of a public transportation network service show a greater range of travel between men and women – the latter being those that have shorter trips. In Alto Trás-os-Montes, where rurality and a system of small and medium-sized cities prevail, mobility behaviour also shows an enlargement of the employment basins, showing a convergence towards the patterns of the other regions. The Algarve displays a stable employment basin dominated by the tourism sector, revealing the almost non-existence of structured public transportation services. In Grande Lisboa – as expected in a metropolitan area – the differences between men and women are fewer in terms of travelling outside the municipality of residence. A common feature is the fact that all the regions reveal the same pattern: the rise of the use of the automobile as a result of the enlargement of the employment basins, increased purchasing power and the lack of flexible and reliable transport services, influencing mode choices in Portuguese society.

This convergence in the 2000s of men and women's mobility patterns is an outcome of EU policies. These increased families' social and economic status; created better living conditions; increased credit for consumption at low interest rates; increased the number of those who held a second residence; and accelerated the changes of choice between small flats and family houses on the outskirts of cities, resulting in the urban sprawl and the spatial fragmentation of the territory. Additionally, individual transport as a modal transport, responds with greater ease and flexibility to the dynamics of the workplace and the quick extension of the employment basins, than the public transport mode. Thus, these patterns of mobility were stimulated by public policies as Portuguese and EU authorities were responsible for the increase of public investment in motorways (profiting from the revenues of gas and motor taxation). Hence, gender convergence in this case is not a successful policy outcome, as we see jobs and families being delocalised as people bought bigger and better houses, but ultimately ended up living in poorer infrastructure sites, with bad or non-existent public transport services or other alternatives – therefore being "forced" to travel by car to their destinations.

With this information, there is now a greater awareness of the fact that women in Portugal are more dependent on public transport than men. However, the overall rise of the use of private modes of transportation is disturbing and unsustainable. As gender-disaggregated data on transportation becomes more available, evidence supporting general trends in gendered mobility patterns and needs is likely to be increasingly supplemented by regional differences. It is this awareness and careful documentation of regional peculiarities that becomes so essential for the development of local, gender-aware transport planning strategies. The specific balance among these will vary from region to region, and policymakers and transport operators need to gather information locally in line with best gender-balancing practice.

In terms of mobility patterns, women travel smaller distances than men, use more public transport and walk more, especially so when they are earn lower incomes. In Portugal, the mobility patterns shown by both men and women in the 2001 and 2011 period, express changes in the nature of society and lifestyle patterns, and are closely associated with the definition of employment areas, verifying that in regions where the spatial interaction is greater, men go out of the county of residence more often than women, associating it with the use of private transport and the relative increase in travel times. Yet, more and more women are using automobiles.

Gender-sensitive and sustainable transport strategies need to be developed and, practical advances can initially be made by improving the quality of household and user surveys and by collecting sex-disaggregated data. Meanwhile, these efforts should be complemented by comprehensive, regionally and locally targeted gender analysis and action plans for transportation. As Beirão and Cabral (2007) revealed, it becomes evident that the urge is to promote policies that reduce private-transport dependence, providing alternatives to driving which might involve an improvement in public transport services (to meet gender differentiated needs and to promote the public transport image as a viable alternative in attracting men as potential users) and stimulating slower modes (e.g. cycling and walking).

The previous differences between men and women in their use of individual transport are disappearing but this is not "good news", at least for environmental concerns (increasing congestion and pollution), especially if we are seeking a low-carbon society. The massive motorized use of transport (car-use) by men and women for commuting, reveals an unsustainable trend that must be at the centre of transport and urban policy development. Despite a general convergence of trends pertaining to the commuting behaviour of men and women, differences will still remain relevant and the need for more directional transport planning for the differenced needs of transportation for men and women is clearly required.

If transport can make a big difference in increasing women's productivity and promoting gender equality – as the Economic Commission for Europe (2009) states – making transport policy more responsive to their needs requires identifying instruments to address those needs, analysing the costs and benefits of those instruments and establishing an appropriate policy framework. But while it is necessary to be aware of the needs and adapt services, it is also true that the expectations created by different factors must be considered. Thus, strategies for planning improved mobility may also need to have more up-to-date data on gender perceptions on the use of the different modes.

Note

1 This differentiation is based on Portuguese local administrative units (LAU): "freguesia" (LAU 1, parish) and "município" (LAU 2, municipalities); each county aggregates several parishes.

References

Beirão, G. and Cabral, J. (2007). Understanding attitudes towards public transport and private car: a qualitative study. *Transport Policy*, *14*(6): 478–489.

Duchène, C. (2011). Gender and transport. Discussion paper no. 2011–11. *The International Transport Forum at the OECD*, Germany. (www.internationaltransportforum.org).

Economic Commission for Europe. (2009). *Report to the United Nations Economic Commission for Europe Executive Committee on the Implementation of the Priorities of the UNECE Reform for Strengthening Some Activities of the Committee*. The Inland Transport Committee and gender issues in transport. ECE/TRANS/2009/7, Seventy-first session Geneva, 24–26 February 2009.

EIGE. (2013). *Reconciliation of Work and Family Life as a Condition of Equal Participation in the Labour Market. Report*. Vilnius: European Institute for Gender Equality, p. 98. (http://eige.europa.eu).

EIGE. (2015). Supporting reconciliation of work, family and private life. Good practices. European Institute for Gender Equality, Luxembourg, Publications Office of the European Union. (http://eige.europa.eu).

EOC. (2007). *The Gender Equality Duty and Local Government: Guidance for Public Authorities in England*, Equal Opportunities Commission, Gender Equality Duty. London: Stationery Office.

Eurostat. (2004). How Europeans spend their time. Everyday life of women and men. Data 1988–2002. *Eurostat Theme 3 Population and Social Conditions*. Luxembourg: Office for Official Publications of the Europeans Communities.

Gaspar, J., Queirós, M., Marques da Costa, N. and Brito Henriques, E. (2009). *Estudo de Diagnóstico e Criação de Indicadores de Género na Área do Território e Ambiente*. Lisbon: CEG, Universidade de Lisboa/FLUL & Comissão para a Cidadania e a Igualdade de Género, p. 175. (www.igualdade.gov.pt/images/stories/documentos/documentacao/relatorios/relatorio_genero_territorio_ambiente.pdf).

Greed, C. (2012). Planning for sustainable transport or for people's needs. *Urban Design and Planning*, *165*(DP4): 219–229. doi: 10.1680/udap.10.00033.

Hasson, Y. and Polevoy, M. (2011). *Gender Equality Initiatives in Transportation* Policy. *A review of the literature*. Women's Budget Forum. Hadassah Foundation, Heinrich Boell Stiftung and European Union. (https://il.boell.org/sites/default/files/gender_and_tran sportation_-_english_1.pdf).

Kalter, M.-J., Olde, H. L. and Jorritsma, P. (2011). Changing travel patterns of women in the Netherlands. *Women's Issues in Transportation, 2009*, Vol. 2. Conference Proceedings. Transportation Research Board, Irvine, California, pp. 179–190. (http://trid.trb.org/view.aspx?id=1101878).

Kunieda, M. and Gauthier, A. (2007). *Gender and Urban Transport*. GTZ Germany: Federal Ministry for Economic Cooperation and Development.

Marques da Costa, N. (2007). *Mobilidade e Transporte em Áreas Urbanas. O caso da Área Metropolitana de Lisboa*. Dissertação de Doutoramento apresentada à Faculdade de Letras de Lisboa, Universidade de Lisboa.

Mashiri, M., Venter, C. and Buiten, D. (2006). *An Assessment of Gender Sensitivity in a Selection of Transport Surveys*. Washington, DC: The World Bank Group. (research space.csir.co.za/dspace/bitstream/.../Mashiri_2006.pdf).

Pitombo, C. S. and Gomes, M. M. (2014). Study of work-travel related behaviour using principle component analysis. *Open Journal of Statistics*, *4*: 889–901. (www.scirp.org/jour nal/ojs).

Polk, M. (2005). Integration of gender equality into transport policy and practice in Sweden. *Research on Women's Issues in Transportation,* Vol. 2: Technical Papers, Report of a Conference, November 18–20, 2004, Transportation Research Board. Göteborg University, Sweden.

Primerano, F., Taylor, M. A. P., Pitaksringkarn, L. and Tisato, P. (2008). Defining and understanding trip chaining behaviour. *Transportation*, *35*(1): 55–72. doi: 10.1007/s11116-007-9134-8.

Queirós, M. and Marques da Costa, N. (2012). Knowledge on Gender Dimensions of Transportation in Portugal. *Dialogue and UniversalismE*, 3(1): 47–69.

Queirós, M., Marques da Costa, N., Morgado, P., Vale, M., Guerreiro, J., Rodrigues, F., Mileu, N. and Almeida, A. (2016). Gender equality and the city: a methodological approach to mobility in space-time. *TRIA*, *17*(2): 143–158. doi: 10.6092/2281-4574/5061.

Rivera, R. (2007). Culture, gender, transport: contentious planning issues. *Transport and Communications Bulletin for Asia and the Pacific*, 76(2007): 20.

Sánchez de Madariaga, I. (2013). Mobility of care: introducing new concepts in urban transport. In I. S. de Madariaga and M. Roberts (Eds.), *Fair Shared Cities: The Impact of Gender Planning in Europe*. Farnham and Burlington, VT: Ashgate, pp. 33–48.

Scheiner, J. (2014). The gendered complexity of daily life: effects of life-course events on changes in activity entropy and tour complexity over time. *Travel Behaviour and Society*, 1(3): 91–105. doi: 10.1016/j.tbs.2014.04.001.

The Scottish Executive Central Research Unit. (2000). *Women and Transport: Moving Forward*. Reid-Howie Associates. The Scottish Executive Central Research Unit, Edinburgh. (www.gov.scot/Resource/Doc/156605/0042069.pdf).

Transgen. (2007). *Gender Mainstreaming European Transport Research and Policies Building the Knowledge Base and Mapping Good Practices*. Copenhagen: University of Copenhagen.

Van der Waard, J., Immers, B. and Jorritsma, P. (2012). *New Drivers in Mobility: What moves the Dutch in 2012 and Beyond?* Prepared for the Roundtable on Long-Run Trends in Travel Demand. Delft, The Netherlands: OECD. (www.internationaltransportforum.org/jtrc/DiscussionPapers/DP201215.pdf).

The World Bank Group. (2010). *Mainstreaming Gender in Road Transport: Operational Guidance for World Bank Staff*. Washington, DC: The World Bank. (www.worldbank.org/transport/).

Transport Scotland. (2017). *Transport and Travel in Scotland, 2016*. Glasgow: Transport Scotland.

6

IMPLEMENTATION OF GENDER AND DIVERSITY PERSPECTIVES IN TRANSPORT DEVELOPMENT PLANS IN GERMANY

Elena von den Driesch, Linda Steuer-Dankert, Tobias Berg, and Carmen Leicht-Scholten

Mobility is a central aspect of participation in daily life, like organizing the purchases of day-to-day consumables or to foster social contacts. As a result, the UN has declared mobility to be a basic right which is an essential precondition for being an active member of society (UN Human Rights Committee, 1999; Hamilton & Jenkins, 2000).

In addition, challenges like climate change, dwindling raw materials, and demographic changes determine the local agendas of policymakers as well as mobility planners. These challenges will influence mobility patterns and affect individual basic rights. Furthermore, the increasing demands for social inclusion are leading to greater reflection upon the sustainable accessibility to different forms of mobility by different social groups (Horx, 2011; Casprig et al., 2013).

It has become increasingly evident that energy, housing, and access to mobility largely determine the living conditions of people. Resources, energy, space, and mobility can therefore no longer be thought of in solely economic and ecological terms, but also social/human terms. Therefore, gender and diversity aspects should be taken into account when designing mobility policy and plans.

In this article, we present the results of an analysis of German Transport Development Plans (TDPs) that was carried out in 2015. We investigated to what extent diverse target groups and their mobility requirements are considered in transport strategy documents of German cities with a population over 200,000. The analysis focuses on two subject areas – visions and measures to be realized – as they represent key elements in planning processes.

The Gender and Diversity Factor in Mobility

Theoretically, the structural category of gender has been recognized as an important inequality issue in mobility research since the 1970s (Law, 1999: 567). Yet research shows that there is still a gap in integrating gender and diversity issues in transportation planning (Hamilton & Jenkins, 2000; Hjorthol, 2008; Sánchez de Madariaga, 2013a). Our research questioned whether transport is still male-dominated "both from an employment point of view and for the values which are embedded" (UNECE, 2009: 2).

Hamilton and Jenkins (2000) came to the conclusion that:

> transport also plays a significant role in either exacerbating or ameliorating the relative disadvantage of women. There is increasing evidence of "transport poverty" and the ways in which this compounds the many other difficulties associated with living on a low income. Poor transport options limit access to employment and social support networks, and to health, recreational and sports facilities, restricting both quality of life and "life chances".
>
> *(Hamilton & Jenkins, 2000: 1799)*

Like gender, other diversity dimensions are not properly scrutinized in transport planning contexts (Norrbom & Ståhl, 1991; Flade et al., 2001; Schlag & Engeln, 2005). Mobility studies have shown that the mobility of users is greatly affected by embodied social categories (Law, 1999; Bauhardt, 2006; Levy, 2013). This research has also brought to light that the category of gender has a huge influence on mobility. Turner et al. (2006) discovered that deliberations in urban planning processes are almost exclusively based on an anticipated "norm" of full-time employed males which implies "blind spots" in mobility planning processes.

In Figure 6.1, Robin Law (1999) shows that gender functions as a social category of inequality and has a great influence on movement in space, access to resources and experiences – as it affects mobility choices – mobility behavior, perception of mobility, as well as experience of mobility.

In accordance with this theoretical approach, the study "Mobility in Germany" (MiD) was able to establish that gender plays a significant role in mobility patterns despite a slow change in gender roles. Thus, women tend to be less mobile than men; they travel less and shorter distances but their travel time is almost equal to that of men (Infas & DLR, 2010). Likewise, while analyzing the modal split, or choice of transportation type, gender-related differences emerge. Hence, women tend to drive a car less frequently than men even though men and women are just as likely to have a driver's license. They have universal access to a car far less than men and they use environmentally friendly modes of transportation like walking, cycling and public transport far more often (Infas & DLR, 2010; Stiewe & Krause, 2012; Ahrend & Herget, 2013).

Because women still spend significantly more time than men performing work that entails caring for other people, their transportation needs, patterns and trip purposes differ from typical male mobility patterns (European Commission, 2013). The

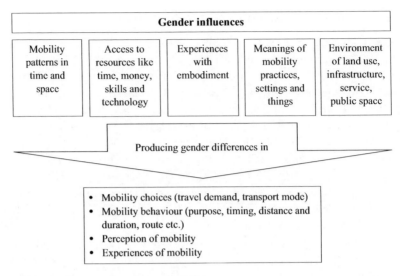

FIGURE 6.1 Influence of gender on mobility

Source: Own elaboration based on Law (1999).

innovative concept "mobility of care" (Sánchez de Madariaga, 2013b) reveals that, especially, mobility patterns related to caring work: i.e. unpaid labor performed by adults – thus men and women – for children, elderly or other dependents who cannot move by themselves, including labor related to the upkeep of households, are often concealed as they are aggregated into other data categories such as shopping, escorting or errands (European Commission, 2013; Sánchez de Madariaga, 2013b).

The fragmentary collection of care or family-based trip chains (Knoll, 2006; Janssen, 2011), as well as the rare gender-sensitive data analysis and visualization of mobility survey results indicate existing "blind spots" or "gender gaps" in transport planning processes (Stiewe & Krause, 2012). Similar problems exist in the field of the presentation of research results, where the aggregation of data conceals the diversity of users' needs in transportation systems. Therefore, data collection concepts in mobility surveys should be reconsidered to ensure gender and diversity-sensitive data gathering as well as analysis.

In addition to gender, there is a range of further categories intersecting with gender, which also affect mobility patterns as well as mobility needs of transport users and must also be taken into account when analyzing transport planning and mobility research. These diversity factors are, e.g. age, income, the presence of children, care work, social status, class, employment (Janssen, 2011; Hoede-maeker et al., 2012; European Commission, 2013), multiple responsibilities related to concurrent employment and care or maintenance work, migration background, phase or circumstance of life, and mental/physical disability or limited mobility (Krause, 2007; Ahrend & Herget, 2013; Levy, 2013). All of these factors are interwoven with each other and represent numerous diversity categories which portray the variety and plurality of users' personal living conditions and associated mobility needs.

Mobility planning must therefore deal with gender and diversity categories in order to prevent people from suffering social exclusion. The recognition of "gender and diversity gaps" in mobility planning processes has enormous potential to ensure the accessibility to and participation in society (Fainstein, 2005; Nussbaum, 2008) by considering the needs of different users in mobility planning concepts (Bauhardt, 2006: 9).

Research Interest, Method and Analysis

Facing these blind spots or gaps in mobility planning and research, the project *buildING|bridges*[1] aims at the development of gender and diversity-sensitive recommendations for mobility planning tools.[2] By analyzing German Transport Development Plans (TDPs) as well as Germany-wide mobility surveys regarding their implementation of gender and diversity issues/diversity categories, research results contribute to a widening of perspective towards different situations, lifestyles, and strategies for coping with everyday life. In this article, the focus is on the analysis of TDPs and their consideration of gender and diversity perspectives.

Transport Development Plans

In Germany, TDPs, also named master plans or transportation plans, are the standard mobility planning documents at the municipal and regional level (Deutsche Gesellschaft für Internationale Zusammenarbeit (GIZ) et al., 2014). They are instruments that include current situations of traffic development in a city in conjunction with concepts and measures for future traffic developments. Moreover, they assist stakeholders in traffic development planning, functioning as a means of communication and providing a mutual interface, which documents progress and problems. Although there are no formalized guidelines about the topics and the extent of TDPs, there are certain key aspects that can be found in the majority of these documents (GIZ, 2014):

- Meaning and significance of mobility for cities and their citizens
- Determining factors that influence transportation development planning
- How these plans intersect with the plans and policies of other planning departments
- The current and desired transportation situations
- Planned measures and their potential effects
- Who are the stakeholders in the planning processes and what are their roles?
- Concepts with future visions and measures.

Furthermore, TDPs describe the transportation developments and the mobility behavior against the backdrop of current basic conditions and parameters such as the legislative basis, as well as social developments like demographic change. Municipalities are not obliged to prepare a TDP (GIZ et al., 2014), although most of the larger German cities produce such documents. The main reason for designing a TDP is to function as a means of communication and documentation as well as a steering tool.

In order to meet the different requirements that result from social, economic, ecological, or infrastructural needs, the TDPs usually have a general orientation, or foundation, in which principles and visions for the future are formulated. In addition, specific steps to achieve the outlined objectives are identified and to some degree hierarchically organized regarding their order of implementation.

In Germany, typical stakeholders of TDPs include: the mobility committee, a separate faction of the city council, the buildings department, but also other project groups like ecology groups and civic associations. Modern instruments of civic participation in TDPs' development processes, for example via online platforms, surveys or citizen walks have also been employed in a few cases (Forschungsgesellschaft für Straßen- und Verkehrswesen (FGSV), 2013).

During a participatory stakeholder process, the plans are voted on, revised, and updated successively over the decades until they are adopted. The planning period varies from process to process, whereas the average period of time constitutes 10 to 20 years. Thus, TDPs must be future-oriented and sustainable, facing global challenges as well as mediating conflicting demands at a local level. Furthermore, as an instrument of transport planning, TDPs are embedded into a legal framework. This framework includes legal texts stating the constraint to implement measures for accessibility in buildings, roads, transport, objects, information etc., to allow access for all citizens regardless of restrictions (Law on equal treatment for people with disabilities (BGG) §4 and §8 (2)).

Moreover, inclusion and participation, as an element of social dimensions, are not guidelines based on moral or social norms but they are legitimized by law. Germany's basic law provides all people with equal opportunities independent of their color, origin, disability or gender and forbids discrimination (BGG §1 and §4).

Furthermore, structural accessibility found its way into public transportation through the Federal Equality Act (Herrmann-Lobreyer, 2007: 28). In addition, paragraph §2, 8 and 9 of the public transportation law of the Federal State of North Rhine-Westphalia includes gender and diversity components:

> (8) During the planning and the configuration of the traffic infrastructure, the vehicles as well as the offers of public transportation, particularly of persons that are sensory handicapped [...] are to be considered according to the Law on Equal Opportunities for Disabled of the Federal Government and the federal states.
>
> (9) Equally the concerns of women, men, persons that care for children, children and cyclists should be taken into account during planning and design of public transport.
>
> *(Law on local public transport in North Rhine-Westphalia (ÖPNVG NRW), 2015 translated)*

Overall Research Questions and Methodological Approach

In the framework of the research project buildING | bridges@research, an analysis of TDPs from German cities with a population over 200,000 was carried out in 2015. The sample of plans was chosen according to the following criteria: the plans were available online and currently valid at the time of analysis. This led to a sample size of 24 TDPs (see Figure 6.2).

The cities of the sample are evenly spread in Germany and the regions mirror different political situations. As there are no explicit legal obligations for the development of TDPs in Germany (GIZ et al., 2014), the analyzed sample of plans turned out to be very different regarding structure, topics, and page length. For example, the TDPs' number of pages varies from about 30 to nearly 800. Since all plans include a future vision as well as a plan of measures, or at least recommendations for action, the analysis focuses on those two subject areas – visions and measures – as they represent key elements in further planning processes.

The main object of research was the consideration and representation of gender and diversity aspects in the TDPs. Hence, major research questions were:

FIGURE 6.2   24 Cities with available TDPs

Source: Own elaboration.

1. Are there gender and diversity aspects that are considered in the TDPs? If yes, to what extent?
2. Are there gender and diversity aspects that are disregarded in the TDPs?
3. How consistent are future visions with specific plans and other policy measures?
4. Which recommendations can be derived for a future gender- and diversity-sensitive transport development plan design?

The examination of TDPs consists of a quantitative as well as a qualitative analysis. Whereas the focus of the first research part is a descriptive data analysis, the qualitative approach is based on content analysis. Research results focus on a contrast between future visions and the recommended measures as the general objectives of transport development processes can diverge considerably from their concrete implementation.

Methods and Research Results

Based on prior theoretical findings regarding the gender and diversity factor in mobility, a set of gender and diversity categories/codes as well as relevant social and environmental topics were developed and used as the basis of analysis. These categories were assigned another set of sub-categories or codings that served as search items in the frame of the computer-based qualitative analysis. The main categories and topics are defined in the following paragraphs and are exemplified by sub-categories for the purpose of clarification. The quantitative analysis was completed by a qualitative content analyses to receive robust results.

Quantitative Analysis

A quantitative analysis of the TDPs explored gives a review of the frequency and distribution of the main gender and diversity categories examined, as well as social and environmental topics (see list of main categories/topics in Figure 6.3) and concentrates on the following research questions:

*   Which categories/topics are taken into consideration frequently/rarely?
*   Are the categories/topics mentioned equally or is there an obvious prioritization of categories/topics?
*   Is there a consistent distribution of categories/topics comparing future visions and measures? Do the measures include the same categories/topics which are addressed in future visions?

To provide a general overview of the distribution of gender and diversity categories in the future visions and measures of the TDPs, Figure 6.3 illustrates the percentage of TDPs including the different categories. The bar chart is arranged

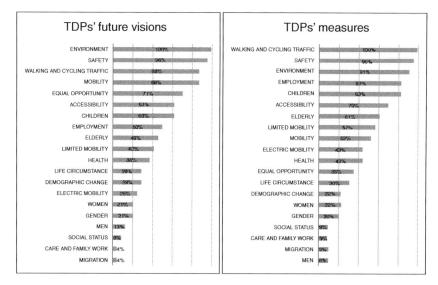

FIGURE 6.3   Percentage of TDPs including the set of categories
Source: Own elaboration.

according to percentage size and also contains the percentage of TDPs dealing with social and environmental topics.

Comparing the TDPs' future vision with its measures, the consideration of categories apparently differs. This indicates that the general objectives and their concrete implementation mentioned are not mutually concordant in all plans. Further analysis shows that there is not a single TDP that covers exactly all the same topics listed in its future visions as well as in its plan of measures/plan of action. There are categories addressed in the goals that are excluded in the implementation plan. In comparison, there are topics which are not part of the future visions but only dealt with in the following measures.

Regarding the quantity of TDPs comprehending the diverse set of categories in Figure 6.2, the issues "environment", "safety" as well as "walking and cycling traffic" are the three main topics in both the future visions and the plans for measures, as they are mentioned in ≥ 88% of the TDPs. On the other hand, the categories "migration", "care and family work",[3] "social status", "gender", "women", and "men" represent the lowest frequency of integration (≤ 22%), whereas the first three mentioned topics are only addressed in fewer than 10% of the samples. There is an obvious tendency towards a prioritization of environment-friendly elements and secure transport planning. In contrast, various gender and diversity categories tend to be neglected or disregarded. Conspicuously, the three most frequent diversity groups discussed are "children" – containing pupil/students and youths – the "elderly" and persons with "limited mobility".[4] They are a subject in ≥ 42% of the TDPs' concept of goals and in ≥ 57% of the plans of measures.

In addition to the high level of discrepancy between the terms mentioned in future goals and the formulated measures, the differences of percentages illustrated in Figure 6.3 are also striking. The social category "equal opportunity" – in terms of equal conditions regardless of the individual life situation and background as well as social inclusion and participation – exhibits the highest discrepancy of integration. Whereas this topic is addressed in 71% of the TDPs' future visions it is only mentioned in 35% of the implementation plans. Likewise, the aspect of "mobility" in terms of mobility requirements, patterns and demands is addressed in 88% of the visions, but merely in 52% of the plans of measures. Another gap becomes apparent regarding the category "employment" which is included in 50% of the TDPs' goals compared to 83% of the implementation plans. Concordant to the theoretical findings mentioned before, the concrete implementation of traffic development measures show a noticeable focus on the mobility needs of employees.

Although the percentage of TDPs that included the categories answers the question of whether the sample mentions the different topics or not, it does not clarify the intensity or quality of usage. Therefore, Figure 6.4 illustrates the absolute frequency of categories addressed in the TDPs' future visions and measures.

Again, the three most frequently used terms in the TDPs are the categories "environment", "walking and cycling traffic", and "safety". The number of mentions is significantly higher compared to other topics of analysis, whereas the

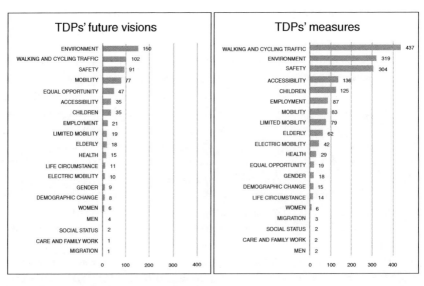

FIGURE 6.4 Absolute frequencies of categories
Source: Own elaboration.

intensity of attention is even higher in the plans of implementation (304–437 codings).

In this regard, looking at the proportion of absolute frequencies, the sizable disregard of the diversity categories "care and family work", "migration", "social status", "men" as well as "women" covering only 1–6 numbers of codings becomes clearly visible. The category "gender" also represents a very small proportion of mentions by comparison (9 codings in the TDPs future visions and 18 codings in the plans of measures).

Altogether, research results of the quantitative analysis illustrate a clear prioritization of ecological topics such as "environment" and "walking and cycling traffic" as well as the aspect of "safety", which indicates a hierarchization that doesn't take into account gender and other diversity categories which also represent a variety of factors that affect a person's mobility patterns as well as mobility needs.

These results of the analyzed TDPs suggest that there may be an implicit political demand to focus on gender and diversity categories. It could be assumed that there are differences depending on the political party leading within the federal state government.[5]

As the theoretical approaches and former research results mentioned in the paragraphs about the gender and diversity factor in mobility have already shown, there are persistent "gender and diversity gaps" or "blind spots" in transport development planning processes that have to be tackled. Because of this, TDPs should set a stronger focus on gender and diversity categories affecting mobility needs and patterns as well as on their intersecting effects in transport planning processes. Moreover, a stronger coherence of structure and implementation of topics in visions and measures is needed as it is required for an equal consideration and integration of diverse target groups.

Qualitative Analysis

As already shown in the quantitative analysis, different codes (or codings) were developed for investigating the previously mentioned gender and diversity categories along with social and environmental topics. These categories allow the identification of similarities and differences in nationwide strategies, as well as to deduce trends and key topics. Using this method also enables one to reflect the image of future cities, which is rooted and interconnected with the transport plans, and to compare this image with the demands and needs of future generations.

By carrying out qualitative content analyses of TDPs,[6] a contextualization of topics becomes possible. This gives a glance at the quality of contents as well as the intensity of a topics' implementation. The analysis is divided into two parts. On the one hand, there is an exploration regarding the guiding principles (future visions) of transport planning. On the other hand, the plans of measures, which should be derived from the guiding principles, are investigated by comparing the visions with the plans for practical implementation.

To analyze the state of implementation concerning diversity perspectives and the reflection of diverse needs in TDPs, the following research questions serve as the basis for proceeding:

- In which context are the categories/topics described?
- How selective are the categories/topics considered?
- To what extent are future needs reflected?

Future Visions in TDPs

The data reveal that there is a strong tendency to make mainstream trends a subject of discussion. Comparable to the megatrend neo-ecology (Horx, 2011), themes that are directly as well as indirectly related to actual key topics, such as environmental protection, conservation of resources, and sustainability, represent a major proportion of the strategy framework and are broadly addressed. In this context, neo-ecology has to be considered as a trend that focuses on the increasing demand for organic products for a lifestyle of health and sustainability (LOHAS), which requires and implies an adjustment of industrial processes to a sustainable and environment-friendly system (Zukunftsinstitut, 2016). The expansion of infrastructure as well as the insistent promotion of walking and cycling, as part of the strategies and objective targets, accentuate the efforts for sustainable mobility. In contrast to this, the topic of "electric mobility" is mentioned inconsistently. Some cities cover this issue quite extensively, whereas other cities don't make it a subject of discussion at all. Electric mobility, when mentioned, is always assessed in connection with environmental topics such as the reduction of emissions (air pollution), reduction of noise, conservation of resources, and enhancement of the quality of life. Only in a few cases is electric mobility put in context with corresponding requirements like infrastructure.

In addition to the topic "environment", the investigation shows a strong focus on dominant groups[7] in the framework of the TDPs – cyclists and pedestrians. However, this strong emphasis of specific groups and their needs and requirements is accompanied by the lack of an intersectional perspective, taking into account non-dominant groups and/or minorities as well as less dominant trends, which are far less covered in the traffic discussions. For example, aspects like gender are barely considered even though there is a sustained discussion concerning aspects like care work. Therefore, it is important to take a closer look at to what extent the different diversity categories (gender, age, disability etc.) are addressed in future visions in the framework of TDPs.

The usage of diversity categories in the guiding principles shows that, in general, the specific diverse needs and perspectives, which represent the people behind topics (e.g. "bicycling") are not mentioned extensively. For example, it is rather astonishing that the most frequently addressed group of people is children, yet people carrying out "care and family work" – adults – are neglected, as the quantitative analysis illustrated. Concerning the category of children, issues like the "promotion of independent and safe mobility of teenagers and children" (City C: 47 – city codes) and the improvement of accessibility in public places and in public transport by taking the needs of pedestrians and children into account (City F: 16), are mentioned.

The qualitative evaluation of the diversity categories "age" and "limited mobility" shows that these topics are hardly taken into account. It appears as if they are only used as buzzwords despite an increased importance of these categories due to demographic change. Regarding the topic "limited mobility", there is no definition, description, or complete enumeration of what can be understood under the term in any of the examined plans. This recognition leads to the assumption that there is a lack of reflection regarding the diverse needs of transport participants. There is also a lack of transparency concerning the question of whose demands are considered and also why. It is important to develop a consistent accessibility concept in order to achieve improvements, especially when considering diverse disabilities.

In addition, this finding is interesting for two reasons. Firstly, experts' reports show, that there has been an increasing consideration of topics like "accessibility" in the last few years (Bundesministerium für Verkehr, Bau und Stadtentwicklung (BMVBS), 2008; Verband Deutscher Verkehrsunternehmen (VDV), 2012), but that there is still a need for implementing barrier-free elements. Furthermore, a study from the federal Ministry of Transport, Building and Urban Affairs (2010) shows that the average number of trips per day, as an expression of mobility, has increased, particularly in the case of older people, compared to the year 2002. The institute for Applied Social Sciences (Infas) and the German Aerospace Center (DLR) conclude: "that 46 million of 281 million trips in total (in Germany in the year 2008) were completed by people aged 65 years or older. That corresponds to a share of the total number of trips of about 16%" (2010: 181). These findings emphasize the increasing importance of taking this group of stakeholders into consideration.

As shown in the quantitative analysis, the diversity category "gender" is rarely mentioned. Using a complementing qualitative analysis, it becomes apparent that the topic of gender is often related directly to the term "gender mainstreaming". Compared to the term "environment", for which concrete examples for reaching the defined targets are mentioned, the explanations in the context of gender are rather short and fairly general. The exemplary objectives "facilitation of mobility regardless of gender and life situation" (City C: 36) as well as statements like: "As part of the gender mainstreaming in particular the special needs of women, families with children, as well as mobility-restricted persons are taken into account" (City M: 7) show that there is a first approach of considering these topics, but when it comes to implementation these topics tend to be neglected.

Moreover, the analysis demonstrates that there is no consistent definition of the term "gender mainstreaming". While on the one hand gender mainstreaming is understood as the diverse requirements of women and men in their social roles (City P: 11, City Q: 10), on the other hand it is defined as "special belongings of women, families with children and people with reduced mobility" (City M: 7) as well as the "consideration of all population groups and life situations" (City M: 17). This could be interpreted as uncertainty concerning the term and its use, meaning that these issues remain vague and are implemented inconsistently.

The diversity category "interculturality" is addressed in only one of the examined future visions. Although the support of integration processes in the form of "offers, which are multi-lingual and take cultural aspects into account, moreover, the integration of citizens with an immigrant background [...], are also for the benefit of many international visitors in the city" (City C: 36).

It can be concluded that the future concepts show a clear trend towards themes that are rooted in the category of environment. In contrast to that, the diverse needs of transport users are recognized only inconsistently.

Plans of Measures in TDPs

The plans of measures are the summarized and practical implementation approach of the future visions. The issues that were discussed in the context of the guiding principles should therefore also be taken into account in the plans of measures.

The plans of measures show the same tendencies previously observed in the future visions: Categories in the context of environment are most frequently mentioned in all of the examined TDPs. The specific measures concerning the topic "environment" are, as already mentioned, almost always in the context of "walking and cycling traffic", but also very often in connection with "safety" as well as "health". In this combination, "safety" aspects shall increase the attractiveness of alternative and more ecological means of transport, whereas the health aspect is mainly mentioned in the context of air quality as well as noise pollution. This tendency is consistent with the findings in the future visions.

In comparison with these findings, the topic "electric mobility", as a possibility for motorized individual transport and as a mobility option for the elderly, is discussed not nearly as intensively as the topic "environment" in terms of eco-friendly transportation planning.

The category "age" is mainly mentioned in the context of "accessibility" but also in connection with the needs of children. Hence, it could be concluded that there is a general assumption that children and the elderly have the same needs. However, research shows that the safety needs of children depend on their body height as well as on their general level of inexperience in traffic situations, whereas the safety needs of elderly people are connected to physically mobility restrictions, a lower level of impulsiveness and lower capacity of reactivity (Funk, 2008; Limbourg & Matern, 2009). This shows a lack of a differentiated consideration as well as a lack of consciousness regarding the variety of user needs in the examined TDPs. Accordingly, the target-group-specific needs are comprehended and implemented insufficiently into practical measures.

As part of the analysis, the consideration of the diversity categories "limited mobility" as well as "accessibility" were examined separately from each other, to investigate the implementation of diverse needs concerning these issues. Nevertheless, the analysis indicates that the topic "limited mobility" is always associated with the diversity category "disability". In this context, the requirements of wheelchair users are mainly discussed, whereas the needs of visually impaired people as well as hearing impaired people are mentioned less frequently. The necessities of people with impairment in the form of baby carriages are mentioned in 35% of all TDPs' measures. The issue of the diversity aspect "interculturality" (migration) was only mentioned in one TDP.

Concerning the subject of "accessibility", research shows that mostly elderly people are mentioned in this context, as are pedestrians and cyclists. The action plan for the implementation of the UN Convention on the Rights of Persons with Disabilities was mentioned in only one of the TDPs. Contrary to the assumption that the topics "limited mobility" and "accessibility" are focusing on the needs identical to the diversity category "disability" and are, therefore, used synonymously, the analysis shows a various and inconsistent classification of the topics in all TDPs.

Comparable to the findings in the framework of the future visions, the topics related to "care and family work" and "gender" are rarely addressed. When mentioned, the gender aspect is almost always directly connected with the gender mainstreaming term, which is not explained in any detail. This result corresponds to the aforementioned findings in the guiding principles. There are no concrete measures connected to questions of gender. One city instead notes that:

> gender-typical patterns can be identified: Boys tend to conquer [the] room, whereas girls rather tend to observe and prefer to be undisturbed rather than in communion with girlfriends. With increasing age, the radius of action widens and the needs and requirements are more differentiated.
>
> *(City Q: 51)*

Including these vague tendencies in behavior entails the risk of stipulating certain manners to a specific group of people, which could lead to a stereotypical and generalized perspective, which might then be reflected in Transport Development Plans. Another city indicates, that:

traffic development planning means to take the different needs of women and men concerning the city, mobility and integration into account in the framework of planning strategies, projects and their evaluation. The actions and measures concept of TDPs must be designed accordingly.

(City T: 33)

Unfortunately, this approach is not supplemented by concrete conclusions. In only one examined plan of measures is gender associated with gender roles and the assumption that behavioral patterns of women and men are the result of the social attribution of gender roles.

Summary of Qualitative Analysis

The qualitative analysis shows that the TDPs exhibit very different qualities concerning the ways in which they address diversity factors. Whereas some plans try to consider a wide range of diversity categories, others only address specific groups like the elderly and children. The understanding of concrete measures presented in all TDPs is heterogeneous, which makes them difficult to compare. The analysis shows that, in general, there is a lack of appropriate measures. This lack is evidenced by identified needs which are not transferred to further implications for structural implementations.

It can be stated that the diverse needs of the target groups in the TDPs' measures are formulated so vaguely that an analysis concerning potential overlaps is not possible. On the one hand, there is a tendency to combine the needs of diverse groups (for example children, the elderly) although there are diverse requirements specific for every diversity category. On the other hand, target groups are discussed separately from one another, which leads to a low level of consideration regarding the aspect of intersectionality,[8] There is a strong tendency to divide target groups into cyclists, pedestrians, bus passengers, etc. Not considered in this scheme are factors like physical and psychological state. Although there seems to be a trend towards the summary of different diversity categories in TDPs, research shows that there are heterogeneous requirements that make a differentiated view necessary (Turner et al., 2006). For example, one study's results indicate a trend towards the individualization of traffic (Horx, 2011). There is a trend towards car ownership among elderly people (Infas & DLR, 2010: 181), whereas on an international level there is a stagnation and even decline concerning the ownership of drivers' licenses among younger people (Institut für Mobilitätsforschung, 2011; Sivak & Schoettle, 2012). Various sources state that public passenger transport is rather unattractive for elderly people because of safety issues as well as usability (Engeln & Schlag, 2001; Limbourg & Matern, 2009).

Another observation is that some cities create incentives for modal choice to influence mobility behavior. In this regard, models like the modal split (PNV-Split),[9] which make it possible to calculate traffic resistance by different transport modes, are used for expressing the traffic resistance and defining measurable targets. The basis for the modal split is often a collection of public available data that does not consider the diversity of requirements. Thus, it seems that the actual modal split is not suitable but has to be adapted, as it is based on general statistics instead of holistic research up to now.

Conclusion and Outlook

The research reported herein delivers two main perspectives referring to the integration of gender and diversity issues in mobility concepts. On the one hand, the analysis of German Transport Development Plans (TDPs) has revealed discrepancies between their visions and their implementation measures. So the assumption arises that formulating visions that integrate gender and diversity perspectives is a question of being "politically correct".

On the other hand, looking at the implementation measures developed in the plans, there is a limited consideration of diverse groups. Combining their needs leads to uninformed decisions that have an impact on marginal social groups. For example, urban municipalities tend to reduce their public transportation offers, which greatly disadvantages unemployed individuals or people with low incomes, as they often do not have access to a car. This development has to be regarded in the context of an emerging occurrence of poverty in old age and phenomena like the Gender Pension Gap[10] (Goebel & Grabka, 2011), which might result in the exclusion of older and/or retired people and elder women in particular (BMVBS, 2010).

Different categories of trips cannot be regarded only as traveling activities because they are linked to social systems. Considering the social dimension as well, we see that there is a wide variety of user groups.[11] For example, women, men, children, employed/unemployed, elderly, people with disabilities, people practicing care work, migrants, etc. all have their own specific and individual needs and requirements in terms of mobility (Mackensen, 1994). Because TDPs are a basic element of transport development processes, there is a clear need to consider gender and diversity categories as fundamental aspects of planning. In contrast to the described necessity to include these perspectives in TDPs, gender and diversity categories, in particular, are vastly neglected in the analyzed sample compared to environmental or ecological topics.

Thus, the development of target-group-oriented mobility concepts that include the requirements of all diverse groups of society is a challenge that has to be faced by urban planners. It is important to implement a diversity perspective not only during the development of Transport Development Plans but also at the beginning of transport planning processes, using a gender and diversity-sensible perspective as an overall leitmotif of the whole cycle of transport planning, in order to ensure a sustainable consideration of themes like accessibility and mobility for all.

Since mobility should entail inclusion and participation, inventions, developments and planning processes should recognize and focus on gender in addition to the different needs as well as the abilities or disabilities of various users. Such a result in Germany would be a paradigm shift, which implements equal opportunities and accessibility in all questions of mobility by taking into account the different lifestyles and coping strategies of daily life on the one hand, and the ecologic, economic as well as international and national policies on the other.

Notes

1 For further information please refer to www.gdi.rwth-aachen.de/forschung/building bridges/.
2 We would like to thank our former colleague Anne Casprig for her work on this project.
3 "Care and family work" includes activities and assignments referred to care, fostering and the maintenance of household, children, family, and persons concerned with high-maintenance needs. It also comprises people facing the double burden of doing care and family work while being employed.
4 The main category "limited mobility" includes persons who are impaired visually, auditory, mentally or concerning movement, as well as persons using equipment like a baby carriage or walking frame.
5 It would be interesting to look at the discrepancy of visions and measures related to the political situation in the federal state governments.
6 For reasons of data protection, direct quotes derived from the examined sample of TDPs are indicated anonymously.
7 In this context "dominant groups" are constellations of people that have characteristics in common, which are discussed publicly and frequently.
8 "The interconnected nature of social categorizations such as race, class, and gender as they apply to a given individual or group, regarded as creating overlapping and interdependent systems of discrimination or disadvantage" (Oxford University Press, 2015).
9 "Mode split involves separating (splitting) the predicted trips from each origin zone to each destination zone into distinct travel modes (e.g., walking, bicycle, driving, train, bus)" (CrimeStat, n.d.).
10 Under the indicator "Gender Pension Gap", the relative difference concerning the pension income of women and men throughout the acquisition phase is summarized (Bundesministerium für Familie, Senioren, Frauen und Jugend, 2011).
11 These groups should not be understood as homogenous. For example, a women can be elderly and unemployed. Thus, a social group embodies several mobility-specific characteristics intersecting with each other.

References

Ahrend, C. & Herget, M. (2013). Verkehrs- und Mobilitätsforschung aus der Genderperspektive. In: Hofmeister, S., Katz, C. & Mölders, T. (Eds.). *Geschlechterverhältnisse und Nachhaltigkeit. Die Kategorie Geschlecht in den Nachhaltigkeitswissenschaften.* Berlin: Verlag Barbara Budrich, pp. 218–227.
Bauhardt, C. (2006). Gender Mainstreaming in der Verkehrspolitik. Anstöße aus der feministischen Verkehrsforschung. In: Friedrich-Ebert-Stiftung (Ed.). *Gleiche Mobilitätschancen für alle! Gender Mainstreaming im Öffentlichen Personennahverkehr.* Zusammenfassung

der Tagung vom 20. 02.2006 in der Friedrich-Ebert-Stiftung, pp. 9–11. Online available at: http://library.fes.de/pdf-files/do/03861.pdf (Accessed on 22.09.2015).

Bundesministerium für Verkehr, Bau und Stadtentwicklung (Federal Ministry of Transport, Building and Urban Development) (BMVBS). (2008). *Hinweise Barrierefreiheit im öffentlichen Verkehrsraum für seh- und hörgeschädigte Menschen.* Bremerhaven: Wirtschaftsverlag NW, Verlag für neue Wissenschaft GmbH.

Bundesministerium für Verkehr, Bau und Stadtentwicklung (Federal Ministry of Transport, Building and Urban Development) (BMVBS). (2010). ÖPNV: Planung für ältere Menschen. Ein Leitfaden für die Praxis. In: *BMVBS-Online-Publikation 09/2010.*

Bundesministerium für Familie, Senioren, Frauen und Jugend (Federal Ministry for Family Affairs, Senior Citizens, Women and Youth) (BMFSFJ). (2011). *Gender Pension Gap – Entwicklung eines Indikators für faire Einkommensperspektiven von Frauen und Männern.* Online available at: www.bmfsfj.de/RedaktionBMFSFJ/Broschuerenstelle/Pdf-Anlagen/gender-pension-gap,property=pdf,bereich=bmfsfj,sprache=de,rwb=true.pdf (Accessed on 22.09.2015).

Casprig, A., Berg, T., von den Driesch, E. & Leicht-Scholten, C. (2013). buildING bridges: Mobilität als Grundlage für Inklusion und Partizipation. In: *Journal Netzwerk Frauen- und Geschlechterforschung NRW*, no. 33 (2013), Essen, pp. 30–36.

CrimeStat. (n.d.). Chapter 15 – Mode Split. Online available at: www.icpsr.umich.edu/CrimeStat/files/CrimeStatChapter.15.pdf (Accessed on 09.11.2015).

Deutsche Gesellschaft für Internationale Zusammenarbeit (GIZ), Federal Ministry for Economic Cooperation and Development (BMZ), Böhler-Baedeker, S., Kost, C. & Merforth, M. (2014). *Urban Mobility Plans: National Approaches and Local Practice.* Bonn: GIZ.

Engeln, A. & Schlag, B. (2001). *ANBINDUNG – Abschlussbericht zum Forschungsprojekt: Anforderungen Älterer an eine benutzergerechte Vernetzung individueller und gemeinschaftlich genutzter Verkehrsmittel.* Stuttgart: Kohlhammer Verlag.

European Commission. (2013). *Gendered Innovations – How Gender Analysis Contributes to Research.* Luxembourg: Publications Office of the European Union.

Fainstein, S. (2005). Feminism and Planning: Theoretical Issues. In: Fainstein, S. S. & Servon, L. J. (Eds.). *Gender and Planning: A Reader.* New Brunswick, NJ: Rutgers University Press, pp. 120–138.

Flade, A., Limbourg, M. & Schlag, B. (2001). *Mobilität älterer Menschen.* Opladen: Leske and Budrich.

Forschungsgesellschaft für Straßen- und Verkehrswesen (Road and Transportation Research Association) (FGSV). (2013). *Hinweise zur Verkehrsentwicklungsplanung.* Köln: FGSV Verlag GmbH.

Funk, W. (2008). *Mobilität von Kindern und Jugendlichen. Langfristige Trends der Änderung ihres Verkehrsverhaltens.* Institut für empirische Soziologie an der Universität Erlangen – Nürnberg. Nürnberg: ifes.

Gesetz über den öffentlichen Personennahverkehr in Nordrhein-Westfalen (Law on local public transport in North Rhine-Westphalia) (ÖPNVG NRW). (2015). Online available at: https://recht.nrw.de/lmi/owa/br_bes_text?anw_nr=2&gld_nr=9&ugl_nr=93&bes_id=3913&aufgehoben=N#det275284 (Accessed on 02.09.2015).

Goebel, J. & Grabka, M. A. (2011). *Entwicklung der Altersarmut.* Online available at: www.diw.de/documents/publikationen/73/diw_01.c.372630.de/diw_sp0378.pdf (Accessed on 02.09.2015).

Hamilton, K. & Jenkins, L. (2000). A Gender Audit for Public Transport: A New Policy Tool in the Tackling of Social Exclusion. In: *Urban Studies*, vol. 37, no. 10, pp. 1793–1800.

Herrmann-Lobreyer, M. (2007). *Die Verbesserung des öffentlichen Personennahverkehrsangebots für mobilitätseingeschränkte Personengruppen mithilfe von Gender Planning am Beispiel der Region Stuttgart*. Online available at: http://elib.uni-stuttgart.de/opus/volltexte/2008/3351/pdf/Diss_komplett.pdf (Accessed on 22.09.2015).

Hjorthol, R. (2008). Daily Mobility of Men and Women – A Barometer of Gender Equality? In: Priya Uteng, T. & Cresswell, T. (Eds.). *Gendered Mobilities*. Aldershot: Ashgate, pp. 193–212.

Hoedemaeker, M., Parik, M., Baldi, B., Qiao, Y., Sahr, C. & Nuñez-Fernández, F. (2012). *GOAL: Profiles of Older People*, First Draft.

Horx, M. (2011). *Das Megatrend-Prinzip: Wie die Welt von morgen entsteht*. München: DVA E-Books.

Infas (Institut für angewandte Sozialwissenschaften) (Institute for Applied Social Sciences) & DLR (Deutsches Zentrum für Luft- und Raumfahrt e.V.) (German Aerospace Center). (2010). *MiD 2008. Mobilität in Deutschland 2008. Ergebnisbericht. Struktur – Aufkommen – Emissionen – Trends*. Bonn and Berlin. Online available at: www.mobilitaet-in-deutschland.de/pdf/MiD2008_Abschlussbericht_I (Accessed on 02.09.2015).

Institut für Mobilitätsforschung. (Eds.) (2011). *Mobilität junger Menschen im Wandel – multimodaler und weiblicher*. Institut für Mobilitätsforschung. Online available at: www.ifmo.de/tl_files/publications_content/2011/ifmo_2011_Mobilitaet_junger_Menschen_de.pdf (Accessed on 29.08.2015).

Janssen, S. (2011). *Mobilität und Gender ... Blick öffnen*. TU International 67, January 2011. Berlin, pp. 20–22.

Knoll, B. (2006). *Verkehrs- und Mobilitätserhebungen. Einführung in Gender Planning*. Dissertation zur Erlangung des wissenschaftlichen Grades Doktorin der technischen Wissenschaft, eingereicht an der Technischen Universität Wien.

Krause, J. (2007). Genderbelange in der Verkehrsplanung. In: Bracher, T., Haag, M., Holzapfel, H., Kiepe, F., Lehmbrock, M. & Reutter, U. (Eds.). *Handbuch der kommunalen Verkehrsplanung*. Berlin: Herbert Wichmann Verlag, pp. 1–33.

Law, R. (1999). Beyond 'Women and Transport': Towards New Geographies of Gender and Daily Mobility. In: *Progress in Human Geography*, vol. 23, no. 4, pp. 567–588.

Levy, C. (2013). Travel Choice Reframed: "Deep Distribution" and Gender in Urban Transport. In: *Environment and Urbanization*, vol. 25, no. 1, pp. 47–63.

Limbourg, M. & Matern, S. (2009). *Mobilität und Alter; Erleben, Verhalten und Sicherheit älterer Menschen im Straßenverkehr*. Eugen-Otto-Butz-Stiftung, Köln: TÜV Media GmbH.

Mackensen, R. (1994). Mobilitätsmuster – Kommunikations- und Mobilitätsbedarf in alters- und geschlechtsspezifischer Differenzierung. In: Forschungsverbund Lebensraum Stadt. (Ed.). *Faktoren des Verkehrshandelns*, Bd. III/1. Berlin: Forschungsverbund Lebensraum Stadt, pp. 363–424.

Norrbom, C. E. & Ståhl, A. (Eds.) (1991). *Mobility and Transport for Elderly and Disabled Persons*. Proceedings of a conference held at Stockholmsmäsan, Älvsjö, Sweden, 21–24 May 1989, organized by the Swedish Board of Transport in co-operation with the Department of Traffic Planning and Engineering, Lund Institute of Technology. Gordon and Breach Science Publishers, Philadelphia, Transportation Studies Volume, no. 13, pp. 770–774.

Nussbaum, M. C. (2008). *Women and Human Development: The Capabilities Approach*. New York: Cambridge University Press.

Oxford University Press. (2015). Intersectionality. Online available at: www.oxforddictionaries.com/de/definition/englisch/intersectionality (Accessed on 09.11.2015).

Sánchez de Madariaga, I. (2013a). From Women in Transport to Gender in Transport: Challenging Conceptual Frameworks for Improved Policymaking. In: *Journal of International Affairs*, vol. 67, no. 1, pp. 43–66.

Sánchez de Madariaga, I. (2013b). The Mobility of Care: A New Concept in Urban Transportation. In: Sánchez de Madariaga, I. & Roberts, M. (Eds.). *Fair Shared Cities: The Impact of Gender Planning in Europe*. London: Ashgate, pp. 33–48.

Schlag, B. & Engeln, A. (2005). Abbau von Mobilitätsbarrieren zugunsten älterer Verkehrsteilnehmer. In: Echterhoff, W. (Ed.). *Strategien zur Sicherung der Mobilität älterer Menschen*. Köln: TÜV Media GmbH. (Schriftenreihe der Eugen-Otto-Butz-Stiftung, Mobilität und Alter, B. 1), pp. 73–98.

Sivak, M. & Schoettle, B. (2012). Update: Percentage of Young Persons With a Driver's License Continues to Drop. In: *Traffic Injury Prevention*, vol. 13, no. 4, p. 341.

Stiewe, M. & Krause, J. (2012). Geschlechterverhältnisse und Mobilität – Welchen Beitrag leisten Mobilitätserhebungen? In: Schrenk, M., Popovich, V., Zeile, P. & Elisei, P. (Eds.). *Tagungsband zur REAL CORP 2012*. Schwechat, Austria: CORP, pp. 321–330.

Turner, J., Hamilton, K. & Spitzner, M. (2006). *Women and Transport Study*. University of East London, Wuppertal Institute for Climate, Environment and Energy. Brüssel: European Parliament.

UN Human Rights Committee. (1999). *CCPR General Comment No. 27: Article 12 (Freedom of Movement)*, contained in CCPR/C/21/Rev.1/Add.9.

UNECE. (2009). *Report to the United Nations Economic Commission for Europe Executive Committee on the Implementation of the Priorities of the Unece Reform for Strengthening Some Activities of the Committee. The Inland Transport Committee and Gender Issues in Transport*. Geneva.

Verband Deutscher Verkehrsunternehmen (association of German transport companies) (VDV). (2012). *Barrierefreier ÖPNV in Deutschland*. 2. Auflage. Düsseldorf: Alba Fachverlag.

Zukunftsinstitut GmbH. (2016). Megatrend Neo-Ökologie. Online available at: www.zukunftsinstitut.de/dossier/megatrend-neo-oekologie/ (Accessed on 06.10.2017).

7

WHY LOW-INCOME WOMEN IN THE US STILL NEED AUTOMOBILES

Evelyn Blumenberg

Introduction

There has been a steady increase in the percentage of US households – even low-income households – with automobiles. This should come as no surprise, since, as many scholars in the US and elsewhere have noted, automobiles make it easier for workers to access employment opportunities and better manage work- and household-supporting responsibilities (Dowling, 2000; Greed, 2008; Murray, 2008; Rosenbloom, 1992; Vance et al., 2004). This paper provides a critical analysis of data and current scholarship on the relationship between low-income women and automobiles. I argue that given the continued dispersion of US metropolitan areas and the growing number of jobs, as well as low-income families living in the suburbs (Kneebone, 2013; Kneebone and Berube, 2013), the evidence suggests that low-income women who do not have access to automobiles are increasingly disadvantaged.

I begin by discussing the history of women and automobiles in the US. I then draw on a diverse body of literature and data to show the increasing importance of automobiles to the lives of low-income women. Their demand for cars emerges from the continued shift in the geography of employment and low-income households, the characteristics of women's work and the labour market, and women's household responsibilities. I next review the growing body of scholarship on the role of automobiles in shaping outcomes for low-income women in the US. Those who are able to access automobiles experience a host of benefits as a result, including better employment opportunities, access to healthier food and greater health-care use.

In the US, there have been relatively few efforts to increase automobile use among low-income households, largely due to the negative environmental externalities associated with driving and, secondarily, due to the high costs of automobile ownership. In the concluding section, I discuss these programmes and policies and their effectiveness. If automobiles are essential to women's livelihoods, policies ought to balance the need for automobiles with broader efforts to reduce their negative environmental impacts.

Women and Cars in the US

Figure 7.1 shows the meteoric rise of automobiles in the US over the past century. While the footprint of cities at the turn of the previous century was substantially smaller than it is today, cars served many of the same purposes. They enabled improved access to destinations – work, friends and family, shopping and recreation – and, therefore, were increasingly popular, despite the initially limited infrastructure to support driving (Walsh, 2008). The number of registered automobiles tripled from 1920 to 1930 and, while the rate of increase declined over time, the total number of registered automobiles continued to grow (Federal Highway Administration, various years). Much of the increase in automobiles was due to consistent growth in the US population; however, the number of cars per household and per capita steadily increased through 2000, declining only slightly in recent years.

From the very beginning, US women – particularly affluent women – used automobiles, participating in women's auto races, taking cross-country trips and

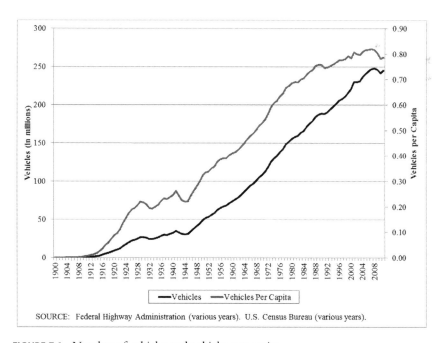

SOURCE: Federal Highway Administration (various years). U.S. Census Bureau (various years).

FIGURE 7.1 Number of vehicles and vehicles per capita

otherwise driving for recreation (Seiler, 2008; Wachs, 1992). Their automobile use was shaped by their gender roles, which, as Seiler (2008, 51–52) writes, prescribed 'the type of driving to which women were directed and the imaginary relationship with the car and the highway they were encouraged to develop'. For example, Walsh (2008, 380) writes that gas-powered automobiles were considered 'a piece of masculine machinery which was difficult and dirty to drive and beyond the capability and fastidiousness of women to operate'. These vehicles were associated with men who were strong enough to operate the cranks necessary to start them and who relied on them to access distant locations (Berger, 1992; Seiler, 2008; Walsh, 2008).

In response to women's mounting enthusiasm for driving, automobile manufacturers quickly mobilised to meet their growing demand for cars. Electric vehicles were specifically marketed to women for their ease of operation and shorter range, suitable for completing household tasks (Bix, 2010; Scharff, 1991; Seiler, 2008; Wachs, 1992). A 1909 advertisement for Baker Electric Vehicles depicts a society woman driving an electric vehicle with the text 'Baker Electrics are safest to drive – easiest to control – simplest in construction, and have greater speed and mileage than any other electrics'. Similarly, an article in the *New York Times* (1915) comments on women and the role of electric vehicles:

> She knows it fulfils all of the demands of her daily routine of calling, shopping and pleasure-seeking. She knows that she likes to run it because there is a certain charm in its simplicity of operation and control – a sort of mild fascination.

Unfortunately, data on women and driving do not go as far back as the early part of the century. However, as Figure 7.2 shows, there has been a consistent increase in female licensed drivers. In 1963, 60 per cent of all licensed drivers were male; by 2012, more than half of all licensed drivers were female. Consequently, the gender gap in licensed driving has narrowed over time. As of 2012, 83 per cent of all women were drivers, compared to 85 per cent of all men. Data by age group suggest that the gender gap in licensed drivers will narrow further as youth age into adulthood. As Figure 7.3 shows, the gender gap in driving is substantial among older age groups; however, among the population under forty years of age, women are slightly *more* likely to drive than men.[1]

At first, for middle- and upper-income women the automobile held the tantalising promise of emancipation from the restrictive confines of the home (Sanger, 1995; Seiler, 2008). Sanger (1995) describes the attitudes of wealthy women who took great delight in the freedom and flexibility associated with the automobile. Additionally, automobiles were viewed as labour-saving devices, enabling women to live and work efficiently (Sutton, 1926). However, as Seiler (2008, 56) notes, the major automobile companies did not want to foster a:

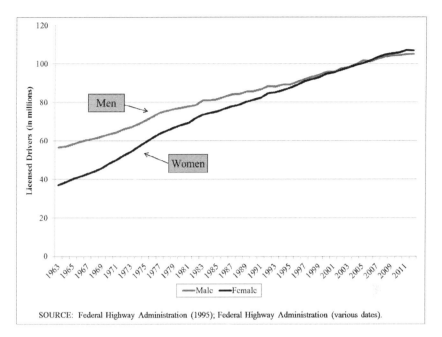

FIGURE 7.2 Licensed drivers by sex

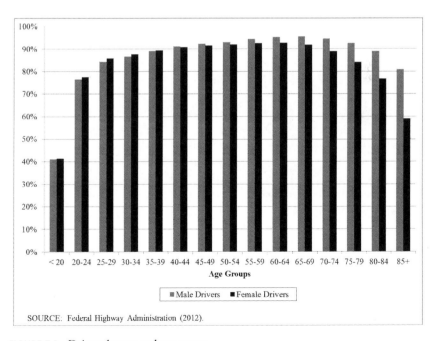

FIGURE 7.3 Drivers by sex and age group

gender revolution', but rather to promote the automobile as the 'proper conveyance for middle-class women's shopping and leisure forays, as it enabled women to move through public space without being subject to the glances and touches of men of other races and classes (a hazard of streetcar and rail travel).

Rather than emancipate women, the automobile seemed to reinforce the sexual division of labour, which for upper-class women meant a separation of spheres – men in the workplace and women in the private sphere of the home (Wachs, 1992). Increasing auto use contributed to the spatial dispersion of urban areas, as the car decoupled residential location and travel from existing streetcar routes (Bottles, 1987; Sanger, 1995). Higher-income households relocated to the suburbs, where large homes and lots left women to carry out their domestic tasks in isolation.

At the same time, automobiles also changed and intensified women's domestic responsibilities. The rise in mass-produced goods deskilled women's domestic responsibilities, as mothers no longer had to produce goods, such as clothing or candles, to grow vegetables or to preserve food (Kendall-Tackett, 2001). Advances in transportation meant that rather than produce household goods, women were simply involved in the repetitive task of buying and delivering goods and services to family members (Cowan, 1983; Kendall-Tackett, 2001). But while technology – in this case, the automobile – may have been *labour*-saving, it was not *time* saving, since automobiles expanded women's responsibilities and the number of chores they needed to complete (Cowan, 1983). Husbands increasingly commuted from their suburban homes to jobs located in the city; their long work days kept them away from the home and shifted additional responsibilities to their wives (Berger, 1992). Additionally, travel by automobile provided evidence of good parenting (Dowling, 2000; Sanger, 1995), with mileage as 'the measure of maternal contribution to familial welfare' (Sanger, 1995, 719). Increasingly, women were judged by the extent to which they chauffeured their children to tutoring, piano lessons, soccer games and other after-school activities. Despite changes in technology, from 1912 to the mid-1960s, the weekly hours of housework for full-time housewives changed little (Connelly and Kimmel, 2010; Ramey and Francis, 2006). Yet over this same period women *increased* the amount of time devoted to child caregiving (Bryant and Zick, 1996; Connelly and Kimmel, 2010; Sayer et al., 2004).

Suburbanisation began in the late nineteenth century with the implementation of the first streetcars, commuter rail lines and omnibuses; yet it accelerated with the introduction and declining costs of automobiles (Kopecky and Suen, 2010). Assembly line production of automobiles in the early twentieth century drove down prices and, in doing so, made automobiles more widely accessible to families beyond the very affluent, enabling the suburbanisation of higher-income households (Walsh, 2008). The costs of automobiles – at least initially – were still substantial and remained out of reach for many low- and some middle-class families. In 1908, the first Model T Ford sold for $825, a price tag equivalent to $21,000 in 2013 dollars (Gross, 1997). Therefore, lower-income families largely lived close to the city centre, where they could rely on modes other than the automobile (Kopecky and Suen, 2010).

Why Low-Income Women (Still) Need Cars

In the 1992 edited collection *The Car and the City*, Sandra Rosenbloom authored a chapter entitled 'Why working families need a car'. This chapter carefully summarised the many benefits of automobiles to working women, particularly those living in the suburbs. These included the flexibility required to travel to suburban destinations – such as jobs – where transit is not readily available, to link work trips to other household-supporting trips (such as to the childcare centre or the grocery store), to chauffeur children to activities that might vary in schedule (e.g. soccer games) and, finally, to quickly respond to the needs of sick children. Subsequently, numerous scholars in the US and elsewhere have noted the many benefits of automobiles to women (Dowling, 2000; Greed, 2008; Murray, 2008; Rosenbloom, 1992; Vance et al., 2004).

In contrast to other developed countries, automobile ownership in the US is almost ubiquitous, particularly among upper-income households (Dargay et al., 2007). As Figure 7.4 shows, 98 per cent of households in the US with incomes

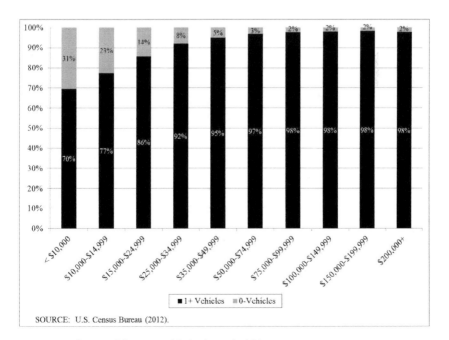

SOURCE: U.S. Census Bureau (2012).

FIGURE 7.4 Automobile ownership by household income

$75,000 or above own at least one automobile, compared to fewer than 80 per cent of households with incomes below $15,000 and 70 per cent of single mothers with incomes below $15,000. Many adults in low-income households *with* automobiles also have limited access to them, since they often live in households where drivers outnumber the number of vehicles. Given the evolving spatial structure of US metropolitan areas, the evidence suggests that women who do not have access to automobiles are even more disadvantaged today than they were twenty-two years ago, when Rosenbloom's chapter was published.

The Suburbanisation of Low-income Families and Employment

Low-income families and employment have decentralised over time, elevating the importance of automobiles in accessing regional opportunities. Less than two-fifths of the US metropolitan population now lives in central-city neighbourhoods, defined as the principal cities of metropolitan areas (US Census Bureau, 2012). Low-income families – those with incomes below the US federally designated poverty line – are also suburbanising (Garr and Kneebone, 2010; US Census Bureau, various years). As Figure 7.5 shows, in 1970 more than 60 per cent of the poor lived in the central city. By 2012, a slight majority of the metropolitan poor (52 per cent) remained in central-city neighbourhoods, motivated by the availability

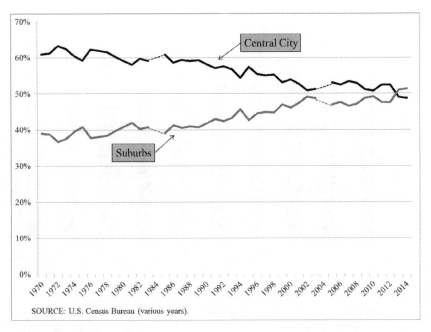

SOURCE: U.S. Census Bureau (various years).

FIGURE 7.5 Central city–suburb residential location of metropolitan poor, United States

of affordable housing and – for those without automobiles – access to relatively high levels of public transit services (Glaeser et al., 2008; US Census Bureau, 2012). Between 2000 and 2011, the number of poor families grew twice as fast in the suburbs as in the large cities that anchor them (Kneebone and Berube, 2013).

Employment Also Continues to Decentralise

From 1998 to 2006, 95 out of 98 US metropolitan areas experienced a decline in the share of jobs located within three miles of downtown, with the largest job increases in areas beyond 10 miles from the central business district (Kneebone, 2009). Today, approximately, 23 per cent of employees in the 100 largest US metropolitan areas work within three miles of the central business district. In contrast, 43 per cent commute to locations more than 10 miles away from the city centre (Kneebone, 2013).

Proponents of the 'spatial mismatch hypothesis' contend that joblessness among low-income residents is due, in part, to residential location in urban areas, where residents are increasingly disconnected from suburban employment opportunities (Kain, 1968). The weight of the evidence suggests that the spatial mismatch contributes to high levels of joblessness among African-American men (Gobillon et al., 2007; Ihlanfeldt and Sjoquist, 1998) and potentially for women as well (McLafferty and Preston, 1996; Thompson, 1997).

Automobiles can help residents of job-poor neighbourhoods overcome their geographic separation from employment. Rather than face the classic 'spatial mismatch', a number of scholars show that low-income, inner-city residents suffer from a modal mismatch: a drastic divergence in the relative advantage between those who have access to automobiles and those who do not (Taylor and Ong, 1995). Even in dense, transit-rich metropolitan areas such as Boston, Detroit, Los Angeles, San Francisco/Bay Area and Tokyo, automobile commuters have a substantial access advantage over transit commuters (Kawabata and Shen, 2006). For example, in the Los Angeles Pico-Union neighbourhood, a high-poverty neighbourhood located adjacent to job-rich downtown, residents with cars have access to five times as many low-wage jobs within a 30 minute commute compared to residents who travel by public transit (Blumenberg and Ong, 2001). A longitudinal analysis of employment access in the Twin Cities shows that the accessibility gap between cars and public transit grew from 1990 to 2000; access by automobile increased at the same time as access by public transit declined (El-Geneidya and Levinson, 2007).

The spatial mismatch is not only a central-city problem. Spatial access to opportunities is also a source of concern for low-income families living in the suburbs of US metropolitan areas, where both residents and employment opportunities are dispersed and transit service tends to be limited. Studies show that less-educated job seekers in dense central-city neighbourhoods have *better* access to jobs than those who live in the suburbs (Shen, 2001).

Low-income families who reside in the suburbs tend to live in areas in which they have access to a below-average number of jobs (Raphael and Stoll, 2001). For suburban families, getting to jobs by modes other than the automobile is difficult, since these neighbourhoods tend to have limited transit service. In an analysis of public transit access in the largest 100 US metropolitan areas, Tomer et al. (2011) found that while 94 per cent of city residents live in neighbourhoods served by transit, only 58 per cent of their suburban counterparts do. Even when there is suburban transit service, service frequency tends to be low.

Women and Employment

Numerous scholars have written on gender disparities in the US labour market. The evidence suggests that the characteristics of women's employment have shifted in ways that make cars increasingly essential to the lives of low-income women. After rising for much of the twentieth century, data from the US Bureau of Labor Statistics show that female labour force participation has changed very little since 1990.[2] It slowly increased from 58 per cent in 1990 to 60 per cent in 2002 and then declined to 57 per cent by 2013, likely due to the lingering effects of the Great Recession. For both men and women, there has been a substantial increase in the number who are unemployed and the number who are not in the labour force, but who continue to be interested in employment (US Bureau of Labor Statistics, various years). While the recession certainly pushed these rates upward, there are still many more women today who are searching for employment than there were in 1990. For example, among women, the percentage of those unemployed increased by 34 per cent from 1990 to 2013 (US Bureau of Labor Statistics, various years). Cars are particularly important to job seekers, as they better enable to travel long distances than other modes and they ease travel to multiple, and oftentimes unfamiliar, destinations (Brooks et al., 2001).

There has also been a substantial increase in the percentage of the workforce that works non-standard hours (Beers, 2000). More than a quarter of all employed women work part-time – twice the percentage of men – suggesting at least one off-peak commute trip (US Bureau of Labor Statistics, 2016). As Figure 7.6 shows, 45 per cent of low-income women travel during non-peak periods, outside of the 6am to 10am rush-hour period: a rate higher than for other groups. Further, the percentage of off-peak travel has increased substantially – for all workers, as well as low-income women – since 1990. Travel by transit during off-peak periods can be difficult, as transit frequency is typically highest during peak periods.

On average, women have less authority in the workplace than men, largely explained by their continued segregation in low-status occupations (Mintz and Krymkowski, 2010). Workers with more workplace authority have greater flexibility than their subordinates (Golden, 2008; Golden, 2009; McCrate, 2005;

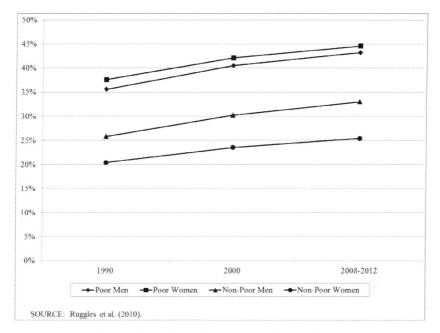

SOURCE: Ruggles et al. (2010).

FIGURE 7.6   Travel to work outside of the morning peak period

Perry-Jenkins, 2005), making it easier for them to leave early or take time off work to attend to household responsibilities. With less workplace flexibility, women – particularly low-wage female workers – must include household-serving trips on their travel to and from work. Compared to men, women are more likely to trip chain – make multiple stops on a single tour. Women make 50 per cent more stops on their way home from work than do men (Mcguckin and Murakami, 2007). Automobiles can better accommodate trip chaining than other modes, providing the speed and flexibility to tightly sequence multiple trips on their way to or from work (Blumenberg, 2004; Rosenbloom, 1992; Roy et al., 2004).

Household Responsibilities

While men are slowly increasing the number of hours that they devote to household responsibilities, data from the American Time Use Survey shows that women still shoulder a far greater burden for the home than men: a finding that holds true for other European countries as well (Sánchez de Madariaga, 2013). On average, US women spend 27 hours per week doing unpaid household work, compared to 16 hours per week for men (Krantz-Kent, 2009). In other words, compared to men, women invest approximately eleven additional hours per week taking care of the home; this includes caring for family members, preparing food, doing laundry and shopping. Among parents in households with children, the number of hours and the gender disparity in time-use increase. Women in households with children spend thirty-eight hours per week on unpaid household work compared to twenty-one hours among men (Krantz-Kent, 2009). Over half of all low-income families are headed by single mothers with children (US Census Bureau, 2012). For these families, the mother is often the only source of both paid and unpaid domestic labour. For low-income women, juggling a complex set of responsibilities can be challenging, with potentially negative effects on children living in the household (London et al., 2004; Roy et al., 2004).

A growing number of studies suggest that automobiles make it easier for low-income families to travel to non-work destinations, which can require extensive trip chaining (Sánchez de Madariaga, 2013). For example, 30.2 million low-income households in the US are located in neighbourhoods that are more than one mile away from a supermarket (US Department of Agriculture, 2009). For these households, automobiles can facilitate longer-distance travel, allowing low-income shoppers to frequent grocery stores outside of their neighbourhoods and enabling them to buy and carry large quantities of groceries at one time (Clifton, 2004; Hirsch and Hillier, 2013; Kerr et al., 2012). Cars also help low-income families more easily reach health-care providers and other services (Bostock, 2001; Guidry et al., 1997) and play an important role in easing travel to day-care centres, schools and training programmes (Brabo et al., 2003; Teske et al., 2009).

The Benefits of Cars to Low-Income Women

Given the many advantages of automobiles for US women, it should come as no surprise that so many low-income women have and use them. Automobile ownership has increased most rapidly among female-headed households (see Figure 7.7). Further, as Figure 7.8 shows, the percentage of workers who commute by automobile has increased since 1960, eliminating the gender gap in automobile use for the commute. As of 2010, 74 per cent of low-income women – those in households with incomes below the poverty line – commuted by automobile: a rate slightly higher than among low-income men (72 per cent). A growing body of scholarship shows that, for low-income women, private automobiles are critical in predicting a diverse set of outcomes, including employment, income, the consumption of healthy food and health-care usage.

Income is one of the largest determinants of automobile ownership (Schimek, 1996). Therefore, employment and the income it provides can enable households to purchase automobiles. Conversely, cars can make it easier to search for, and regularly commute to and from, jobs and, therefore, have a positive effect on employment-related outcomes, including income. Even studies that control for the simultaneity of car ownership and employment consistently show an

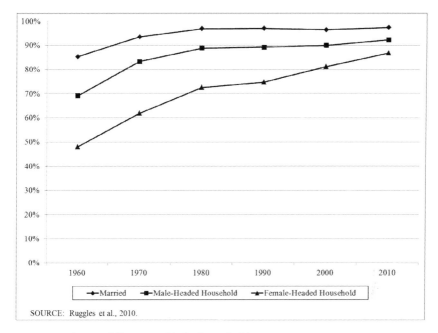

FIGURE 7.7 Automobile ownership by household type

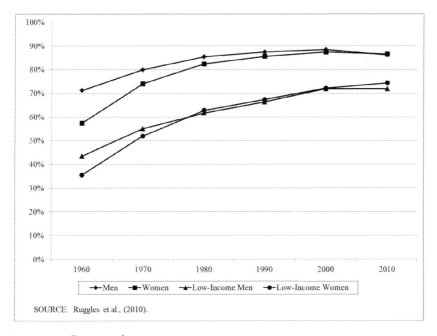

FIGURE 7.8 Commute by car

independent and positive effect of automobile ownership on economic outcome, such as employment rates, the likelihood of leaving welfare and earned income. Due to the availability of data, many of these studies focus on outcomes for welfare participants – largely poor, female-headed households dependent on government cash assistance (Baum, 2009; Cervero et al., 2002; Gurley and Bruce, 2005; Lucas and Nicholson, 2003; Ong, 2002). In contrast, studies on the relationship between public transit and women's employment outcomes show mixed findings (Alam, 2009; Gurmu et al., 2008; Ong and Houston, 2002; Sanchez et al., 2004).

A small number of studies use the longitudinal data of welfare recipients to examine the relative effects of automobile *and* transit access on employment and outcomes for welfare recipients (Cervero et al., 2002; Gurley and Bruce, 2005; Sandoval et al., 2011). These studies find that public transit access was not a significant predictor of desired outcomes: exit from welfare and/or enhanced employment. In contrast, after controlling for a rich set of household-level socioeconomic and neighbourhood characteristics, automobile access remained a significant correlate of employment and welfare exits. Therefore, for low-income women, automobiles appear to be a far more powerful determinant in job acquisition and job retention than public transit. A growing body of scholarship suggests that automobiles may contribute to improved outcomes for low-income families in areas other than the labour market, such as access to food and health services (D'Angelo et al., 2011; Guidry et al., 1997; Yang et al., 2006).

Increasing Women's Access to Cars

Despite the growing evidence of the importance of automobiles to low-income women, there have been relatively few policy efforts to increase their access to them. In the US, many policymakers routinely oppose policies and programmes that might be perceived as promoting automobile use, thus contributing to traffic congestion, air pollution and sprawl. Moreover, there are concerns regarding the role of automobiles in contributing to excessive household transportation expenditure burdens. Recent efforts to enhance transportation options for the poor, therefore, have focused on public transit. For example, in 1998, the US Congress passed the Job Access and Reverse Commute (JARC) programme, allocating federal funds to projects that connect inner-city residents to suburban employment centres (49 USC § 5309). From 1999 to 2001, only 5 per cent of these funds were allocated to programmes that facilitated automobile purchases (Sanchez and Schweitzer, 2008). The remaining 95 per cent was used to establish and enhance fixed-route transit (59 per cent), demand responsive service (20 per cent), guaranteed ride-home programmes (7 per cent) and for outreach and marketing (21 per cent).

Recent studies of the effect of JARC-sponsored transit programmes show that participants benefited from these programmes; however, their overall effect on welfare usage and employment appeared modest (Sanchez and Schweitzer, 2008;

Thakuriah et al., 2008). Public transit works best in dense urban areas, where origins and destinations are proximate and, therefore, travel times are reasonably short. In the US, only 4 per cent of neighbourhoods fit this description (Blumenberg et al., 2015) – a percentage likely much smaller than in other developed nations. In the US, urban planners are actively working to increase residential and commercial densities, particularly in neighbourhoods surrounding public transit. In the long run, these structural changes to city form will make it easier to access opportunities via public transit. Low-income families should benefit from these land-use changes, provided they are not priced out of these neighbourhoods as a consequence of the gentrification that has accompanied some of these developments (Pollack et al., 2010).

In the short run, however, in the US, automobiles remain a necessary link between low-income women and their access to opportunities. A few US automobile policies and programmes appear promising. One effective strategy is the removal of regulatory barriers to automobile ownership and, in particular, the lifting of the vehicle asset limitation associated with some government social benefit programmes (Hurst and Ziliak, 2006; Lucas and Nicholson, 2003; Sullivan, 2006). Additionally, some social programmes provide user-side subsidies to better enable their low-income participants to afford the cost of travel, both by public transit *and* automobile (National Resource Center, n. d.; US Departments of Transportation, Health and Human Services, 1998).

Policies that focus on public benefit programmes appear helpful, yet do not go far enough, since only a fraction of the poor (30 per cent) receive any form of government assistance (Ruggles et al., 2010; author's calculations). Federal and state governments have offered a few other auto programmes. Individual development accounts (IDAs) are matched saving accounts that can help families save for and purchase various assets, including – in some programmes – vehicles (Stegman and Faris, 2005). Some states, such as California, offset the operational costs associated with automobile ownership by providing state-sponsored low-cost automobile insurance and low-income vehicle repair programmes to bring vehicles into compliance with emissions requirements.

Finally, the non-profit and private sectors have developed programmes and products that increase low-income families' access to automobiles. Non-profit organisations have stepped in and, as of 2006, established 151 low-income automobile programmes (National Economic Development Law Center, 2006). In addition to selling or donating vehicles to low-income families, these programmes often provide ancillary services, including ongoing car-repair support, consumer protection from price gouging, referrals to job training or family support services and financial literacy training. Although they tend to be small, these programmes have been effective in increasing automobile ownership rates among participants (Brabo et al., 2003).

The private sector has also played a role in reducing the costs of auto travel by providing programmes and services that enable low-income households to pay only for the travel that they use. For example, programmes such as car sharing and ride sharing (e.g. Uber, Lyft) allow travellers to pay per mile of travel, providing many of the benefits of automobiles (e.g. speed, door-to-door service, flexibility) without the high costs of ownership (National Research Council, 2005; Shaheen et al., 2009). Similarly, rather than charging a flat fee, some automobile insurance companies now allow drivers to pay per mile travelled. This payment structure benefits low-income drivers, who, on average, travel fewer miles than higher-income drivers (Brobeck and Hunter, 2012).

In conclusion, the evidence suggests that although more and more families – including low-income families – have access to automobiles, those who do not are increasingly disadvantaged. Low-income women without cars are significantly less likely to find employment and to have access to the many destinations (grocery stores, schools, health clinics, day-care centres, etc.) that guarantee an adequate quality of life. As discussed above, there are a few promising programmes and policies to increase low-income women's access to automobiles. However, many stakeholders are wary of these efforts, worrying that they send the wrong message. For example, in a recent Streetsblog article, Schmitt (2014) writes:

> Every additional car on the road adds to traffic congestion and slows down buses. Every additional parking space spreads destinations farther apart, making places tougher to traverse on foot. Giving a poor family a car might help that specific household, but it would harm others at the same time.

Schmitt and others who share this perspective argue that an increase in low-income drivers will negatively affect those who are already on the road – disproportionately, higher-income drivers. Yet it is lower-income families – those with limited opportunities and choices – who will benefit the most from increased access to automobiles. In the short run – until access to opportunities by transit rivals that of automobiles – low-income travellers should not be relegated to inferior modes of travel simply because of the driving propensities of higher-income travellers. If automobiles are essential to women's lives, policies ought to carefully balance women's need for automobiles with broader efforts – aimed at travellers of all incomes – to address their negative effects.

Notes

1 Gender differences among seniors are likely due to historical gender differences in licensing, as well as contemporary differences in driving cessation (Rosenbloom, 2001).
2 The labour force participation of men has declined in recent years, reducing the labour-force participation gap between men and women from 19 per cent in 1990 to 13 per cent in 2013.

References

Alam, B. M. (2009). 'Transit accessibility to jobs and employment prospects of welfare recipients without cars. A study of Broward County, Florida, using geographic information systems and an econometric model', *Journal of the Transportation Research Board*, 2110, 78–86.

Baum, C. (2009). 'The effects of vehicle ownership on employment', *Journal of Urban Economics*, 66, 151–63.

Beers, T. (2000). 'Flexible schedules and shift work: replacing the 9-to-5 workday', *Monthly Labor Review*, 6, 33–40.

Berger, M. (1992). 'The car's impact on the American family', in M. Wachs and M. Crawford (eds), *The Car and the City: The Automobile, the Built Environment, and Daily Urban Life*, Ann Arbor, University of Michigan Press, 57–74.

Bix, A. (2010). 'A car for the "weaker sex"?', *OAH Magazine of History*, 24, 42.

Blumenberg, E. (2004). 'En-gendering effective planning: spatial mismatch, low-income women, and transportation policy', *Journal of the American Planning Association*, 70, 269–81.

Blumenberg, E., Brown, A., Ralph, K., Taylor, B. D. and Voulgaris, C. (2015). *Typecasting Neighborhoods and Travelers: Analyzing the Geography of Travel Behavior among Teens and Young Adults in the U.S*, Los Angeles, Lewis Center for Regional Policy Studies.

Blumenberg, E. and Ong, P. (2001). 'Cars, buses, and jobs: welfare participants and employment access in Los Angeles', *Transportation Research Record*, 1756, 22–31.

Bostock, L. (2001). 'Pathways of disadvantage? Walking as a mode of transport among low-income mothers', *Health and Social Care in the Community*, 9, 11–18.

Bottles, S. (1987). *Los Angeles and the Automobile*, Berkeley, University of California Press.

Brabo, L. M., Kilde, P. H., Pesek-Her Riges, P., Quinn, T. and Sanderud-Norquist, I. (2003). 'Driving out of poverty in private automobiles', *Journal of Poverty*, 7, 183–96.

Brobeck, S. and Hunter, J. R. (2012). *Lower-income Households and the Auto Insurance Marketplace: Challenges and Opportunities*, Washington, Consumer Federation of America.

Brooks, F., Nackerud, L. and Risler, E. (2001). 'Evaluation of a job-finding club for TANF recipients: psychosocial impacts', *Research on Social Work Practice*, 11, 79–82.

Bryant, W. K. and Zick, C. D. (1996). 'Are we investing less in the next generation? Historical trends in time spent caring for children', *Journal of Family and Economic Issues*, 17, 365–92.

Cervero, R., Sandoval, O. and Landis, J. (2002). 'Transportation as a stimulus of welfare-to-work private versus public mobility', *Journal of Planning Education and Research*, 22, 50–63.

Clifton, K. J. (2004). 'Mobility strategies and food shopping for low-income families: a case study', *Journal of Planning Education and Research*, 23, 402–13.

Connelly, R. and Kimmel, J. (2010). *The Time Use of Mothers in the United States at the Beginning of the 21st Century*, Kalamazoo, W.E. Upjohn Institute for Employment Research.

Cowan, R. S. (1983). *More Work for Mother: The Ironies of Household Technology from the Open Hearth to the Microwave*, New York, Basic Books.

D'Angelo, H., Suratkar, S., Song, H., Stauffer, E. and Gittelsohn, J. (2011). 'Access to food source and food source use are associated with healthy and unhealthy food-purchasing behaviours among low-income African-American adults in Baltimore City', *Public Health Nutrition*, 14, 1632–39.

Dargay, J., Gately, D. and Sommer, M. (2007). 'Vehicle ownership and income growth, worldwide: 1960–2030', *Energy Journal*, 28, 143–70.

Dowling, R. (2000). 'Cultures of mothering and car use in suburban Sydney: a preliminary investigation', *Geoforum*, 31, 345–53.

El-Geneidya, A. and Levinson, D. (2007). 'Mapping accessibility over time', *Journal of Maps*, 3, 76–87.

Federal Highway Administration. (various years). *Highway Statistics*, Washington, US Department of Transportation.

Garr, E. and Kneebone, E. (2010). *The Suburbanization of Poverty: Trends in Metropolitan America, 2000 to 2008*, Washington, The Brookings Institution.

Glaeser, E. L., Kahn, M. E. and Rappaport, J. (2008). 'Why do the poor live in cities? The role of public transportation', *Journal of Urban Economics*, 63, 1–24.

Gobillon, L., Selod, H. and Zenou, Y. (2007). 'The mechanisms of spatial mismatch', *Urban Studies*, 44, 2401–27.

Golden, L. (2008). 'Limited access: disparities in flexible work schedules and work-at-home', *Journal of Family Economic Issues*, 29, 86–109.

Golden, L. (2009). 'Flexible daily work schedules in the U.S. jobs: formal introductions needed?', *Industrial Relations*, 48, 27–54.

Greed, C. (2008). 'Are we there yet? Women and transport revisited', in T. P. Uteng and T. Cresswell (eds), *Gendered Mobilities*, Aldershot, Ashgate Publishing, 243–56.

Gross, D. (1997). *Forbes® Greatest Business Stories of All Time*, Michigan, John Wiley & Sons, Inc.

Guidry, J. J., Aday, L. A., Zhang, D. and Winn, R. J. (1997). 'Transportation as a barrier to cancer treatment', *Cancer Practice*, 5, 361–66.

Gurley, T. and Bruce, D. (2005). 'The effects of car access on employment outcomes for welfare recipients', *Journal of Urban Economics*, 58, 250–72.

Gurmu, S., Ihlanfeldt, K. R. and Smith, W. J. (2008). 'Does residential location matter to the employment of TANF recipients? Evidence from a dynamic discrete choice model with unobserved effects', *Journal of Urban Economics*, 63, 325–51.

Hirsch, J. A. and Hillier, A. (2013). 'Exploring the role of the food environment on food shopping patterns in Philadelphia, PA, USA: a semiquantitative comparison of two matched neighborhood groups', *International Journal of Environmental Research in Public Health*, 10, 295–313.

Hurst, E. and Ziliak, J. P. (2006). 'Do welfare asset limits affect household saving? Evidence from welfare reform', *The Journal of Human Resources*, 41, 46–71.

Ihlanfeldt, K. R. and Sjoquist, D. L. (1998). 'The spatial mismatch hypothesis: a review of recent studies and their implications for welfare reform', *Housing Policy Debate*, 9, 849–92.

Kain, J. (1968). 'Housing segregation, negro employment, and metropolitan decentralization', *Quarterly Journal of Economics*, 82, 175–97.

Kawabata, M. and Shen, Q. (2006). 'Job accessibility as an indicator of auto-oriented urban structure: a comparison of Boston and Los Angeles with Tokyo', *Environment and Planning B: Planning and Design*, 33, 115–30.

Kendall-Tackett, K. A. (2001). *The Hidden Feelings of Motherhood: Coping with Stress, Depression, and Burnout*, Oakland, New Harbinger Publications.

Kerr, J., Lawrence, F., Sallis, J. F., Saelens, B., Glanz, K. and Chapman, J. (2012). 'Predictors of trips to food destinations', *International Journal of Behavioral Nutrition and Physical Activity*, 9, 58.

Kneebone, E. (2009). *Job Sprawl Revisited: The Changing Geography of Metropolitan Employment*, Washington, The Brookings Institution.

Kneebone, E. (2013). *Job Sprawl Stalls: The Great Recession and Metropolitan Employment Location*, Washington, The Brookings Institution.

Kneebone, E. and Berube, A. (2013). *Confronting Suburban Poverty in America*, Washington, The Brookings Institution.

Kopecky, K. A. and Suen, R. M. H. (2010). 'A quantitative analysis of suburbanization and the diffusion of the automobile', *International Economic Review*, 51, 1003–37.

Krantz-Kent, R. (2009). 'Measuring time spent in unpaid household work: results from the American time-use survey', *Monthly Labor Review*, July, 46–59.

London, A. S., Scott, E. K., Edin, K. and Hunter, V. (2004). 'Welfare reform, work-family tradeoffs, and child well-being', *Family Relations*, 53, 148–58.

Lucas, M. T. and Nicholson, C. F. (2003). 'Subsidized vehicle acquisition and earned income in the transition from welfare to work', *Transportation*, 30, 483–501.

McCrate, E. (2005). 'Flexible hours, workplace authority, and compensating wage differentials in the US', *Feminist Economics*, 11, 11–39.

Mcguckin, N. and Murakami, E. (2007). 'Examining trip-chaining behavior. Comparison of travel by men and women', *Journal of the Transportation Research Board*, 1693, 79–85.

McLafferty, S. and Preston, V. (1996). 'Spatial mismatch and employment in a decade of restructuring', *The Professional Geographer*, 48, 420–31.

Mintz, B. and Krymkowski, D. H. (2010). 'The ethnic, race, and gender gaps in workplace authority: changes over time in the United States', *The Sociological Quarterly*, 51, 20–45.

Murray, L. (2008). 'Motherhood, risk and everyday mobilities', in T. P. Uteng and T. Cresswell (eds), *Gendered Mobilities*, Aldershot, Ashgate Publishing, 47–63.

National Economic Development Law Center. (2006). 'Low-income car ownership programs: 2006 survey', www.insightcced.org/uploads/publications/assets/LICO2006surveyreport.pdf (accessed 21 June 2016).

National Research Council. (2005). 'Car-sharing: where and how it succeeds' (TCRP Report 108), Washington, The National Academies Press.

National Resource Center. (n.d.). *An Inventory of Federal Funding for Coordinated Transit and Human Services Transportation*, Washington, National Resource Center for Human Service Transportation Coordination.

New York Times. (1915). 'More and more women are driving their own electrics', 4 July 1915, X11.

Ong, P. (2002). 'Car ownership and welfare-to-work', *Journal of Policy Analysis and Management*, 21, 239–52.

Ong, P. M. and Houston, D. (2002). 'Transit, employment, and women on welfare', *Urban Geography*, 23, 344–64.

Perry-Jenkins, M. (2005). 'Work in the working class: challenges facing families', in S. M. Bianchi, L. M. Casper and R. B. King (eds), *Work, Family, Health, and Well-Being*, Mahwah, Lawrence Erlbaum, 453–72.

Pollack, S., Bluestone, B. and Billingham, C. (2010). *Maintaining Diversity in America's Transit-Rich Neighborhoods: Tools for Equitable Neighborhood Change*, Boston, Dukakis Center for Urban and Regional Policy.

Ramey, V. A. and Francis, N. (2006). 'A Century of Work and Leisure' (NBER Working Paper No. 12264), Cambridge, National Bureau of Economic Research.

Raphael, S. and Stoll, M. A. (2001). 'Can boosting minority car-ownership rates narrow inter-racial employment gaps?', *Brookings-Wharton Papers on Urban Affairs*, http://urbanpolicy.berkeley.edu/pdf/RS2001PB.pdf (accessed 21 June 2016).

Rosenbloom, S. (1992). 'Why working families need a car', in M. Wachs and M. Crawford (eds), *The Car and the City: The Automobile, the Built Environment, and Daily Urban Life*, Ann Arbor, University of Michigan Press, 39–56.

Rosenbloom, S. (2001). 'Sustainability and automobility among the elderly: an international assessment', *Transportation*, 28, 375–408.

Roy, K. M., Tubbs, C. Y. and Burton, L. M. (2004). 'Don't have no time: daily rhythms and the organization of time for low-income families', *Family Relations*, 53, 168–78.

Ruggles, S., Alexander, J. T., Genadek, K., Goeken, R., Schroeder, M. B. and Sobek, M. (2010). *Integrated Public Use Microdata Series: Version 5.0* [Machine-readable database], Minneapolis, University of Minnesota.

Sánchez de Madariaga, I. (2013). 'Mobility of care: introducing new concepts in urban transport', in I. Sánchez de Madariaga and M. Roberts (eds), *Fair Shared Cities: The Impact of Gender Planning in Europe*, Farnham, Ashgate, 33–48.

Sanchez, T., Shen, Q. and Peng, Z. (2004). 'Transit mobility, jobs access and low-income labour participation in U.S. metropolitan areas', *Urban Studies*, 41, 1313–31.

Sanchez, T. W. and Schweitzer, L. (2008). *Assessing Federal Employment Accessibility Policy: An Analysis of the JARC Program*, Washington, The Brookings Institution.

Sandoval, J. S. O., Cervero, R. and Landis, J. (2011). 'The transition from welfare-to-work: how cars and human capital facilitate employment for welfare recipients', *Applied Geography*, 31, 352–62.

Sanger, C. (1995). 'Girls and the getaway: cars, culture, and the predicament of gendered space', *University of Pennsylvania Law Review*, 144, 705–56.

Sayer, L. C., Bianchi, S. M. and Robinson, J. P. (2004). 'Are parents investing less in children? Trends in mothers' and fathers' time with children', *American Journal of Sociology*, 110, 1–43.

Scharff, V. (1991). *Taking the Wheel: Women and the Coming of the Motor Age*, Albuquerque, University of New Mexico Press.

Schimek, P. (1996). 'Household motor vehicle ownership and use: how much does residential density matter?', *Journal of the Transportation Research Board*, 1552, 120–25.

Schmitt, A. (2014). 'The problem with prescribing "access to cars" in the fight against poverty', *Streetsblog USA*, http://usa.streetsblog.org/2014/04/04/the-problem-with-prescribing-access-to-cars-in-the-fight-against-poverty/ (accessed 21 June 2016).

Seiler, C. (2008). *Republic of Drivers: A Cultural History of Automobility in America*, Chicago, University of Chicago Press.

Shaheen, S. A., Cohen, A. P. and Chung, M. S. (2009). 'North American carsharing 10-year retrospective', *Journal of the Transportation Research Board*, 2110, 35–44.

Shen, Q. (2001). 'A spatial analysis of job openings and access in a U.S. metropolitan area', *Journal of the American Planning Association*, 67, 53–68.

Stegman, M. A. and Faris, R. (2005). 'The impact of IDA programs on family savings and asset holdings', in M. Sherraden (ed), *Inclusion in the American Dream: Assets, Poverty, and Public Policy*, Oxford, Oxford University Press, 216–37.

Sullivan, J. X. (2006). 'Welfare reform, saving, and vehicle ownership. Do asset limits and vehicle exemptions matter?', *The Journal of Human Resources*, 41, 72–105.

Sutton, G. W. (1926). 'The woman at the wheel: the help a car can be in home-making', *Pictorial Review*, 28, 69.

Taylor, B. and Ong, P. (1995). 'Spatial mismatch or automobile mismatch? An examination of race, residence, and commuting in U.S. metropolitan areas', *Urban Studies*, 32, 1453–73.

Teske, P., Fitzpatrick, J. and O'Brien, T. (2009). *Drivers of Choice. parents, transportation, and School Choice*, Bothell, Center on Reinventing Public Education, University of Washington.

Thakuriah, P., Sriraj, P. S., Sööt, S. and Persky, J. (2008). 'Economic benefits of employment transportation services' (final report), Chicago, University of Illinois at Chicago, Urban Transportation Center.

Thompson, M. A. (1997). 'The impact of spatial mismatch on female labor force participation', *Economic Development Quarterly*, 11, 138–45.

Tomer, A., Kneebone, E., Puentes, R. and Berube, A. (2011). *Missed Opportunity: Transit and Jobs in Metropolitan America*, Washington, The Brookings Institution.

US Bureau of Labor Statistics. (various years). 'Labor force statistics from the current population survey', www.bls.gov/cps/cpsaat08.htm (accessed 21 June 2016).

US Census Bureau. (2012). 'American community survey', www.census.gov/programs-sur veys/acs/ (accessed21 June 2016).

US Census Bureau. (various years). 'Current population survey', March and Annual Social and Economic Supplements, www.census.gov/programs-surveys/cps.html (accessed 21 June 2016).

US Census Bureau. (various years). 'Population estimates program', Population Division, www.census.gov/popest/ (accessed 21 June 2016).

US Department of Agriculture. (2009). 'Access to affordable and nutritious food: measuring and understanding food deserts and their consequences', (report to Congress), Washington, Economic Research Service.

US Department of Labor. (2016). '2015 current population survey', Washington, DC, Bureau of Labor Statistics. www.bls.gov/cps/cpsaat08.htm#cps_eeann_ftpt.f.1 (accessed 10 August 2016).

US Departments of Transportation, Health and Human Services (1998). 'Use of TANF, WtW, and job access funds for transportation', http://workforcesecurity.doleta.gov/dmstree/tegl/tegl98/tegl_10-98a2.pdf (accessed 10 August 2016).

Vance, C., Buchheim, S. and Brockfeld, E. (2004). 'Gender as a determinant of car use: evidence from Germany' (paper delivered to the Research on Women's Issues in Transportation conference, Chicago, 18–20 November).

Wachs, M. (1992). 'Men, women, and urban travel: the persistence of separate spheres', in M. Wachs and M. Crawford (eds), *The Car and the City: The Automobile, the Built environment, and Daily Urban Life*, Ann Arbor, University of Michigan Press, 86–100.

Walsh, M. (2008). 'Gendering mobility: women, work and automobility in the United States', *History*, 93, 376–95.

Yang, S., Zarr, R. L., Kass-Hout, T. A., Kourosh, A. and Kelly, N. R. (2006). 'Transportation barriers to accessing health care for urban children', *Journal of Health Care for the Poor and Underserved*, 17, 928–43.

PART II

Engendering Planning for Urban Justice

8

PUBLIC TOILETS

The Missing Component in Designing Sustainable Urban Spaces for Women

Clara Greed

Public toilets are essential to creating accessible, sustainable, and equitable urban spaces for all men and women. But women experience greater toilet problems, as explained in this chapter which discusses the reasons for the continuing unequal and impractical nature of public toilet provision for women. Men generally have twice the level of provision as women, resulting in long toilet queues for the Ladies toilets. Although women have fewer facilities than men, their biological needs are greater. Menstruating women need toilet facilities more often, as do menopausal, pregnant, and elderly women with urinary and incontinence problems. The historical and cultural roots of the problem are discussed. But contemporary diversity and equality agendas do not necessarily benefit women either. The chapter discusses the trend towards seeing gender as a continuum, not a binary, resulting in the desegregation of public toilets, which may deflect attention from meeting women's long-standing demands for better toilet provision. Do Gender-Neutral Toilet (GNT) trends recognise women's biological differences, including menstruation, and ensure their right to privacy, equality, and dignity? Public toilet provision is not only a complex sociological issue but also a vital physical component of cities and their infrastructure. In conclusion, ways in which planning policy and urban design can improve toilet provision for women are presented.

Introduction: Public Toilets and Sustainable Urban Spaces

Creating sustainable urban spaces for all implies that all sorts of people have the right to enjoy, travel to, and stay within urban space. The original definition of sustainability included the requirement of social equality for everyone (UN, 1992). Everyone, male and female, needs the toilet. But particular problems are experienced by the elderly, those with disabilities, and those responsible for babies and small children. But this chapter specifically concentrates on the effect that the lack of suitable and available public toilet provision has upon women and thus their chances of being able to freely access our towns and cities, and it also discusses problems of mainstreaming gender into both urban planning and sanitation (Greed, 2005; Taylor et al., 2017). Although toilet provision is a basic equality issue, gender-equality requirements are widely flouted in respect of toilet provision for women (Sommer et al., 2016). It is argued that unequal toilet provision remains a violation of women's human rights. But this is a controversial topic that incorporates debates about the relationship between gender, biology, and sexuality.

Public toilet provision remains a major, but often unrecognised and invisible, issue in creating urban spaces which are accessible to all. Lack of facilities restricts the time and distance women can travel from home, holding them back by 'the bladder's leash' (Cooper et al., 2000; Kitchen and Law, 2001). Women are the ones who are likely to be out and about within urban space, travelling on public transport more than men, and often accompanied by children or by elderly and disabled relatives, all of whom have specific toilet needs (Cavanagh and Ware, 1991; Greed, 2012). But women have less toilet provision than men, both in terms of the distribution and availability of facilities and the level of pro-vision per block. On average, over twice as much toilet provision has been given to men as women (BSI, 2010; ICC, 2011; Penner, 2013; Anthony, 2017) Moreover, the design of the toilets that are available scarcely takes into account women's 'different' biological characteristics and requirements (Bichard and Ramster, 2011; Drakeford, 2012; Ramster et al., 2018). For example, around a quarter of women of childbearing age will be menstruating at any given time (Jewitt and Ryley, 2014), and will therefore need the toilet more often (Jewitt and Ryley, 2014). In spite of this, even if equal floor space is provided for the women's and men's side of the average public toilet block, men are likely to have twice the number of 'places to pee' because a whole row of urinals can be provided in the same space where only a few cubicles can be fitted in (Penner, 2013). Queues build up because of lack of facilities and also because women take twice as long to use the toilet than men, because of biological consider-ations, the need to access a cubicle, and to deal with more clothing than men (Kira, 1975). So, 'if you want to know the true position of women in society look at the queue for the toilet'. The so-called 'solution' to queuing, of desegre-gating male/female toilets, will not necessarily reduce queues, especially if no additional facilities are provided. Instead, it will have other negative effects on women, as will be explained. Likewise, introducing Gender-Neutral Toilets (unisex toilets) without any consideration of women's different design require-ments is not necessarily a step towards greater gender equality for women. But men may experience GNTs as the height of luxury compared with traditional basic male public toilets and urinals. In fact, renaming both the Ladies and the Gents as Gender-Neutral facilities results in greater pressure on women's toilets whilst women themselves are unable to use the Gents toilet if it predominantly consists of urinals. Some local authorities have taken the easy option of keeping the Gents as it is, and only renaming the Ladies toilets as Gender Neutral, which increases toilet inequality for women (Ramster et al., 2018).

Public toilets may be defined as comprising both traditional 'on-street', local authority public toilets and 'off-street' toilets to which the public has right of access, for example in restaurants or department stores, which, together, are defined as 'away from home toilets' by the British Toilet Association (BTA, 2001; Greed, 2003). The BTA subsequently defined them as 'Publically *Available* Toilets' (PATs) (Kemp (ed.), 2010). This definition is problematic as it suggests that users are a unitary group all equally able to access the toilet, when clearly there are many gender, class, appearance, and disability factors which determine a person's chances of actually accessing a particular toilet, and so the term 'Publically Accessible Toilets' is seen to be more realistic (Bichard and Ramster, 2011).

The lack of public toilets has often been raised in respect of urban planning policy and accessibility issues (Greed, 1994, 2003, 2012, 2016). Yet toilet provision is not a required component of UK planning law or development plan production. Rather, toilets are the responsibility of operational technical departments, concerned with street cleansing, highway maintenance, and which are generally male-dominated and not renowned for their social awareness (Fisher, 2008). Therefore, in the concluding section I recommend a strategic, high-level strategic approach to toilet provision to be carried out by more spatially and socially aware urban planning authorities.

A Diversity of Perspectives Shaping Provision

The first part of this chapter seeks to explain the nature of, and reasons for, the inadequate toilet provision for women, with reference to historical, legislative, and urban policy factors. For example, the sexist late nineteenth- and early twentieth-century public health legislation which still limits women access to the toilet will be explained. The chapter particularly relates to the United Kingdom, along with international comparisons. In the second part, the cultural factors which legitimise toilet discrimination towards women are highlighted, with particular reference to menstruation and women's 'other' bodily functions. Not only have these biological 'differences' often been ignored in contemporary toilet debates, but they have been the reason to see women variously as dirty and unclean, inferior to men, and of such little importance that 'special' toilet facilities for them have been considered an unwarranted expense and unnecessary luxury.

One would have imagined that the modern-day emphasis upon equality, gender, diversity, and human rights would have led to the acknowledgement and rectification of women's toilet problems. But, as will be explained in the third section of the chapter, the situation is more complex. It has often been said of public toilets that, 'all human life is there' as toilets are places where gender, biology, and sexuality intersect. Public toilets are 'contested spaces' used by a range of different sorts of people, each with their own toilet agenda and needs, including women, those with disabilities, people of different ethnicities and religious beliefs, the elderly, parents with babies and small children, and those of different sexualities (Greed, 2006). But, gender overarches all demographic and cultural minorities within society (Reeves, 2005).

But it is argued that we should give greater importance to the biological differences and toilet requirements of women. As will be explained, the word 'gender' has increasingly been seen as a cultural construction, which has become divorced from, or even used as a replacement for, the very real physical and biological differences between the majority of women and men. Second-wave feminists stressed that 'women' were not born but were socially constructed to take on particular gendered roles which were not necessarily linked to the biological differences between women and men. Much of feminist theory and protest was based upon believing in this fundamental binary division between women and men, with men holding dominant power through patriarchy. But in recent years there has been a fundamental cultural turn away from seeing gender as a binary factor to seeing it as a continuum, and in the process – still extant – biological differences have become marginalised.

In the fourth and last section, ways in which town planners and urban designers might mainstream toilet provision, especially for women, into planning policy and development plans are discussed. The fact that women's toilet needs are different and more diverse than men's has design implications at both the individual toilet-building level (that is the toilet block) and for city-wide planning policy. This section will look at 'planning for toilets' at the city-wide, local district, and toilet-block levels, along with the constraints of planning law.

The implementation of change through the planning system is not an easy task (in the UK at least). The expansion of the diversity and equality agendas has not necessarily been good for women and gender considerations often come very low on the pecking order, or are seen as detracting from sustainability policy, although gender equality is a key component of sustainability. Some local planning authorities have over 37 different minority and diversity categories and so gender – and more specifically women – are lost in the morass (Greed, 2005). Ostensibly, 'planning is for people' (Broady, 1968), but there has been little awareness of the physical, corporeal needs and biological characteristics of different groups within society (Bichard, 2014). Likewise, urban geography has been rather reticent about the 'city and the body', including bodily functions (Longhurst, 2000), particularly in respect of disability and gender differences. Municipal authorities have always been keen to deal with technical sewerage and infrastructural issues, but are less enthusiastic about recognising the importance of toilet users and their excretory functions, which create sewage in the first place (Fisher, 2008).

Historical, Legislative and Attitudinal Constraints

Local authorities were first given powers to provide public toilets in the UK under the 1875 Public Health Act (Greed, 2003). But provision for women was far less than for men. Most of the engineers, architects, and decision makers in Victorian times were men. They had little concern with women's needs or were embarrassed by the unseemly topic of women's public conveniences. Respectable middle-class women were not meant to be out on the street on their own, or to need toilets, resulting in what Penner (2001) calls 'unmentionable suffering'. Not providing females' public toilets was seen as a way of protecting women's modesty, dignity, and privacy (Overall, 2007), and guarding men from female pollution of public space (Browne, 2004). One of the key campaigns of the women's Suffrage movement was for toilets for women and the Ladies Association for the Diffusion of Sanitary Knowledge campaigned hard to change attitudes (Greed, 2003, p. 104).

In contrast, it was considered quite acceptable to provide street urinals, and blocks of men-only toilets for 'the working man' to use on his way to the factory. But nothing was provided for working class women going to the factories and mills (Cooper et al., 2000). Even today new male street urinals are being installed, such as the Urilift, which is meant to combat male street urination caused by late-night binge drinking. Apparently, they are for the purpose of 'street cleansing', so they are not technically 'public toilets' and not subject to equality laws that require 'equal' provision of public services for women and men (Greed, 2003, p. 91).

From the beginning, there was little consideration of the need to create accessible, well-designed toilets. Greater emphasis was often put upon technical plumbing considerations rather than user need and many Victorian public toilets were built underground, down steps, in convenient proximity to the main sewers. This resulted in countless generations of people – especially women with pushchairs, the elderly, and those with disabilities – having difficulty accessing public toilets (Cavanagh and Ware, 1991). In the twentieth century, toilet law was consolidated in the still-extant 1936 Public Health Act, which gives local authorities permissive, but not mandatory, powers to build toilets. Under Section 87, Subsection 3, local authorities were empowered to charge such fees as they think fit '*other than for urinals*'. So women had to pay to urinate and men did not, although in some locations men were charged to use cubicles in the Gents too (Penner, 2001). Payment was enforced by 'penny in the slot mechanisms' on cubicle doors. Full-height metal turnstiles at the entrance to women's toilets, but not men's, were also a common sight right up until the 1960s in England, making access difficult (Cavanagh and Ware, 1991).

Following a heated campaign, the 1965 Turnstile Removal Act abolished the use of turnstiles and many local authorities made their toilets free. But this Act only applied to local-authority-run toilets, and they still exist at many railway stations. Owing to government funding cutbacks, turnstiles are re-appearing at the entrances to public toilets, especially in London where you may have to pay 50 pence to use the toilet. The 2012 London Local Authorities Act revoked the rule prohibiting turnstiles in the capital. Both men and women can now be charged owing to a rather perverse understanding of the 2010 Equality Act, which interprets 'equality' as charging everyone to use the toilet, rather than making it free for everyone! Modern turnstiles are waist height and based on a softer 'paddle system' but can still be a major barrier, especially if they are narrow, for women who are pregnant and indeed for anyone, male or female, with pushchairs, luggage, or who is elderly or does not fit in the narrow entrance space available. But it has long been shown that women are the majority of people with pushchairs, indeed pushchairs outnumber wheelchairs 15–1 (Goldsmith, 2000), and overall women have particular difficulties accessing public toilets (Bichard, 2014).

The principle of providing fewer toilet facilities for women than men was embodied in the early legislation, and carried through into modern building regulations and the British Standards Institute requirements (BSI, 2006). Gender inequality has been embedded in all aspects of toilet legislation and design. But queues for the Ladies toilets are often blamed on women, for 'taking too long' or 'not going before you went out' or seen as a joke (Stanwell-Smith, 2010), when in reality they have fewer facilities. Likewise, toilet cubicles are often narrow and poorly designed, but women might be blamed for being too fat or having too much shopping with them (Greed and Daniels, 2002). Some men may also have trouble using cubicles for similar reasons. But the great difference is that women always have to use cubicles whereas men have urinals available too, which offer less restricted space.

Space within the cubicle is so limited that the edge of an inward-opening door often touches the outer rim of the toilet pan. Women have to get into the cubicle, close the door, and then do a three-point turn to position themselves over the toilet seat. There is usually a giant toilet-roll holder located directly above the toilet pan, so that women need to do a limbo dance to sit down. Such an arrangement could only be designed by front-facing urinators (male sanitary engineers). In comparison, in the USA, cubicles (stalls) are more generous in terms of internal floor space (ICC, 2011). But privacy is often limited in North American toilets because of the huge gap under the door and vertical gaps at the sides. These gaps were originally introduced to discourage male homosexual activity within toilets, with little regard to women's privacy and embarrassment (Anthony, 2017). 'Disabled toilets' (accessible cubicles) are often used by those who cannot fit into the regular toilets (including pregnant women, larger women, those with small children and push chairs, and anyone with luggage). But entry is often restricted and usually there is only one disabled toilet alongside the regular toilets. So a large number of people fall outside the abled/disabled binary because they are 'disenabled' by the narrow, inaccessible design of 'normal' toilets (Hanson et al., 2007).

The Cultural Roots of Under-Provision

Dirt and Disgust

Both men and women view toilets as sites of disgust, dirt, disease, sex and disorder (Pain, 1997; Barcan, 2005). The toilet is a source of embarrassment, and not a worthy subject for open debate or policymaking. Toilets are generally seen as a taboo subject within society because of the association with excretion and the baseness of our bodily existence. Women's toilets and excretory functions are seen as even dirtier (than men's), because women are seen as 'other', falling on the wrong side of the clean/dirty, pure/impure, moral/immoral, body/spirit, gender/biology binaries that have deep roots in Western philosophy and religion (Eliade, 1948; Douglas, 1966).

Many women are wary of using public toilets, preferring to 'hold on' which may lead to future urinary problems. Women are concerned about 'catching germs from the toilet seat', a not-unjustified concern, although one is more likely to catch gastro-diarrhoeal infections from toilet door handles than STDS from sitting on the seat (Salley, 1996; Greed, 2006). Research shows around 80% of women 'hover' over the seat to urinate when in public toilets, whereas they prefer to sit when using their toilet at home. Hovering contributes to residual urine retention in the bladder by 150% and reduces the rate of urine flow by 21% and contributes to the development of continence problems (Parazzini et al., 2003). But, as Barcan (2005) observes, men's toilets are actually physically dirtier than women's and smellier, but as they say, 'you can't smell yourself'.

Menstruation was always seen as shameful and embarrassing and it has only been in recent years that the topic has been broached within toilet-research circles (Taylor et al., 2017).

Ignoring the fact that at any one time around a quarter of all women of childbearing age will be menstruating, the absence of the provision of facilities for them to deal with their periods and change sanitary protection is a major factor in limiting women's access to urban space. The chances of streptococcal toxic-shock syndrome from sanitary protection is increased if there are no toilets available to change tampons (WEN, 2012). The low priority given to menstruation is evidenced by the inclusion of a plastic bin for the disposal of 'sanpro' (sanitary protection items), in women's toilets. This bin is often put right beside the toilet pan, touching the seat, restricting women's chances of sitting on the toilet (Williams, 2009). Such bins are often overflowing and infrequently emptied. If menstruation were taken seriously a ducted sanpro-disposal system would be built into the cubicle.

The problems are even greater in the developing world. Of the nearly 7 billion people in the world, around 2 billion lack not only toilets but accessible water supply, and electricity too, and in many developing countries such sanitation as exists is very basic (George, 2008). Sarah Jewitt, a social geographer, comments that the 'geographies of shit' are seldom discussed because of taboos about human waste in general (Jewitt, 2011; Sim, 2012). But women suffer even greater sanitary disadvantage. The United Nations' 'Sustainable Development Goals' (SDGs) introduced in 2016 (www.isdgs.org/) have sought to bring attention to women's specific toilet needs. Subsection 6.2 states that by 2030 the aim is 'to achieve access to adequate and equitable sanitation and hygiene for all and to end open defecation, paying special attention to the needs of women and girls and those in vulnerable situations'. But little mention is made of menstruation. Fifty per cent of girls in Africa do not continue with school when they start menstruating (Jewitt and Ryley, 2014). Those who persevere are likely to be absent for up to 5 days every month, because of the absence of school toilets specifically for girls, a lack of washing and changing facilities, and privacy.

New Contenders: Allies or Detractors?

After years of fighting for equal toilet provision for women and recognition of their 'different' biological toilet needs, new gender paradigms are challenging the very concept of separate toilet provision for women (Gershenson and Penner, 2009). The binary sexual division, upon which second-wave feminism was based, is being questioned (Mayer, 2017, pp. 91, 315) as traditional societal beliefs are being challenged by a new relativism. There has been a cultural turn towards seeing gender as a continuum. Individuals can now self-define their gender and can transition from male to female (or vice versa). Public toilets have been critiqued as problematic for trans users because they are the ultimate gender-segregated, binary public spaces (Skeggs, 2001; Valentine, 2002; Browne, 2004; Kogan, 2007; Cavanagh, 2010; Doan, 2010; Longhurst and Johnston, 2010; Molotch and Noren, 2010).

The move to GNTs (Gender-Neutral Toilets) has been welcomed by some as a means of making public toilets more flexible and inclusive to all genders, and is promoted as a way of reducing queues for the Ladies. Some modern (fourth-wave) feminists are optimistic that bringing women and men together will actually improve provision for all (Mayer, 2017) and have promoted integrated school toilets (Slater et al., 2016). But many women have expressed concerns about the impact upon women and girls of desegregating toilets (Jeffreys, 2014; Cunningham, 2016). Doreen Massey, the social geographer (Massey, 1984) stated that 'to be male is to occupy space', so there is no such thing as gender-neutral public space, and in shared spaces women usually lose out. The public toilet block has long been the only safe separate space for women in the city of man; a sanctum away from the male gaze. The emphasis upon gender neutrality has sidelined the toilet needs, biological differences, and personal experiences of women. The lack of consideration of women's (toilet) issues within the transgender movement has been seen by some old-time feminists as sexist, patriarchal and part of the ongoing 'the war against women', albeit in a new guise. For example, Kathleen Sloan states *'the gender identity movement erases women'* and empowers men to enter women-only spaces (Sloan, 2016; McGuire, 2017, pp. 166–168, 253; Jeffreys, 2014).

In the USA, toilets are already being desegregated, under Title IX legislation, to accommodate transsexual people. Title IX of the Education Amendments Act 1972 introduced the regulation that no person should be excluded from educational facilities on the basis of their sex. According to Justice Ruth Ginsberg – one of the drafters of Title IX in the 1970s – it was introduced to counter sexism towards women, and was instrumental in opening up educational and sports opportunities to women (McGuire, 2017, pp. 11, 131, 176, and Chapter 9 on toilets). In May 2016, President Obama sent a 'Dear Colleague' (presidential policy advice note) to all public educational bodies, stating that Title IX was to be re-interpreted, so that nobody was to be excluded on the basis of their chosen gender. This resulted in the widespread desegregation of school, college, and public building facilities, including restrooms, showers, and changing rooms (Gersen, 2016).

As a result, women's toilets are potentially no longer exclusively for women. Whilst originally aimed at accommodating a very small minority of transgender people (and others who feel 'gender incongruent'), Title IX potentially enables any men who choos to say that they identify their gender as 'female' to enter female restrooms, without verification. This has created a great deal of concern amongst women because of fears regarding privacy, loss of dignity, embarrassment, and personal safety. This is especially so amongst women who are wary of men (in the toilet) because of previous sexual attacks. Everyday sexism and harassment does not stop at the toilet door (Bates, 2014). Toilet desegregation has all sorts of worrying implications for both women and men, but women's and men's views and needs have not been fully considered within the new gender identity agenda still in its infancy. The media and academia often portray women's toilet concerns as reactionary, conservative, religious, fundamentalist, homophobic, transphobic, even unreasonably androphobic. But one needs to be mindful of the context of what is still a highly sexist, potentially violent, and discriminatory society towards women. Women's toilets always attract a range of ill-intentioned men ranging from male voyeurs and illicit photographers to those likely to molest women. Many women are fearful of potentially predatory straight men entering their facilities (Pain, 1997; Greed, 2003).

Providing a block of individual cubicles, that is single GNTs, each with its own separate doors and washing facilities, in addition to (not instead of, or at the expense of) separate Ladies and Gents toilets, removes the problem of choosing 'which' toilet to use and provides the ultimate privacy for whoever wants it, and is preferable to simply renaming all the existing toilets 'for everyone'. Nevertheless, women are concerned about the vulnerability of small children who often have to be left outside the small cubicles, in desegregated toilet blocks, whilst mothers often keep the door ajar, as do women with luggage that won't fit in the cubicle. Even if there are individual cubicles, men and women still share, and queue in, a common access corridor to the cubicles.

Young women just starting their periods are often very embarrassed about anyone finding out they are menstruating. Being expected to share with men in public toilets, or with boys at school, is likely to result in them staying at home when their period takes place. A toilet colleague, Susan Cunningham, who has served on British Standards toilet committees, comments:

> Women, on average, are menstruating for 40 years of their lives. With each period lasting for approximately 5 days in each 28, that means they are dealing with intimate sanitary issues for 65 days for each of those 40 years. I can assure you that, when I was coping with my periods, I would have regarded anything other than a toilet solely for women, as being the wrong toilet. Many women (more women than men) are quietly coping with problems associated with bladder and bowel control. Sometimes, 'accidents' happen, and in those circumstances, anything other than a toilet solely for women is the wrong toilet.
>
> *(Cunningham, 2016)*

In the UK, the Gender Recognition Bill, which is currently subject to public consultation, will also enable any man to choose which toilet they use (Government Equalities Office, 2018). This proposed legislation would allow any person to self-define themselves as male or female without the need for medical certification of transgender status, potentially allowing any man to enter women-only spaces such as toilets, showers, sports clubs, and women's rape refuges (GEO, 2015). In April 2017 the Barbican Arts Centre in London jumped the gun, and took down the Ladies and Gents signs on its theatre toilets and renamed them, 'Gender-Neutral Toilets' and Gender-Neutral Toilets with Urinals' respectively. This resulted in furious rows over even longer queues for the Ladies, as men joined the line for the erstwhile Ladies toilet (Grafton-Green, 2017). This reduced the chances of women being able to use the already limited numbers of cubicles, whereas the men still had the option of using the urinals. None of this improved the situation for women, who already suffer inadequate toilet provision at theatres. For example, the highly successful satirical musical, *Menopause the Musical* did not come to London because Jeanne Linders, its writer, producer, and lyricist would not take it to the West End in protest against the inadequate provision of toilets for women in London theatres as most of her audiences are menopausal women in their forties and fifties: an age group that needs to use the toilet frequently (Parazzini et al. 2003).

A range of articles and letters in March and April 2017 in the newspapers summed up the concerns many women have regarding desegregating public toilets and the new gender agenda. For example, Jenni Murray in her BBC's *Woman's Hour* radio programme agreed with Germaine Greer's views that transgender men are not really women and was reprimanded by the BBC. The Barbican GNT toilet riots led to further media alarm. The consensus was that '*transgender women do not understand what being a real woman is*' with particular reference to menstruation and that '*a transgender woman cannot know the hot roar of menopause*'. Many contributors believed that such individuals take with them '*all the male privileges and entitlements that those born male take for granted*' and this has, inevitably, adversely affected women, particularly in allowing men to take over women's toilets (for examples of these widely held views by women see Daily Telegraph, 2017).

But, according to Stonewall, and the government (Gender Equality Office, 2018) only around 5,000 people have undertaken transition, mainly male to female, with a further 165,000 who feel they are in the wrong gender, whereas women comprise half the population. Transgender rights seem to have taken priority over other diversity factors too, such as women's legal right to privacy and religious considerations. For example, some Islamic, Hindu, and Orthodox Jewish women are forbidden to share public space so intimately with male strangers, especially when menstruating, and so are effectively barred from public toilets. Clearly, there needs to be more policy finesse in recognising women's concerns, and those of other minority groups, whilst balancing this with the requirements of transgender people (Plaskow, 2016, p. 750).

The needs of the small transgender minority have been taken so seriously that public toilets are being desegregated. In contrast, women have suffered immeasurably, for hundreds of years, because of inadequate toilet provision. More than feeling 'uncomfortable' they have been greatly inconvenienced by having to queue for inadequate facilities, with negative health implications for the pregnant and elderly in particular. But, no government has as yet recognised the very real toilet discrimination towards women of desegregating public toilets, or rushed through legislation to increase women's toilet provision (Taylor et al., 2017). Because the situation was not thought through, women are even worse off due to the way GNTs have been introduced: by simply desegregating existing toilet blocks without any design modifications, given that women have far less provision (than men) to share with other toilet users to start with. Little consideration has been given to how this affects women who seem to be expected to give up their toilet space, dignity, safety, and privacy without complaint.

Proponents of GNTs often give the impression that women are over-reacting because there are already many types of desegregated toilets in use. There are degrees of toilet 'sharing' with a diverse range of users, but this is different from total mixing in public situations. Most people share toilets at home, but with family members and visitors, not complete strangers. Single-user, self-contained individual 'unisex' cubicles with their own door are common in many coffee shops, and on planes and trains. These may be seen as a preferable form of GNT, than situations where existing rows of toilet cubicles which are only separated by flimsy partitions (with gaps under the walls) are simply desegregated without modification. But, whatever the arrangement, many women do not like sharing unisex facilities with men as 'they spray the seat' and 'male the floor wet' (Greed and Daniels, 2002; Ramster et al., 2018). For example the APC (Automatic Public Convenience) that is the stand-alone automatic on-street toilet is generally seen as just a urinal for men, which are often dirty because of malfunction of the cleaning mechanisms, and their design makes them difficult to use by women (Bichard and Ramster, 2011). But women are much more concerned about situations where inside a toilet block, all the cubicles (with minimal dividing walls) are entirely desegregated. Some women and men simply cannot 'go' in situations where everyone can hear, smell and see everyone else (Soifer, 2001). Arguments that desegregating toilets will create more flexibility and reduce toilet queues need to be balanced against the fact the queues may get shorter because GNTs will drive some women and men away, and reduce their freedom and mobility (Greed, 2012, 2016). There is also greater pressure on already limited disabled toilet facilities, as some trans people see them as a safer alternative to the Ladies or the Gents (Ramster et al., 2018).

Clearly the situation is complex, but the official British Standards Institute, which provides government-endorsed regulations on toilet provision, still requires separate male and female toilet facilities, based upon years of detailed research and mathematical calculations. As a member of the BS6465 Sanitary Installation Committee (BSI, 2010), which undertakes public consultation and draws on current toilet research when updating the standards, it is clear, from public feedback on the standards, that sex-segregated toilets are what the majority of people want. The main complaint is that there are not enough facilities for women and the committee has been working to rectify this historical bias in favour of women (BSI, 2010, and ongoing quinquennial updates). Rather than totally desegregating existing toilets, or building new gender-mixed toilets, it is better to provide a range of alternatives. For example, at the new Storyhouse Arts Centre in Chester there are ample male and female traditional toilets, plus doors which have 'Gender Neutral' marked on them, containing individual 'unisex' cubicles, as well as separate accessible toilets and baby changing facilities. More toilets of all sorts would also help reduce queues.

In contrast to increasing desegregation in the West, the need for separate toilets for girls and women, as discussed earlier, is a very high development priority in the rest of the world. The United Nations Report on *The Human Right to Safe Drinking Water and Sanitation* states that gender-specific toilets should be provided, especially in schools, where privacy to deal with menstruation becomes a major factor in determining whether girls attend school or drop out. It requires all public toilet facilities are provided in a manner appropriate to local cultural and religious habits and requirements, with gender segregation being seen as a priority and a basic principle in achieving equality for women (Albuquerque and Roaf, 2012, pp. 35, 153–154). Paragraph 2.1.2 of the UNICEF document, *Core Questions and Indicators for Monitoring WASH in Schools in the Sustainable Development Goals*, on applying SDG 6 to toilet provision specifies that separate school toilets should always be provided for girls (UNICEF, 2016).

As a member of the UN, and signatory to key UN directives on sanitation, gender, and equality, including the Sustainable Development Goals, the UK cannot ignore these requirements and see themselves as 'above' international human rights law and UN directives in respect of women's toilet provision. Indeed all EU nation-state governments should be applying these UN requirements through subsidiarity. This UN-level requirement for separate toilets for women and girls applies to all countries, (not just developing countries) and thus, arguably, takes precedence over UK and USA toilet desegregation policies and laws within in the global policy hierarchy (Greed and Johnson, 2014, pp. 18–22).

A Toilet Planning Spatial Strategy

What is the role of planning in all of this? And how can toilet policy, especially for women, be mainstreamed into urban planning policy? Most local planning authorities do not include toilet provision requirements within their urban policies or development plans (Greed, 2016). This undermines health policies, economic development, social inclusion, and environmental sustainability. If the government wants to create accessible, equal, sustainable, healthy cities, and to get people out of their cars and back to public transport, cycling and walking, then adequate public toilets are essential: they are 'the missing link' in creating healthy sustainable, accessible, equitable, and inclusive cities (Bichard et al., 2003; Hanson et al., 2007). Inadequate toilet provision, especially at railway stations, in major thoroughfares, and town centres, undermines people's mobility and chances of freely accessing and moving around in the city as a whole.

Macro Level (City-Wide Policies)

It is vital to adopt a high-level strategic spatial policy approach to toilet provision. Planners, with their spatial awareness and methodological skills, are particularly suited to produce such a strategy. Plan-making has three basic stages, namely, SAP = Survey > Analysis > Plan. Applying this approach to the development of toilet policy, the toilet planner needs to 'survey' the existing situation of the area, identify problems, note lack of facilities, and estimate future demand trends, whilst taking into account gender and other demographic factors. The ratio and numbers of male/female facilities will differ according to the location and gender composition of the users, for example over 70% of people in shopping centres are likely to be female, whereas 80% are likely to be male, at least in many sports venues, and this is reflected in the British Standards recommendations (BSI, 2010). Undertaking this exercise in a rational manner would reveal the extent and nature of the problems and the pent-up demand for public toilets. Public toilets cannot be provided everywhere because of cost and space-availability constraints. Therefore a spatial hierarchy of toilet provision would need to be developed to enable facilities to be targeted to area need. Both spatial (geographical location) and temporal (patterns and peaks of usage in time) factors need to be taken into account in developing a hierarchy of provision. Social, equality, and demographic considerations should also be taken into account, for example, as to whether existing facilities cater mainly for women, or men; whether there is likely to be a demand for women's toilets, men's urinals, disabled facilities, or GNTs in particular locations, and the levels of accessibility and demands of an ageing population.

The central area is the main focus of the city's business and retail activities, and the part of the city that tourists are likely to visit. Historically, the main transport routes in UK cities radiate out from the city centre, with downtown railway and bus stations being the main gateways to the rest of the city. Toilets need to be provided in all city centres and transport termini, including at least one 24-hour facility. In such downtown locations, a comprehensive range of toilet facilities might be provided in toilet 'super blocks'. There are major differences between daytime and evening users in city centres, where 'the evening economy' of pubs, clubs, and bars in the UK attracts large numbers of predominantly young, male drinkers, with attendant problems of street urination. The installation of male street urinals for night-time users, may reduce street urination, but does not help women and daytime users or anyone who wants privacy.

Rather than looking to the West, the East might provide better guidance and examples on how to plan for toilets at the strategic level. A restroom revolution is being achieved as a result of policy enlightenment and the work of toilet organisations such as the Japan Toilet Association and Taiwan Toilet Association, and similar organisations in China, Malaysia, and Singapore (WTO, 2015). Their governments have invested heavily in toilet provision, often with a higher level of provision for women: for example ratios of 2 to 1, or even 3 to 1, in favour of women are common in Japan. In the city of Toyama, Japan, public toilet policy and location is included in the city's development plan, alongside other land uses and forms of development (Miyanishi, 1996). Within Europe, Zurich has produced a spatial 'WC Master Plan' (Zurich, 2004), and Vienna's city planning department is integrating public toilet provision into its plan-making system, as part of its programme of mainstreaming gender into all aspects of urban planning (Vienna, 2015, p. 49; Sánchez de Madariaga and Roberts, 2013).

Meso Level: District Planning

At the district and local neighbourhood level, fewer facilities are needed, but provision should be linked to needs generated by local shopping centres, car parks, and transport termini. A combination of local pubs, hot food takeaways, clubs, pubs, taxi ranks, and bus stops, results in a potential 'toilet hotspot'. In smaller settlements, rural areas, and outlying suburbs some toilet blocks should be provided to ensure coverage. In addition, there are large numbers of mobile 'away from home' workers, lorry and bus drivers, care workers, tourists, and private motorists passing through who may be desperate to find somewhere to park and use the loo.

First, it is important to identify the nature of the local area and the different types of would-be toilet users, which might include, for example, local shoppers, public transport users, school children, people visiting local pubs, clubs, and sports facilities. Each of these user groups will have different characteristics in terms of age and gender requirements. It is not enough to suggest – as many male planning officers suggested (as was often recorded in previous research) – *'well they could always use the pub'* (Greed and Daniels, 2002). If the majority of daytime users are mainly women shoppers, including pensioners, women out on their own, or with small children and babies, then on-street public toilets with disabled provision, baby changing facilities, and a higher level of women's toilets are needed, rather than expecting everyone to use just one unisex toilet in the local coffee shop.

Micro Level: Toilet Block Design

Public toilets should be proudly visible as a key component of accessible urban spaces. Some local authorities hide theirs behind bushes and down dark footpaths. Such seclusion inevitably attracts vandalism, anti-social behaviour, and, potentially, attacks on women. Instead, public toilets should be located in prominent positions with good surveillance all around. Drawing on the principles of inclusive urban design and place-making, at this most detailed level of urban planning, 'legibility' (ease of finding the toilets) and accessibility are particularly important (I'DGO, 2009). The Restroom Association of Singapore, for example, stresses the importance of initial design plus ongoing maintenance, cleaning, and good management, to ensure the toilets are usable (WTO, 2015). If vandalism and disrepair are neglected, this is a sure sign that nobody is watching and nobody cares, whereas, in contrast, well-maintained facilities can actually contribute to the regeneration of the image of the area as a whole (Pain, 1997). Much modern toilet design seems to be more concerned about designing-out crime, often resulting in additional barriers, such as narrow modern turnstiles, vandal-proof toilet fixtures (like metal lavatory pans without seats, no support rails, and minimal washing facilities) that all create a non-user-friendly, anti-woman environment for users (Kemp, 2010).

Planning Law

Many of the issues discussed are toilet design and management matters, and may not appear to be within the remit of planning law, but are still the responsibility of the local authority or commercial provider (Drakeford, 2012). Planners have often determined that 'women's issues' are not a land-use matter but are *ultra vires* because gender is not seen as being within the scope of planning law because it is seen as *social* not *spatial* (Greed and Johnson, 2014, Chapters 2 and 15). But toilet provision is a planning matter if poor toilet design restricts many people from accessing urban space and reduces urban sustainability.

Under-provision of toilets in public buildings and spaces should also be revealed by the operation of the government's PSED (Public Sector Equality Duty). Under the PSED there is a specific requirement for gender considerations to be mainstreamed into town planning policy and practice, and also into the provision of facilities and public services that are publically funded: including facilities, such as toilets, whose provision is not mandatory. Also, buildings that discriminate in their design in providing less facilities for women than men, do not meet Supplementary Planning Guidance requirements on Equalities. If gender equality were mainstreamed into all aspects of planning departments' work, then toilet inequalities would soon be flagged up. The Royal Town Planning Institute's Code of Professional Conduct requires practising planners to apply equality, diversity, and human rights principles to their work (Greed, 2005). By using their professional judgement and expertise, planners exercise considerable discretionary power to decide which non-statutory issues are relevant to planning policy (Greed, 2012).

The Way Ahead

In conclusion, toilet decision makers and designers, who are still mainly male, need to take seriously these legal requirements to take women's toilet needs into account. Women, as toilet users, need to talk about toilets and explain their specific needs regarding menstruation, pregnancy, and other biological differences, and to discuss openly their concerns over loss of privacy, dignity, and safety. There needs to be open, frank discussion between all parties, toilet providers/ users, male/female, gay/straight, trans/born, old/young, abled/disabled, with/ without children, menstruating/menopausal, inter alia, as to the implications of introducing GNTs. The impact of expecting everyone to use the same toilets needs to be assessed. Unlike racial desegregation, gender desegregation is not a mark of progress, as separate toilets are provided for good historical and biological reasons. The right for women to have their own public toilets was a hard-won right.

To sum up, simply changing existing segregated toilets into Gender-Neutral Toilets does not increase the overall number of toilets, or compensate for the unequal levels of provision currently experienced by women. Nor does such a move guarantee increased provision of women-related facilities to meet their 'different' toilet needs in terms of menstruation, menopause, pregnancy, and the greater level of baby and child toileting duties still undertaken predominantly by women.

To help create change, more women need to get into the male-dominated professional areas of sanitation and toilet design, so that they can shape the agenda of the toilet providers rather than suffering as toilet users. In the USA, thanks to the efforts of women architects and toilet activists campaigning for 'potty parity', not just an 'equal' ratio of 1:1, but 2:1 in favour of women to reduce queues, has been achieved in over 20 states (Anthony and Dufresne, 2007; Anthony, 2017, pp. 121–158). Likewise in France, the government has been taking toilet equality seriously, promising to make all public toilets free (Damon, 2009) influenced, in part, by the resurgence of the ideas of Lefebvre regarding 'la droit à la ville' (the right to the city) (Greed, 2016). It is essential to mainstream gender considerations into toilet policy at the highest level of policymaking, rather than leaving it to male technicians and plumbers with no sociological awareness (Greed, 2005; Fisher, 2008). Gender must not be treated as an abstract disembodied concept, separate from biology. It must be related to the realities of the differences in bodily functions between men and women, and thus the particular needs of men and women need to be respected. From a planning perspective toilets need to be mainstreamed into urban policy, because they are physical land uses, which have implications for creating sustainable urban spaces for all.

References

Anthony, Kathryn (2017). *Defined by Design: The Surprising Power of Hidden Gender, Age and Body Bias in Everyday Products and Places*, New York: Prometheus Books, Chapter 6, 'A Taboo Topic: Restroom Revolution', pp. 121–158.

Anthony, Kathryn and Dufresne, Megan (2007). 'Potty Parity in Perspective: Gender and Family Issues in Planning and Designing Public Restrooms', *Journal of Planning Literature*, Vol. 21, No. 3, pp. 267–294.

Barcan, Ruth (2005). 'Dirty Spaces: Communication and Contamination in Men's Public Toilets', *Journal of International Women's Studies*, Vol. 6, No. 2, pp. 7–23.

Bates, Laura (2014). *Everyday Sexism*, London: Simon and Schuster.

Bichard, Joanne (2014). *Extending Architectural Affordance: The Case of Publicly Accessible Toilets*, London: University College London, Doctoral Dissertation.

Bichard, Joanne, Hanson, Julienne and Greed, Clara (2003). *Access to the Built Environment – Barriers, Chains and Missing Links: Review*, London: University College London.

Bichard, Joanne and Ramster, Gail (2011). *Publically Available Toilets: An Inclusive Design Guide*, London: Royal College of Art.

Broady, Maurice (1968). *Planning for People*, London: NCSS/Bedford Square Press.

Browne, Katherine (2004). 'Genderism and the Bathroom Problem: (Re)materialising Sexed Sites, (Re)creating Sexed Bodies', *Gender, Place and Culture*, Vol. 11, No. 3, pp. 331–346.

BSI (2006). *BS 6465: Sanitary Installations: Part 1: Code of Practice for the Scale of Provision, Selection and Installation of Sanitary Appliances*, London: British Standards Institute.

BSI (2010). *Sanitary Installations: Part 4: Code of Practice for the Provision of Public Toilets*, London: British Standards Institute.

BTA (2001). *Better Public Toilets: The Provision and Management of 'Away from Home' Toilets*, Winchester: British Toilet Association.

Cavanagh, Sheila (2010). *Queering Bathrooms: Gender, Sexuality and the Hygienic Imagination*, Toronto: University of Toronto Press.

Cavanagh, Sue and Ware, Vron (1991). *At Women's Convenience: A Handbook on the Design of Women's Public Toilets*, London: Women's Design Service.

Cooper, Annabelle, Law, Robin, Malthus, Jane and Wood, Pamela (2000). 'Rooms of Their Own: Public Toilets and Gendered Citizens in a New Zealand City, 1860–1940', *Gender, Place and Culture*, Vol. 7, No. 4, pp. 417–433.

Cunningham, Susan (2016). Letter to *Cleanzine Online Magazine*, 20. 10.16 www.theclean zine.com/pages/12490/we_have_mail_mixed_washrooms_we_dont_think_so/which refers to www.thecleanzine.com/pages/12296/leader/

Daily Telegraph (2017). www.pressreader.com/uk/the-daily-telegraph/20170307/ 282037621956215

Damon, Julien (2009). 'Les Toilettes Publiques: un droit à mieux amenagement', *Droit Social*, No 1, pp. 103–110 ('Public toilets: the right for better provision' in *Human Rights Journal*).

de Albuquerque, Catarina and Roaf, Virginia (2012). *On the Right Track: Good Practices in Realising the Rights to Water and Sanitation*, London: United Nations, Human Rights to Water and Sanitation Declaration, UN Special Rapporteur Report, p. 35.

Doan, Petra L. (2010). 'The Tyranny of Gendered Spaces – Reflections from beyond the Gender Dichotomy', *Gender, Place & Culture*, Vol. 17, No. 5, pp. 635–654.

Douglas, Mary (1966). *Purity and Danger: An Analysis of the Concepts of Pollution and Taboo*, London: Ark.

Drakeford, Mark (ed.) (2012). *Public Health Implications of Inadequate Public Toilet Facilities – Report of Evidence*, Cardiff, National Assembly of Wales: Health and Social Care Committee, www.senedd.assembly.wales/documents/s6040/Public%20Health%20Implica tions%20of%20Inadequate%20Public. Accessed 11.01.2016.

Eliade, Mircea (1948). *The Sacred and Profane: The Nature of Religion*, New York: Harcourt, 1987, originally 1948.

Fisher, Julie (2008). 'Women in Water Supply, Sanitation and Hygiene Programmes', *Municipal Engineer*, Vol. 161, No. ME4, pp. 223–229.

GEO (2015). *Providing Services for Transgender Customers: A Guide*, London: Government Equalities Office.

George, Susan (2008). *The Big Necessity: Adventures in the World of Human Waste*, London: Portobello Press.

Gersen, Jeannie Suk (2016). 'The Transgender Bathroom Debate and the Looming Title IX Crisis', *New Yorker*, May 24th. www.newyorker.com/news/news-desk/public-bath room-regulations-could-create-a-title-ix-crisis

Gershenson, Olga and Penner, Barbara (eds.) (2009). *Ladies and Gents: Public Toilets and Gender*, Philadelphia: Temple University Press.

Goldsmith, Selwyn (2000). *Universal Design: A Manual of Practical Guidance for Architects*, Oxford: Architectural Press, 2000.

Government Equalities Office (2018). *Reform of the Gender Recognition Act: Government Consultation*, London: Government Equalities Office, issued July 2018, www.gov.uk/govern ment/consultations/reform-of-the-gender-recognition-act-2004

Grafton-Green, Patrick (2017). 'Barbican to Review Its Gender-neutral Toilets after Furious Row Breaks Out', *Evening Standard*, Thursday 6 April 2017, www.standard.co.uk/ news/london/barbican-to-review-genderneutral-toilets-after-furious-row-over-long-queues-for-women-a3509136.html

Greed, Clara (2003). *Inclusive Urban Design: Public Toilets*, Oxford: Architectural Press.

Greed, Clara (2005). 'Overcoming the Factors Inhibiting the Mainstreaming of Gender into Spatial Planning Policy in the United Kingdom', *Urban Studies*, Vol. 42, No. 4, pp. 1–31, April.

Greed, Clara (2006). 'The Role of the Public Toilet: Pathogen Transmitter or Health Facilitator', *Building Services Engineering Research and Technology Journal*, Vol. 27, No. 2, pp. 127–140.

Greed, Clara (2012). 'Planning and Transport for the Sustainable City or Planning for People', *Journal of Urban Design and Planning*, Vol. 165, June, No. DP4, pp. 219–229.

Greed, Clara (2016). 'Taking Women's Bodily Functions into Account in Urban Planning Policy: Public Toilets and Menstruation', *Town Planning Review*, Vol. 87, No. 5, pp. 505–523.

Greed, Clara and Daniels, Isobel (2002). *User and Provider Perspectives on Public Toilet Provision*, Bristol: University of the West of England, Occasional Paper 13, in association with the Nuffield Foundation.

Greed, Clara (1994). *Women and Planning: Creating Gendered Realities*, London: Routledge.

Greed, Clara and Johnson, David (2014). *Planning in the United Kingdom: An Introduction*, London: Palgrave Macmillan.

Hanson, Julienne, Bichard, Joanne and Greed, Clara (2007). *The Accessible Toilet Resource Manual*, London: University College London.

I'DGO (2009). *Pedestrian Friendly Neighbourhoods*, Edinburgh: I'DGO (Inclusive Design for Getting Outdoors), A Research Report on Older People's Well Being and Getting Outdoors, by L. Mitchell and E. Burton. www.idgo.ac.uk/useful_resources/publica tions.htm

ICC (2011). *Global Guidance for Practical Public Toilet Design*, New York: International Code Council.

Jeffreys, Sheila (2014). 'The Politics of the Toilet: A Feminist Response to the Campaign to Degender a Women's Space', *Women's Studies International Forum*, Vol. 45, pp. 42–51.

Jewitt, Sarah (2011). 'Geographies of Shit: Spatial and Temporal Variations in Attitudes Towards Human Waste', *Progress in Human Geography*, February 14, 2011, Vol. 35, No. 5, pp. 608–626.

Jewitt, Sarah and Ryley, Harriet (2014). 'It's a Girl Thing: Menstruation, School Attendance, Spatial Mobility and Wider Gender Inequalities in Kenya', *Geoforum*, Vol. 56, pp. 137–147.

Kemp, Gillian (ed.) (2010). *Publically Available Toilets Problem Reduction Guide*, Welwyn Garden City: Hertfordshire Constabulary Crime Prevention Design Service in association with the British Toilet Association.

Kira, Alexander (1975). *The Bathroom*, Harmondsworth: Penguin.

Kitchen, Rob and Law, Robin (2001). 'The Socio-spatial Construction of (In)accessible Public Toilets', *Urban Studies*, Vol. 38, No. 2, pp. 287–298.

Kogan, Terry (2007). 'Sex-Separation in Public Restrooms: Law, Architecture, and Gender', *Michigan Journal of Gender and Law, Michigan University*, Vol. 14, No. 1, online available at: http://repository.law.umich.edu/mjgl/vol14/iss1/1

Longhurst, Robyn (2000). *Bodies: Exploring Fluid Boundaries*, London: Routledge, Critical Geographies Series.

Longhurst, Robyn and Johnston, Lynda (2010). *Space, Place, and Sex: Geographies of Sexualities*, New York: Rowman and Littlefield.

Massey, Doreen (1984). *Spatial Divisions of Labour: Social Structures and the Geography of Production*, London: Macmillan.

Mayer, Catherine (2017). *Attack of the 50 ft Women: How Gender Equality Can Save the World*, London: Harper Collins.

McGuire, Ashley (2017). *Sex Scandal: The Drive to Abolish Male and Female*, Washington: Regnery Publishing, Salem Media Group.

Miyanishi, Yutaka (1996). *Comfortable Public Toilets: Design and Maintenance Manual*, Toyama: City Planning Department, Japan.

Molotch, Harvey and Noren, Laura (2010). *Toilet: Public Restrooms and the Politics of Sharing*, New York: New York University Press.

Overall, Christine (2007). 'Public Toilets: Sex Segregation Revisited', *Ethics and the Environment*, Vol. 12, No. 2, pp. 71–91, September 2007.

Pain, Rachel (1997). 'Social Geographies of Women's Fear of Crime', *Transactions of the Institute of British Geographers*, Vol. 22, No. 2, pp. 231–244.

Parazzini, Fabio, Chiaffarino, Francesca, Lavezzari, Maurizio and Giambanco, Vincenzo (2003). 'Risk Factors for Stress, Urge and Mixed Urinary Incontinence in Italy?', *International Journal of Obstetrics and Gynaecology*, Vol. 110, pp. 927–933.

Penner, Barbara (2001). 'A World of Unmentionable Suffering: Women's Public Conveniences in Victorian London', *Journal of Design History*, Vol. xiv, No. 1, pp. 35–52.

Penner, Barbara (2013). *Bathroom*, London: Reaktion Books.

Plaskow, Judith (2016). 'Taking a Break: Toilets, Gender and Disgust', *South Atlantic Quarterly*, Vol. 115, No. 4, pp. 748–754.

Ramster, Gail, Greed, Clara and Bichard, Jo-Anne (2018). 'How Inclusion Can Exclude: The Case of Public Toilet Provision for Women', *Built Environment*, Vol. 44, No. 1, pp. 52–77.

Reeves, Dory (2005). *Planning for Diversity: Planning and Policy in a World of Difference*, London: Routledge.

Salley, Nicola (1996). 'A Bacteriological Investigation of the Public's Perception of Public Toilets', *Environmental Health Congress*, Harrogate, 2-5 September, 1996, Chartered Institute of Environmental Health.

Sánchez de Madariaga, Inés and Roberts, Marion (eds.) (2013). *Fair Shared Cities: The Impact of Gender Planning in Europe*, London: Ashgate.

Sim, Jack (2012). 'I Give a Shit: Inaugural Address' Durban: World Toilet Organisation Conference, see his speech at www.youtube.com/watch?v=_sYq20OJlUA

Skeggs, Beverley (2001). 'The Toilet Paper: Femininity, Class and Mis-recognition', *Women's Studies International Forum*, Vol. 24, No. 3, pp. 295–307.

Slater, Jen, Jones, Charlotte and Procter, Lisa (2016). 'School Toilets: Queer, Disabled Bodies and Gendered Lessons of Embodiment', *Gender and Education*, pp. 1–15, see shura.shu.ac.uk/13896/ and www.tandfonline.com/doi/full/10.1080/09540253.2016.1270421

Sloan, Kathleen (2016). 'The Gender Identity Movement Erases Women' *Delaware Online*, June 22, see https://stoptranschauvinism.wordpress.com/2016/06/24/the-gender-iden tity-movement-erases-women/

Soifer, Steven (2001). *Shy Bladder Syndrome*, Oakland: Harbinger (Maryland).

Sommer, Marnie, Chandraratna, Sahani, Mahon, Therese and Phillips-Howard, Penelope (2016). 'Managing Menstruation in the Workplace: An Overlooked Issue in Low and Middle Income Countries', *International Journal for Equity in Health*, Vol. 15, No. 86, pp. 1–5, see www.ncbi.nlm.nih.gov/pmc/articles/PMC4895811/, doi:10.1186/s12939-016-0379-8

Stanwell-Smith, Rosalind (2010). 'Why Public Toilets are No Laughing Matter', *Perspectives in Public Health*, Vol. 130, No. 1 (Leader comment, p. 13).

Taylor, Julie, Cavill, Sue and Reed, Brian (2017). 'Mainstreaming Gender into the WASH Sector: Dilution or Distillation?', *Gender and Development*, Special Issue on Sanitation, Vol. 25, No. 2, pp. 185–204.

UN (1992). *The Rio Declaration: On Environment and Development*, New York: United Nations.

UN (2015). *Sustainable Development Goals*, New York: United Nations, see https://sustaina bledevelopment.un.or/topics. Accessed 15.11.2015.

UNICEF (2016). *Core Questions and Indicators for Monitoring WASH in Schools in the Sustainable Development Goals*, New York: UNICEF with WHO.

Valentine, Gill (2002). 'Queer Bodies and the Production of Space, Chapter 9', *Handbook of Lesbian and Gay Studies*, Diane Richardson and Steven Seidman (eds.), London: Sage, pp. 145–160.

Vienna (2015). *Manual for Gender Mainstreaming in Urban Planning and Development*, Municipal Department 18, Urban Development, see www.wien.gv.at/stadtentwicklung/stu dien/pdf/b008358.pdf. Accessed 15.11.2015.

WEN (2012). *Seeing Red: Sanitary Protection and the Environment*, London: Women's Environmental Network.

Williams, Elaine (2009). *User-Product Interaction: Users and the Design of Public Convenience Sanitary-ware Products in the UK*, Loughborough: Universit of Loughboroughy, Department of Design and Technology, Doctoral Thesis.

WTO (2015). *World Toilet Organisation Campaigns*, Singapore: WTO, link to publications at http://worldtoilet.org/media/resource-portal/. Accessed 15.11.2015.

Zurich (2004). *Master Plan ZuriWC, Band 1 and 2*, Zurich, City Planning Department, see www.stadt-zuerich.ch/gud/de/index/gesundheit/gesundheitsschut_hygiene/zueriwc. html. Accessed 15.11.2015.

9

ARE SAFE CITIES JUST CITIES?

A Perspective from France

Claire Hancock and Lucile Biarrotte

Introduction

This chapter aims to analyse current developments in French urban policy in the light of international literature on spatial justice and fair-shared cities. It makes particular reference to the implementation of gender mainstreaming policies and the integration of traditionally disempowered minority groups in urban planning processes. While dominant understandings of "sustainability", in France, still concentrate on environmental and economic aspects, we see greater concern for social sustainability being introduced by stealth, by way of international and European discussions and commitments. Our hypothesis is that the integration of gender concerns into political discourse, and the application of gender mainstreaming in urban policies, opens a breach in the French universalist consensus. Consequences are likely to be wide-ranging and need to be carefully investigated as they unfold in the coming years.

It is hard to dispute that French cities, like cities in the Western world, have been designed and run by White, middle- and upper-class, able-bodied, and mostly straight, males, with the interests and activities of White, middle- and upper-class able-bodied, and mostly straight, males foremost in their mind (Coutras 1987, 1996, 2003, Greed 1994, Kanes Weisman 1994). However, this limited, normative idea of the city manager, in addition to the normative idea of the citizen, are being increasingly challenged by the implementation of "gender mainstreaming"[1] as well as improved "participative democracy" (Humain-Lamoure 2010, Gardesse 2011, 2014). In this context it seems important to consider what forms of difference are being taken into account in the rethinking of urban planning, transportation, housing policies, and city management. It is equally important to show what other forms of difference remain "below the radar", unacknowledged, misrecognized, and may even suffer greater exclusion as a result of this rethinking.

The issues we address, on the basis of current developments in France, are the following: how to reinscribe spatial justice in cities, in the context of a country in which "difference" still has a problematic status? To what extent does universalism still dictate a normative view of belonging and citizenship? How to acknowledge difference in a way that does not define some publics and some neighbourhoods as "specific", "vulnerable", or in need of help, and others as "undesirable", "problematic" and in need of policing? How to carry out gender mainstreaming in urban planning in ways that neither stereotype women (as sexual prey, victims of violence, or mothers and carers) and essentialize gender roles, nor construct undesirable publics and problem areas? In other words, how to construct a "gendered right to the city" (Fenster 2005) that does not overrule other rights to the city? Is there a way of dealing, through space, with conflicting and overlapping logics of discrimination and exclusion, and in what ways can more inclusive cities be designed?

We aim to cast some light on the relative absence of France from debates about gender and planning, as well as on the quite specific ways in which these are being reinterpreted in the French context, and applied in two of the larger metropolitan areas.

Inclusiveness without the Acknowledgement of Difference

Neither the literature on the "just city" (Marcuse 2009, Fainstein 2010, Soja 2010), nor the growing literature on "fair-shared cities" (Sanchez de Madariaga & Roberts 2013), address the French case. In fact, it is as if France were a "blind spot" for both literatures, with few exceptions, for reasons which we argue are all but coincidental. The difficulty of including French cities in such discussions is inherently linked to specificities of French political discourse and values, and the way these translate into urban policy. Put simply, there exists a typically French universalistic belief that, if difference is ignored, discriminations will simply go away (see Amiraux & Simon 2006, Palomares 2013). This entails a collective refusal to acknowledge certain approaches to inequalities, particularly those perceived as imports from the United States and Great Britain.

French specificity owes a lot to the fact that the unbridled "neoliberal" forces at play in other countries and cities may be less important in accounting for ongoing urban changes than an encompassing (French) "Republican" ideal. Republican principles do not allow for the recognition of communities or forms of difference between citizens: the first article of the French Constitution states that the Republic "shall ensure the equality of all citizens before the law, without distinction of origin, race or religion". Accordingly, the State does not permit the production of any disaggregated statistical data by racial group or religious affiliation, leaving little scope to target differentiated groups of the population, in particular the ones facing racism. However, because women are, unlike other discriminated groups in France, actually counted, and therefore visible in statistics, their claims are more difficult to dismiss as unsightly "communitarian" claims, their under-representation in the spheres of power and decision-making being easy to document and argue (Sénac 2012). This accounts for the fact that the first and arguably only political measures analogous to "affirmative action" were taken with a year 2000 law to ensure better representation of women in elected positions.[2] This takes place in a national context about which a 2015 report to the European Parliament underlined "the lack of political will from the government, the lack of training for officials in the public administration and the reluctance of social actors and social partners to embrace the gender equality agenda" (Lépinard & Lieber 2015, p. 8). While quota schemes have ensured a gradual improvement of the proportion of women elected to municipal councils (over 40%), only 16% of French mayors are women.

This Republican model does not mean that neoliberalism is irrelevant to the understanding of urban change in France. Rather, it means that models framed and tested on Anglophone countries cannot be smoothly transferred to the French case. The ways in which national contexts, institutions, policymakers, and academics reinterpret and appropriate injunctions from international and European institutions suggests the need for sustained exploration. The French context has tended to claim its "cultural exception" as a bulwark against all things global, conflated with Anglo dominance and with unchallenged neoliberal drives. There has therefore been much soul-searching over how one can make certain approaches, like gender mainstreaming, compatible with French culture and practices, because the status quo is not perceived as problematic, but actually as praiseworthy and brave resistance to "political correctness".

In addition, there exists in France a form of "virtuous racism" (Guénif-Souilamas 2004b) from which even feminist movements are not immune. There is a widespread belief that Muslim women are the primary victims of sexism and misogyny in France as well as internationally (see Scharff 2011 for a discussion of Britain and Germany). In France, the movement *Ni Putes Ni Soumises* ("Neither Whores nor Submissives") was created in 2003 as a grassroots organisation in deprived neighbourhoods and protested violence against women. It was subsequently embraced and co-opted by mainstream political parties (Guénif-Souilamas 2004a). It contributed to a specific view of the geography of sexism and gender violence, as primarily found in the poorer neighbourhoods with high proportions of immigrant and/or Muslim populations (see Hancock 2008). Many unresolved postcolonial tensions underlie social issues: minority rights, the framing of Muslims as second-class citizens and a "threat" to national identity, and questions of gender, in particular the "protection of brown women from brown men", play a major part in these tensions (Hancock 2011a).

On January 20, 2015 in the aftermath of the journalist killings which shocked France on January 7, 8 and 9, French Prime Minister Manuel Valls pronounced a discourse about the "territorial, social and ethnic apartheid" he or some of his advisors had suddenly become aware of. He also mentioned the words "relegation" and "ghetto" and went on to underline the "daily discriminations (encountered by those who) do not have the right name, the right skin colour, or are women". Suddenly turning one's concern to "protecting women" after a terrorist attack is by no means unprecedented, as Susan Faludi brilliantly demonstrated in her analysis of the highly gendered narrative of heroes and victims that spread in the US after September 11, 2001 (Faludi 2007). Indeed, the protection of women (children, and/or families, "widows and orphans") is one of the tropes that pop up in "securitarian" discourse with great regularity. In France however, it is deeply steeped in a postcolonial culture, and all about designating "enemies", whether external or internal. It also sits rather uncomfortably with the indictment of forms of racial or ethnic discrimination which Valls performed in the same speech, as we shall see.

Territorializing Equality policies, Ensuring Safety?

The "territorializing" of equality policies in France, and the ways in which it resonates with Lefebvre's historical reflections on "the right to the city", have been discussed elsewhere (Hancock 2017, Blanchard et al. 2017). This section will address the way in which urban policies and policies for the equality of women and men have begun to overlap in the French context.

There was, in the past decade, a trend for making women of Maghrebi origin responsible for the Politique de la Ville (urban policy, targeted specifically on "problem" neighbourhoods) in French governments. Starting in 2007 with former leader of *Ni Putes Ni Soumises* Fadela Amara, in the right-wing Fillon government, this continued in 2014 with Najat Vallaud-Belkacem briefly taking on the ministry of Cities alongside the ministry of Rights of Women, only to be succeeded by Myriam El-Khomri later in the year. While there have been discussions of the reasons why non-White personalities who became part of French governments are much more likely to be women than men (Sénac 2012), the nomination of women in that particular capacity seems profoundly meaningful.[3]

The conflation of urban and gender issues became most obvious in 2014, the year the High Council for the Equality between women and men[4] published a report calling for the "territorialization" of gender-equality policies, with emphasis on remote rural areas and areas targeted by the Politique de la Ville.[5] While rightly pointing out that locally dependent groups such as carers and single mothers are disproportionately suffering from inadequate provision of public services and transportation in parts of the country, the report also presumed an overlap of gender and territorial inequalities significant enough to deal with both simultaneously.

The 2014 reboot of the Politique de la Ville added "territorial discriminations" (based on place of residence) as one of the legally prohibited forms of discrimination

(Hancock et al. 2016). The body responsible for urban policy merged with the one handling regional development and attractivity policies[6] and with the National Agency for Social Cohesion and Equal Opportunities,[7] in a single "Commissariat Général à l'Egalité des Territoires" (CGET).[8] "Equality of territories" was therefore seen as the overarching objective, or means, to ensure equality not only between neighbourhoods, but also between people. The CGET headed the renewal of the "Contrats de ville", the documents establishing the projects and objectives which the State funds for the 2014–2020 period in deprived neighbourhoods (the Quartiers Politique de la Ville, QPV, with substantially revised perimeters). It made available on its website four methodological guides to help local authorities navigate four "transversal priorities": citizen involvement ("conseils citoyens"), youth, anti-discrimination measures and "equality between women and men".[9]

Meanwhile, calls were increasingly being heard, from both academics and activists, to adopt new perspectives with respect to deprived neighbourhoods. They emphasizes the "pouvoir d'agir" (agency) of their inhabitants, with references to "empowerment" that both resonate with feminist theory and take specific overtones in a country in which "the top-down tradition" (Fainstein 2010, p. 65) has gone virtually unchallenged in urban planning and city management. This touches on the way expertise on urban issues is constructed in France, with little recognition of the knowledge of inhabitants, considered as illegitimate and unqualified to take part in decision-making (Bacqué et al. 2010, Carrel 2013, Bacqué & Biewener 2013, Bacqué & Mechmache 2013). Of course, this is not the case in France only (Listerborn 2007, Deboulet & Nez 2013). The context, therefore, particularly in deprived neighbourhoods where inhabitants have limited means to organize and weigh on policymaking, is not just of an under-representation of women in planning processes, but of an under-representation of all segments of the population.

In France, the concern for the "empowerment" of women seems to be enlisted systematically on the side of those arguing for further control and security measures in deprived neighbourhoods. Listerborn (2016) considered several cities in Sweden and Canada to warn of the effects of depoliticizing the issue of women's safety. First raised by grassroots feminist groups, the issue was subsequently diverted as part of city marketing techniques. Foregrounding the eradication of fear through urban design, she argues, became a way of avoiding discussion of gendered power relations. In particular, it obscured what studies throughout the world tend to show, which is that home settings are far more dangerous for women than public space, since they are where most violence against women and sexual assaults take place. Listerborn also emphasizes that it is systematically the experiences of fear of some types of women which are taken into account and considered as valid, with racialized, working-class women receiving less consideration. Marylène Lieber (2016) reaches similar conclusions in her investigation of who complains of street harassment, and insists on the necessity of an intersectional approach.

Listerborn goes on to show how the focus on "safety" tended, in the first decade of the 21st century, to divert funding from associations and agencies assisting women to policies of "crime prevention through environmental design", in particular in North America where "terrorist threats" became the major concern (on the ways in which "terrorism" is constructed to obscure major forms of threat and gendered violence, see Pain 2014). Furthermore, "safety" became a major selling point for new housing targeted at middle and upper-class people (Listerborn 2016). Thus the concern for "women's safety" became a commodity and a forerunner of gentrification of some central city areas. This is how feminist claims can be co-opted by property developers and planners to disguise exclusionary projects, which tend to displace the "undesirable" (Froment-Meurice 2016), as "inclusive". In France, these policies take place alongside drives to make deprived neighborhoods more "mixed", as part of objectives of "mixité sociale" that have been shown to have perverse effects (see Kirszbaum 2013, Kipfer 2016).

Gender on Municipalities' Agenda

Against this backdrop, some French cities have been working in the last decade on the implementation of United Nations (UN) and European Union (EU) directives on gender mainstreaming in urban planning (Loup 2006). Some of the earliest attempts to bring gender equality to bear on planning took place in 2001 in Paris, with two districts (arrondissements) linking a security-oriented approach of public spaces to the elimination of violence against women (Lieber 2002). A few safety audits took place, one of them especially targeting women, because it was organized by the elected official in charge of gender equality. But nothing came out of this experience because technical staff was not involved in the audits. The different services of the municipality were not on the same page at all, and the people in charge were derided and criticized for their activist stance. When the claims came from the grassroots, they were not heard, and when they came from the top, they had to appear more gender-neutral, in order to gain credibility. In one of the districts, the head of the police department went so far as to write to the Mayor in order to state that those audits would not be taken into account as serious diagnostic tools for public space security.

If planning programs aimed at women can have empowering effects on many levels, there are also plenty of threats and perverse effects that can follow. The actors trying to implement a gender approach often face a lot of obstacles, in particular in administrative public services. The setting of such approaches needs several joint elements, like strong political and popular support, and key actors within the professional system, discussing the methods and results with the targeted public, instead of imposing them from the top (Biarrotte 2012). Actors have to work with inhabitants and local associations, but they also need to convince other professionals (especially the ones in technical services, like infrastructures and urban planning department) of the need to implement non-discriminatory approaches. This calls for both specific and integrated approaches, including training and advocacy to explain and convince. But this work cannot be done without support from the upper administrative hierarchy, the elected councillors, and a real budget.

If similar experiences took place in other French cities, no major official program was implemented in France until recently. Some research projects started to give more visibility to the articulations of gender issues and city management, noticeably in Bordeaux (A-Urba & ADES-CNRS 2011), Lyons (GRePS & Vinet 2013), and today with research-action projects in Greater Paris. One can refer for instance, to "La ville côté femmes" in Gennevilliers, a former industrial "banlieue" west of Paris (urbaines.hypotheses.org). Advocacy from personalities and feminist groups like the associations Genre et ville (Gender and the city), or the collective Stop Harcèlement de Rue (Stop Street Harassment), and the consultancy firm Maturescence, also brought the question into local public debate. The municipality of Paris, under newly elected Mayor Anne Hidalgo, stated its intention to catch up and set the pace:[10] an ambitious 8-point plan was laid out in March 2015, including a point providing for "international leadership", and one about the necessary "reconquering of public space" on behalf of women[11] (www.paris.fr/actualites/l-egalite-femmes-hommes-un-enjeu-de-cohesion-sociale-2066). Partly as a result of this impetus, Paris acquired its first guidelines for "gender and public space" in October 2016 in a guide inspired by handbooks produced in Vienna, Berlin and Barcelona, aimed at "urbanists, planners and people in charge of public space".[12]

While research projects in France have generally dealt with large cities (Bordeaux, Grenoble, Lyons, Rennes and others), the concern of municipalities and of the French government tends to focus on the deprived areas targeted by the Politique de la Ville. Both academics such as Elise Vinet, who works closely with the municipality in Lyons, and freelance researchers such as Chris Blache who jointly heads the collective Genre et ville, have voiced to us their discomfort with being repeatedly asked to investigate those areas, without being given the means to conduct comparative research in less deprived areas, where they suspect gender issues are no less likely to arise. Employees of the municipality of Aubervilliers, who work in a department in charge of gender issues and anti-discrimination policies, confessed their annoyance to us in an interview (June 2015): they were repeatedly asked about the "specific" type of problems they encountered in one of the municipalities of Parisian "banlieue" with the highest proportion of foreign-born inhabitants.

The way French cities are currently implementing actions is somewhat disconnected from the approaches that have been tested in other countries. Most striking is the way the initiative seems to come from central government, which is making money available through the General Commission for Territorial Equality (CGET). Since 2012 one of the major elements of this implementation are incentives to organize "marches exploratoires de femmes" (women's audit walks), involving women from deprived neighbourhoods in walks during which they assess the urban environment, point out problematic aspects of their local areas and suggest improvements. Though these may sound analogous to "take back the night" explorations organized by feminists in other countries and/or other times, this policy implemented to engage women in urban planning is actually inspired by a Montréal municipal program. This phenomenon is due both to the proximity that French language permits and to a certain conception of citizenship that makes Québec culturally closer than the United States, permitting a smoother transfer of ideas and public policy models (Biarrotte 2012, 2014).

Nevertheless, the way women's audits are implemented in France underlines many of the problems caused by the adaptation of foreign policy models to new cultural and political contexts. Montréal has been a city of pioneering experimentation for including women in urban planning decisions, in order to empower them on every level of decision-making, from the political to the civic, including the professional level. The program called "Femmes et Ville" was developed over almost a decade, with multiple partnerships and a strong bottom-up dynamic. This led to the collective creation of methodologies like women urban audits, and to the publication of evaluation and professional guides (Michaud et al. 1993, Paquin & Michaud 2002). The comparison of those guides with the one published by the French government (Secrétariat Général du Comité Interministériel des Villes 2012) demonstrates a direct filiation. But unlike what happened in Montréal in the 1990s, tools are reused in France in a "top-down" manner, trying to impose priorities dictated by professionals, with no real adaptation to the actual claims. Moreover, in the French context the guide is used as an end in itself, and not necessarily linked to a wider program questioning women's under-representation in public space. It is also a top-down attempt to insert gender issues into the political agenda, even if it claims to answer the legitimate expectations of women living in those areas (Secrétariat Général du Comité Interministériel des Villes 2012, p. 4), in contrast to the Canadian context where all the work had been done from a bottom-up perspective. When programs are implemented in such a way, other risks can appear, like the reinforcement of stereotypes about women, but also about certain types of populations, especially when only deprived areas are targeted.

However, merely involving women in highly controlled experiments is clearly insufficient to actually implement a gender-sensitive approach. Reports from the organizers of "marches exploratoires" in the urban area of Saint-Etienne[13] point to the fact that some women who took part arrived with notes handwritten by their husbands who did not want to miss the opportunity to express a grievance or request a change. While this could be interpreted as a means of muscling one's way back into a space of expression designed for women, it actually also points to the fact that some men might legitimately feel that their views are also insufficiently taken into account.

Women as "Experts of the Local"?

Earlier research has shown that while municipalities may be asking for data on discrimination or self-censorship on the basis of gender, research participants may want to discuss other forms of discrimination they encounter on the basis of race, origin, religion or class (Bouamama et al. 2013, GRePS & Vinet 2013). Where local governments are rightly concerned with sexist or homophobic violence and forms of interpersonal violence, inhabitants may also want to point out other forms, like institutional or systemic violence of which city authorities may be unaware because they unwittingly participate in them (for instance in processes of consultation). There is evidence, from the case of the "Femmes et Ville" programme conducted in Montréal, that foregrounding women's issues and demands in urban planning quite often means foregrounding white, middle-class, straight women's priorities, with consequences in terms of the gentrification of some urban areas, and the eviction of other publics deemed undesirable (like sex workers). A similar process has been described in the Netherlands as "genderfication" (Van den Berg 2012, Van den Berg & Chevalier 2017), with the foregrounding of the interests of "families" and/or "children" being used as arguments to rule out or displace uses of public space deemed incompatible with family life. The women most empowered by such policies seem to be those with the highest social and cultural capital to begin with, while non-white women, lesbians, women with less conventional lifestyles, working-class women, benefit less and remain peripheral to the decision-making process.

When such women are explicitly invited to take part in the process of defining difficulties and shaping policy responses, they are designated as experts on their own local neighbourhood only, and rarely asked to formulate claims or demands on a wider level. It is as though their legitimacy and citizenship were of a purely local scale, not likely to exert itself at a city-wide level. There is a striking resemblance between these occurrences and what has been criticized in NGOs' and international organizations' foregrounding of women or gender issues in development policies in the Global South (Bertrand 2011). These policies assign women a merely "local" role and deny them claims and participation at other decision-making levels. There are distinct echoes of this in the official handbook on "marches exploratoires", which are described as "a walking diagnostic tool to draw on women's expertise as users"—though there is no discussion of the reason why women are "expert users", but not men. This resonates with Coutras's criticism of the "grands ensembles", or post-war massive new urban developments (many of which are now part of the areas targeted by the Politique de la Ville). They granted women a role as "guardians of the local", with specific duties with respect to their neighbourhoods. This was in keeping with 1950s' notions of gender roles, but bound to lead to "urban crisis" as women increasingly took on work outside the home, just as men were massively losing their jobs (Coutras 1987, 1996). While research has consistently addressed the women of the "grands ensembles'" "feelings" or "emotions" (Huguet 1965, Kaminski 1978), the idea that they might actually hold opinions and become agents of city-making has only recently come under consideration.

The geographical assignation of gender issues to "banlieue" neighbourhoods, in France, has been one of the mechanisms whereby French society as a whole has allowed itself to remain in denial about sexism, misogyny, violence against women and sexual minorities, being rife throughout French society and French cities. The "urban crisis" ("crise urbaine") diagnosed by Coutras (1996) has been increasingly seen as a crisis in gender relations, but strictly located in "problem" areas characterized (though that aspect was conspicuously absent from Coutras' analysis) by high proportions of immigrant inhabitants. In other words, the current orientations of this policy imply that gender issues in public space take place, or have their place, only or mostly in deprived neighbourhoods targeted by the Politique de la Ville. This resonates with a European-wide tendency to see sexism and misogyny as "located" in such neighbourhoods, and the preserve of "brown men" of immigrant origin, and which needs further critical examination.

There is therefore a risk of stigmatization of other publics, like young men of immigrant origin, or of the instrumentalization of some women against other types of public, considered as undesirable in public spaces, like sex workers,[14] who might also be women, but not be considered as entitled to an opinion. The way marches are organized in France has not always steered clear of the danger of the stigmatization of both other types of users of public space (irresponsible drivers, uncivil youths, drug dealers, etc.), and of specific neighbourhoods. In some cases, participating women are asked to publicly confirm what the national or local authorities already presumed, that their neighbourhoods are hotbeds of crime, anti-social behaviour, out-of-control youths, and dysfunctional families, with the foregrounding of "security" as a theme to such marches in many ways predetermining the findings. This takes place in a context in which repeated attempts have taken place to enlist women of these neighbourhoods *against* the men of the very same neighbourhoods—their fathers, sons, nephews, brothers, or cousins—and frame their resistance to these attempts as alienation and inability to escape their "culture" (Manier 2013). Nor can one argue that there are no specifically gendered issues affecting men in these neighbourhoods, when they have disproportionate trouble finding employment, when they are primary targets of arbitrary "stop-and-search" on the part of the police, and experience incarceration at extremely high rates (concerns voiced by the women of Le Blanc-Mesnil). It therefore seems urgent to rethink many of these policies in a more intersectional perspective, by taking into account how race and class in particular intersect gender. This does not weaken or dilute gender policies, it actually seems to be the only way to make them widely acceptable and therefore sustainable. This is particularly true in contexts such as France where concern for "women's safety" is often feigned in the most nationalist and Islamophobic movements to justify repression and exclusion of Muslim and/or racialized citizens (Hancock 2017). This is consistent with a French tendency to pit minorities against one another, for instance by depicting anti-racism as inconsistent with anti-sexism. Intersectionality therefore appears as a particularly daunting challenge in a French context in which minorities have often been considered as in competition with each other, rather than having converging interests in questioning the status quo (Fassin & Fassin 2006, Delphy 2008).

Conclusion

While the previous French government seemed determined to push gender issues to the foreground, it did not escape a tendency to use them against minorities. There is still a tendency in France to consider gender equality as a distraction, if not a decoy, from the major social issues of inequality and class struggle. To wit, on the left, "societal" changes (such as the right to wed for gay couples) are opposed to real "social" change. There is the sense that left-wing credentials are easily bought by pandering to "special interests" groups such as the LGBTIQ and women's rights groups. This reflects a failure to understand the extent to which being part of a "minority" does not preclude being working-class, or poor—and a misrecognition of the extent to which it exposes to specific violence, not only in public space, but also on the job or housing market, as well as in the home. Systemic violence, inflicted by institutions and governments, is a no less significant aspect of oppression than interpersonal aggressions (Young 1990).

Thinking in terms of "spatial justice" may help resolve these tensions, we suggest, if "spatial justice" is taken to refer to the accessibility to all of urban space, urban environments of comparable quality, and participation in decision-making processes (Hancock 2011b)—and not to an equalizing of territorial development as it often is, mistakenly, in the French context. This requires accepting the idea that groups of people suffer discriminations, rather than "territories", and that this cannot be effectively dealt with through area-based measures. Recognition of minorities, as theorized by Nancy Fraser (2000), seems to be a crucial missing element to this understanding of spatial and social justice. What is needed is a recognition of women and people of immigrant origin as "full partners in social interaction", entitled to "participatory parity", not as minorities to be protected or civilized. What is most striking in the steps being taken towards gender planning in French cities is that they once again take place as dispensations from above, with all the fragility that comes from such measures, likely to be reversed when governments change. There is a failure to build such policies in bottom-up manners, relying on citizens' input and participation, which appears to reduce women and other discriminated groups to the role of onlookers rather than fully fledged actors in the making of cities.

Notes

1 See for example the documents by the European Union and Commission: *Mainstreaming Gender into the Policies and the Programmes of the Institutions of the European Union and EU Member States* (2013) and *Manual for Gender Mainstreaming* (2008).

2 See the law on parity in politics: Loi n° 2000–493 du 6 juin 2000 tendant à favoriser l'égal accès des femmes et des hommes aux mandats électoraux et fonctions électives.
3 With the recent political change and Philippe government, both women's rights and Politique de la Ville have been deprived of Ministries and massively defunded.
4 Haut Conseil à l'Egalité entre les femmes et les hommes, also known as HCE.
5 Sabathier, R., 2014. *Combattre maintenant les inégalités sexuées, sociales et territoriales dans les quartiers de la politique de la ville et les territoires ruraux fragilisés. Rapport du groupe de travail EGAliTER*, Rapport EGAliTER. HCEFH.
6 Délégation à l'Aménagement du Territoire et à l'Attractivité Territoriale, also known as DATAR.
7 Agence nationale pour la Cohésion Sociale et l'Egalité des Chances, also known as ACSé, active in areas such as integration and anti-discrimination.
8 General Commission for Territorial Equality.
9 Ministère de la Cohésion des Territoires, n.d. "Élaborer son contrat de ville, Cadres de référence" URL www.ville.gouv.fr/?elaborer-son-contrat-de-ville. Accessed on June 29, 2017.
10 Full disclosure: both authors of this chapter are part of a group funded by a Parisian programme, Paris 2030, to carry out exploratory research on gender issues, from quantitative perspectives (as municipal statistics are rarely made available in gender-disaggregated forms) as well as qualitative ones (policy analysis and more ethnographic research using visual methods). The final report of this two-year project entitled "Le Pari(s) du genre" will be available on the website parisdugenre.fr alongside a webdoc under construction in 2017–2018.
11 Mairie de Paris, (2016) L'égalité femmes/hommes: un enjeu de cohésion sociale URL: www.paris.fr/actualites/l-egalite-femmes-hommes-un-enjeu-de-cohesion-sociale-2066 (accessed on June 29, 2017).
12 This guide can be found here www.paris.fr/actualites/la-ville-de-paris-devoile-le-premier-guide-referentiel-sur-le-genre-l-espace-public-4138.
13 Presentation given as part of a workshop on gender and planning at the University of Lyons, May 16, 2015.
14 One of the 8 points of Anne Hidalgo's March 2015 Plan for equality, for instance, is the "struggle against the prostitutional phenomenon", in conformity with the French Socialist party's abolitionist stance.

References

Amiraux, V. & Simon, P. (2006). "There are no minorities here: Cultures of scholarship and public debate on immigrants and integration in France", *International Journal of Comparative Sociology*, 47:3–4, 191–215.

A-Urba & ADES-CNRS. (2011). *Usage de la ville par le genre*, Bordeaux, France, Agence d'Urbanisme de Bordeaux.

Bacqué, M.-H. & Biewener, C. (2013). *L'empowerment, une pratique émancipatrice*, Paris, La Découverte.

Bacqué, M.-H. & Mechmache, M. (2013). "Le pouvoir d'agir. Pour une réforme radicale de la Politique de la Ville", rapport au ministre délégué chargé de la Ville, juillet.

Bacqué, M.-H., Sintomer, Y., Flamand, A., & Nez, H. (eds.) (2010). *La démocratie participative inachevée.* Paris, Adels, Yves Michel.

Bertrand, M. (2011). "Quand femme rime avec local: Logique de promotion ou nouveau confinement dans les villes africaines", *Justice Spatiale/Spatial Justice* 3, www.jssj.org/article/quand-femme-rime-avec-local-logique-de-promotion-ou-nouveau-confinement-dans-les-villes-africaines/

Biarrotte, L. (2012). « *Femmes et ville* » *à Montréal. Un programme municipal genré et ses conséquences urbaines* (Mémoire de Master 1), Paris, 1 Panthéon-Sorbonne.

Biarrotte, L. (2014). *La ville en rose? Genre et féminisme en aménagement : conséquences théoriques
et pratiques* (Mémoire de Master 2), Paris, 1 Panthéon-Sorbonne.

Blanchard, S., Chapuis, A., & Hancock, C. (2017). "*Banlieusard.e.s* claiming a right to the
city of light: Gendered violence and spatial politics in Paris", *Cities*, online,
doi:10.1016/j.cities.2017.03.007.

Bouamama, S. et Collectif de Femmes du Blanc-Mesnil. (2013). *Femmes des quartiers populaires. En résistance contre les discriminations*, Paris, Le Temps des Cerises.

Carrel, M. (2013). *Faire participer les habitants? Citoyenneté et pouvoir d'agir dans les quartiers
populaires*, Lyon, ENS éditions.

Coutras, J. (1987). *Des villes traditionnelles aux nouvelles banlieues. L'espace public au féminin*,
Paris, SEDES.

Coutras, J. (1996). *Crise urbaine et espaces sexués*, Paris, Armand Colin.

Coutras, J. (2003). *Les peurs urbaines et l'autre sexe*, Paris, L'Harmattan.

Deboulet, A. & Nez, H. (2013). *Savoirs citoyens et démocratie urbaine*, Rennes, Presses Universitaires de Rennes.

Delphy, C. (2008). *Classer, dominer: qui sont les Autres?* Paris, La Fabrique.

Fainstein, S. (2010). *The Just City*, Ithaca, Cornell University Press.

Fainstein, S. & Servon, L. (2005). *Gender and Planning: A Reader*, New Brunswick, Rutgers
University Press.

Faludi, S. (2007). *The Terror Dream: Myth and Misogyny in an Insecure America*, New York,
Metropolitan Books.

Fassin, D. & Fassin, E. (2006). *De la question sociale à la question raciale*, Paris, La Découverte.

Fenster, T. (2005). "The right to the gendered city: Different formations of belonging in
everyday life", *Journal of Gender Studies*, 14:3, 217–231.

Fraser, N. (2000) "Rethinking recognition", *New Left Review*, 3, May–June, 107–120.

Froment-Meurice, M. (2016). *Produire et réguler les espaces publics contemporains. Les politiques
de gestion de l'indésirabilité à Paris*, doctoral dissertation, Université Paris-Est and Université de Genève.

Gardesse, C. (2011). *La concertation citoyenne pour le projet de réaménagement des Halles de Paris,
2002–2010. Les formes de démocratisation de l'action publique en urbanisme et ses obstacles*,
doctoral dissertation, Institut d'Urbanisme de Paris.

Gardesse, C. (2014). "The fraught 'ménage à trois' comprising public actors, private players
and inhabitants involved in the urban production process: Why it is hard to deploy participative arrangements in French urban development projects", *Urban Studies*.
doi:10.1177/0042098014555631.

Gilbert, P. (2011). 'Ghetto', 'relégation', 'effets de quartier'. Critique d'une représentation
des cités", *Métropolitiques*, 9 February, www.metropolitiques.eu/Ghetto-relegation-
effets-de.html

Greed, C. (1994). *Women and Planning: Creating Gendered Realities*, London and New York,
Routledge.

GRePS & Vinet, E. (2013). *Etude-action sur les discriminations multifactorielles envers les femmes dans
trois quartiers prioritaires lyonnais. Non/-recours aux offres socio-éducatives et de loisir, place dans
l'espace public et ethnicisation des rapports sociaux (de sexe)*, Groupe de recherche en psychologie
sociale. Université Lumière Lyon 2; Ville de Lyon; Région Rhône-Alpes, Lyon, France.

Guénif-Souilamas, N. (2004a). "Ni pute, ni soumise ou très pute, très voilée: Laïcité d'en
haut, féminisme d'en bas", 81–88 in C. Nordmann (ed.), *Le foulard islamique en questions*,
Paris: Amsterdam.

Guénif-Souilamas, N. (2004b). "La Française voilée, la beurette, le garçon arabe et le musulman laïc. Les figures assignées du racisme vertueux", 109–132 in N. Guénif-Souilamas (ed.), *La République mise à nu par son immigration*, Paris, La Fabrique.

Hancock, C. (2008). "Spatialities of the secular: Geographies of the veil in France and Turkey", *European Journal of Women's Studies*, 15:3, 165–179.

Hancock, C. (2011a). "Le corps féminin, enjeu géopolitique dans la France postcoloniale", *L'Espace politique*, n°14, http://espacepolitique.revues.org/index1882.html

Hancock, C. (2011b). "Genre, identités sexuelles et justice spatiale", *Justice Spatiale/Spatial Justice*, 3, www.jssj.org/archives/03

Hancock, C. (2015). "The republic is lived with an uncovered face—And a skirt: (Un) dressing French citizens", *Gender, Place and Culture*, 22:7, 1023–1040. doi:10.1080/0966369X.2014.958061.

Hancock, C. (2017). "Feminism from the margin: Challenging the Paris/*banlieue* divide", *Antipode*, 49:3, 636–656.

Hancock, C., Lelévrier, C., Ripoll, F., & Weber, S. (eds.) (2016). *Discriminations territoriales, entre interpellation politique et sentiment d'injustice des habitants*. Editions l'Œil d'Or, collection Critique et cité.

Haut Conseil à l'Egalité entre les femmes et les hommes. (2014). "Combattre maintenant les inégalités sexuées, sociales, territoriales dans les quartiers politique de la ville et les territoires ruraux fragilisés", Report published on June 19, 2014.

Haut Conseil à l'Egalité entre les femmes et les hommes. (2015). "Avis sur le harcèlement sexiste et les violences sexuelles dans les transports en commun", Report published on April 16, 2015.

Huguet, M. (1965). "Les femmes dans les grands ensembles. Approche psychologique de cas d'agrément et d'intolérance", *Revue Française de Sociologie*, 6:2, 215–227.

Humain-Lamoure, A.-L. (2010). *Faire une démocratie de quartiers?* Paris, Bordeaux, éditions Les Bords de l'Eau.

Huning, S. (2013). "Ambivalences of gender planning", *Métropolitiques*, www.metropolitiques.eu/Ambivalences-of-Gender-Planning.html

Kaminski, P. (1978). "Les femmes dans les grands ensembles", *Economie et statistique*, 96, 71–77.

Kanes Weisman, L. (1994). *Discrimination by Design: A Feminist Critique of the Man-Made Environment*, Urbana and Chicago, University of Illinois Press.

Kipfer, S. (2016). « Neocolonial urbanism? La rénovation urbaine in Paris », *Antipode*, 48:3, 603–625.

Kirszbaum, T. (2013). «La rénovation urbaine comme politique de peuplement », *Métropoles* [En ligne], 13, mis en ligne le 01 décembre 2013. URL: http://metropoles.revues.org/4769

Lépinard, E. & Lieber, M. (2015) The Policy on Gender Equality in France, report to the European Parliament's Directorate General for Internal Policy, FEMM Committee.

Lieber, M., (2002) "Les marches exploratoires à Paris", in *Table ronde: Les marches exploratoires, et après?* Presented at the 1er Séminaire international sur la sécurité des femmes—Tisser les liens, Montréal, Québec, Canada.

Lieber, M. (2016). "Qui dénonce le harcèlement de rue? Un essai intersectionnel de géographie morale", in E. Lépinard, M. Roca & F. Fassa (eds.), *Les usages de l'intersectionnalité*, Paris, Presses Universitares de France.

Listerborn, C. (2007). "Who speaks? And who listens? The relationship between planners and women's participation in local planning in a multi-cultural urban environment", *GeoJournal*, 70, 61–74.

Listerborn, C. (2016). "Feminist struggle over urban safety and the politics of space", *European Journal of Women's Studies*, 23:3, 251–264. doi:10.1177/1350506815616409.

Loup, M. (2006). *Prendre en compte le genre dans la révision du SDRIF : Lutter contre les inégalités entre les femmes et les hommes dans l'aménagement du territoire*, Paris: Région Ile-de-France.

Manier, M. (2013). "Cause des femmes *vs* cause des minorités: Tensions autour de la question des "femmes de l'immigration" dans l'action publique française", *Revue Européenne des Migrations Internationales*, 29:4, 89–110.

Marcuse, P. (ed.) (2009). *Searching for the Just City: Debates in Urban Theory and Practice*, London, Routledge.

Michaud, A., Lahaise, M.-D., & Hénault, M. (1993). *Guide d'enquête sur la sécurité des femmes en ville*, Montréal, Ville de Montréal, Service des loisirs, des parcs et du développement communautaire, Module du développement communautaire.

Pain, R. (2014). "Everyday terrorism. Connecting domestic violence and global terrorism", *Progress in Human Geography*, 38:4, 531–550.

Palomares, E. (2013). "Le racisme: Un hors-champ de la sociologie urbaine française?", *Métropolitiques*, 11 September, www.metropolitiques.eu/Le-racisme-un-hors-champ-de-la.html

Paquin, S. & Michaud, A. (2002). *Guide d'aménagement pour un environnement urbain sécuritaire*, Montréal, Ville de Montréal.

Sanchez de Madariaga, I. & Roberts, M. (2013). *Fair-shared Cities: The Impact of Gender Planning in Europe*, Farnham, Ashgate.

Scharff, C. (2011). "Disarticulating feminism: Individualization, neoliberalism and the othering of 'muslim women'", *European Journal of Women's Studies*, 18:2, 119–134.

Secrétariat général du Comité interministériel des villes. (2012). "Guide méthodologique des marches exploratoires. Des femmes s'engagent pour la sécurité de leur quartier", Cahiers pratiques Hors-Série.

Sénac, R. (2012). *L'invention de la diversité*, Paris, Presses Universitaires de France.

Soja, E. (2010). *Seeking Spatial Justice*, Minneapolis, University of Minnesota Press.

Van den Berg, M. (2012). "Femininity as city marketing strategy. Gender bending Rotterdam", *Urban Studies*, 49:1, 153–168.

Van den Berg, M. & Chevalier, D. (2017). "Of 'city lounges', 'bans on gathering' and macho policies—Gender, class and race in productions of space for Rotterdam's post-industrial future", *Cities*, online.

Young, I. M. (1990). *Justice and the Politics of Difference*, Princeton, Princeton University Press.

10

EVERYDAY LIFE EXPERIENCES OF AFGHAN IMMIGRANT WOMEN AS REPRESENTATION OF THEIR PLACE OF BELONGING IN AUCKLAND

Roja Tafaroji

Introduction

In the context of the genderSTE objectives,[1] this chapter offers the perspective of the 'outsider' in order to contribute to our understanding of changing societies and the role of newcomers. It highlights the challenges, opportunities, different insights, and experiences that newcomers offer.

Gender, race, and ethnicity have been found to be important constitutive categories of power relations in structuring inequality in societies (Gilbert 1997). Numbers of feminist scholars have studied the different experiences of women in cities (see Beebeejaun 2017, Chouinard and Grant 1995, Fenster 1999, Jarvis et al. 2009, Kail and Irschek 2008, Sanders 1990, Whitzman et al. 2013). They found that women's daily lives in cities are influenced and shaped by different layers of power relations of the dominant society. This then affects both their position in, and their relation to, their living place. The relationship between people and places, according to environmental psychologists like Proshansky and his colleagues (1983), contributes to the (re)identification process of people in their living places. Through the (re)identification process, therefore, women attain a sense of belonging to their living places.

The focus of this research is to identify and discuss the everyday life experiences of Afghan immigrant women based on their conceptions of places they use and experience in Auckland, being the main gate for immigrants in New Zealand (Auckland Council 2012). The chapter starts with a brief review of the existing literature on the historic position of immigrant women worldwide. Then it focuses on the everyday life experiences of eight Afghan immigrant women in Auckland. Drawing on empirical work carried out as part of a PhD research fieldwork study[2] conducted by the author of this chapter, the second section of the chapter explores the meaning of 'home' as the central place of the daily lives of Afghan women. This section continues with a discussion about the position of participants in the place through analysing different layers of identity interacting with their everyday life experiences in Auckland.

Women's Position in Their Daily Lives

The history of human life demonstrates that women have been excluded in terms of their access to power, knowledge and advantageous situations (Fenster 2005, Hillier 2002, McDowell 1983, 1992, McDowell and Court 1994, McDowell and Sharp 1997, Sandercock 1995,). Feminists would argue that women have been traditionally oppressed and obliged to take on traditional women's roles and responsibilities in the private sphere and have been excluded from public life. They have been expected to do the everyday tasks of cooking, laundry and childcare, and learn to navigate, or become functionally familiar with the (male-dominated) public sphere of the capitalist marketplace (Brooks 2007). As De Beauvoir (1972 [1949]) observed, women as a group have been socially defined as the 'other' while men constructed them as their own objects living in a man's world under the influence of their power. However, considering women as a homogenous group ignores the many differences within the group and universalises the various approaches. For instance, the tendencies of first-wave feminists to consider women and men as two groups with exactly the same subjectivities in society (Hekman 1999a, 1999b), and attempts by second-wave feminists to break down the 'gendered public-private split' (Wesselius 2000) show how different experiences of different men and women influenced by different power relations could be underestimated. Third-wave feminists, among them Sandra Harding and Uma Narayan, insist on approaching 'otherness' as cultural differences to draw attention to 'issues of language, class, racial, ethnic, sexual and gender differences' (Narayan and Harding 2000, p. 48). They explain the importance of recognising both sameness and difference between women. Accordingly, third-wave feminists, among them postmodernist feminists, started to focus on the different experiences of women in the constructed dominant society (Fraser and Nicholson 1989, Hooks 1984, Mann and Patterson 2016, Wesselius 2000).

Postmodern thinkers argue that the structures of every power relation in a society reproduce differences between people (Bauman 1992, 2005, Keith et al. 1993, Soja 1989, 1996). Historically, this has been done through separating people based on different layers of their identity including their race, ethnicity, and gender, among others. The competitive nature of power, particularly in dominant male-oriented cultures of the era of capitalism, brings about segregation within the labour market (Charles 2011). Patterns of the division of labour divide people's living and working places. This has led to the maintenance and perpetuation of patriarchal power and dominance in those societies through inclusion and exclusion of specific groups during decision-making processes (Hillier 2002).

International immigration also influences patterns of social inclusion and exclusion through modifying the process of (re)production of difference. The process of social division and social production of difference includes various types of differentiation, including gender, race, class and nation (Keith et al. 1993).

Hence, exclusion from public life is a common experience for many women; although not exclusive to their gender, it differs with respect to their class, race, ethnicity, and aspects of their everyday life experiences. In this regard, 'immigrant women' are subject to exclusion as a result of the intersection of their gender, race, ethnicity, religion, and culture.

Afghan Women as Subjects of Migration

Globally, women have played a major part in changing demographic immigration flows since the mid-1990s.[3] Afghan women make up almost half of the Afghan population in New Zealand and Auckland. This pattern is consistent with the proportion of the female and male population in total living in Auckland (Figure 10.1).

Afghan immigrants are one of the most sizeable groups of the Muslim population in New Zealand (see Table 10.1 for recent figures). This is a result of civil war, the Taliban regime and the war in Afghanistan following the 11 September 2001 attacks in the United States. A group of asylum seekers from

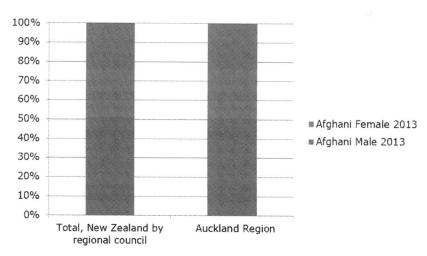

FIGURE 10.1 Population of Afghan women in comparison to Afghan men in Auckland and New Zealand, according to the 2013 Census

Source: Own elaboration after Statistics New Zealand (2013).

TABLE 10.1 Refugee quota Branch Arrival Statistics for
2014–2015 in New Zealand Auckland

Nationality	New Zealand	Auckland
Myanmar	2333	957
Iraq	684	415
Afghanistan	**650**	**221**
Palestine	149	146
Sri Lanka	230	112
Eritrea	196	103
DR of Congo	197	98
Burundi	79	62
Sudan	140	51
Ethiopia	86	40
Somalia	92	40

Source: Own elaboration after MBIE (2016).

Afghanistan who were fleeing from the Taliban were accepted by the New Zealand government after they were refused entry to Australian waters. This was in August 2001, when Prime Minister Helen Clark decided to settle Tampa[4] Afghan asylum seekers (Beaglehole 2013, Magee 2011).

In subsequent years, Afghan family members were relocated through the Refugee Quota Programme, and nearly one-third of them now live in Auckland (Gruner and Searle 2011, Magee 2011). Following 11 September 2001, the stories of Muslims from non-Western countries integrating as immigrants into Western countries changed markedly and have been affected by the mainstream media's reporting of national security and terrorism in Western European countries (Ahmad 2006, Lahav 2003). The following graph (Figure 10.2) demonstrates how the immigration pattern of Afghan refugees and asylum seekers as a considerable part of Muslim immigrants has changed since 2001, influenced by global events.

Afghan Immigrant Women: Subject to Exclusion

A study of the experiences of migrants and refugees in New Zealand (Strategic Social Policy Group 2008) suggests that women from specific backgrounds, including Afghanis, can be subject to exclusion as well as discrimination as a result of wanting to preserve their own culture, including how they appear in public (their dress, worn symbols and skin colour), how they communicate (talking their language) and interact with others, and how they practise their beliefs and religion. Accordingly, in the following section, I will examine aspects of the identity of Afghan women that play important roles in their resettlement process in Auckland.

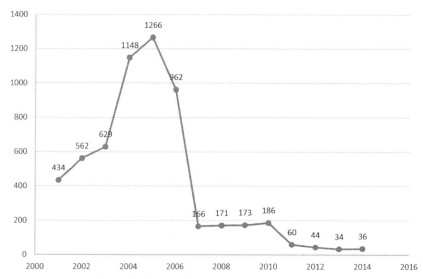

FIGURE 10.2 Number of Afghan refugees and asylum seekers by the year of arrival in New Zealand

Source: Own elaboration after UNHCR Statistical Online Population Database.

Research about the situation of Afghan women as immigrants in Western countries suggests that although they may change their socio-spatial settings, they still have a tendency to carry on their traditional roles and responsibilities in their families and communities (Bhanji 2011, Khan 2002, Lipson and Miller 1994, Rostami-Povey 2007a). Historically, this is a result of their life experiences under the influence of the patriarchal culture in Afghan families. These experiences have been aggravated by experiences of exile as a result of civil war in Afghanistan from 1992 to 1996, and when the Taliban[5] captured the capital city of Kabul in 1996 (Baker 2010, Bhanji 2011, Ghasemi 1998). Following a century of war, exile and (economic, social, and ideological) oppression, the majority of these women left their hometowns and country as a response to perceived and serious threats to their survival and to seek a 'better life'. On the other hand, they experience their daily lives in the context of Western countries where globalization is evident and (neo)liberal policies highly promote individualism and personal identity as well as independence in people's daily lives (Elliott and Lemert 2009, Woodward et al. 2008).

Afghan immigrant women (with a refugee background), like other citizens, are supposed to conform to the expectations that are constructed by the dominant norms and values of the host society. These expectations and responsibilities provide these women with different and sometimes contradictory situations in their new living places. Each category of these responsibilities takes place during the daily lives of Afghan women while they interact with their host society. Different socio-spatial interactions with different degrees of power and influence create and develop different situations of participation, assimilation, and isolation for newcomers in their host society (Faist 1999). Each of these situations illustrates levels of inclusion and exclusion of immigrants in their new living places. Hence, there is always potential for some Afghan immigrant women to manage the changes and (re)build their own places within their host society, while others become isolated either from their communities or from the host society. Accordingly, to explore the way Afghan women meet the expectations of both their ethnic culture and that of the host society, and also to interpret their level of integration, it is crucial to understand how they interact during their everyday life experiences in the city.

Everyday Life and Belonging to Place

Researchers who are interested in the subjective existence of people in their living places, acknowledge the importance of the everyday life experiences of people in developing a sense of place, belonging and identity in a city (Altman et al. 1980, Buttimer and Seamon 1980, Lefebvre and Levich 1987, Marcus 1992, Perkins and Thorns 2012, Rapoport 1976, Relph 1976, Tuan 1974). Everyday life experience, indeed, is conceptualised as the observable manifestation of social existence, the cyclical and rhythmic events over a variety of time periods and the ritualised and habitual engagement with others to participate in activities within a certain temporal duration in particular spaces (Sztompka 2008). In his distinguished book *The Practice of Everyday Life*, de Certeau (1988) considers everyday life as the ordinarily practised activities in the city, most importantly the activity of walking. Lefebvre (1996a, 1996b) focuses on everyday life as the opportunity for people to use and participate in decision-making processes as their right to the city. Inevitably, therefore, everyday life involves interactions between people and places.

According to the Canadian geographer Edward Relph (1976), people and places gain their meanings and identities from each other. He argues that this reciprocal identification process is necessary for both people and places to create, maintain, and recreate their character. This is in accordance with Henri Lefebvre's conceptualisation of urban space, in which he characterises the city as a realm of 'partnership' between people and places as everyday life is being experienced (Goonewardena et al. 2008, Lefebvre 1991, 1996a). Lefebvre (1991, 1996b) believes that production and reproduction of social relations are influenced more by the forces of different lived experiences in the city than by the dominant ideology. However, a feminist analytical approach contends that Lefebvre underestimates the gendered aspects of everyday life as he does not recognise the patriarchy embedded within power relations which works differently for women's and men's experiences (Fenster 2005). Concerning this critique, Fenster (2005) explains how different narrations of the everyday life experiences of men and women in the city highlight their different expressions of interacting with and belonging to urban spaces. Young (1989) introduces the notion of 'differentiated citizenship', Nira Yuval-Davis (1997, 1999) terms it 'multi-layered citizenship', and finally Purcell (2003) classifies it within the reorientation of citizenship. What is common to all these studies is that the scholars acknowledge the deficiency of thinking in terms of one set of people with similar characteristics. This results in the 'ideal of universal citizenship of the liberal democracy approach' (Fenster 2005, p. 218). Instead, they point to the necessity of accepting the importance of different identities and multiple communities.

Exploring Everyday Life Experiences of Afghan Women in Auckland

Fieldwork was conducted between 2013 and 2015 to study the everyday life experiences of a small group of Afghan immigrant women in Auckland, New Zealand. This study focused on the sense of belonging and attachment and the relations of Afghan women to places.

In order to evaluate Afghan immigrant women's attachment to their new place, a multi-modal qualitative methodology involved semi-structured deep interviews, as well as participant observation during the interviews in public spaces. The participants were chosen from Afghan women who live in Auckland, from different age groups, education and occupational backgrounds, and their specific ethnicity within the Afghan community. According to the Department of Labour of New Zealand, immigrant youths[6] are divided into three groups based on their generation: 'first-generation immigrants' are immigrant youths who were born overseas and immigrated to New Zealand after the age of 12. '1.5-generation immigrants' are known as immigrant youths who were born overseas and immigrated to New Zealand by the age of 12. There is another group of immigrants who are signified as 'second-generation immigrants'. They are New Zealand-born youths with both parents born overseas (Ward 2008). The latest group is not the focus of this study. Seven women (five women from 1.5-generation and two women from first-generation immigrants) agreed to be interviewed. The first interview questions asked about their immigration story. Then further questions asked about their familiarity with the city. Finally, participants were asked to narrate their everyday life experiences in the city as they were related to the category of attachment and belonging to space. After exploring their everyday life experiences, I concluded my understanding on the gendered aspects of attachment to their places of experience in the city. As mentioned earlier, patriarchal power relations evident in the private lives of Afghan women are affected by the history of patriarchal culture in Afghanistan and have been playing the most important role in the formation of their presence in public life.

Drawing from place-attachment theory (Giuliani 2003, Hidalgo and Hernandez 2001, Low and Altman 1992, Manzo and Devine-Wright 2014, Marcus 1992), people, place, and the process of attachment are the pivotal threefold variables contributing to place-attachment, which provide answers to the questions who, what, and how of place-attachment. Also, urban sociologists identify three levels of home, neighbourhood, and city as places of attachment, belonging and identity (Manzo and Devine-Wright 2014). Place-attachment as a methodological approach (not just theoretical) enables researchers to understand and analyse the level and depth of attachment of individuals and communities to places. It is important to specify whose place-attachment is going to be analysed in order to apply the most suitable framework for the research.

To study the way Afghan women attach themselves and belong to places in Auckland, it is important to identify central places of their daily lives constructed by their cultures. According to studies of Afghan culture and the situation of Afghan women (Baker 2001, 2010, Khan 2002, Moghadam 1992, Rostami-Povey 2007a, UN Women 2013), 'home' is the pivotal place of women in Afghan culture. So as not to isolate the discussion in the way that Lefebvre did when he dismissed the gender aspects of everyday life to explain everybody's right to the city, firstly I highlight Afghan women's right to their home (as representation of private life), where their central place of use and participation is.

Afghan Women's Right to the 'Home'

Studies show that people can relate to their place of dwelling, which is prototypically known as 'home' (Lewicka 2014, Marcus 1995, Moore 2000, Rybczynski 1986). People's sense of belonging to 'home' is 'a symbol of continuity and order, rootedness, self-identity, attachment, privacy, comfort, security, and refuge' (Lewicka 2011, p. 211). Tuan (1975) insists on the 'home' place as 'the centre of meaning', which is constructed by experience.

Also, 'home' as the private realm is central to the Afghan collective culture (Mohammad 2005). The reviewed literature, and existing studies on Afghan culture, and the situation of Afghan women in their culture, suggest that the place of home – which is defined within the private realm of daily life – is the main place of the everyday life experiences of Afghan women (Baker 2010, Emadi 2005, Khan 2002, Moghadam 1992, Rostami-Povey 2007b, UN Women 2013). However, this is not exclusive to Afghan culture and is more or less applicable to many other societies (even to Western societies).[7] 'Home' is defined as the place of 'being' and 'becoming' for Afghan women, like many other women from other societies in the world. Therefore, I inspect Afghan women's sense of belonging to 'home' as the initial place where they perform the roles and responsibilities expected from them in their culture.

Afghan women of first-generation immigrants have specific roles and responsibilities expected of them by the individualistic, liberal society in which they resettle. It is argued that those responsibilities are different from and sometimes incompatible with the ones they carry in their own culture (Lipson and Miller 1994). They immigrate with or without their male counterparts and families.

Those who accompany their families, particularly those who settle in urban contexts, are expected to be loyal to their family and community values. On the other hand, they have to survive, often with low incomes, unemployment, or underemployment, language barriers, integration into society, immigration loans and funding constraints (Bhanji 2011). To manage their financial situation, particularly as newcomers, these Afghan women need to play a role in the finance of the family. They need to work outside the house where the social norms of the host society are dominant. To overcome language barriers, they may have to participate in English classes outside their community, in a place which has its own regulations and norms. These new experiences may bring some contradictions and incompatibilities into contact with their Afghan culture and its value system.

I begin the discussion of the meaning of the 'home' place by drawing on extracts of the quotations from the participants of the first generation of immigrants. As a first-generation immigrant, Banoo, who came to New Zealand three years ago on her own, considers New Zealand as a home place for herself and her children who are not here yet.

(TRANSLATION)[8] BANOO: Well, New Zealand is like my new home now ... because I feel safe here ... no one pries into other people's business. Everyone is busy with their own business. No matter who is studying what, who is working where, who is doing what ... no one talks behind the other one, there's nothing like these things here, ... so I feel very comfortable here ...

Banoo considers safety and individual freedom as the most important aspects of making a place feel comfortable. Prioritising individuation and privacy, she refers to her experience of living as an Afghan woman within a patriarchal culture that took away her freedom of choice.

Soraya, another participant Afghan woman from the first-generation of immigrants migrated with her three sons to New Zealand when she was 45 years old. Although she has lived most of her life in Iran since she was six years old, grew up there, and got married there, all her life's milestones and experiences were strongly culturally constructed as an Afghan woman. Soraya stated during the interview that as Afghan immigrants in Iran, she and her family did not have legal access to many public resources and services such as education and employment. This is, nevertheless, the same case for the majority of Afghan immigrants who are identified as illegal immigrants in Iran (Hoodfar 2008). Consequently, Soraya became more and more determined to leave Iran. As a result of the United Nation's decision to send her and her family to New Zealand, she has been living in Auckland for three years.

During the interview, Soraya appreciates the way that she has been acknowledged by the host society, and she has not experienced this before. Likewise, she explains that for her, a place where people acknowledge each other with respect is the place that she calls 'home'. She refers to those people as family members or other members of the public.

(TRANSLATION) SORAYA: Well, in my opinion, a person's home must be a calm place. To me, calmness is very important. Home should be a place where one's needs and desires are met there … well home is where respect is, respect between family members, or respect among other members of the public … it doesn't matter where it is, but respect is very important. When there's respect at home, people don't misbehave with each other, everyone has a good feeling …

Both women (Banoo and Soraya) associate their ideal place with 'home', a place which has specific values for them as places to feel comfortable, safe, and respected in. Young (2005) identifies (1) safety, (2) individuation, (3) privacy, and (4) preservation as normative values of 'home' and says they should be accessible to everyone. She describes these values in order to advocate the value of the right of people to home, particularly for refugees in the host society whose chance to maintain their familial and community culture and history has been threatened through destabilisation of their homes in their country of origin (Young 2005).

The meaning of home is different for the participant Afghan women from another generational group who were born overseas but came to New Zealand by the age of 12 (1.5-generation immigrants). The following quotations demonstrate how the younger group of participants describe the place called 'home' and to what extent it is culturally based. Sadjida is a young Afghan girl who arrived in Auckland at the age of 10 (1.5-generation immigrant) with her mother and two other siblings (one older brother and one younger sister). She is in her early 20s and just graduated from the University of Auckland. When I asked her about the meaning of the 'home' place for her, Sadjida referred to her everyday relationships and interactions with people whom she cares about. She described how these relationships make her feel safe and at ease.

SADJIDA: I guess it should have very of a childhood memories …, like, you know, that's what with me home would be. Home is a place where you feel more comfortable in, where you go to, to forget your other worries, you know, forget about the things and remember the good times, and have a lot of memories where you have your families around too, you know, things like that, friends and how often do you go to that place, and how long have you been there, so that's what I feel like home and also the people you care about! (Laughs quietly.) The people you care about [their] values as the place, that's where home would be, that is where they are, the people [who] care about you and the way you value themselves, that's what, you know, a home would be …

Henna, who has lived in Auckland for 15 years, described her conceptualisation of a place called 'home' as follows.

HENNA: The places that I used to it and I'm comfy that I can do what I like to, I don't get forced by people or … not forced like they tell me 'oh, this', but I feel that I get forced by this, so I didn't feel so.

Having a sense of familiarity with the place and its components as well as a sense of freedom and not to feel 'forced' are key factors of a place in which Henna would feel being at 'home'. Henna explained how this sense of place familiarity gives her a sense of comfort.

HENNA: I don't like new … I would get used to it, but after few times, but I prefer not going to a new place and trying new things.

Meena and Taiba arrived in New Zealand when they were eight years old (1.5-generation immigrants). They have journeyed to Afghanistan a few times in recent years. Experiencing life in Afghanistan gave them the opportunity to be with the people they know, and to do things that give them a sense of comfort and safety. They refer to their country of origin as 'back home', a place in which they feel a sense of comfort and safety through being with the familiar people of the same culture. Therefore, even after having life experiences in New Zealand, they refer to the importance of the sense of familiarity with the place and the people in order to call a particular place a 'home' place.

MEENA: I think of a place of comfort, you know, a place where I feel like … I can be however I want to and not feel uncomfortable … and … having like a good company, you know, who is around me …
TAIBA: I think … for a place to [be] call[ed] home, it should have more people from my country, especially the people that I'm really close to, like when I go back home [Afghanistan], the most thing that I enjoy is like with being with the family, friends or families that are familiar with me, or I know them, because … the familiarity is very important to me, … also it should be … safe, and obviously has all the facilities that I need it. So you don't have the hardship of going through everyday life.

Sophia, another participant of the 1.5 generation of immigrants, referred to the importance of 'having someone' there as the main characteristic of the 'home' place.

SOPHIA: having someone in the house …

In the following extract from her interview, Sophia explained how her feeling of rootedness in New Zealand has been shaped by the aspect of familiarity. She mentioned that the sense of familiarity leads to her feelings of safety and happiness in the place.

SOPHIA: I think people are still important ... You think of a home, it's not
   like ... for some people it's like the ... which is important as well, like seeing
   the green, the cleanliness, the environment, you know, the nature ... So for
   example, if I go to another country, even when I went to Australia, and ... you
   know, I was there for few weeks and then I came back, I would feel born in
   New Zealand, because this is where I'm used to ... you know? ... So it's
   about like getting used to somewhere with the environment, the nature, and
   then mostly the people, so, you know, if your family is somewhere or you
   got used to there or your friends or your husband, you know, you feel more
   home in that place and that ... And other elements like nature, the weather,
   the environment ...

ROJA: So and is that enough for a place to feel like home for you?

SOPHIA: Yeah to feel safe, to feel happy.

These quotations from the findings of the fieldwork study suggest that the
'home' place becomes the expressive setting of the individual and the collective
beliefs, norms, and values of the participants. Therefore, the 'home' place,
according to Hayden (Hayden 1995) is a 'cultural landscape' which is inseparable
from familial and community relationships. The findings from this study also
advocate the idea that the 'home' place is Afghan women's place of belonging.
Home place for the participants of this study is where they can experience comfort and relief – comfort as a result of feeling safe and secure, and relief as
a result of being in mutual care and companionship with the people surrounding
them. The participants' sense of belonging to their home place is drawn from
their right to their home. Home, then, is a foundational place of belonging and
identity for the participant Afghan women. Therefore, it is important to highlight the aspects of place which shape their sense of belonging and identity.

Afghan Women's Position in the Place: Inclusion or Exclusion?

Historically, women have been subject to subordination and confinement by
dominant patriarchal structures within power relations (Engels and Morgan
1972, Walby 1989). 'One of the major criticisms of the concept of patriarchy is
that it cannot deal with the differences between forms of gender inequality at
different times and places, nor with the diversity of the experiences of women'
(Walby 1989, p. 217). Although this construction has been confronted and
objected to by feminist movements, particularly in Western countries, the patriarchal structure of power is working to enforce and subordinate women, especially in the public life of the city. This historical conception has been practised
for a long time in Afghanistan, where women have been excluded from public
life and confined to taking on reproductive roles at home: the private territory
of life.

On the other hand, adapting to the space of 'home' as their so-called territory, Afghan women have gained a sense of belonging and identity regarding their specific right to the home. Referring to Afghan women's conceptualisation of 'home' earlier in this chapter, this study confirms that home is the place for their bodily experience and representation (Young 2005). This is their place of lived reality to reproduce and preserve. Afghan women acknowledge 'home' as their place to perform all the tasks and responsibilities associated with their roles as Afghan women in the family. Subsequently, family becomes the social structure that Afghan women interact with during their daily lives. All at once, they become disconnected from their place of belonging through immigrating to another country. Unlike the advantage that they gain by approaching a better life in a better socio-economic and spatial situation, they lose a strong emotional and rooted part of every human relation, which is 'home' (Wastl-Walter et al. 2003). Therefore, Afghan women encounter more conflictive experiences while coping with the feeling of homelessness as it is defined, as well as losing strong relationships with family and all the experiences, memories, and feelings rooted in childhood. Thereafter, it is expected for them to become excluded from the public life of their host society as a result of a crisis in their identification process. Their exclusion is because they lose strong links between their body, their mind, and the place they used to interact with during their everyday lives.

However, referring to the given definition and approach of 'everyday life' by Henri Lefebvre earlier in this chapter, Afghan women experience their daily lives as being influenced by different aspects of their identities, including gender, race, ethnicity, religion, and their stage of life, among others. Their everyday life experiences are also influenced by their individual and social position in the specific time of their presence in a specific place. It means that their experience in time and place needs to be interpreted and analysed based on different aspects of identity which contribute to their positionality and their relation to space. It results in different encounters and interactions between people and places. One could discuss the identification process of Afghan immigrant women in relation to a place contributes to the development of their sense of belonging and attachment to that place in the host society.

Generally, Afghan women (from both first- and 1.5-generation immigrants) experience the everyday tasks of their public life as contradictory to their cultural values. However, their inclusion or exclusion is represented through (re) building their multi-layered identity, including their religion, gender, culture, and ethnicity influeneced by different layers of power relations in the host society. In fact, they create different modes of being through intersecting different layers of identity according to the different occasions of daily life. Moreover, apart from their religion and culture, the identification processes of Afghan immigrant women in their new living places are also influenced by their stage of life which impacts age, education, job, etc. Therefore, I differentiate between

two generations of Afghan immigrant women to analyse their use of and participation in the public life of the city.

Most of the participant Afghan women among the 1.5-generation immigrants
either study or work in the city. As educated working Muslim women, they are
also concerned with their religion as an important aspect of their identity. They
do not seem to see any clash between their religious values, the rules they are
expected to adhere to, and their desire to study and work.

TAIBA: em I would be happy with my education side, but I wouldn't be happy
          with the lifestyle that I have. So that lifestyle is so, so bad for the girls, they
          have to do all the house work, and there's so many … like things that you
          need to do. but I would probably like it if I am even obliged to study, because
          you know to be honest … actually, if I was allowed to study and take my
          own decisions in back home, and there wouldn't be the society stopping me
          and … I would be able to do the things that I'm doing now here, then
          I would be happy to be back there. Because it's my home country and it's my
          own language, my own people, and I have like … so many families
          there … and when I went, the three months that I went there [to Afghani-
          stan], I enjoyed my life so much. Because in here it's so tired, depressing you
          know like … I don't know it's just the city, it's just … , and there, is just
          people full of laughter, they enjoy life, they don't care. In here you have to
          think about little things that you have to do to improve your life. There, they
          don't care. Those three months that I went there, I enjoyed it so much. I was
          like 'Wow I wanna have this life', but then again when I was thinking of my
          education, I would say 'No, I wanna have … I wanna be able to study my
          own major and be able to like not depend on people' …

Although Taiba appreciates her chance to study here in New Zealand, she
does not underestimate her inclination to live with her people in Afghanistan.
However, she sounds more determined to finish her studies and not to become
a dependent woman at home.

Furthermore, after being told about the situation of their families and their
parents back in Afghanistan, these young participant Afghan women have
become more determined to use the chance of living here to appreciate fully
the hardships and risk their parents experienced. Meena, who was born in Iran
after her family migrated from Kabul to Tehran before coming to New Zealand,
describes her gratitude for what her family has done during their immigration
journey in the following manner.

MEENA: I mean they always talk about how they … were you know back in Iran,
          and then you know how we should [laughed] we should like you know learn
          from … what they went through and be grateful, I mean we are grateful!
          You know what they went through, and then it's you know what we are not

going through it you know … ! But … they do talk about those things, and you know it's like you know … we should be happy …

The intonation of her voice and repetition of words is an indication of not being sure about the way she intends to appreciate her parents; it is also a sign of the domination of family over the decision-making process.

Again, this is in accordance with their community-based values. They see their way of participation in the public life of the city as an advantage to their religious and ethnic community, because this would prove the egalitarian and progressive nature of Islam (Ramji 2007). Hence, they contribute to the society but only as long as their familial and community values are being fulfilled. There follow some examples of young Afghan women who have changed or modified their decision in favour of their familial and community norms and values.

Sadjida explains her decision not to go to another city in New Zealand to study for a post-graduate diploma that would afford her better job opportunities. She withdrew her application as a result of a family decision to avoid being overwhelmed by the Afghan community's culture of gossip.

SADJIDA: So, because my family was here in Auckland, I needed to live by my own in Hamilton to study in the university. But you know … we have a relative in Hamilton, but my mom didn't like me to go and stay with them in their place … and there is a very small Afghan community there who know my family here, and if I wanted to go and stay in a hostel or places like that as a lonely young Afghan girl, they might say gossips and talk about me like 'Oh why is she alone?' or 'No it's not good for a young Afghan girl to live alone' or things like that you know? … these kinds of gossips are like nightmares for everyone in the community. So, we were thinking that all of us move to Hamilton which at the end of the day it didn't sound rational you know … so I just cancelled my plan to study there and I continued looking for some jobs which are easier to adapt like … you know I mean according to my family situation in here.

Another example comes from Taiba, who explains how her way of dressing in public is in line with her religious and community values.

TAIBA: When I know that it's a public space and I'm with the Afghans, I prefer wearing like a modest clothes, so I wear like long dress, or maybe skirt. I kind of like avoid wearing jeans, and I also avoid wearing short dresses. but if I know that … the place where I go is mostly other people, I would prefer wearing short dress or jeans … things like that, but make-up for me is like anyone whoever is there, even I put make-up when I'm home … [Laughed quietly.]

Therefore, community and family determine the way that these Afghan women contribute to the public life of the city. Afghan women are more involved in self-advancement for themselves as well as their families and their communities (religious or ethnic). Therefore, the relation of Afghan women (from both first- and 1.5-generation immigrants) to public spaces in Auckland depends on the capacity of those places to embrace community bonds.

In theorising spatial triads, Lefebvre defines (social) space as a social product based on norms, values and meanings which affects spatial experiences and perceptions of the space (Lefebvre 1991). According to Lefebvre (1991) and Soja (1996), the first space is the physical or perceived space, while the second space is described as mental or conceived space. Regarding Lefebvre's conception of social space as a third space, Soja formulated and developed 'thirdspace' to conceptualise 'cumulative trialectics' (Soja 1996). It provides this opportunity to renegotiate boundaries and cultural identity. This is in accordance with Homi Bhabha's theory of cultural hybridisation as an alternative in post-colonial cultures (Bhabha 1990, 1994). 'Thirdspace' is defined to contest dominant norms and set up a new place of discourse for the representation and meaning of use and participation in the place. Therefore, grounding my thinking on Lefebvre's (1991) spatial understandings of power and Soja's conceptualisation of 'thirdspace', I am likely to refer to 'thirdspace' as an in-between position. Recognizing this in-between position as the space of discourse and interaction, Afghan immigrant women create their own sense of place and belonging which can appear as an intensification of their identity. Afghan immigrant women re-actualise their culture, which is raised from their memories in specific places. Their different experiences in public spaces based on their community bonds to those places create their own sense of home and belonging. In this regard, Sandercock (1995) reminds us of bell hooks' interpretation of 'space of radical openness' as a place in which more than one identity is included, so it is the place for different individuals and communities to experiment, to redefine home, and to rethink territories and boundaries based on their different conceptions of the place. Also, Anzaldúa (1999) explains the struggle of women from different cultures in a new place as an ongoing process in order to be identified by and attached to a new way of life and culture. It also expresses their need to exist, explore, and to go further.

Moreover, Massey (in Keith et al. 1993) describes the conceptualisation of space within the process of social relations which are dynamic in nature. Therefore, everyday life experiences of Afghan immigrant women contribute to the creation of a sense of place and belonging for them in their host society of Auckland.

Conclusion

According to the fieldwork study, Afghan immigrant women position themselves between the cultural place of Afghan community and the place of the dominant culture in their host society. In this in-between position, Afghan immigrant women experience their daily lives as being influenced by different intersecting aspects of their identity, including gender, race, ethnicity, religion, and their stage of life, among others. The intersection between different aspects of their identity represents itself in the daily life experiences of Afghan immigrant women, comprising their clothing, their language, their foods, and their behaviour in their host society. Also, their use of place and their interaction and participation in public life as a collective presence sets up another kind of representation in the city. They construct their own conceptual territories through their collective use and appreciation of the space within the city of the host society.

Afghan immigrant women rebuild their sense of belonging and identities through their daily actions and interactions within the place, although in a different position to others. The precedence of community and familial roles, as well as responsibilities to the new society, determine Afghan women's relation to their new place. It is an influential factor for Afghan women (of both first- and 1.5-generation immigrants) in Auckland. It also affects the way they redefine new territories for their daily activities alongside locals. In rebuilding their identities during their routine life, Afghan women are neither completely assimilated into the dominant lifestyle nor do they totally adjust to the cultural norms of Afghanistan. Hence the binary notion of exclusion or inclusion cannot be applied to their position in Auckland simply because of their different positioning from others. Indeed, they do interact with their surroundings according to their daily life requirements. They deliver meaning to those places in which their sense of belonging and attachment is created and developed. Further research could usefully explore policies which can create places which have the capacity and potential to recognize and embrace different representations of Afghan immigrant women in the public life of their Western host societies.

Notes

1 GenderSTE stands for Gender, Science, Technology and Environment, a COST policy-driven network that joined over 200 scholars and policymakers from 40 countries between 2012 and 2016. Its initiator and Chair was Inés Sánchez de Madariaga from Universidad Politécnica de Madrid (Sánchez de Madariaga 2016).
2 Discourses of everyday life experiences of Afghan women are taken from a fieldwork study that Roja Tafaroji conducted for her PhD research project between 2013 and 2015.
3 Industrialization and its aftereffects brought about global competition for goods and services which has altered the labour market. As a result, there has been an increased demand for women in different parts of the Western world in different fields such as nursing and teaching (Champion 1994, Fry 2006, United Nations Department of Economic and Social Affairs, Population Division 2013). This has changed the pattern of the division of labour between men and women all over the world and contributed to the gradually obtained independence of women as they attempt to gain control over their mobility and standard of living.
4 *Tampa* was a Norwegian freighter that rescued Afghan asylum seekers in 2001. They were refused entry to the country by the Australian government.

5 The Taliban (Pashto: طالبان ṭālibān), is an Islamic fundamentalist political movement in Afghanistan. Women were affected in a cruel way by the Taliban's interpretation of Islam once it was in power in Afghanistan (between September 1996 and December 2001). Under the Taliban's harsh version of Islamic law, women were not permitted to work outside their homes. Even their simple presence in public spaces, such as when shopping and visiting relatives' places, resulted in many limitations and obstacles if they did not have a male accompanying them (Baker 2010, Bhanji 2011, Ghasemi 1998, Khan 2002).

6 The term 'migrant youth' is used along with 'national youth' as arbitrary terms in a report for Migrant and Refugee Youth Settlement and the Social Inclusion Series by the Department of Labour in New Zealand. This categorization of migrant youths has been made by a larger international project (International Study of Ethno-Cultural Youth), which was established to examine a range of intercultural variables, acculturation attitudes, discrimination issues, and (psychological and social) adaptation (Ward 2008). So, *age of arrival* and *place of birth* have been considered as influential factors in acculturation and the adaptation process of immigrant youths in the host society. In this research, the age of 12 as the cut-off age is defensible, considering that it shows significant differences between research participants in terms of their chances to access education and schools.

7 The privatization of women by men within the household has been a historic process. The 'home' place has been defined by male power as a space in which to control women who are bodies and objects of sexuality (Kristeva 1986). It subsequently became the dominant male ideology worldwide by offering the excuse that 'women cannot be self-controlled' because of their fluid, overblown sexuality.

8 The participants who belong to the first generation of immigrants, Banoo and Soraya, were interviewed in Farsi, their native language, according to their preferences. The translation from Farsi to English is provided by the author, Roja Tafaroji.

References

Ahmad, F. (2006). British Muslim perceptions and opinions on news coverage of September 11. *Journal of Ethnic and Migration Studies*, 32(6), pp. 961–982.

Altman, I., Wohlwill, J.F. and Rapoport, A. (1980). *Human behavior and environment: advances in theory and research: environment and culture*. New York: Plenum Press.

Anzaldúa, G. (1999). *Borderlands: La Frontera*. San Francisco, CA: Aunt Lute books.

Auckland Council. (2012). *The Auckland plan*. Auckland, NZ: Auckland Council.

Baker, M. (2001). *Families, labour and love: family diversity in a changing world*. Vancouver: UBC Press.

Baker, A. (2010). Afghan women and the return of the Taliban. *Time Magazine*, 9.

Bauman, Z. (1992). *Intimations of postmodernity*. London and New York: Routledge.

Bauman, Z. (2005). *Liquid life*. Cambridge, UK and Malden, MA: Polity.

Beaglehole, A. (2013). *Refuge in New Zealand: a nation's response to refugees & Asylum seekers/ by Ann Beaglehole*. Otago: Otago University Press.

Beebeejaun, Y. (2017). Gender, urban space, and the right to everyday life. *Journal of Urban Affairs*, 39(3), pp. 323–334.

Bhabha, H. (1990). The third space: interview with Homi Bhabha. In Ders. (Hg), ed., *Identity: community, culture, difference*. London: Lawrence and Wishart, pp. 207–221.

Bhabha, H.K. (1994). *The location of culture*. London and New York: Routledge.

Bhanji, R.M. (2011). Resiliency amidst the fragmented lives of Afghan refugee women. PhD diss., https://macsphere.mcmaster.ca/bitstream/11375/11258/1/fulltext.pdf

Brooks, A. (2007). Feminist standpoint epistemology: building knowledge and empowerment through women's lived experience. In: B. Hesse, N. Sharlene and L.L. Patricia, eds, *Feminist research practice: a primer*. Thousand Oaks, CA: Sage Publications, pp. 53–82.

Buttimer, A. and Seamon, D. (1980). *The human experience of space and place*. London: Croom Helm.

Champion, A.G. (1994). International migration and demographic change in the developed world. *Urban Studies*, 31(4–5), pp. 653–677.

Charles, M. (2011). A world of difference: international trends in women's economic status. *Annual Review of Sociology*, 37, pp. 355–371.

Chouinard, V. and Grant, A. (1995). On being not even anywhere near 'the project': ways of putting ourselves in the picture. *Antipode*, 27(2), pp. 137–166.

De Beauvoir, S. (1972 [1949]). *The second sex*. Harmondsworth: Penguin.

De Certeau, M. (1988). *The practice of everyday life*. Berkeley, CA: University of California Press.

Elliott, A. and Lemert, C. (2009). *The new individualism: the emotional costs of globalization revised edition*. New York: Routledge.

Emadi, H. (2005). *Culture and customs of Afghanistan*. London: Greenwood Publishing Group.

Engels, F. and Morgan, L.H. (1972). *The origin of the family, private property, and the state*. New York: Pathfinder Press.

Faist, T. (1999). 2 developing transnational social spaces; The Turkish-German example. In: L. Pries, ed, *Migration and transnational social spaces*. Aldershot: Ashgate Publishing Ltd, pp. 36–43.

Fenster, T. (1999). *Gender, planning, and human rights*. London: Psychology Press.

Fenster, T. (2005). The right to the gendered city: different formations of belonging in everyday life. *Journal of Gender Studies*, 14(3), pp. 217–231.

Fraser, N. and Nicholson, L. (1989). Social criticism without philosophy: an encounter between feminism and postmodernism. *Social Text*, (21), pp. 83–104.

Fry, R.A. (2006). *Gender and migration*. Washington, DC: Pew Hispanic Center.

Ghasemi, M.E. (1998). Islam, international human rights & (and) women's equality: Afghan women under Taliban rule. *Southern California Review of Law and Women's Studies*, 8, p. 445.

Gilbert, M.R. (1997). Feminism and difference in urban geography. *Urban Geography*, 18(2), pp. 166–179.

Giuliani, M.V. (2003). Theory of attachment and place attachment. In: M. Bonnes, T. Lee and M. Bonaiuto, eds, *Psychological theories for environmental issues*. Aldershot: Ashgate, pp. 137–170.

Goonewardena, K., Kipfer, S., Milgrom, R. and Schmid, C. (2008). *Space, difference, everyday life: reading Henri Lefebvre*. New York: Routledge.

Gruner, A. and Searle, W. (2011). *New Zealand's refugee sector: perspectives and developments, 1987–2010- at a Glance*. Wellington: Department of Labour.

Hayden, D. (1995). *The power of place: urban landscapes as public history*. Cambridge, MA and London: The MIT Press.

Hekman, S.J. (ed.) (1999a). *Feminism, identity, and difference*. Portland, OR: Frank Cass Publishers.

Hekman, S.J. (1999b). *The future of differences: truth and method in feminist theory*. Malden, MA: Polity Press in association with Blackwell Publishers Ltd.

Hidalgo, M.C. and Hernandez, B. (2001). Place attachment: conceptual and empirical questions. *Journal of Environmental Psychology*, 21(3), pp. 273–281.

Hillier, J. (2002). *Shadows of power: an allegory of prudence in land-use planning*. New York: Routledge.

Hoodfar, H. (2008). The long road home: adolescent Afghan refugees in Iran contemplate 'return. In: J. Hart, ed, *Years of conflict: adolescence, political violence and displacement*. Oxford: Berghahn Books, pp. 165–185.

Hooks, B. (1984). *Feminist theory: from margin to center*. Boston, MA: South End Press.

Jarvis, H., Cloke, J. and Kantor, P. (2009). *Cities and gender*, 1st ed. London: Routledge.

Kail, E. and Irschek, E. (2008). Fair shared city: gender mainstreaming planning strategy in Vienna, 2008, Paper presented at the Gender and Urban Policies, Strategies for Gender mainstreaming and local governance.

Keith, M., Pile, S., Harvey, D., Smith, N., Katz, C., Bondi, L., Radcliffe, S., Revil, G., Massey, D., Hesse, B., Soja, E., Hooper, B. and Golding, S. (1993). *Place and the politics of identity*. London: Routledge.

Khan, A. (2002). Afghan refugee women's experience of conflict and disintegration. *Meridians*, 3(1), pp. 89–121.

Kristeva, J. (1986). *The Kristeva reader* (edited by T. Moi). New York: Columbia University Press.

Lahav, G. (2003). Migration and security: the role of non-state actors and civil liberties in liberal democracies, *Second Coordination Meeting on International Migration*. New York: United Nations, Department of Economic and Social Affairs, Population Division.

Lefebvre, H. (1991). *The production of space*. Oxford and Cambridge, MA: Blackwell.

Lefebvre, H. (1996a). *The right to the city*. Oxford: Blackwell Publishing, pp. 63–181.

Lefebvre, H. (1996b). *Spaces and politics: Writings on cities*. Cambridge, MA: Blackwell Publishing.

Lefebvre, H. and Levich, C. (1987). The everyday and everydayness. *Yale French Studies*, (73), pp. 7–11.

Lewicka, M. (2011). Place attachment: how far have we come in the last 40 years? *Journal of Environmental Psychology*, 31(3), pp. 207–230.

Lewicka, M. (2014). In search of roots: memory as enabler of place attachment. In: L. Manzo and P. Devine-Wright, eds, *Place attachment: advances in theory, methods, and applications*. London and New York: Routledge, pp. 49–60.

Lipson, J.G. and Miller, S. (1994). Changing roles of Afghan refugee women in the United States. *Health Care for Women International*, 15(3), pp. 171–180.

Low, S.M. and Altman, I. (1992). *Place attachment*. Boston, MA: Springer.

Magee, J. (ed.) (2011). *New to New Zealand: ethnic communities in Aotearoa: a handbook*, 5th ed. Hamilton, NZ: Ethnic New Zealand Trust.

Mann, S.A. and Patterson, A.S. (2016). *Reading feminist theory: from modernity to postmodernity*. New York: Oxford University Press.

Manzo, L.C. and Devine-Wright, P. (eds.) (2014). *Place attachment: advances in theory, methods and applications*. London and New York: Routledge.

Marcus, C.C. (1992). *Environmental memories. Place attachment*. Boston, MA: Springer, pp. 87–112.

Marcus, C.C. (1995). *House as a mirror of self: exploring the deeper meaning of home*. Berkeley, CA: Conari Press.

Immigration New Zealand. (2016). The refugee and protection unit: refugee quota branch (RQB) resettlement statistics. Retrieved from https://www.immigration.govt.nz/about-us/what-we-do/our-strategies-and-projects/supporting-refugees-and-asylum-seekers/refugee-and-protection-unit

McDowell, L. (1983). Towards an understanding of the gender division of urban space. *Environment and Planning D: Society and Space*, 1(1), pp. 59–72.

McDowell, L. (1992). Doing gender: feminism, feminists and research methods in human geography. *Transactions of the Institute of British Geographers*, 17(4), pp. 399–416.

McDowell, L. and Court, G. (1994). Gender divisions of labour in the post-Fordist economy: the maintenance of occupational sex segregation in the financial services sector. *Environment and Planning A*, 26, p. 1397.

McDowell, L. and Sharp, J.P. (eds.) (1997). *Space, gender, knowledge*. London, New York and Arnold: John Wiley & Sons.

Mohammad, R. (2005). Geographies of Muslim women: gender, religion, and space. In: G. Falah and C. Nagel, eds, *Geographies of Muslim women gender: gender, religion, and space*. New York: Guilford Press, pp. 178–200.

Moghadam, V.M. (1992). Patriarchy and the politics of gender in modernising societies: Iran, Pakistan and Afghanistan. *International Sociology*, 7(1), pp. 35–53.

Moore, J. (2000). Placing home in context. *Journal of Environmental Psychology*, 20(3), pp. 207–217.

Narayan, U. and Harding, S. (2000). *Decentering the center: philosophy for a multicultural, postcolonial, and feminist world*. Bloomington, IN: Indiana University Press.

Perkins, H.C. and Thorns, D.C. (2012). *Place, identity and everyday life in a globalizing world*. London: Palgrave Macmillan.

Proshansky, H.M., Fabian, A.K. and Kaminoff, R. (1983). Place-identity: physical world socialization of the self. *Journal of Environmental Psychology*, 3(1), pp. 57–83.

Purcell, M. (2003). Citizenship and the right to the global city: reimagining the capitalist world order. *International Journal of Urban and Regional Research*, 27(3), pp. 564–590.

Ramji, H. (2007). Dynamics of religion and gender amongst young British Muslims. *Sociology*, 41(6), pp. 1171–1189.

Rapoport, A. (1976). *The mutual interaction of people and their built environment*. The Hague: Mouton Editions.

Relph, E. (1976). *Place and placelessness*. London: Pion.

Rostami-Povey, E. (2007a). Afghan refugees in Iran, Pakistan, the UK, and the US and life after return: a comparative gender analysis. *Iranian Studies*, 40(2), pp. 241–261.

Rostami-Povey, E. (2007b). *Afghan women: identity and invasion*. London: Zed Books.

Rybczynski, W. (1986). *Home: a short history of an idea*. New York: Viking.

Sánchez de Madariaga, I. & M. Roberts (eds.) (2013) *Fair Shared Cities. The Impact of Gender Planning in Europe*. Ashgate, Aldershot-New York.

Sánchez de Madariaga, I. (ed.) (2016). Advancing gender in research, innovation & sustainable development. COST Network genderSTE, Fundación Universidad Politécnica de Madrid, Madrid.

Sandercock, L. (1995). Voices from the borderlands: a meditation on a metaphor. *Journal of Planning Education and Research*, 14(2), pp. 77–88.

Sanders, R. (1990). Integrating race and ethnicity into geographic gender studies. *The Professional Geographer*, 42(2), pp. 228–231.

Soja, E.W. (1989). *Postmodern geographies: the reassertion of space in critical social theory*. London and New York: Verso.

Soja, E.W. (1996). *Thirdspace: journeys to Los Angeles and other real-and-imagined places*. Cambridge, MA: Blackwell.

Strategic Social Policy Group. (2008). *Diverse communities: exploring the migrant and refugee experience in New Zealand*. Wellington, NZ: Ministry of Social Development.

Sztompka, P. (2008). The focus on everyday life: a new turn in sociology. *European Review*, 16(1), pp. 23–37.

Tuan, Y. (1974). *Topophilia: a study of environmental perception, attitudes, and values.* Englewood Cliffs, NJ: Prentice Hall.

Tuan, Y. (1975). Place: an experiential perspective. *Geographical Review*, 65(2), pp. 151–165.

UN Women. (2013). *"Like a bird with broken wings" Afghan women oral history, 1978–2008.* Kabul: United Nations Entity for Gender Equality and The Empowerment of Women, Afghanistan Country Office.

United Nations. Department of economic and social affairs, population division (2013-last update). *Trends in international migrant stock: the 2013 revision- migrants by age and sex* [Homepage of United Nations], [Online]. Available: www.un.org/en/development/ desa/population/theme/international-migration/index.shtml [August 25, 2015].

Walby, S. (1989). Theorising patriarchy. *Sociology*, 23(2), pp. 213–234.

Ward, C. (2008). *The experiences of migrant youth: a generational analysis.* Wellington, NZ: Department of Labour.

Wastl-Walter, D., Va´radi, M.M. and Veider, F. (2003). Coping with marginality: to stay or to go. *Journal of Ethnic and Migration Studies*, 29(5), pp. 797–817.

Wesselius, J. (2000). "Woman" in the plural: negotiating sameness and difference in feminist theory. In: J.H. Olthuis, ed, *Towards an ethics of community: negotiations of difference in a pluralist society.* Waterloo: Wilfrid Laurier University Press, pp. 74–90.

Whitzman, C., Legacy, C., Andrew, C., Klodawsky, F., Shaw, M. and Viswanath, K. (2013). *Building inclusive cities: women's safety and the right to the city.* London: Routledge.

Woodward, I., Skrbis, Z. and Bean, C. (2008). Attitudes towards globalization and cosmopolitanism: cultural diversity, personal consumption and the national economy. *The British Journal of Sociology*, 59(2), pp. 207–226.

Young, I.M. (1989). Polity and group difference: a critique of the ideal of universal citizenship. *Ethics*, 99(2), pp. 250–274.

Young, I.M. (2005). *On female body experience: "throwing like a girl" and other essays.* New York: Oxford University Press.

Yuval-Davis, N. (1997). Women, citizenship and difference. *Feminist Review*, 57(1), pp. 4–27.

Yuval-Davis, N. (1999). The "multi-layered citizen". *International Feminist Journal of Politics*, 1(1), pp. 119–136.

11

GENDER MAINSTREAMING IN THE REGIONAL DISCOURSE OVER THE FUTURE OF THE RUHR METROPOLITAN AREA

Implementation of Gender Mainstreaming in Planning Processes

Jeanette Sebrantke, Mechtild Stiewe, Sibylle Kelp-Siekmann, and Gudrun Kemmler-Lehr

Introduction: Gender Mainstreaming as an Important Strategic Approach

The realities of life – whether of men or women, the young or the elderly, of families and singles – are complex, and are thus demanding for urban and regional planning. Gender mainstreaming[1] is primarily a political guideline promoting equal opportunities between the sexes and demographic groups in all spheres of life. Gender mainstreaming:

> means the development, organization and evaluation of decision-making processes with the aim of getting all stakeholders and players involved in policy-making to incorporate the gender perspective into all political and administrative measures at all levels. In each policy area and at all levels the different starting conditions and impacts on gender should be considered in order to achieve genuine equality between women and men.
>
> *(Schweigert 2001: 1267)*

With *gender planning*, a strategic approach to spatial planning has evolved since 2000. Under it, equal opportunities and gender mainstreaming have become a goal of comprehensive, effective and sustainable planning. It is about gender issues in spatial planning. Gender relations need thus to be addressed at all planning levels. This includes, for example, collecting gender-specific data and analyzing women's and men's lifestyles to develop gender criteria and actively involve women. Women's participation, bringing in their (professional) experience and those of professional women and actors who are involved in the process, is an essential requirement for achieving more equal opportunities in the planning sector, a domain which is predominantly still dominated by male decision makers (see, for example, the planning department head in the Ruhr Metropolitan Area).

The term "gender" refers to the "social dimension of sex associated with particular role ascription and task allocation – not to the biological gender (sex)" (Ehrhardt 2003: 13). That means that gender refers to the economic, social, and cultural attributes and chances associated with being male or female and reflecting social reality. Interaction between individuals, groups, and society enables this form of sexuality to exist – and to socially change.

Rational Reasons for Gender Planning

Gender mainstreaming in planning is meant to identify gender roles and the different living conditions of women and men in society, because structural disadvantages still exist for women in many areas. Whether in lifestyles or daily routines, significant differences exist in the appropriation and use of space and in mobility behavior.

In the Ruhr Metropolitan Area, the different living conditions of women and men are to be seen, in particular, on the labor market and in their respective social situations. In the *Woman's Atlas Ruhr*, Ruth Kampherm emphasizes that though women living in the region are more integrated in the labor market (i.e. a higher labor force participation rate), the labor market is still segmented by gender (see Kampherm 2000: 50, Lessing 2010: 138–155). As Claudia Horch writes in *WomanRuhrMan*:

> Despite the ongoing transformation into a service economy, women's share of jobs in the Ruhr region doesn't increase – compared to the state (NRW). More and more they find themselves in "part-time- and mini-jobs, precarious and temporary employment". It is a cause for concern that women account for three-quarters of low-income earners and that now almost every fourth child under 15 years is living off social security benefits. This development highlights the indispensability of economic, structural and social policies matched to the respective labor market situations of women and men in the Ruhr Metropolitan Area.
>
> *(see Horch 2010: 389)*

These differences are reflected in the social space structure, as seen in the "poor" city districts of the Ruhr Metropolitan Area where women of all ages, single parents and especially families with many children are having to get by on low incomes. The consequent settlement and neighborhood development challenges can only be solved in the context of urban and regional planning as well as regional development. Planning issues such as housing, infrastructure facilities, mobility and the quality of open spaces play a decisive role in determining the region's viability and environmental quality.

> Gender mainstreaming [in the planning context] is mainly an analytic and planning method aimed at improving the quality of planning and project development processes. Though gendered regional development may seem complicated at first glance, it does not entail any major increase in work. It does however consistently question the effects on women and men in every planning project, making planning more targeted and ultimately enhancing its quality.
>
> *(Horch 2010: 391f.)*

The effectiveness of planning, social processes, and their impacts are also different issues that need to be focused on. The aim is to develop matching equality policies and strategies. In some areas, the living conditions of men and women are similar or even reversed (in education and training, for instance, boys and young men must be particularly encouraged). Women are – beyond the areas of acquisition, transfer income, and working conditions also less represented in wealth, ownership, professional (management positions) or social status (power and influence in politics, business, media). Moreover, women account for a high proportion of unpaid household work (see Lessing 2010: 138–155).

Women remain primarily responsible for looking after the family and doing the housework, whether they are employed or not. Though any increase in women's employment – especially mothers – leads to greater economic independence, it usually also leads to a double burden on women, whereas conditions for men remain constant. Gender mainstreaming in planning and social processes aims to regard these structural differences carefully and sharpen the focus on them. Therefore, demands on the living environment and the surrounding areas increase (see Bölting & Schneiders 2010: 278 ff.). This brings differentiated spatial planning issues into focus alongside social situations, people's age, or ethnic background.

Legal Basis for Gender Mainstreaming in Germany

The actual implementation of equal rights[2] and the implementation of gender mainstreaming in political spheres of activity – for example, in spatial planning and planning administration – are highly different and require a more long-lasting process. Of importance here are the political environment and the legal anchoring of equal opportunities and gender mainstreaming, based on Germany's federal structure, by a Cabinet decision from 1999. The Federal Republic of Germany's government acknowledges gender mainstreaming as a universal guiding principle of their actions.

In 2000, an inter-ministerial working group became responsible for implementing gender mainstreaming at various action and planning levels: The Building Code, in its amended 2004 version, states in §1 (Section 6, Sentence 3) that, particularly during the preparation of development plans, account needs to be taken of:

> the social and cultural needs of the population, in particular those of families, the young and the elderly and those with handicaps, as well as to the requirements of the education system and the need for sports, leisure and recreational facilities.

§1 (Section 2) of the Spatial Planning Act (ROG 2008) stipulates "sustainable spatial development, which leads [...] to a balanced order with equivalent living conditions [...]", and in §2 (Section 2, Sentence 3 ROG 2008) the "ensuring of equal opportunities in the sub-regions". Here it says "The provision of services and infrastructure of general interest, and in particular access to facilities and services of primary care for all population groups, has to be ensured to maintain equal opportunities in the sub-regions in an appropriate manner" (§2, Section 2, Sentence 3 ROG 2008).

The Federal State Planning and the still-valid North Rhine-Westphalia state development plan (LEP NRW) – a 10-year multidisciplinary, integrated spatial development concept for North Rhine-Westphalia – declares in Section I: New Challenges: "The special needs of women, elderly, disabled people, children and adolescents must be considered" (LEP NRW 1995: 5). It goes on to state in Section II (A.II, section 4): "Measures of spatial and settlement's structural development should be taken into account regarding the future population development and the needs of women, the elderly, the disabled and of children and adolescents" (LEP NRW 1995: 6).

The new draft LEP NRW states in its introduction:

> In addition to the spatial specifications there are further functional and social goals to be achieved, in particular at subsidiary planning levels and in permit-granting and approval processes. With regard for instance to the consistent implementation of the gender and disability mainstreaming approach in the context of subordinate planning, a review of the different effects on sexes and on the social participation of people with disabilities is required.
>
> *(Staatskanzlei des Landes Nordrhein-Westfalen 2015: 1)*

The regional planning and regional development refer to the state's requirements mentioned above and the need to substantiate them at its planning level.

Activities Aimed at Implementing Gender Mainstreaming in the Planning Administration

In addition to the above-mentioned legal enshrinement, activities are increasingly taking place to establish gender mainstreaming as a guiding principle in planning for everyday life. In fact, local authorities – with the assistance at the federal level – are involved in the implementation of gender mainstreaming and enriching it with best practice examples. The 2003–2005 ExWoSt research project Gender Mainstreaming in Urban Planning developed practical examples in many cities, demonstrating how gender mainstreaming can be implemented in urban development and open-space planning, and, furthermore, how the gender perspective can be actively and visibly incorporated into routine municipal planning work and concrete projects. Based on selected model cities (Dessau, Pulheim, Bremen), the research project, funded by the Federal Ministry of Transport, Building and Urban Development and carried out by the Federal Institute for Research on Building, Urban Affairs and Spatial Development, has defined transferable strategies for integrating gender mainstreaming into routine administrative activities, as well as target agreements and measurable success criteria (see the Difu website). As a result, a number of good examples and implementation strategies exist for everyday municipal planning.

By contrast, only a few approaches exist at the levels of regional planning and regional development for implementing gender mainstreaming in planning processes and involving (specialist) women. In her essay "The city is the region – regional development must be gender-balanced", Sabine Baumgart wrote about experiences from other regions (Hannover, Rhineland-Palatinate and the Stuttgart region):

> While women's issues started entering the planning policy debate at the municipal level in the early 1990s, this applies to the regional level [...] to a very different extent. Selected examples show that though this topic has been on the political and instrumental agenda in some Federal States for many years, by spatial planning actors who are dealing with. It is still not 'mainstream', i.e. it is not taken into account in routine planning work.
>
> *(Baumgart 2010: 362)*

Interim Conclusion – Current Status of Gender Mainstreaming in Administrative Practice

Up till now, planning routines for handling the gender perspective in the fields of regional development and regional planning have been missing. An advanced "objective perspective" is required, both for identifying existing opportunities and for remedying deficits and disadvantages for women and men. The aim of using the gender perspective is to achieve greater quality and efficiency in spatial planning (a "win-win"). Therefore, a lot of convincing work is needed to strengthen women's participation at all levels. While there is already awareness of the importance of a gender perspective in regional planning, there is often little or no structural anchoring of gender mainstreaming within administrations. In this respect, qualified staff for substantive processing are needed, together with management support.

The Ruhr Regional Association (RVR) is considering gender mainstreaming at three levels, internally and within the framework of the regional discourse about developing the Ruhr Regional Plan. The RVR has played a pioneering role here, giving gender mainstreaming high priority right from the start.

The Ruhr Metropolitan Area and the Ruhr Regional Association

The Ruhr Metropolitan Area is located in the west of Germany and in the heart of Europe. A lot of important transit corridors cross the area. More than 5 million inhabitants live in an area of over 4,400 square kilometers, spread over 53 cities and municipalities. Together with Istanbul, Greater London, Île-de-France, Moscow and the Madrid Metropolitan Area, the Ruhr Metropolitan Area is thus one of the biggest agglomerations in Europe (see RVR 2014b: 13 and Figure 11.1).

With the mission of supporting the area's development, the Ruhr Regional Association – a communal administration union – comprises 11 independent Ruhr cities (Bochum, Bottrop, Dortmund, Duisburg, Essen, Gelsenkirchen, Hagen, Hamm, Herne, Mülheim a. d. Ruhr and Oberhausen) as well as four districts (Ennepe-Ruhr, Recklinghausen, Wesel and Unna) as seen in Figure 11.2.

Legal reforms in the period 2004–2007 saw the state parliament of North Rhine-Westphalia reassigning planning competences for the Ruhr Metropolitan Area to the Ruhr Regional Association. Having taken over regional planning on

FIGURE 11.1 The Ruhr Metropolitan Area and other metropolises in Europe
Source: ILS 2015, internal working material.

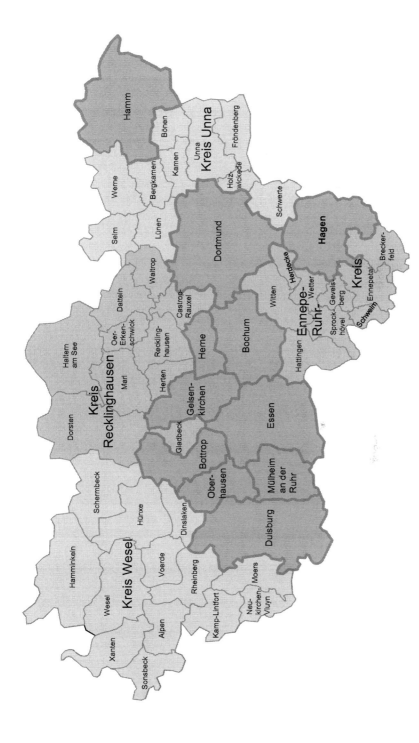

FIGURE 11.2 Cities and districts of the Ruhr Metropolitan Area

Source: Ruhr Regional Association.

31 October 2009, the Ruhr Regional Association is able to create an integrative regional plan for the entire region again for the first time in more than 40 years, setting down a conditional framework for the region's spatial development over the next 15 years (see RVR 2014a: 13). The RVR is thereby responsible for both formal regional planning and informal regional development.

Formal planning instruments are statutory planning instruments – their definitions and targets are binding. The regional plan devolves its binding effect on the subordinate authorities. By contrast, informal planning instruments (here for regional development) refer to various types of voluntary cooperation in the form of working groups as well as concrete conceptual plans that are not formalized. Such plans are not binding for citizens or other public authorities and institutions, though they can lead to a self-imposed commitment.

In the field of regional development, the RVR is the provider of such important infrastructural projects as the *Industrial Heritage Trail* and the *Emscher Landscape Park*, Europe's biggest regional park. The Ruhr Regional Association's legal tasks include the regional promotion of trade, industry, and tourism, the protection and development of open spaces, forests, and green areas, as well as public relations work and the preparation of climate and geological data for the Ruhr Metropolitan Area. Under the amended (12 May 2015) law governing the RVR, tasks such as the connection of local European work (and European subsidies policy) and traffic development planning were added (Article 1, §4 RVRG 2015).

Furthermore, the RVR is the seat of the Ruhr Parliament (the Association's assembly) which consists of community politics delegates. As a regional council, the Ruhr Parliament decides on amendments to and realignments of the regional plan for the Ruhr area. Under the 12 May 2015 amendment, Ruhr Parliament delegates will be elected directly by the area's inhabitants from that date (Article 2, §10 RVRG 2015). Both the Parliament itself and its future direct elections are a novelty in Germany.

Gender Mainstreaming – A Goal and Cross-Cutting Issue for Regional Planning in the Ruhr Regional Association

Taking account of gender mainstreaming has a long tradition in the RVR. It is enshrined in the law establishing the RVR in §10, sentence 9 (Formation of the Association Assembly); §13, sentence 1 Point 4 (Tasks of the Association Committee) and in §17 (Tasks of the Equal Opportunities Officer), as amended on 3 February 2014 (last amended on 12 May 2015). This means that the inclusion of the gender perspective is explicitly demanded by the head of administration.

The RVR's organizational and human resources development foresees the following structures for permanently integrating gender mainstreaming into everyday business: The Association has an Equal Opportunities Officer, a women's advancement plan, an in-house Equality Working Group as well as a referee with the explicit task of integrating gender into spatial planning. An interdepartmental Gender Working Group, dealing in-depth with the Association's planning topics, also looks at where and how gender mainstreaming aspects can be incorporated. Moreover, there is an intense cooperation with the Women's Network Ruhr.

The Women's Network Ruhr (FNW): A Platform for Active Participation

Founded in 2002, the Women's Network Ruhr (FNW) is an informal regional network supporting the active participation of the region's gender experts and equal opportunities officers. One of the aims of the member women was the participation in the mission statement process of City Region Ruhr 2030.[3]

Such informal regional women's networks are a reaction to the lack of women's presence and gender-focused topics in a region. Therefore, women's networks strive for women's active involvement in regional development processes[4] (see Bock 2001: 58).

Genesis and Structure of the Network

The foundation of the FNW goes back to an initiative discussed in the summer 2002 workshop "Women create a model for the region" held in Essen by the then Ruhr Municipal Association (now named Ruhr Regional Association). Participants successfully pursued the goal of launching a gender mainstreaming-oriented development within the City Region Ruhr 2030 project and of participating in the inter-municipal City Region Ruhr planning process.[5]

Following the workshop, the FNW was founded, bringing together committed actors from the region again. Since the late 1980s, there have been many women's activities and participation initiatives in the Ruhr area in the context of such projects as Agenda 21 and the International Building Exhibition (IBA Emscher Park). In 1989 the Working Group Women and Planning was established from former women's initiatives,[6] acting as an official advisory working group for the IBA Emscher Park. Between 1989 and 1998 it developed gender criteria and indicators aimed at strengthening gender-sensitive planning and construction. In addition, the Working Group worked intensively on individual pilot projects and on implementing women's housing projects. The dedicated work of the FNW follows in this "tradition" and experience.

The FNW is currently made up of 140 women with planning, gender, and planning-science backgrounds. They work in equality authorities, city administrations, Ruhr institutions, state ministries, universities, churches, offices, associations, or initiatives and mostly live in the Ruhr Metropolitan Area or in the state of North Rhine-Westphalia.

Structurally, it was and is important for the FNW to be institutionally integrated: FNW coordination and organization is in the hands of the RVR Equal

Opportunities Officer and a three-member panel of spokeswomen. Highly accepted by RVR management, the network operates independently and autonomously and is open to all women interested in gender issues within the region.

Objective, Commitment and Contributions

The aim of the FNW is to incorporate gender mainstreaming as a guiding principle in processes, projects, and administrational activities within the region and its municipalities. With its activities, the FNW wants gender-sensitive working methods and strategies to become common practice and routine in local and regional planning as well as in the academic world. The region's diversity serves as the basis for FNW topics and issues.[7] One of the first gender projects was the Ruhr Valley, with its cycle trail, in which the results of FNW fieldwork and expertise (see "On Gender traces in the Ruhr Valley", FNW 2003) were fed into local and regional processes.

The FNW regularly looks critically at planning-relevant issues from a gender perspective and selects topics on the agenda in the Ruhr Metropolis and in North Rhine-Westphalia. It organizes training workshops and events in collaboration with the RVR or e.g. with the Faculty of Spatial Planning at TU Dortmund (see Figure 11.3).

Furthermore, the FNW has issued written statements on draft bills, for example on the review and amendment of the 2004 law governing the RVR, with a view to anchoring gender mainstreaming. The FNW is a body responsible for public affairs (TÖB) for the regional land-use plan of six Ruhr municipalities and regularly gives opinions on planning processes. It is striving to participate in this capacity in the future Ruhr Regional Plan.

In the 13 years of its existence the network has established itself as a qualified partner for the implementation of gender mainstreaming in the RVR and region's planning and has raised its profile through organizing joint events and issuing publications. Building on its long experience, the FNW has actively participated in the RVR's regional discourse to develop the new Ruhr Regional Plan. FNW experts have been involved in the discourse from its beginning, taking part in individual events with their own contributions (available in the RVR's respective publications). This forms a solid base for entrenching gender-related aims and contents in the Ruhr Regional Plan (formal level) and for incorporating gender-related topics and projects in the RVR's Spatial Development Action Program for the Ruhr Metropolitan Area on regional development (informal level) currently being compiled.

The Regional Discourse ... on the Road to the Future of the Ruhr Metropolitan Area

Now in charge of public regional planning, the RVR focuses on the Ruhr Metropolitan Area as a unit in terms of planning. Strategic conceptual aims of regional development and general spatial implementation of regional planning are considered

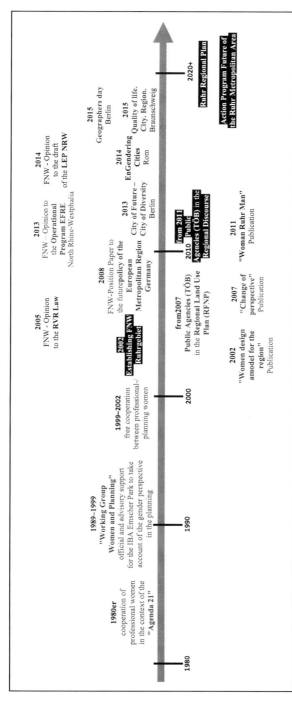

FIGURE 11.3 Timeline – FNW activities

Source: RVR 2015, internal working material.

together. The above-named Spatial Development Action Program for the Ruhr Metropolitan Area is being developed in parallel with the Ruhr Regional Plan for the Ruhr Metropolitan Area. In this context, the regional discourse was introduced to boost transparency and communication. It constitutes a new approach to "strategic regional planning", emphasizing the importance of informal planning structures. The (expert) public has been integrated since 2011 through the intensive participation of associations, expert institutions, business, agriculture, politics, civil society, and the local Ruhr municipalities and districts. The professed goal is to come up with a plan "by the region for the region". The region's development potential and current challenges are being identified and goals are being worked out (see RVR 2014a: 13). Topics include settlement development, industry, trade, agriculture and forestry, traffic and mobility, energy supplies, open spaces, and tourism, cultural landscapes, education, as well as the issue of water. Equal opportunities/gender mainstreaming and adjustment to climate and demographic change are cross-sectional goals and need to be considered in all fields.

The regional discourse thus stands for transparency, intensive participation, and communication, the incorporation of the expert knowledge of the municipalities concerned and research organizations, as well as the integration of associations, clubs, and institutions. New planning principles resulting from a new planning philosophy are being used as a basis. Formal and informal planning instruments are being considered as interrelated and developed accordingly.

Gender Mainstreaming in the Regional Discourse – from the Outset

When the regional discourse was initiated there was consensus that equal opportunities/gender mainstreaming had to be integrated from the outset (see RVR 2014: 153). As a result, the implementation of gender mainstreaming is set on three levels:

1. Structural
2. Content
3. Process.

The structural level refers to the embedding of gender mainstreaming in the existing law of the Ruhr Regional Association (RVRG), especially in the section on organization and human resource development. At the process level, gender mainstreaming is incorporated (see Figure 11.4) into all participation forms (i.e. regional forums, expert dialogues, international competition of concepts, future forums).

At the content level, the Ruhr Regional Plan (as a formal result of the preceding regional discourse) and the Spatial Development Action Program for the Ruhr Metropolitan Area (as an informal result of the preceding regional discourse) are influenced by the insights and concrete results of the above-mentioned participation opportunities.

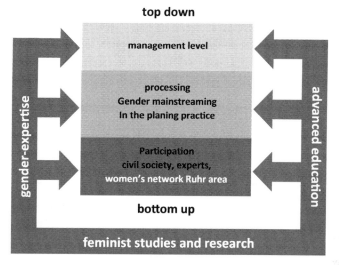

FIGURE 11.4   Process, content, and participation
Source: RVR 2015, internal working material.

Implementation at Structural Level (Organization and Human Resources Management)

The successful implementation of gender mainstreaming is dependent on whether its principles are fully accepted and promoted by decision makers. The head of the RVR administration and the responsible politicians have decided to incorporate gender issues in the regional discourse over the Ruhr Regional Plan and the RVR's future regional development (see RVR 2014a: 153). The RVR's Equal Opportunities Officer and the RVR's professional planner with her explicit gender scope have been actively involved and act as multipliers of the FNW's work. In addition, the internal interdepartmental Gender Working Group has accompanied the different stages of the regional discourse. Figure 11.4 shows how gender mainstreaming is embedded into the RVR's top-down and bottom-up planning processes and how it is accompanied by education and training and backed up by gender expertise and the results of feminist research.[8]

Implementation at Process Level (Participation)

Figure 11.5 illustrates the entire regional discourse process, which started in 2011 with district and municipal interviews with all 53 cities and four districts.

The diagram in this figure describes the process itself with its particular types of events aimed at creating the Ruhr Regional Plan as a formal outcome and the Spatial Development Action Programs for the Ruhr Metropolitan Area as an informal one. This process includes the competition of ideas are represented in the upper section of the graph. The planning instruments (like settlement area monitoring, open-space

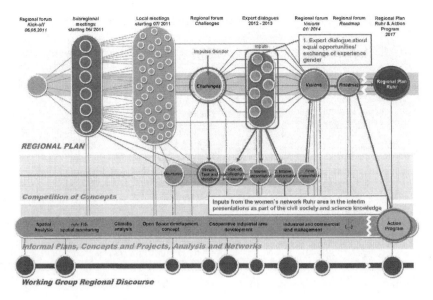

FIGURE 11.5   Regional discourse components
Source: RVR 2014a, supplied by authors.

concepts, etc.) which accompany and support the entire process can be seen in the lower part of the illustration, with the associated Working Group Regional Discourse.

In all discourse process and participation formats, gender mainstreaming concerns were integrated from the outset. For instance, in the "Regional Forum" *Challenges* (2011) an external gender expert was invited to present the spatial requirements and criteria from a gender perspective. The following 11 expert dialogues took place from April 2012 to March 2013:

1. Exchange of experience: Gender/Equal Opportunities
2. Regional greenways
3. (Large-scale) retail
4. Agriculture and forestry
5. Traffic and mobility
6. Energy and climate
7. Recreation and tourism
8. Cultural landscapes
9. Open space
10. Water
11. Settlement development.

The dialogue about gender/equal opportunities was deliberately scheduled before the other ten dialogues to sensitize stakeholders to the different gender perspectives. Furthermore, the RVR continued to intensely involve citizens, regional players, and academia by calling for a *competition of ideas* on the future of the Ruhr Metropolis. In a collaborative process to establish a development perspective covering the entire region, five internationally staffed planning teams were given the challenge of developing visions for the region. In the announcement for this competition, one requirement was to take explicit account of the diverse lifestyles of women and men and the different planning cultures (see RVR 2013: 5, 14). Furthermore, equal opportunities and gender mainstreaming were discussed and addressed in the various future forums of the *competition of ideas* (see Figure 11.5).

Another component of the *competition of ideas* was the RVR's call for *1,000 Ruhr Ideas*. Launched in cooperation with a major local newspaper, the idea was to have citizens develop ideas and visions for the whole Ruhr Metropolis. Citizens submitted some 430 creative ideas and suggestions to the five international planning teams and the political bodies (expert committee and Ruhr Parliament) (see RVR 2014a: 30).

In addition to *Ruhr Ideas*, a second call – *Ruhr Knowledge* – targeted academia (universities, colleges, research institutes, and institutions). The FNW took part in both calls (*1,000 Ruhr Ideas* and *Ruhr Knowledge*) (see Digression: Loveable und livable quarters – living portraits in this chapter). The evaluation of all submitted ideas involving a gender perspective confirmed the current topics in gender studies: Safety in public spaces, the quality of housing and the living environment, mobility/accessibility opportunities, the desire for togetherness, leisure, and open space.

The entire regional discourse is being evaluated in-depth by the responsible planning committee and is being politically decided by the Association Assembly (the Ruhr Parliament) thereby politically legitimizing gender mainstreaming. In the Working Group Regional Discourse with its mainly local representatives and its mission to assist and advise the RVR in the matters associated with the regional discourse, an FNW representative is also involved in order to open up opportunities for dialogue.

Implementation at Content Level (Gender Criteria and Issue)

All 11 expert dialogues, the regional forums, the *competition of ideas* as well as its outcomes related to gender criteria have been documented in publications now available as work material for further planning.

Findings from the First Regional Forum – *Challenges*:

Indication for the mission statement process:

- The Ruhr Metropolitan Area needs gender-sensitive images (role models) depicting life and work in the region (counteracting the outdated male-dominated image of Ruhr coal miners and steelworkers).

Indication for the data collection:

- Current working and living patterns need to be recorded separately and made transparent.

Indications for new perspectives – what they need to consider:

- The everyday conditions of women and men
- Structural disadvantages – especially for women
- Structural change achievements (who benefits and how?)
- Involvement and participation.

In all 11 specialized dialogues, FNW representatives presented the gender perspective. The findings of three of the dialogues are listed exemplarily here.

Findings from *Experiences of Gender/Equal Opportunities*:

Principles and qualities contributing to equal opportunities were worked out for spatial development. These include:

- Integrated concepts
- Mixed use
- Good accessibility, public transport services
- Decentralized supply/jobs
- Housing close to green areas/recreational spaces.

To achieve broad participation, empowerment is necessary in order to gain consensus among different disciplines or citizens and sectoral planning; it requires a common understanding and appropriate event formats.

Findings from the Expert Dialogue *Traffic and Mobility*:

- Gender-sensitive mobility planning in terms of methodology/content/processes (impact assessment)
- Gender-specific statistics/mobility analysis
- Consideration of different everyday mobility patterns of women/men, good public transport accessibility
- Representation and participation of users and experts in mobility plans.

Findings from the Expert Dialogue *Settlement Development*:

1. Develop living environment and places of residence gender-sensitively.

2. Gender-specific data collection and spatial analysis in order to visualize structural disadvantage.
3. Qualities for the integrated planning of housing, work, leisure, utilities and infrastructure which are oriented on the everyday lives of women/men/families/communities.

The main findings of the expert dialogues and the *competition of ideas* are to be found in "Perspectives for the Spatial Development of the Ruhr Metropolitan Area", a position paper supported by all concerned regional players and has been decided by politics. The position paper serves as a basis for developing the Ruhr Regional Plan (as a formal planning instrument) and the Spatial Development Action Program for the Ruhr Metropolitan Area (as an informal planning instrument) and is thus a guideline for future regional development by the RVR (see Figure 11.6 and RVR 2014a. 154).

In the Ruhr Regional Plan, gender mainstreaming will be incorporated in the preamble, general principle, goals, and guidelines.

From a current perspective it can be concluded that the gender perspective reinforces the context of justification (gender check) and consequently has a high relevance for assessments, for instance:

* Greater focus on inner development
* Settlement development only with regard to existing infrastructure
* Open spaces close to housing
* Guaranteed high-quality public transport infrastructure connections.

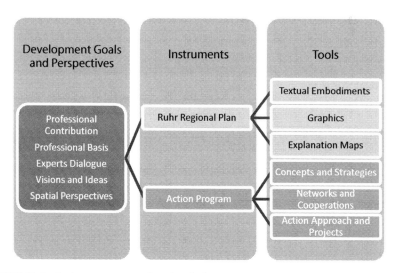

FIGURE 11.6 Action program and regional plan
Source: RVR 2014a, internal working material.

Once the decision to adopt the Ruhr Regional Plan and the Action Program For the spatial development Ruhr Metropolitan Area has been taken, the RVR can start implementing the regional projects. The two papers will also constitute the basis for local projects, with the option of realizing the gender perspective in their respective fields of action. The gender-oriented dialogue will thus be continued at various levels.

A First Conclusion – Gender Mainstreaming in the Regional Planning of the Ruhr Metropolitan Area

For the Ruhr Metropolitan Area, the challenges shaping the future lie on the one hand in its declining population and on the other hand in the difficult financial situation of its cities and municipalities, which allows little scope for action. It is important to prioritize the continuing need to restructure social and structural adjustment measures and infrastructure projects within the region. This is only possible with broad regional consensus – hand in hand with stakeholders and the population in general on the basis of an innovative and dialogue-oriented regional development concept. The Ruhr Metropolis has taken this path under the declared regional governance assumed by the Ruhr Regional Association on taking over responsibility for regional planning and regional development in 2009. At the launch event for the regained regional planning in 2010, regional governance was highlighted as a pioneering method and underlined by expertise (see Horch 2010: 386).

The above-mentioned regional discourse has been consistently conducted with the participation of local and regional players as well as civil society actors under the counterflow principle to detect and identify the Ruhr-specific resources for shaping the future and defining the mission statement process. With the *competition of ideas*, civil society, a variety of citizen initiatives and networks as well as those from academia were included. In both cases, equal opportunities and gender mainstreaming were consistently seen as a cross-cutting issue from the outset.

Although experience and related networking structures already existed in the region, the RVR was well aware of the fact that the region's future development was dependent on the successful adoption of a gender perspective. In his welcoming speech at the Ruhr Regional Association's 2007 event Change of Perspective – Gender Mainstreaming in Regional Development, Regional Director Heinz-Dieter Klink stated:

> It is and remains the goal of the RVR, hand in hand with its member municipalities, to provide decent working and living conditions for the people of the Ruhr and to make the area more attractive for in-migrating men and women.

With the incorporation of gender mainstreaming in a dialogue-oriented regional planning process along with its numerous topics (from settlement development, mobility, etc. to specialist technical and social subjects), the RVR is treading new ground in regional development and planning. It is important to ensure that stakeholders such as the FNW participate. In addition, highly motivated managers and employees are needed in planning administrations, together with similarly motivated regional players, to develop routines and matters of course in the sense of a gender mainstreaming strategy in the everyday planning work. Moreover, in order to sustainably implement gender mainstreaming in governance, mutual trust plays a very important role.

Since the (gender) objectives and contents of regional-level planning are perforce very general, this task places high demands on everyone concerned – internal (RVR) and external (stakeholders, municipalities, politicians). Opinion-making and acceptance are repeatedly demanded in the context of many discussions. As an ongoing process, the implementation of gender mainstreaming is therefore characterized by the following features:

- Gender mainstreaming/gender justice from the outset
- Support by the region's professional planners and equal opportunities officers (i.e. the FNW)
- Learning together and from one another as a permanent process.

This approach should be based on already existing gender objectives and criteria for the RVR's regional projects and should be developed and mediated for municipal projects. For the consistent incorporation of gender mainstreaming in regional strategies – at both regional and local level – and in technical issues, gender-specific analyses are required (data collection and data analysis). For communication and sensitization in the regional context of planning and politics, visualized gender-specific regional analyses in the form of maps and plan statements are essential too. For this, as well as for gender monitoring with a continuous compilation and updating of regional gender-specific data, appropriate structures (including human capacities) and responsibilities need, accordingly, to be established within the planning administration.

Digression

A contribution to the Ideas Competition: Loveable und livable quarters – living portraits

This contribution of the women's network – based on exemplary living portraits of women in the Ruhr area – broaches the issue of an innovative methodology to better capture housing needs. It was important to focus on the quality of housing and the living environment. Of particular interest was their suitability for everyday use, coupled with the question: How can negative developments be stopped and how can positive approaches be strengthened? Starting out from the following three key questions the individual life situation was situated:

Where do I live now? What's important to me? Which visions do I have for 2030? It was also important to note negative developments as well as to indicate positive living (environment) situations. The innovative methodology presupposes an awareness of women's own housing situations: This is one of the minimum criteria for planning participation.

Using this autobiographical and emotionally centered method, the resulting essays provide insights into personal living and life patterns; they include wishes and needs and thus contribute to a new participation culture. In particular, they reflect a part of the lives of women of different ages, with different family relationships and different professional and income levels conditions. All women live and/or work in the region. The promise to open up complex issues by permitting personal feelings and criticisms increases the diversity of planning and positively highlights gender mainstreaming. Against this background, the portraits are currently being expanded to include men from the region.

Using these living portraits, stakeholders can arbitrarily set priorities vis-à-vis other qualitative methods. The portraits allow them to revise the written word from a certain distance. Any revision can be explained or concealed. Furthermore, the author is locatable directly in the text by the addressee. The impressions reached in this way underlie, principally, the interpretation of the reader. Any filters that might arise from the interpretation or editors of the contribution are minimized. In all the living portraits, the authors are illustrated by self-taken images, by what was particularly important, by the choice of the subject, the time of recording and the positioning.

Despite the variety of living portraits and the visions of the future (2030), the following quality criteria and opinions are consistently highlighted in all living portraits – and are also important from a gender perspective:

- Practicality of housing and living environment
- Affordable housing and housing diversity
- Short walk to local amenities and social infrastructure offerings
- Good access to public transport and a good cycling and walking infrastructure
- Close-by, usable, and unencumbered green and recreational areas
- Facilities and networks for joint activities and civic engagement in the neighborhood.

The following additional knowledge from the living portraits has a certain "signal effect" for the region: The demographic change and image change which have taken place in many neighborhoods through refurbishment or demolition work are individually experienced in very different ways by the authors who live there (positive – negative – indifferent). Alongside the realities of life, it seems that subjective feelings and value systems play a role here too.

Notes

1 The concept of gender mainstreaming was first discussed in 1985 at the 3rd UN World Conference on Women in Nairobi, and was developed and established in 1995 at the 4th UN World Conference on Women in Beijing as a strategy of new instruments for gender equality policies. With the 1997/1998 Amsterdam Treaty, EU Member States undertook to apply gender mainstreaming in their policies.

2 Enshrined in Article 3, Section 2, Sentence 2 of the 1949 Basic Law (GG) of the Federal Republic of Germany (last amended on 23 December 2014): "Men and women have equal rights. The state promotes the actual implementation of equal rights for women and men and works towards the elimination of existing disadvantages".

3 Eight cities of the Ruhr region (Bochum, Dortmund, Duisburg, Essen, Gelsenkirchen, Herne, Mülheim/Ruhr and Oberhausen) and the University of Dortmund's Faculty of Spatial Planning participated in the national competition "City 2030" and started by defining a common regional mission statement in 2001.

4 As a result of her research on regional women's networks, Stephanie Bock wrote in 2001: "Regional women's networks represent alliances of different women's and gender political actors. To the 'inside' they act in a socially supportive manner as informal networks and serve as sources of information and contacts. To the 'outside' they participate actively in the politics of regional development and policy processes based on a feminist understanding. Their aims are on the one hand to strengthen the public presence of women in the region and on the other hand to promote the implementation of gender policy content in regional policy fields of action" (Bock 2001: 58).

5 "Gender mainstreaming" was enshrined as a principle for the mission statement process of *Ruhr City Region 2030* and is included in the documentation for the mission fair – vastness – organized by the *Ruhr City Region 2030*, from February 5, until 7 February 2003 (Städteregion Ruhr 2003: 11).

6 1989 – in the first year of the International Building (IBA) Emscher Park – a workshop with the theme "More power and influence of women in the planning" was initiated by dedicated professional women and equal opportunities officers of the region. In addition, a working group Women and Planning – with institutional involvement in the IBA-Company – was founded. This was led from 1989–1998 by IBA employees. With the completion of the IBA and the resolution of the IBA committees the work of the working group Women and Planning also ended and it was for a successor – if possible also sought a new institutional links, which then found itself at the Ruhrgebiet communal Association (KVR) in 2002 with the establishment of the Women's Network Ruhr.

7 Important fields of action of the Women's Network Ruhr and examples of network activities include, for example, the relevant contribution of the publication Woman-RuhrMan (2010: 58f) since 2002. See list under www.metropoleruhr.de/regionalver band-ruhr/ueber-uns/gleichstellungsarbeit/frauennetzwerk.html.

8 Feminist research distinguishes itself by the fact that their professional issues and research methods include equality, human dignity and self-determination of women. It aims to make female history and achievements visible and to demonstrate the unequal status of women and men in society and promote equality. It is not limited to women's studies, but is implemented in many research projects worldwide.

References

Bauhardt, Christine (2004). *Entgrenzte Räume. Zu Theorie und Politik räumlicher Planung.* Wiesbaden.

Baumgart, Sabine (Hrsg.) (2010). Die Stadt ist die Region. Regionalentwicklung muss geschlechtergerecht sein. In: *FrauRuhrMann*, pp. 359–367. Essen. Klartext Publisher.

Bock, Stephanie (2001). *Regionale Frauennetzwerke –Frauenpolitische Bündnisse zwischen beruflichen Interessen und geschlechterpolitischen Zielen.* Kassel.

Bölting, Torsten; Schneiders, Katrin (2010). Lebenswelten von Frauen und Männern im Quartier. In: *FrauRuhrMann*, pp. 278–304. Essen. Klartext Publisher.

Broschüre Gender Planning (2002). *Arbeitskreis Broschüre Gender Planning* (Hrsg.). First Edition. Kaiserslautern.

Deutsche Institut für Urbanistik (Difu) (2015). Gender Mainstreaming im Städtebau. Website www.difu.de/publikationen/difu-berichte-42005/gender-mainstreaming-im-staedtebau.html [Last accessed on September 16, 2015].

Ehrhardt, Angelika (2003). Gender Mainstreaming – wo es herkommt, was es will und wie es geht. In: Jansen, Mechtild; Röming, Angelika; Rohde, Marianne (Hrsg.): *Gender Mainstreaming. Herausforderung für den Dialog der Geschlechter*, Second Edition, p. 13. München.

Frauennetzwerk Ruhrgebiet (Hrsg.) (2003). Auf Genderspuren im Ruhrtal – Von Lokführerinnen, Arbeiterfrauen und Burgfräulein. Erfahrungsberichte und Ergebnisse der Ruhrtal-Radtour. Essen.

Frauennetzwerk Ruhrgebiet (Hrsg.) c/0 Regionalverband Ruhr (2007). Perspektivwechsel – Gender Mainstreaming in der Regionalentwicklung. Essen.

Greiwe, Ulla; Kelp-Siekmann, Sibylle (2005). Gender Mainstreaming – Leitlinie auch in regionalen Prozessen. Die Implementierung des Leitbildes am Beispiel des Frauennetzwerks Ruhrgebiet. In: *RaumPlanung 123*, pp. 259–263. Dortmund.

Greiwe, Ulla; Kelp-Siekmann, Sibylle (2010). Informelle Frauennetzwerke – Wie kommt Gender in den Mainstream. In: *FrauRuhrMann*, pp. 54–61. Essen. Klartext Publisher.

Horch, Claudia (2010). Mit gutem Beispiel voran. Innovative regionale Entwicklungsstrategien müssen Frauen und Männer im Blick haben. In: *FrauRuhrMann*, pp. 385–393. Essen. Klartext Publisher.

Jansen, Mechtild; Röming, Angelika; Rohde, Marianne (Hrsg.) (2003). *Gender Mainstreaming – Herausforderung für den Dialog der Geschlechter.* München.

Kampherm, Ruth (2000). *Frauenatlas Ruhrgebiet, Kommunalverband Ruhrgebiet.* Essen.

Lessing, Petra (2010). Frauen – geringer beschäftigt, bezahlt und abgesichert. In: *FrauRuhrMann*, RVR (Hrsg.). pp. 138–155. Essen. Klartext Publisher.

Pohlmann-Rohr, Birgit; Selter, Regina (2007). Der Arbeitskreis Frauen und IBA –ein Rückblick. In: Becker, Ruth; Greiwe, Ulla (Hrsg.): *Internationale Bauausstellung Emscher Park –eine Chance für Frauen? Studien Netzwerk Frauenforschung NRW Nr.4.* Dortmund, Second unchanged Edition, pp. 74–81 and pp. 109–134.

Regionalverband Ruhr (Hrsg.) (2013). *Ideenwettbewerb Zukunft Metropole Ruhr. Auslobung.* Essen.

Regionalverband Ruhr (RVR) (Hrsg.) (2010). *FrauRuhrMann – Lebenswelten von Frauen und Männern in der Metropole Ruhr.* Essen. Klartext Publisher.

Regionalverband Ruhr (RVR) (Hrsg.) (2014a). Ideenwettbewerb Zukunft Metropole Ruhr. Ruhr.impulse. Essen.

Regionalverband Ruhr (RVR) (Hrsg.) (2014b). Website www.metropoleruhr.de/en/home/ruhr-metropolis/data-facts.html [Last accessed on September 18, 2015].

RVR- Gesetz in der Fassung der Bekanntmachung vom 03. Febr. 2004 (GV.NRW. S. 96), zuletzt geändert durch Gesetz vom 12. Mai 2015 (GV.NRW. S.435).

Schweigert, Birgit (2001). Alles Gender – oder? Die Implementierung von Gender Mainstreaming auf Bundesebene, In: Internationale Betriebswirtschafts- und Volkswirtschaftslehre (IBV), Nr. 20, p. 1267.

Staatskanzlei des Landes Nordrhein-Westfalen (2015). Landesentwicklungsplan Nordrhein-Westfalen. Entwurf Juni 2013. Website www.nrw.de/landesplanung/ [Last accessed on September 16, 2015].

Städteregion Ruhr 2030 (City Region 2030) (2003). *Unendliche Weite*, p. 11. Essen.
The North Rhine Westphalia State Development Plan LEP NRW (1995).

Further Information

www.metropoleruhr.de
www.metropoleruhr.de/regionalverband-ruhr
www.metropoleruhr.de/regionalverband-ruhr/regionaler-diskurs
www.ideenwettbewerb.metropoleruhr.de
www.metropoleruhr.de/regionalverband-ruhr/ueber-uns/gleichstellungsarbeit/
www.frauennetzwerk.html

12

AN ANALYSIS OF EU URBAN POLICY FROM THE PERSPECTIVE OF GENDER[1]

Sonia De Gregorio Hurtado

Introduction

Cities have been part of the focus of EU policy since the end of the 1980s. Due to the awareness of the relevance of urban issues in achieving the objectives of the treaties, a complex process of policy-building has taken place within EU institutions since. This has led to the definition of what we could call today the "European Union's urban policy" or the "urban dimension of EU policy".

In order to understand the process of policy construction that has taken place over the last three decades, it is relevant to mention that the European Union does not have powers in the field of urban issues. The legislative capacity in this regard lies in the hands of the Member States. Consequently, over the years, urban issues within EU policy have been drafted using a number of non-compulsory policy tools of different types, produced and launched by different stakeholders (the European Commission, the European Parliament, the Committee of the Regions, the Informal Meeting of Ministers of Urban Development, organisations such as Eurocities, etc.).

These tools consist mainly of: (i) written documents (policy documents such as EC communications, case studies of best practices, guidelines, etc.); (ii) instruments for urban regeneration launched by the European Commission (the Urban Pilot Projects – UPP – and the URBAN Community Initiative), co-funded by the Structural Funds; and (iii) URBACT, a programme aimed to develop knowledge, practical experience, and capacity in networks of cities that work around a specific policy challenge, considered relevant to sustainable urban development in the context of the Europe 2020 strategy (European Commission, 2010).

There are also other instruments, initiatives, and programmes that have exerted an influence on the definition and development of the urban dimension in EU policy. However, those mentioned here are the most specific and visible ones. They have produced the most demonstrable results, and they have been launched within this specific policy domain over the last three decades (De Gregorio Hurtado, 2017).

This process of policy-building has led to the construction of a concept of "sustainable/integrated urban development" that has been integrated within the policy tools mentioned through the development of a specific policy discourse. This work is aimed at understanding how the gender perspective has been introduced into the EU's policy discourse on urban matters over the last 15 years.

In order to achieve this objective, it is important to take into account that in 1999 the Treaty of Amsterdam (signed in 1997) came into force. It brought new insight into gender issues at Community level, as for the first time it introduced the concept of gender mainstreaming within the Treaty. This new approach to equal opportunities included multiple new provisions strengthening EU competence in this policy area. The Treaty moved equal opportunities on from a focus on equal pay to become a central objective of EU political commitment. As a result, equal treatment between women and men now represents a fundamental right enshrined in EU law (Booth and Bennett, 2002: 2). For Pollack and Hafner-Burton (2000) the most far-reaching provision in the new Treaty was the revision of Articles 2 and 3 that made equal opportunities for women and men a central objective of the Union.

As a result of the adoption of this, from that moment on, the gender perspective became integrated within many policy areas where the EU was politically active. Today, 15 years after the adoption of the gender-mainstreaming approach in the Treaty, the current level of implementation of this perspective within the different policy areas is highly heterogeneous: some policy fields have integrated or have started to mainstream gender (e.g. gender is now mainstreamed within EU research policy), while others have not yet started this process.

The results of this research indicate that the gender dimension has not yet been introduced into EU urban policy: a policy field that sets down the guidelines for sustainable urban development in EU territory. In turn, that lays the basis of the criteria on how EU cities contribute to support the daily life of their citizens through all the initiatives that are co-funded by the Structural Fund under the EU Cohesion Policy.

The main contribution of this study consists of identifying the lack of implementation of gender mainstreaming in the urban policy of the EU. It is relevant to shed light on this to: (i) raise awareness of this gap; (ii) start a process aimed at exploring the reasons that explain the situation; and (iii) contribute to acquiring knowledge aimed at facing limitations and obstacles in order to bring about a transformation. All this is considered significant in the context of the urban dimension of the Cohesion Policy in the period 2014–2020, under which initiatives and programmes for urban development are being launched in the different Member States, particularly with the support of "the European Regional Development Fund (ERDF), in which Member States are now obliged to earmark at least 5% of their national ERDF allocation [...] to support integrated sustainable urban development strategies" (European Commission, 2015: 3).

The awareness of this lack of implementation could give rise to policy action oriented to introducing the dimension of gender into all the urban initiatives co-funded by the Structural Funds, which would have a beneficial impact on EU cities in the short and medium term. This is particularly vital, as many of these tools are aimed at regenerating urban areas, and the integration of the gender dimension within urban regeneration can contribute to strengthening social interaction and reducing social exclusion (García-Ramón et al., 2004), which is an explicit objective of EU urban policy (see, for example, European Commission, 2011).

This study has the following structure: the second part introduces the approach adopted by the research and establishes the conceptual framework for the analysis, the third part explains the methodology, the fourth part develops the discussion, and the fifth gathers the conclusions and their implications, including recommendations for policy action in the short and medium term, aimed at integrating the gender perspective in EU urban policy.

Conceptual and Methodological Frameworks for a Critical Approach to EU Urban Policy from the Viewpoint of Gender

In 1998, one year after signing the Treaty of Amsterdam, the European Commission published a policy document (communication) that exerted a relevant impact on the development of the EU's urban dimension (Cullingworth and Nadine, 2006). It was entitled Sustainable Urban Development in the European Union: A Framework for Action (European Commission, 1998). The document had as its main objective "to stimulate better coordination of existing Community actions" that affected urban areas (Cullingworth and Nadine, 2006, 382). To achieve this objective, it took into account the legal changes that were taking place within the Union at that moment, in order to develop an urban policy framework consistent with the overall policy scenario and EU political objectives. Consequently, it mentioned the Treaty of Amsterdam as one of the main legal changes taking place in the EU context, explaining the consequences that this new framework would have for urban matters in the EU. In fact, the implications for cities as regards much of the content of the Treaty were addressed by the document (social cohesion, sustainable urban development, etc.). It is relevant to highlight that it did not mention the need to implement the gender-mainstreaming approach within the context of urban policies or urban planning.

It is worth underlining that a first and superficial look at the document might give the reader the impression that gender was considered implicitly in the text's policy discourse. This is because the document follows a general discourse that underlines equality as a policy objective of the EU, but this is a concept of equality biased from the perspective of gender, which takes equality to mean sameness, concealing the fact that the social construction of gender entails women and men having different needs and expectations regarding public and private spaces (housing) in cities.

By doing this, the document fails to consider gender as a driver of discrimination in the field of urban policies. While it does not consider discrimination on a gender basis, it does mention discrimination due to sex, race, or ethnic origin, religion or belief, disability, age, or sexual orientation, as forms of existing inequality in EU urban areas which have to be tackled through anti-discrimination measures in order to achieve social cohesion and equality (European Commission, 1998). The use and selection of words do not have neutral effects: as a result, gender is left out of the policy discourse and the definition of the policy problem, ignoring the impact that the social construction of gender has on EU citizens who live in urban areas (almost 72%, according to the European Commission (European Commission, 2014)).

Evidence gathered by the literature on gender and urban issues shows that gender differences have not always been considered within urban planning. Historically, the work of planners and policymakers has adopted a universal tone, focussing on a male reference point as the implicit norm (Fainstein and Servon, 2005). This implicit understanding of urban planning has given rise to cities that do not support the needs and expectations of different groups of citizens in the same way, particularly the needs and requirements of those who have most of the responsibility for the burden of child-bearing and care-giving: caring for children and other adults (older relatives and relatives with disabilities), as well as housework (care work) (Sánchez de Madariaga, 2004). The care work which sustains society has been socially assigned to women, and even if things are changing slowly it is women who perform this work. For example, in the EU women spend an average of 26 hours per week on care and household activities, compared with 9 hours for men (European Commission, 2014). At the same time, in 2013, only 63% of European women held jobs in paid employment (ibid.). The Europe 2020 strategy considers an objective to increase this percentage by 2020 (European Commission, 2010) by promoting gender equality.

The dual role of women in society (as responsible for care work and as workers in wage-earning jobs) determines the needs and expectations they have regarding urban environments and housing, since public and private environments shape the way we live our lives, how easy we can move from home to school to work; how our social relationships are aided by urban design; what our perception of safety in urban environments is; and whether or not we can embark on a professional career, etc. Ignoring how town planning can contribute to providing a satisfactory response to women's needs reproduces gender inequalities in society, and particularly in cities, as "the built environment plays a role in shaping gendered identities, practices and power relations" (Burgess, 2008: 113).

The integration of the gender perspective in urban policies "redefines existing issues in important ways, and makes women visible not only as subjects of planning but also as active participants in planning and policy-making processes" (Fainstein and Servon, 2005: 4), which can contribute significantly to reshape the urban dimension of EU policy; an issue that has a real potential to improve the quality of life of all citizens and to achieve the EU objective of social cohesion. This is because the integration of gender into urban policies would result in a more sustainable, equal and accessible built environment for all citizens (Greed, 2005a).

From this viewpoint, we can thus state that the analysis of the EC Communication Sustainable Urban Development in the European Union: A Framework for Action shows that by excluding the gender issue from the definition of the policy problem it is biased from a gender perspective. By doing this, the document not only contradicts the gender vision set down by the Treaty of Amsterdam, it also demonstrates a lack of attention to the substantial body of research already undertaken. The observation of this fact focussed the research on understanding whether the subsequent policy tools (which have been relevant in the construction of EU urban policy) had applied a similar approach – excluding gender from the policy problem they define – or had included it in their policy discourse on urban matters. This would enable us to ascertain whether the biased discourse in the 1998 document had developed over time.

In order to obtain a general overview of this issue, this research ran an empirical study that consisted of reviewing a selection of the written policy tools that have played a relevant role in the definition and development of EU urban policy through the years, using discourse analysis methodology. This methodology was selected because it enables studying the construction of the policy discourse. This is because it sheds light on how the discourse can enhance or avoid the inclusion of certain keywords, concepts, and ideas. The analysis of policy discourse shows us that it plays an ideological role through justification, ambiguity, hidden, and unsaid postulations (Pasqui, 2014). It builds and enhances some concepts and contributes to the definition of the policy problem, while deliberately leaving out some others (concealing or excluding them). The "linguistic turn in Western philosophy" evidenced this representational force of language: the performative and constructive function of language gives it a strong political meaning, playing a key role in the construction of politics, as "the actors can choose the language in light of their communicative intent so that they can better make use of the power of language to construct certain reality" (Sun, 2007).

The research reported here adopts its conceptual framework from the literature, particularly Fainstein and Servon, 2005; Jarvis and Kantor, 2009; Sánchez de Madariaga, 2004; Sánchez de Madariaga and Roberts, 2013; Reeves et al., 2012; and Greed, 1994, 2005a, 2005b. The method applied has been designed so that it is able to help understand if the discourse developed by the documents launched in the context of the urban policy of the EU has integrated the gender perspective.

Method

As stated, the method selected is discourse analysis. In order to apply it to achieve the objective of the study, we selected a number of the afore-mentioned policy tools (written policy documents) to analyse the policy discourse encoded in them. Each of the policy documents has been considered a unit of analysis (Sayago, 2014). The policy tools analysed have been selected on the basis of the following criteria:

- They are considered and recognised by different stakeholders as having exerted relevant influence over the definition of EU urban policy over time.
- They are documents drafted over the period 1999–2013, during the programming periods of the EU Cohesion Policy 1994–1999, 2000–2006, 2007–2013, so that the evolution of the policy discourse can be analysed.
- They are documents of different types: EC-produced political documents, best practices launched for benchmarking, and guidelines/position papers by the Member States, documents drafted by EU experts and published by the EC.
- All of these are written documents in which EU policy discourse has been encoded within the language used. They enable policy discourse to be analysed through the written language.

The following are the policy instruments analysed over the different periods of the EU's Cohesion Policy.

- **Period 1994–1999** (the study has only considered documents published after the Treaty of Amsterdam was signed):

  o Sustainable Urban Development in the European Union: A Framework for Action (European Commission, 1998).

- **Period 2000–2006**:

  o Partnership with the Cities. The Urban Community Initiative (European Commission, 2003).

- **Period 2007–2013**:

  o Leipzig Charter on Sustainable European Cities (Informal meeting of Ministers of Urban Development, 1997).
  o Cities of Tomorrow. Challenges, Visions, Ways Forward (European Commission, 2011).

o   Urban Development in the EU: 50 Projects Supported by the European Regional Development Fund during the 2007–2013 Period (European Commission, 2013).

In order to achieve its objective, the study has constructed a research protocol aimed at testing the policy discourse encoded within all the policy tools studied. The protocol has identified a set of analytical categories, formulated as questions, constructed on the basis of the review of the literature on the relevance of integrating the gender perspective in urban policies. It has enabled us to analyse the different units of analysis in a homogeneous way, so that comparison of approaches across the different programming periods was possible. The set of analytical categories/questions has been constructed on the basis of the following criteria:

• They have been selected through a review of the literature on the relevance of integrating the gender perspective in urban policies and planning, and a number of manuals for implementation, edited by different institutions: Fainstein and Servon, 2005; Sánchez de Madariaga and Roberts, 2013; Reeves et al., 2012; Greed, 1994, 2005a, 2005b; Jarvis and Kantor, 2009 and the following manuals for implementation: Berlin Handbook (Senatsverwaltung für Stadtenticklung year not given), Sánchez de Madariaga, 2004; Damyanovic et al., 2013; and RTPI, 2003.

This has enabled us to identify categories oriented to understand which gender-related concepts, ideas and key words could be: (i) making present the gender perspective; (ii) introducing concepts and ideas biased from a gender perspective; (iii) substituting gender, building up on perspectives that might seem to be equivalent but which are reductive or conceal the implications of gender differences in urban areas.

• They are aimed at adopting the approach to gender in research made explicit by Fainstein and Servon (2005: 6): "gender is not the only lens that allows us to look at planning and policy issues from another perspective". Other analytical categories such as race, class, age, etc. must be interrelated with gender in order to gain an overall and comprehensive understanding of societies which planning has an impact on.
• They have been constructed taking into account the "primary problems" pointed out by Eichler (1998), regarding biased research and public policy from the perspective of gender.[2]

The protocol included the following analytical categories, formulated as questions:

- Does the document explicitly introduce the concept of gender mainstreaming?
- Does the document mention "gender"? If yes, what is the meaning of/ approach to "gender"? How many times is this word mentioned?
- Does the document introduce the gender dimension of town planning and urban policies, even if indirectly/implicitly? If yes, how is it introduced?
- Does the document mention "equal opportunities"? How?
- Does the document mention "social cohesion"? How?
- Does the document mention "social diversity"? How?
- Does the document mention "women" and "sex"? How?
- Does the document mention other concepts relevant to the analysis? What are they?
- Does the document include relevant statistics with data disaggregated by sex that takes gender implications into account in urban areas?
- Does the document highlight the necessity of taking into account that women and men might benefit differently from an urban policy proposal?
- Does the document mention the need to identify and provide an answer to the different needs of women and men regarding urban public places, public facilities, mobility, and housing?
- Does the document include recommendations aimed to ensure gender equality through all the stages of the policy process (decision-making, definition of objectives, policy design/planning, policy implementation, and evaluation)?

After the analysis of each written document, the research observed and compared the results with the aim of understanding the policy discourse on gender that has been encoded within the documents from the different periods of the Cohesion Policy. The aim was to identify potential development or transformation of the discourse over time. Afterwards the study discussed the results from an overall and comparative approach.

Answering the Question: Has Gender Been Mainstreamed in the Documents Launched from EU Urban Policy?

As mentioned above, the document entitled Sustainable Urban Development in the European Union: A Framework for Action (European Commission, 1998) ignored gender as a social category of analysis to be included in urban policies and planning through the implementation of gender mainstreaming, as established by the Treaty of Amsterdam. Leaving gender out of the definition of the policy problem resulted in a policy tool that provided guidelines for sustainable urban development in which the implications of gender differences were not taken into account. From the perspective taken by this work it can be said that it gave rise to a biased concept of sustainable urban development, based on a reductive idea of European society.

Considering the "primary problems" pointed out by Eichler (1998), regarding biased research and public policy from the perspective of gender, it can be said that the document is characterised by a problem of "gender insensitivity" that consists of ignoring gender as a fundamental social variable. As she points out, gender insensitivity may or may not be a result of an androcentric bias, and in most cases it is difficult or impossible to tell because, typically, gender insensitivity is based on a conception that considers gender as too unimportant to be mentioned. According to her, it is relevant to identify gender insensitivity, as this is "an important precondition for identifying and correcting other forms of sexism in research" (Eichler, 1998: 82) and public policy. The observation of the subsequent UE policy tools analysed demonstrates that the approach identified in this communication by the EC has not changed over time and can be found even in the more recent tools. In the following paragraphs, we describe the most important results of the discourse analysis.

The only document analysed that explicitly mentions the term "gender mainstreaming" is Partnership with the Cities: The Urban Community Initiative (European Commission, 2003). It introduces gender mainstreaming in the following terms:

> The two key elements of the general principle of equal opportunities laid down in the Community Treaties are the ban on discrimination on grounds of nationality and equal pay for men and women. Equal opportunities are intended to apply to all Community policies, especially through the "gender mainstreaming" approach. Gender mainstreaming should ensure that measures and operations financed by the Structural Funds take into account their effects on the respective situations of women and men.
>
> *(Ibid.: 47)*

In the quotation, the concept of "gender mainstreaming" is linked to a narrow concept of "equal opportunities" that focusses on overcoming discrimination on the basis of nationality and equal pay for men and women. This fact reduces the cross-sectional nature of gender mainstreaming set down in the Treaty of Amsterdam (equality and equal opportunities for women and men regarding any issue), and its transformational capacity in urban areas. This is particularly so, if associated with the Structural Funds that allocate financial resources to specific initiatives to improve EU cities.

Interestingly, none of the subsequent documents analysed explicitly or implicitly mention the implementation of gender mainstreaming in urban policies.

Similarly, the dual social role of women (as responsible for most of the care work and as workers in wage-earning jobs) is not mentioned in the policy tools reviewed, even if it is recurrently pointed out by the literature (e.g. Fainstein and Servon, 2005; Reeves et al., 2012; European Commission, 2014) and the documents drafted on EU social policy, as a major driver of inequality in our society.

Many of the tools analysed point to equal opportunities for men and women as a necessary step to increase the number of women in the EU's work force. For example, the document Cities of Tomorrow mentions that an Agenda for new skills and jobs has been launched in the EU with the aim of achieving a 75% employment rate for women and men for the 20–64-year-old age group by 2020 (European Commission, 2011: 4). This approach to equal opportunities between women and men is the same as in the Europe 2020 strategy: the documents point out equal opportunities for men and women as necessary for a more competitive work force but fail in proposing guidelines and measures to achieve it through urban policies.

From the different documents analysed we have found words that conceal or replace the gender perspective with a narrow idea of equal opportunities or equity between men and women as regards urban planning and policy:

- The word "parents" is used in a sense that assumes that parents and mothers are groups that have the same needs with regard to urban areas, public facilities, public transport, etc.
- The word "family" is used similarly. Observing that a very common case of gender insensitivity is to consider the family as the smallest unit of analysis (familism), Eichler considers familism to be a source of (gender) bias (Eichler, 1998). Familism is often found in the document Cities of Tomorrow.
- The document *Cities of Tomorrow* conceals gender differences in the use of urban areas using terms such as "people" and "child-friendly city".

The absence of biased gender dimension seems to contradict the general discourse of all the documents analysed; a discourse heavily based on the general concepts of social inclusion and social equality. Contradiction also lies in the fact that the most recent policy tools to be analysed agree in considering the demographic challenge as one of the threats to achieving sustainable urban development in the EU, pointing out that this problem has to be addressed in terms of a wide range of policy fields that include action from the domain of urban policies.

For example the document *Cities of Tomorrow* recognises that "as fertility remains considerably below replacement rates, in most EU Member States the relatively small EU population growth still observed is mainly due to migration flows" (European Commission, 2011: 15). However, it fails to mention the relevance of the gender issue regarding the demographic challenge, something that ignores the evidence on the importance of gender equality policies in addressing this issue, even if it was recognised by the Commission in 2006 (European Commission, 2006).

It should be noted that none of the tools analysed use disaggregated statistics by gendering the data and indicators they used to set the overall picture of the

EU city. This data is needed as the basis to establish the social scenario to which the guidelines, general ideas, and concept of sustainable urban development will be applied. As a consequence, it can be said that the guidelines for achieving more sustainable cities in the EU are biased from the perspective of gender.

From the documents analysed, no mention has been found of the fact that women and men benefit differently from policy proposals. Policy discourse takes equality to mean sameness. This is a major issue to be taken into account, since the promotion of gender equality is enshrined in EU legislation, which regulates the funds, as an overarching principle. Particularly for the budget period of the Cohesion Policy 2007–2013, the EU presented as an obligation the introduction of the principle of equal opportunities between women and men and non-discrimination in action funded by the Structural Funds. Specifically, the EU rules on the Structural Funds and the Cohesion Fund stated that:

> Member States and regions should pursue the objective of equality between men and women at all stages of the preparation and implementa-tion of programmes and projects. This may be done through specific actions to promote equality or combat discrimination, as well as by taking careful account of how other projects and the management of the funds may affect women and men.
>
> *(European Commission, 2005: 14)*

Moreover, none of the documents explicitly include recommendations that will help to ensure gender equality through urban planning and related policies at all levels and throughout the complete policy development (decision-making, defin-ition of objectives, policy design, policy implementation, or assessment). In some cases they include guidelines to achieve equal opportunities that will help achieve gender equality but as an indirect effect. Regarding this point, we should mention Zibell's (2013) analysis of the *Leipzig Chart* from the perspective of gender. For her, this policy tool does not contribute to transforming the values and ideas that determine the decision-making, design and implementation processes that repro-duce gender stereotypes in the EU: "the setting in which the changes are envis-aged continues to have patriarchal implications" (Zibell, 2013: 80). In this way it adopts the traditional androcentric perspective, which not only reproduces urban areas that maintain gender differences but is also an approach that fails to encom-pass the perspective of gender mainstreaming (integrating gender throughout the whole policy process at all levels) within policy processes.

Conclusions and Policy Implications

The analysis undertaken revealed that the urban dimension of EU policy has failed to integrate the gender dimension in its policy discourse, while other topics (for example, climate change or the demographic challenge) have been integrated within the concept of sustainable urban development, built up over the different periods of the Cohesion Policy. In fact, the study led to this first and most important conclusion: the gender dimension has not been integrated within the policy tools analysed. Since they are representative of EU discourse on urban issues during the last periods of the Cohesion Policy (1994–1999, 2000–2007, 2007–2014), it is possible to state that gender mainstreaming has not been integrated within the urban dimension of the EU policy, which contradicts the mandate of the Treaty of Amsterdam and the objective of social equity within the Union (particularly the concept of equal opportunities between men and women).

This review also shows that the lack of a gender dimension in these policy tools seems to be "justified" by the development of a rhetoric based on the inclusion and repetition of concepts such us: social cohesion, social equality, equal opportunities, family-friendly city, etc. However, the view embraced by the policy discourse does not integrate gender, as it fails to understand and implement the cross-sectional nature of this concept.

The review of the results shows that even if the policy tools analysed mention that the objective is to create cities for everyone, these are characterised by a "male by default" perspective that conceals the gender implications of urban policies. By doing this, the documents contribute to perpetuating gender discrimination by, for example, concealing the different needs and expectations of men and women as regards their urban environments, and how fair urban areas can empower women.

The policy tools reviewed fail to build a vision of cities that aims to address the needs of all, regardless of their gender. Interestingly, other factors of difference such us age, physical health or ethnic group, are taken into account and mentioned frequently.

Consequently, the concept of sustainable urban development embodied in the policy discourse adopted by these tools, should be reviewed from this point of view. This is important in order to comply with EU gender equality policy, as mentioned above, and particularly to integrate a more comprehensive approach to urban issues, where gender is considered a relevant social category of analysis in understanding how urban policies could enhance the daily life of citizens, and how they benefit women and men differently.

In the context of the budget period for the EU Cohesion Policy (2014–2020), Member States are deciding (in agreement with the EC and the regions) how EU guidelines on urban matters will be integrated into their national and regional projects. If gender is not integrated within the EU policy discourse (i.e. embedded within the policy discourse in documents produced in the field of urban policy), which guide Member States in their urban strategies, this aspect will not be mainstreamed into the programmes and projects to be co-funded by the Structural Funds for sustainable urban development in the coming years.

As the literature reveals (Tofarides, 2000; Gelli and Tedesco, 2001; De Gregorio Hurtado, 2012), EU-produced policy instruments exert a relevant influence upon the definition of urban policy in the Member States, particularly in those that have been less active regarding this public policy domain (Carpenter, 2013). Consequently, the new budget period could represent an opportunity to incorporate the gender-mainstreaming view within urban policies at country, regional and, especially, local level. This would contribute to complying with the Treaty mandate on this issue and to funding (through the Structural Funds) sustainable urban development and urban regeneration strategies that contribute to achieving fairer cities for all. Adopting this vision would also contribute importantly to the current context of construction of the Urban Agenda for the European Union (De Gregorio Hurtado, 2016).

Notes

1 A part of this study was developed under a short-term scientific mission funded by COST Action Gender, Science, Technology and Environment – genderSTE – at the Center of Interdisciplinary Gender Studies of the University of Trento in 2016. Professor Sánchez de Madariaga, Chair of genderSTE, suggested the idea and provided scientific advice. The author thanks Professor Poggio and her team from Trento for their inputs to the methodology. Portions of this chapter have been already published in the *Journal of Research in Gender Studies*, 7(1).
2 Eichler establishes four primary problems and three secondary problems regarding sexist research. She applies her own study to the research. In this analysis, the problems identified by Eischler are applied to policy documents.

References

Booth, C. & Bennett, C. (2002). Gender mainstreaming in the European Union: Towards a new conception and practice of equal opportunities? *The European Journal of Women's Studies*, 9(4), 430–446.

Burgess, G. (2008). Planning and the gender equality duty: Why does gender matter? *People, Place & Policy Online*, 2(3), 112–121.

Carpenter, J. (2013). Sustainable urban regeneration within the European Union: A case of 'Europeanization'? In Leary, M. E. & McCarthy, J. (eds.) *The Routledge Companion to Urban Regeneration*, pp. 138–147. London: Routledge.

Cullingworth, B. & Nadine, V. (2006). *Town and Country Planning in the UK*. Oxon: Routledge (first edition 1964).

Damyanovic, D., Reinwald, F. & Weikmann, A. (2013). *Gender Mainstreaming in Urban Planning and Urban Development*. Vienna: Urban Development Vienna.

De Gregorio Hurtado, S. (2012). *URBAN Policies of the European Union from the Perspective of Collaborative Planning. The URBAN and URBAN II Community Initiatives in Spain*. PhD diss., Technical University of Madrid.

De Gregorio Hurtado, S. (2016). Integrating the gender perspective in the Urban Agenda for the European Union. State of the art and upcoming challenges. *TRIA*, 17, 203–218.

De Gregorio Hurtado, S. (2017). Is EU urban policy transforming urban regeneration in Spain? Answers from an analysis of the Iniciativa Urbana (2007–2013). *Cities*, 60, 402–414.

Eichler, M. (1998). *Non-Sexist Research Methods*. Boston: Allen and Unwin.

European Commission. (1998). *Sustainable Urban Development in the European Union: A Framework for Action*, COM(98) 605. Brussels.

European Commission. (2003). *Partnership with the Cities: The Urban Community Initiative*. Luxembourg.

European Commission. (2005). *Cohesion Policy in Support of Growth and Jobs: Community Strategic Guidelines, 2007–2013*, COM (2005)0299. Brussels.

European Commission. (2006). *The Demographic Future of Europe: From Challenge to Opportunity*. Brussels.

European Commission. (2010). *Europe2020: A Strategy for Smart, Sustainable and Inclusive Growth*. Brussels.

European Commission. (2011). *Cities of Tomorrow: Challenges, Visions, Ways Forward*. Brussels.

European Commission. (2013). *Quality of Life in Cities: Perception Survey in 79 European Cities*. Brussels.

European Commission. (2014). *Report on Progress on Equality between Women and Men in 2013. 2013 Report on the Application of the EU Charter or Fundamental Rights*. Brussels.

European Commission. (2015). *European Structural and Investment Funds. Guidance for Member States, Programme Authorities and Cities. Article 7 on Integrated Sustainable Urban Development of the Regulation 1301/2013 on the European Regional Development Fund*. Brussels.

European Council. (2006). *Council Regulation (EC) N 1083/2006 Laying Down General Provisions on the European Regional Development Fund, the European Social Fund and the Cohesion Fund and Repealing Regulation (EC) N 1260/1999*, Official Journal of the European Union L210/25 of 31-7-2006. Brussels.

Fainstein, S. S. & Servon, L. J. (2005). *Gender and Planning: A Reader*. New Brunswick, NJ and London: Rutgers University Press.

García-Ramón, M. D., Ortiz, A. & Prats, M. (2004). Urban planning, gender and the use of public space in a peripheral neighbourhood of Barcelona. *Cities*, 21(3), 215–223.

Gelli, F. & Tedesco, C. (2001). *Governments and Modes of Governance in the U.S. and the European Cities: The Change in Urban Policies*. Presentation in the Conference Area-based initiatives in contemporary urban policy, Danish Building and Urban Research Association. Copenhagen, 17–19th May 2001.

Greed, C. (1994). *Women and Planning: Creating Gendered Realities*. London: Routledge.

Greed, C. (2005a). An investigation of the effectiveness of gender mainstreaming a means of integrating the needs of women and men into spatial planning in the United Kingdom. *Progress in Planning*, 64, 243–321.

Greed, C. (2005b). Overcoming the factors inhibiting the mainstreaming of gender into spatial planning policy in the United Kingdom. *Urban Studies*, 42(4), 719–749.

Informal meeting of ministers on urban development. (1997). *Leipzig Chart*. Leipzig. Available at: http://ec.europa.eu/regional_policy/archive/themes/urban/leipzig_charter.pdf (accessed 5-4-2016).

Jarvis, H. & Kantor, P. (2009). *Cities and Gender*. New York: Routledge.

Pasqui, G. (2014). Urban Policies in Europe. Discourses, Rhetoric and Dispositifs, Presentation at the New Urban Language Congress, organized by the Escuela Técnica Superior de Arquitectura: Madrid, 25–27th June 2014.

Pollack, M. A. & Hafner-Burton, E. (2000). Mainstreaming gender in the European Union. *Journal of European Public Policy*, 7(3), 432–456.

Reeves, D., Parfitt, B. & Archer, C. (2012). *Gender in Urban Planning: Issues and Trends*. Nairobi: UN-Habitat.

Royal Town Planning Institute (RTPI). (2003). *Gender Equality and Plan Making. The Gender Mainstreaming Toolkit*. London: RTPI.

Sánchez de Madariaga, I. (2004). *Urbanismo Con Perspectiva De Género*. Seville: Junta de Andalucía-European Social Fund.

Sánchez de Madariaga, I. & Roberts, M. (2013). *Fair Shared Cities: The Impact of Gender Planning in Europe*. Farnham and Burlington, VT: Ashgate.

Sayago, S. (2014). El análisis del discurso como técnica de investigación cualitativa y cuantitativa en las ciencias sociales. *Cinta Moebio*, 49, 1–10.

Sun, J. (2007). *Language, Meaning, and World Politics: The Language of the Bush Administration and the Iraq War*. Harvard: Fellows' Papers. Weatherhead Center for International Affairs. Harvard University.

Tofarides, M. (2000). The multi-level gatekeeper system: The case of the European Union's Urban Policy Experiment. PhD diss., European University Institute.

Zibell, B. (2013). The model of the European City in the Light of Gender Planning and Sustainable Development. In Sánchez de Madariaga, I. & Roberts, M. (eds.) *Fair Shared Cities: The Impact of Gender Planning in Europe*, pp. 75–90. Farnham and Burlington, VT: Ashgate.

13

GENDER MAINSTREAMING URBAN PLANNING AND DESIGN PROCESSES IN GREECE

Charis Christodoulou

Introduction

Greece is represented on European Union (EU) boards that work on improving the quality and efficiency of Research and Structural Funds in terms of gender equality. The national organization responsible, the General Secretariat for Gender Equality (GSGE) at the Ministry of Interior, is a member of the European Community of Practice on Gender Mainstreaming ESF (European Structural Fund impact on employment, social inclusion, and training). Although no reports on this representation and contribution are widely available, gender-mainstreaming policy and action in Greece has focused on issues of employment, education, and health, combating domestic violence, access in public administration, equity in representation in local authorities, women's empowerment and consultation, etc. (GSGE 2013–1417). These fields of interest have truly reflected the critical areas of concern as adopted at EU-level since the late 1990s following the *Beijing Platform for Action* (UN Women 1995). They are still being refined in the local context along the Sustainable Development Goals in the *2030 Agenda for Sustainable Development* (UN 2015). The *National Programme for Substantive Gender Equality 2010–2013* (GSGE 2010) also had several pillars of action. The first pillar considered enhancement and implementation of core legislation on civic equity as a horizontal policy. The specialized policies for gender equality,[1] coupled with gender policymaking institutions, was its second pillar. A third pillar referred to gender mainstreaming for all public policies in general, through changes in the policies and actions of all ministries. The *National Action Plan on Gender Equality 2016–2020* (GSGE 2017) developed the same policy areas in collaboration with representatives of civil society, academia, and public administration to define concrete objectives and synergies with stakeholders. Thus, GSGE received positive European attention in the 2017 *Annual*

Report of the European Commission on Gender Equality (EC 2017, 43, 52–53) for actions taken to deal with discrimination issues faced by refugee women and their children, as well as for the *National Action Plan on Gender Equality 2016–2020* (GSGE 2017).

However, in the sector of environment, urban development, urban planning, and urban design there has been little or no progress in practice in the last decade, even though an overall *gender-mainstreaming strategy* has been developed by GSGE since 2010 and forwarded to the national, regional and local levels (GSGE 2011a, 2011b, discussed later in this chapter). Spatial planning, environmental protection and management in Greece lacks adequate pragmatic focus in the various levels of administration authorities (Evangelidou et al. 2005) despite the fact that these are principles embedded in the country's constitution. Moreover, on one hand, urban development is not recognized as a field of public policy priority in the overall endeavour of gender equality. Hence, no reference to urban planning policy was found in the *National Action Plan on Gender Equality 2016–2020* (GSGE 2017). On the other hand, gender mainstreaming in urban planning and design requires both urban planning expertise and gender insight – the combination of which needs to be further elaborated in practice. It is important to bridge the gap between academic approaches and policy paths – stemming from international, mostly European directives, with actual realities in Greek cities, as well as the gap between administrative and professional practices in urban planning and design.

This chapter briefly reviews the critical stages of direct and indirect attempts to raise gender awareness in urban planning and design in recent years in Greece. It aims to build *a hypothesis* of actual gender mainstreaming urban planning and design in the Greek context and outline the relevant directions of action. Thus, it contributes to the ongoing national and European discussion of the topic. It is argued that the emphasis should be put on the actual planning procedures and design processes by intersecting discourses and fields of otherwise separate practice. A new set of questions for future research and practice are put forward. Finally, it concludes that the issues at stake are not only institutional and knowledge-based, but depend on the creative mobilization of all actors involved.

Gender Awareness in the Greek City Discourse and Urban Policies

In the 1990s there were a small number of projects that either acknowledged or identified gender issues from a feminist standpoint and incorporated the gender perspective into processes at the local level. Examples include a participatory regeneration project in Thiva in Attica in collaboration with the National Technical University of Athens (Vrychea & Laurent 1992) and, later, part of a comprehensive approach to combat social exclusion adopted in EU-funded projects such as "Quartiers en Crise" and "Poverty" carried out by consultants and local authorities in instances between elected members and policymakers (Christodoulou 2015, 55–59, 96–100). They were exploratory attempts to deal with the profound and obvious dynamics of women's perceptions of urban realities, local power relations, and women's precious involvement in supporting the implementation processes.

Feminist approaches supported the challenge of bringing gender issues into planning and formulated the hypotheses of case research and urban analysis. They dealt with actual problems within urban projects that otherwise would never have been funded. These were *sui generis* exceptional paradigms, outside of the dominant planning policies applied. They were evaluated on their own terms without adequate feedback or spinoffs into official urban policies. However, they have produced a legacy in the Greek city discourse of urban geographical research (mostly in the capital, Athens) on real-world intersections of gender with issues of immigration, segregation, and the dominant perceptions of gender and everyday life. All these have enriched our understanding of urban transformations beyond academic approaches (see Vaiou 2002, 2004, Lykogianni 2008, Vaiou & Stratigaki 2008, Arapoglou & Sayas 2009, Pantelidou-Malouta et al. 2009, Stratigaki & Vaiou 2009). This strand of research has been very critical, in recent years, of austerity policies, representing the effects of measures, and actual status and survival strategies of women which might otherwise remain out of sight and undocumented (see Vaiou 2014, Lada 2016).[2] However, mainstream urban planning and design in Greece has remained unaffected and in an uneasy relationship with these urban realities in times of economic recession.

The Greek spatial planning system is a hierarchically and centrally controlled system (i.e. government controlled). It has been formulated according to specific articles in the Greek Constitution, where the State is responsible for 'ekistics' and it has always been 'worlded' by a political tradition of clientelism. In the wording of the EU Urban Compendium (EC-DG Regio 2000, 15) the case of the Greek spatial planning system 'is dominated by an emphasis on purely physical aspects'. It 'has a strong architectural flavour and concern with urban design, townscape and building control' (EC-DG Regio 1997). It belongs in the so-called 'urbanism' planning tradition. The key concepts are 'the statutory town plan, its never-ending extensions, the building conditions attached to it, the building permit, and the existence of extensive out of plan areas, where building can take place under a variety of conditions'.[3] Nationwide planning standards (density, plot-ratio development, social infrastructure provision, and allocation, etc.) frame and structure new neighbourhood projects. Thus, the main concerns of urban policies are, on the one hand, the interface between private and public land ownership, and, on the other, the development rights of landowners.

The planning controls in physical terms are exercised through long-term processes that wholly transcend the scale of locally managed urban projects and encourage random property development – thus they have produced small-grain mixed-use urban areas. Widespread unauthorized settlements and constructions of all kinds restrict the scope of official urban planning, while at the same time cities and towns on the whole face severe problems in the provision of technical and social infrastructure. The market–state relations of small and large capital investments in urban space have allowed little space for the expression of civil society. Long-term top-down processes and procedures of urban planning and the implementation of urban projects and construction works remain obscure for laypeople. Such processes and procedures are usually described as 'bureaucracy in planning'. Social aspects of spatial planning are rendered of secondary importance, not only by the average citizen but also by central and local administration, because political power relations prevail in the public discussion and final top-down decision-making. Sustainability rhetoric has been incorporated in the statutory framework since the 1990s (Laws 2508/97 and 2742/99) – mostly related to urban regeneration and spatial planning, but complex principles of sustainability were never contextualized in practice. It is mainly construction works – coarse and large-scale – that orient local and national development. Urban development has continued to take place incrementally at a piecemeal pace, consolidating market and client-oriented objectives. All these elements sum up the Greek version of 'path dependency' in the planning of urban projects and interventions.

This chapter is not meant to provide an exhaustive critical description of the pros and cons of the Greek planning system and city design. Only the main specifics of the spontaneous and co-evolutionary urban development processes in the Greek context are highlighted to support a gender-mainstreaming hypothesis further on. Given the successive Economic Adjustment Programs (EAPs),[4] orchestrated by the European Commission, the European Central Bank, and the International Monetary Fund – and imposed by Greek governments since 2010 – the whole of the urban planning and development process has fallen under a gradual reconstitution towards neoliberalization in order to facilitate large capital investments in urban development. New legislation on the reconstitution of the urban planning system enacted in July 2014 (Law 4269/14) did not integrate gender insights, or social inclusion, or environmental sustainability issues into the agenda. On the other hand, gender issues in the design of urban space were previously covered indirectly, partly as a by-product of guidance provided for other objectives, e.g. the design of playgrounds in the neighbourhood and designs for all to ensure access for vulnerable groups.[5] This form of *dispersed guidance* in separate policy documents and legal notices does not form a stable starting point from which to evolve and control gender-mainstreaming design processes.

Within this discussion it is important to make reference to the implemented urban projects in Greek cities within EU-funding frameworks or initiatives. EU-funded projects have had the most effective results in urban regeneration and in-fill development, as they have usually been decided on strict implementation rules, i.e. budgets, schedules, and deadlines, demarcation of development areas, etc. stemming from EU horizontal policies and funding regulations. Yet the bulk of urban policies, strategies, and projects have been implemented without being affected by analytical gender criteria. During the 4th Programming Period of the European Structural Funds (2007–2013), operational programs – sectoral and regional ones – were supposed to facilitate the development of projects that promote gender equality. In Greece, however, in the implementation phase of urban infrastructure (public open space, social facilities, etc.) the gender equality and non-discrimination criterion was to be fulfilled – at all scales and objectives – only in general terms, as part of a checklist for EU-funding eligibility. The positive or neutral effect of the project was to be described only briefly as part of technical form-filling activities. In the current period of ESF (2014–2020) result indicators for projects are required regarding the numbers of women and men beneficiaries in order to screen projects in relation to the horizontal policy of non-discrimination and gender budgeting. However, no real attention is paid to the complexity of gender issues in practice. Responsible public administration officials are not gender-aware enough to advance or evaluate the projects in terms of actual gender equality beyond stereotypes. The features of urban projects are usually determined by engineers, planners and economists that are not actually in the targeted groups required to be trained in the issues of gender awareness because they do not fall outside the groups usually required to enact gender-equality policy in Greece.

In conclusion, gender awareness within urban policies and formal urban planning is almost non-existent, even though a series of urban-research projects from the standpoint of gender have provided a whole new understanding of how Greek cities actually integrate gendered spatiality. However, there is no reflection of this research and knowledge to be found in gender mainstreaming within urban policies. In addition, EU-funded projects aren't developed, implemented and assessed on the basis of qualitative gender criteria.

Gender Mainstreaming Urban Policies and Planning – Practical Tools

Across Europe there has been a recent proliferation of documents in the form of handbooks and guides about urban planning and design, not only related to gender mainstreaming. Widely-known gender-mainstreaming handbooks give specific directions for how to deal with gender in urban planning and design. As one goes through the gender mainstreaming *Handbook of the Senate of the City Government of Berlin* (Women's Advisory Committee 2011) or the Spanish language book *Urbanismo con perspectiva de género* (Sánchez de Madariaga 2004), one realizes the depth and width of the spectrum of active urban policies developed as part of an overall administrative structure of services related to urban and housing planning, design, and management. These handbooks are based and structured on analytical criteria of gender integration in urban plans and projects in relation to their characteristics. Likewise, the Royal Town Planning Institute *Toolkit* and good practice notes (RTPI 2003, 2007) are based on the multi-stakeholder framework of planning processes in the United Kingdom. These both emphasize processes in planning and gender-relevant intersections. In the *Handbook of Gender Mainstreaming Urban Planning and Development in Vienna* (Damyanovic et al. 2013), the mature approach combines legal aspects with the many design and planning aspects of the city's Urban Development Plan, STEP 2025. On the one hand, gender mainstreaming is provided as an overview of comprehensive planning processes and a strategy ahead of planning and urban development, combining gender-related goals with urban quality criteria. On the other hand, methods and instruments for various planning projects and design objects are prescribed in specific detail. In the Finnish *Guide* for gender-mainstreaming development programmes and projects (Haataja et al. 2011), emphasis is put on systematic gender-awareness raising in all project phases, critically considering views of all stakeholders (authorities, project actors) beyond stereotyped assumptions. All in all, gender-mainstreaming guides in planning reflect the specificities of each planning context and governance as these have been formulated historically and are advanced and applied locally. They also correspond to different concepts of space suitable for different lifestyles, routines, and everyday lives as gender is explicitly transacted by culturally defined issues of age, life stage, immigration, employment, and vulnerability, etc. in diverse contexts. As proposed by Horelli (2017), engendering urban planning requires diverse ways of dealing with varying types of planning.

As far as manuals, handbooks, and guides of practice are concerned, in Greece there is no strong tradition of their use in any policy sector. However, there is some progress in this form of policy action in terms of gender. GSGE has made a huge endeavour in top-down gender-awareness raising in public administration through guidance. It is not surprising that this effort to raise gender awareness has produced a significant number of guidance tools since 2010, the year that austerity measures were launched and special spending was cut in the framework of EAP, if we consider that these policies were decided and funded by the EU. Targeting gender-mainstreaming policies on a national, regional, and local level as a whole gender-mainstreaming strategy – a *Model System* – has been elaborated (see Karamessini 2015, 271 for a critical review). At the same time, respective *Implementation Guides* were compiled to direct public policies at all levels (GSGE 2011a, 2011b, 2011c). They proposed measures to be undertaken by each ministry in Action Plans for Ministerial and Regional policies in the 4th ESF Programming Period, one of which was the constitution of gender committees with the participation of gender experts. The latter were not fostered in practice. In the responsible Ministry of Environment, Energy and Climate Change, key programs were proposed along the axes of energy saving and environmental crisis management. These were finally only linked to mainstream planning processes and top-down decisions. Another program axis was the improvement of the quality of the urban

environment, and especially of citizens' – men and women – different transportation needs and conditions in big cities, as well as matters of green development.
Little is known about the results of these programs as evaluation reports were not
published. The same goes for regional policies on energy management, public
health and quality of life in cities. The gender perspective was never enacted in
qualitative terms.

On the other hand, important statutory measures have been taken at the local
level by the Ministry of Interior, Decentralization and e-Government in the
framework of an overall reformation of local and regional government in
2010–2011 ('Kallikratis' Program of 3852/2010 Law). Responsibilities and decision-making powers in social policies were transferred to the Municipal and
Regional Administration. Local and regional offices and committees on gender
equality within social policies were expected to be constituted in order to act as
one-stop points of coordination – advising, informing and networking all stakeholders, including public workers, citizens, women groups, etc. to pursue
gender equality and gender mainstreaming across local and regional policies,
regulations, and programs. Based on the 'Kallikratis' Program it is obligatory to
integrate gender-equality measures in the Regional Operational Plans, while this
remains provisional for municipalities. At the regional level of governance, it
seems that gender mainstreaming is often lost between the lines of social policies
in general, or that the people responsible are not suitably trained or open-
minded enough to think creatively about Greek cases of gender (in)equality
status. Not all local authorities seem to realize or want to activate this potential
and it is important who staffs these units and what their stance and experiences
are. Thus, no results are expected in the long term unless a proactive stance in
identifying and controlling concrete steps is adopted.

Targeted at local-level actions, the GSGE has produced two *Implementation Guides*
in the framework of the National Program of Effective Gender Equality 2010–13
(GSGE 2010): a short one in relation to the *European Charter for Equality of Women and
Men in Local Life* (CEMR 2006) and one in relation to the *Model System of Gender
Mainstreaming* municipal policies (GSGE et al. 2011, GSGE 2011c). The direct audience is the whole of the municipalities in the country, with those that have signed the
European Charter for Equality of Women and Men in Local Life as a priority (Stratigaki
2014).[6] The guides are structured around the themes of the European Charter and at
the same time they refer to relevant Greek legislation, with a good number of interesting ideas about integration and transcription of the whole gender agenda in the Greek
context. Main topics and themes belong to the fields of the environment, quality of
life, housing, mobility, planning, and sustainable development. Emphasis is put on the
role of women in suitable development and on the direction towards providing solutions to urban issues in everyday life that should cater for the needs of all citizens –
men and women – beyond the general good. Proposed axes of intervention are related
to public space (such as the creation of green networks, transformation of vacant plots
into children's playgrounds, public lighting for improving the sense of security, the

creation of niches to take a rest in the city) and mobility by means of public transport in relation to itineraries, schedules and vulnerable groups. Physical interventions are supported by 'soft' interventions, such as strategies for changing dominant mentalities, training programs for municipal employees involved in social equity and relevant social services, networking, and collaboration with civil society and support of women's participation in decision-making. The guide also proposes integrating all gender-mainstreaming actions in the obligatory – since 2006 – Local Operational Program and the relevant annual Action Program and budget. Last, but not least, the guides provide a short methodology of phasing-in gender mainstreaming and actions in good time at the local level, as well as structuring gender-impact assessments in relation to women's representation, access to resources (time, information, financial power, career, IT etc.), and rights, etc.

These guides are a very good start to frame gender mainstreaming in statutory terms, as it is imperative, in local administration in Greece, to oblige public workers to take charge! However, reference to legislation is restricted to the overall administration of local authorities and does not refer to urban planning and design-specific statutory frameworks. Additionally, in the guides there are topics that have been directly transcribed from the international discourse that do not fit well into the powers of Greek municipalities. For example, urban transportation is not a responsibility of municipalities. Therefore it is transport agencies and central governmental offices that should be mobilized to implement gender-improved services. Another example is housing production, which in Greece is a field of design and construction implemented solely by private entrepreneurs. Control and regulation happens only through general building regulations, commonly applied across the whole country. So, again, it is private developers and ministerial offices that should be persuaded to change, e.g. housing typologies to cover for new housing realities. The most obvious field of gender-mainstreaming design in Greece seems to be the design of public space where the responsibility lies mostly in municipalities in the form of public works. The informative, knowledge-based guides elaborated by GSGE are important but, in order to provoke action, stakeholders in the Greek context should be more concretely referred to with a focus on the actual processes and procedures stemming from planning legislation and design regulations. Concise handbooks with analytical design criteria and a focus on processes following the European experience could serve as useful tools to inspire and direct technical staff (planners, engineers, architects) taking part in decision-making at a local and regional scale.

Gender Mainstreaming Urban Planning and Design in Greece – A Hypothesis

As mentioned before, the urban planning system in Greece is embedded in rather inflexible institutions and long-term, top-down, non-publically interactive decision-making processes (Evangelidou et al. 2005). The main question remains: how can gender issues be drastically incorporated into the planning processes, urban design end-products, and urban management? This is the starting point of my hypothesis to gender mainstream urban planning and design in Greece. We should move to a more detailed *how* of gender mainstreaming beyond a top-down briefing. Gender mainstreaming in urban planning and design should be context-specific and at the same time procedure-specific to achieve progress in reform and transformation.

To introduce gender awareness across the whole of urban planning processes, one has to open up explicitly the planning phases and procedures as officially prescribed in relevant legislation as well as usually enacted in practice. One should break the bureaucratic and technocratic shell, and describe and explain to laypeople and local collectives – women and men of all ages and identities – what is going on, critically discuss and scrutinize issues beyond stereotypes, invite people to participate and to express their own aspects and interests of living in a specific area that might otherwise be kept in silence. There is a need to allow a bottom-up push in participation by providing citizens – women in particular – with reasons to set goals and produce results for their own cities and living environments. This is a matter of civic emancipation and democratization within the perspective of sustainable cities and resilient urban management.

To start with women's participation, the obligatory public display of official town plans before being finally authorized should be modernized in a more democratic and technologically current way. Participation should allow women's voices to be expressed more fully at all phases of urban change, new developments, or regeneration projects. New communication technologies and social networking could provide the platform for parallel wider public expression. Public-space allocation is designated in long-term planning procedures, and public-space re-configuration is considered to be solely a technical issue, anchored on property rights. Processes are kept top-down and remain obscure to laymen and laywomen. One should provide more short-term and direct impact development or intervention stages in everyday life. There is a need to check, follow-up, monitor, and evaluate continuously to open and democratize these processes.

Building policies for gender awareness in administrative procedures related to urban planning and design in recent years has been inconsistent because it has been taken over first by GSGE, and later by the ministries, regions, and municipalities that do not consider or tackle gender issues as a priority. There must be a horizontal collaboration of all stakeholders. So, there is the matter of *who* is going to take over the challenge and coordinate it in praxis? On one hand, following the European Charter definition (CEMR 2006):

> local and regional authorities represent the levels best placed to combat the persistence and the reproduction of inequalities, and to promote a truly egalitarian society. They can, through their competences, and through co-operation with the whole range of local actors, undertake concrete actions in favour of equality of women and men.

They also have statutory responsibilities in social policies. On the other hand, local authorities in the Greek context are most often narrow-minded and tied up with local and national political strings, lacking the statutory responsibilities at all levels of planning decisions. But elected members in local authorities could easily be allured by the political gains related to the improvement and inclusiveness of urban quality of life. Moreover, "gender planning competence is part of the planning competence of each individual planning discipline, such as landscape, spatial planning, architecture, geography and traffic planning" (Damyanovic 2009). Thus, the ongoing and prosthetic experience of experts is more likely to have results in gender-mainstreaming practices of area-based development (Beall & Todes 2004a, 2004b).

These facts lead my hypothesis towards an agile twin agent: a mobile expert team in engendered urban planning and design that could collaborate with a local focus group of dynamic representative citizens – women, and willing gender-sensitive municipal planners and designers in continuous feedback and mutual training. There is a need to inform and train all relevant actors, planners, and designers in how to challenge stereotyped roles, needs, and behaviours in urban space and to surpass the statutory and informal processes to provoke change. To gender mainstream policies, one needs the gender-conscious and gender-informed stances of citizens, professionals and practitioners involved in urban planning and design processes alike, and not gender experts in general or from other policy fields.

Although gender-equality issues were not on the agenda in the aforementioned 2014 planning reform, procedures have been accelerated over time as the levels of planning (strategic and physical) have been simplified, and there is an opportunity in urban design practice to define the actual form and function of new development projects. This provides possibilities of women's empowerment and participation in decision-making at the local level. Because new planning standards and patterns are expected by the ministerial services responsible, there is still time to go beyond quantitative general programmatic planning standards and integrate qualitative criteria of sustainable gender-sensitive cities, e.g. social and functional mix, and prescribe gender-aware criteria for issues such as neighbourhood regeneration as well as the repair of urban sprawl. Finally, local and regional committees should be given the responsibility and authority to screen the Municipal and Regional Programmes of Technical Works and relevant budgets using gender-aware approaches and qualitative gender-aggregated data. Through the so-called 'gender lens' one could assess and prevent actions that consolidate inequality and thereby act correctively on projects and interventions, aligning public and private investment with gender equity in regions, cities, and towns. Thus, a broadened list of actors involved in the production of urban space, together with a specialized handbook for technical staff and elected members should be comprehensively compiled.

Beyond top-down administrative steps to engender planning processes, there are several directions of research that it is important to support in order to delve into actual gendered urban realities and bring about change in mainstream understanding. There are several factors that need to be researched and analyzed with regard to gender perspectives. Greek cities are in a period of devolution and in need of regeneration and reconstruction in densely built parts, as well in the diffused parts in the periphery, as the dream of living in suburbs has been smashed or cancelled. In the recent crisis period, EAPs' austerity measures have brought upheaval to Greek society. New urban phenomena arise that provide the city with new potential in spatial-environmental and socio-economic constitutive terms, i.e. vacant lots and buildings, solidarity networks, citizens' initiatives (Christodoulou & Lada 2017). At the moment, there are processes in families and social interactions in everyday life that keep life going in unprecedented and unknown ways, made possible through a new adaptation of the south-European welfare regime (Musterd et al. 1999). In another direction of research, one could focus on the decision-making processes and assess the results of the works of the new municipal and regional gender committees (of 'Kallikratis' administration reform) in local gender-mainstreaming urban interventions and inequity prevention.

Brief Conclusion

The issues at stake concerning gender-mainstreaming urban design and planning in Greece are both contextually institutional and knowledge-based. To advance an engendered framework of steps and fields of action, procedural guidance and control should be reinforced by means of qualitative gender criteria at all phases of a project so that all stakeholders build a deeper understanding and conceptualization of the complexity of interactions at the local level. In that, the training of professionals and focused research on urban conditions that are arising stand out as prerequisites for the creative mobilization of all actors involved in an updated conceptualization of sustainable and inclusive urban environments.

Notes

1 The fields of policies considered in the second pillar of the *National Programme for Substantive Gender Equality 2010–2013* are: (1) violence against women, (2) multiple discrimination, (3) reproductive and sexual health, (4) employment, (5) fostering women's participation in decision-making and civil society, (6) mass media, and (7) arts and culture.
2 Notice also that the Closing Remarks of the UN Committee on the Elimination of Discrimination against Women in the 2013 Report of the Greek Government (CEDAW 2013) included serious concerns about the lack of data and research on the negative effects of the crisis on all aspects of women's life in Greece. This report made no reference to policies related to the environment, but pointed out the negative impacts on housing provisions with the closing down of the only workers' housing organization in Greece (OEK) and the significant cutbacks of the operation and maintenance of nurseries and child-care facilities.

3 Greek words have been erased.
4 Usually referred to as "bail-out packages" or "memoranda".
5 These were elaborated and forwarded by offices responsible in the Ministry of Environ-
   onment, Planning and Public Works – later renamed as the Ministry of Environment
   and Climate Change, and the Ministry of Interior.
6 A good number of local authorities (all regions of the country and 153 municipalities –
   out of 325 in all) signed and agreed to adopt the Charter for Equality on the Local
   Level after continuing campaigns run by GSGE since 2011. By the end of 2016 the
   number of Municipalities that signed the Charter rose to 202 (source: GSGE).

References

Arapoglou, V. & I. Sayas. (2009). Gender aspects of the segregation in Athens: Economic
   restructuring, feminization of employment and immigration. In Emmanouel, D.,
   Zakopoulou, E., Kaftantzoglou, R., Maloutas, T. & Hadjigianni, A. (eds.) *Social and
   Spatial Transformations in Athens of the 21st Century*. Athens: National Centre for Social
   Research, pp. 103–128 [in Greek].
Beall, J. & A. Todes. (2004a). Headlines and head-space: Challenging gender planning
   orthodoxy in area based urban development. *IDS Bulletin*, Vol. 35, No. 435.4 (Reposi-
   tioning Feminisms in Development), pp. 43–50.
Beall, J. & A. Todes. (2004b). Gender and integrated area development projects: Lessons
   from Cato Manor, Durban. *Cities*, Vol. 21, No. 4, pp. 301–310.
CEDAW. (2013). *Concluding Observations on the Seventh Periodic Report of Greece Adopted by
   the Committee at Its Fifty Fourth Session*, 11 February–1 March. Geneva: Office of the
   United Nations High Commissioner for Human Rights (OHCHR) – Committee on
   the Elimination of Discrimination against Women (CEDAW).
CEMR. (2006). *The European Charter for Equality of Women and Men in Local Life*. Innsbruck:
   Council of European Municipalities and Regions.
Christodoulou, C. (2015). *Landscapes of Sprawl. Urbanization and Urban Planning. The Periph-
   ery of Thessaloniki*. Thessaloniki: University Studio Press [in Greek].
Christodoulou, C. & S. Lada. (2017). Urban design in the neoliberal era: Reflecting on the
   Greek Case. *Journal of Urban Design*, Vol. 22, No. 2, pp. 144–146.
Damyanovic, D. (2009). Gender Mainstreaming as a strategy for sustainable urban planning
   procedures. Paper presented in *"City Futures" International Conference*, Madrid.
Damyanovic, D., F. Reinwald & A. Weikmann. (2013). *Gender Mainstreaming in Urban
   Planning and Urban Development*. Vienna: Urban Development Vienna, Municipal
   Department 18 (MA 18) – Urban Development and Planning. Available at: www.wien.
   gv.at/stadtentwicklung/studien/pdf/b008358.pdf.
EC. (2017). *2017 Report on Equality between Women and Men in the EU*. Belgium: European
   Union.
EC-DG Regio. (1997). The EU Compendium of spatial planning systems and policies.
   Regional Development Studies, 28, European Commission-DG Regional Policy and
   Cohesion, Brussels.
EC-DG Regio. (2000). The EU Urban Compendium of spatial planning systems and pol-
   icies – Greece. Regional Development Studies, 28G, European Commission-DG
   Regional Policy and Cohesion, Brussels.
Evangelidou, M., K. Kallis, E. Basoukea, T. Moysiadou & N. Chlepas. (2005). *Study of Spa-
   tial Planning Levels and Relevant Designation Procedures – Part A*. Athens: Technical Cham-
   ber of Greece.

GSGE. (2010). *National Programme for Substantive Gender Equality 2010–2013*. Athens: GSGE-Ministry of Interior.

GSGE. (2011a). *Implementation Guide of the Model System of Gender Mainstreaming Policies of Central Government (Ministries)*. Document produced in the framework of the EU-funded project "Creation of Methodologies and Instruments of Integration, Monitoring and Control of Gender Mainstreaming All Public Policies", Athens: GSGE [in Greek].

GSGE. (2011b). *Implementation Guide of the Model System of Gender Mainstreaming Policies of Regions*. Document produced in the framework of the EU-funded project "Creation of Methodologies and Instruments of Integration, Monitoring and Control of Gender Mainstreaming All Public Policies", Athens: GSGE [in Greek].

GSGE. (2011c). *Implementation Guide of the Model System of Gender Mainstreaming Policies of Municipalities*. Document produced in the framework of the EU-funded project "Creation of Methodologies and Instruments of Integration, Monitoring and Control of Gender Mainstreaming All Public Policies", Athens: GSGE [in Greek].

GSGE. (2013–1417). Ministry of interior & administrative reconstruction, general secretariat for gender equality, *Press Releases* www.isotita.gr/category/deltia-typou/ [Accessed 22 July 2017].

GSGE. (2017). *National Action Plan on Gender Equality 2016–2020*. Athens: Ethniko Typografeio [in Greek].

GSGE, E. Mari & D. Birbas (2011). *Implementation Guide of The European Charter for Equality of Women and Men in Local Life*. Athens: GSGE [in Greek].

Haataja, M.-L., E. Leinonen & S. Mustakallio. (2011). *Gender Mainstreaming in Development Programmes and Projects. Guide for Authorities and Project Actors*. Finland: KoulutusAvain Ltd., WoM Ltd., Ministry of Employment and the Economy.

Horelli, L. (2017). Engendering urban planning in different contexts-successes, constraints and consequences. *European Planning Studies*, Vol. 25, No. 10, pp. 1779–1796.

Karamessini, M. (2015). Structural crisis and adjustment in Greece. Social regression and the challenge for gender equality. In Karamessini, M. & Rubery, J. (eds.) *Women and Austerity: The Economic Crisis and the Future for Gender Equality*. Athens: Nissos Publications, pp. 239–273 [in Greek].

Lada, S. (2016). Gendered aspects of the crisis: Vulnerable bodies, bare lives. In Exhibition Catalogue #ThisIsACo_op – the Greek Pavilion at the 15th International Architecture Exhibition 'La Biennale di Venezia'. Athens: Association of Greek Architects (SADAS – PEA)/Ministry of Environment and Energy, General Secretary of Spatial Planning and Urban Environment.

Lykogianni, R. (2008). Tracing multicultural cities from the perspective of women's everyday lives. *European Urban and Regional Studies*, Vol. 15, No. 2, pp. 133–143.

Musterd, S., C. Kesteloot, A. Murie & W. Ostendorf. (1999). *Urban Social Exclusion and Modes of Integration. Literature Review*. Amsterdam: Amsterdam Centre for the Metropolitan Environment, Report n.1.

Pantelidou-Malouta, M. & A. N. Kapekaki. (2009). Evolution of perceptions of gendered relations in Athens, 1988–2006. In Emmanouel, D., Zakopoulou, E., Kaftantzoglou, R., Maloutas, T. & Hadjigianni, A. (eds.) *Social and Spatial Transformations in Athens of the 21st Century*. Athens: National Centre for Social Research, pp. 247–278 [in Greek].

RTPI. (2003). *Gender Equality and Plan Making: The Gender Mainstreaming Toolkit*. London: Royal Town Planning Institute.

RTPI. (2007). *Good Practice Note 7: Gender and Spatial Planning*. London: Royal Town Planning Institute.

Sánchez de Madariaga, I. (2004) *Urbanismo con perspectiva de género*, Seville: Junta de Andalucí - European Social Fund.

Stratigaki, M. (2014). The European charter for equality of women and men in local life: A window of opportunity for gender equality, Presentation in *"Engendering Cities" International Conference*, Rome, 25–26 September.

Stratigaki, M. & D. Vaiou. (2009). *The Gender of Immigration*. Athens: Metechmio [in Greek].

United Nations. (2015) *Transforming Our World: The 2030 Agenda for Sustainable Development*, United Nations, A/RES/70/1.

United Nations Women (UN WOMEN). (1995). *Beijing Declaration and Platform for Action – Beijing+5 Political Declaration and Outcome*. New York: UN [2014 Reprint].

Vaiou, D. (2002). In the interstices of the city: Albanian women in Athens. *Espace, Populations, Societes*, Vol. 2002–3, pp. 373–385.

Vaiou, D. (2004). (Re)constituting the urban through women's life histories. In Droogleever, J., Cristaldi, F. & Fortuijn, J. D. (eds.) *Gendered Cities: Identities, Activities, Networks – A Life Course Approach*. Rome: IGU – Home of Geography, Publications Series 6. Rome: Società Geografica Italiana, pp. 171–182.

Vaiou, D. (2014). Tracing aspects of the Greek crisis in Athens: Putting women in the picture. *European Urban and Regional Studies*, Published online before print March 26.

Vaiou, D. & M. Stratigaki. (2008). From 'Settlement' to 'integration', informal practices and social services for women migrants in Athens. *European Urban and Regional Studies*, Vol. 15, No. 2, pp. 119–131.

Vrychea, A. & C. Laurent (eds) (1992). *Participatory Design: Theoretical Research, History of Ideas and Practices, Methodological Approaches*. Athens: National Technical University of Athens – Technical Chamber of Greece [in Greek].

Women's Advisory Committee of the Senate Department for Urban Development. (2011). *Gender Mainstreaming in Urban Development*. Berlin: Senatsverwaltung für Stadtentwicklung.

PART III
Tools for Engendering Planning

14

GENDERING THE DESIGN OF CITIES IN AOTEAROA NEW ZEALAND

Are We There Yet?

Dory Reeves, Julie Fairey, Jade Kake, Emma McInnes, and Eva Zombori

Introduction

This chapter combines the voices of five women from Aotearoa New Zealand. Eva Zombori, private sector consultant, contributes by setting out and critiquing the planning and urban design legislative framework in Aotearoa New Zealand. Julie Fairey, local board member for Puketepapa, writes from her personal experience of working as a local-body politician and advocating for women's equality. Emma McInnes, one of the founders of Women in Urbanism, writes about the passion and energy which has led to the growth of this influential advocacy group concluding with a list of changes cities need to make. Jade Kake, Māori architect, writes about the role of Māori women in the built-environment professions, their challenge and issues. Finally, Dory Reeves looks at what role education should play in developing the built-environment professionals of the future. Please note that there is a Glossary of terms used at the end of the chapter.

Aotearoa New Zealand was one of the founding members of the United Nations, playing a key role in drafting the Universal Declaration of Human Rights and ratifying the Convention on the Elimination of all Forms of Discrimination against Women (CEDAW) in January 1985, albeit six years after it was adopted by the UN General Assembly (Statistics NZ, 2013; UN, 2014). So despite New Zealand's recognised track record of having a history of openness to gender equality (Curtin, 2014), Equal Employment Opportunities Commissioner Jackie Blue reflected, during the 2014 International Women's Day, that the whakapapa, or history on women's suffrage, shows that equality 'is still some years away' (Blue, 2014).

New Zealand has been slow to acknowledge its responsibility for the universal sustainable development goals and SDG5, equality for women (UN, 2015). Speaking on behalf of the New Zealand delegation to CEDAW, Jan Logie said that New Zealand was 'absolutely committed to the 2030 Agenda' (Logie, 2018). As of 2018, however, New Zealand has yet to commit in practical ways to the New Urban Agenda (UN, 2016).

The discourse around women's equality promoted by the Ministry of Women's Affairs in New Zealand focuses on three key issues: violence against women, the fact that women are the majority of those earning at or below the minimum wage, and a lack of representation at the top tables. Gender-analysis frameworks, such as the 'Full Picture' tool, used to facilitate the systematic integration of gender into government policy were actually introduced in the 1980s but they have not been widely used up till now. What has been lacking is a holistic and joined-up approach which recognises that, unless the planning and design of cities and towns are gendered, women will not achieve gender equality.

Writing in 2011, Rachel Simon-Kumar (2011) spoke of gender continuing to lose ground and pointed to three processes at work: (1) invisiblisation, when women's issues become framed as gender-neutral or as issues that matter to both men and women; (2) when the concept of women becomes dissolved in the public discourse into specific identities; and (3) backlash against gender and feminist issues. In New Zealand, the Māori cultural dimension must be added. Despite gender being strongly embodied in the way that Māori understand the world (Salmond, 2015), organisations like The Māori Women's Welfare League or Te Rōpū Wāhine Māori Toko I te Ora were established in the early 1950s – following the mass movement of Māori from rural to urban areas – to focus on health and education issues (MWWL, 2015). In political dealings with the government, mana tane (male) claims have tended to be affirmed and protected whilst mana wāhine (women) have not, leading to claims of the subordination of gender to culture (Irwin, 1993).

Planning Legislation in New Zealand – Eva Zombori

When analysing New Zealand planning legislation from a gender perspective, the overwhelming conclusion that one comes to is that there is little to be said other than to list instances of omission. This is true both of the major operative legislation and the subsidiary local plans and design guideline documents.

The fundamental pieces of legislation concerning town planning in New Zealand are the Resource Management Act (RMA), (Public Act, 1991) and the Local Government Act (LGA) (Public Act, 2002b). The main purpose of the RMA, as cited in Section 5 (1), is 'to promote the sustainable management of natural and physical resources'. As such, the Act was never conceived as an enabler of the social aspects of urban planning. Section 5 (2) defines sustainable management as 'managing the use, development, and protection of natural and physical resources in a way, or at a rate, which enables people and communities to provide for their social, economic and cultural wellbeing and for their health and safety'. Criteria based on environmental impact are stressed as the basis for plans (Regional Policy Statements and District Plans) and development decisions, leading to the notion of effects-based planning. There is a presumption that, within certain parameters, any activity is permissible provided the environmental effects are no more than minor (Vallance et al., 2005: 719; Higgins, 2010: 4).

Although the social aspect of planning was recognised in Section 5 (2) of the RMA legislation, there is no definitive interpretation of 'social and cultural wellbeing', which leaves the area in which gender would naturally be addressed undetermined. Consequently, the emphasis of planning in New Zealand has continued to be on the environmental and economic effects of development. Although the RMA, since its enactment, has been amended numerous times – most recently in 2017 – none of the changes have addressed gender issues. Similarly, the current amendments before parliament deal with other aspects of the legislation, and gender matters remain unaddressed.

Although the RMA does not explicitly include a gender perspective, it 'explicitly recognizes the role of Māori culture and the principles of the Treaty of Waitangi as being of national importance, and provides for consideration of iwi (local tribes) management plans where these have been prepared' (Higgins, 2010: 5, citing Harmsworth, 2005).

The LGA 2002 has been recognised as a major influence on the planning regime, explicitly promoting social, economic, environmental and cultural community wellbeing. But whereas attempts were made to define cultural wellbeing (MfE, undated), there has been no attempt to define social wellbeing.

Under the LGA 2002, local government is responsible for involving Māori in decision-making processes and enhancing Māori capacity to participate by providing enhanced Māori representation. Furthermore, Schedule 10 of the LGA requires that a long-term plan must include a council's plans in terms of fostering Māori capacity to participate in the decision-making process, and an annual plan must include a statement on what has been done to foster this capacity.

Today, the statement of intent for the Ministry for the Environment (MfE) states that the focus is on positive ageing, pay, employment equity and disability. All have a direct impact on women, although even within the MfE the issues are seen as concerning employment or economic factors rather than issues which specifically address gender equality.

> While integrating equality and diversity at a strategic planning level, work programmes will continue around positive ageing, pay and employment equity and disability. We will also collect information on our workforce profile and report on information and trends to measure and support equality and diversity.
>
> *(MfE, undated)*

A significant part of a city's spatial organisation falls within the realm of urban design, and the way in which urban design rules and guidelines are applied determines whether the 50 percent of the population who are female have the same ability to use and enjoy the environment as the 50 percent who are male. Extensive research has been carried out internationally on what makes a city 'woman friendly', stressing the importance of factors such as shade and ergonomic street furniture available in areas where people are expected to spend time; adequate supply of public toilet facilities; appropriate mix of land uses so that facilities and services are easily accessible without private vehicle transport. None of these gender-specific insights have been incorporated into or inform gendered urban design guidelines operative in New Zealand.

The most significant and comprehensive national design guideline was the Urban Design Protocol, produced by the Ministry for the Environment and first published in 2005. The intention was for this document to be reviewed in 2014, but this review has not yet eventuated and the Urban Design Protocol document cannot currently be found on the Ministry for the Environment website. This design guideline did not contain sections specifically concerned with children, the elderly or women. It did make reference to women explicitly in relation to safety, reflecting long-standing work undertaken to promote Crime Prevention through Urban Design in New Zealand (MfE, 2005). The initial focus on creating well-designed medium–density housing schemes has one reference to women in connection with Crime Prevention through Environmental Design (CPTED) on page 10. However, the description of social impact analysis (SIA) page 18–19, mentions people generally rather than gender specifically. The same applies to the *Auckland Design Manual* (ADM) which is a non-statutory design guidance document supplementing the operative district plan for the city. The document provides guidance based on international best practice examples but it does not contain references to women nor their specific needs. Some design guidance within the manual contains a high level of detail on housing and street design, but overall it provides a more generic set of urban design guidelines. It should be noted, however, that the ADM contains CPTED principles as well as a section on Te Aranga design principles which are a set of outcome-based principles founded on intrinsic Māori cultural values and designed to provide practical guidance for enhancing outcomes for the design environment (Auckland Council, undated). In summary, this brief review highlights the lack of gender-specific references in current planning and urban design legislation and guidance and, as we know from experience elsewhere, this lack of legislative framework means there are gaps in provisions.

Women in Local Politics – Julie Fairey

Aotearoa New Zealand is recognised internationally as the first nation to give women the franchise to vote in national elections: in 1893. We had the first female mayor in the then British Empire in Onehunga – part of Auckland – in

1894, and have now had three female prime ministers, with the most recent having a baby while in office. From the outside it might look as if Aotearoa New Zealand has no glass ceiling blocking women from power and influence, but that is far from the reality for many women and girls seeking input to the local government decisions that most impact their daily lives.

My own experience as an elected member of Auckland Council began in 2010. At that time Auckland had just started a new unitary council, bringing together a regional council and seven district or city councils for the first time. Twenty ward councillors and a mayor were elected to represent the region, and 149 local board members were voted in to give a local voice to each of 21 local board areas. I was one of two women elected to the six-member Puketāpapa Local Board, in Mt Roskill, on Auckland's isthmus. In that 2010 election, 41 percent of those elected across the 170 positions were women: 38 percent on the regionally focused Governing Body, and 42 percent on local boards. Only three of the 21 local boards had more women than men, with a further four having a balance of male and female. Two-thirds were majority men.

Fast forward to the most recent elections in 2016 and the gender balance at Auckland Council had improved slightly overall, although women were only a third of the Governing Body. In total, 46 percent of those voted in were female, and just over half of the local boards had majority women or a balance. Representation at the local board level was nearly even, with 72 women elected and 77 men. (To date, no one who openly identifies as being of non-binary gender has been elected to Auckland Council.)

Representation at the decision-making table matters, and can make a real difference to the organisational culture as well as the priorities of a council. But those elected need to include not just women but also feminists who recognise that there is value in bringing a gender lens to the work of local government. While more women, and a broader diversity of women, are now elected to Auckland Council, much of the power in regard to planning and the resources to implement that planning is still held by men. There has been recognition that there are some sectors of the community who tend to be under-represented in traditional council consultation processes such as hearings and submissions, as well as at the elected level. These are in part addressed by appointed advisory panels, covering youth, seniors, Pacific people, ethnic communities, those with disabilities, the rainbow community and those living in rural areas, as well as the statutorily required Independent Māori Statutory Body to give a voice to tangata whenua. Structures to deliberately seek and include the perspectives of women are yet to come.

My own experience has been that when I have raised the need to ensure some representation for women on working parties, the response has been largely negative, followed by a suggestion that I do it, even though other women might be more able or qualified. 'Why would we need to appoint a woman?' is the reply, sometimes from other women too. I have observed a lack of understanding from elected members of the value that a gendered perspective can bring. Usually the question is 'how much will this cost?' rather than 'how do we best do this?'

In July 2018, Auckland Council's Community Development and Safety Committee considered a request to make Auckland a City for CEDAW, and publicly commit to eliminating all forms of discrimination against women. The committee of 15 includes only two women. As I write, they have requested a report to inform future decision-making. In 2015 the proposal was turned down, so this is actually encouraging progress! The Governing Body also commissioned research in 2017 into how the council can be more inclusive, which may provide real results for women's participation and influence in future.

If development at the regional level is modest, the leadership of women in local boards has been more encouraging. Local boards are a unique local government structure in Auckland, matching up more with the previous district councils than with the much less powerful community boards. Most local board members are paid enough to consider the role as a half-time job, with the 21 chairs remunerated at a full-time level. This means people who could not afford to participate in the past have been able to put themselves forward and know that the compromise affecting other parts of their lives will be more about time rather than money (or indeed both).

While the powers that local boards have are somewhat limited by law, regional policies and Council-Controlled Organisations (particularly in transport), nonetheless there are real opportunities to create and realise a community vision. In my own area of Puketapapa the local board worked for many years on planning for a suburb with an old quarry at its heart, ultimately playing a powerful role in winning a compromise for the community that will deliver better urban design outcomes and much-needed housing close to a town centre and public transport routes. Local boards are resourced to be strong advocates, and effective decision makers, and in my opinion more and more people are being elected who see the positive potential of the Council's role as a facilitator and enabler for the community it serves, and not just as a regulator and distributor of grants.

Another important aspect of local boards, which hopefully gives women and other marginalised groups more input, is how close they are to their communities, and the open and innovative engagement processes they run. Every three years, each local board produces a local board plan for their area. In the first term, public views were largely gathered by written submissions and hearings, but the third term was very different. Most local boards tried new approaches, reflecting a wish to gather more input than in the past and reach parts of their communities who often had not engaged with council decision-making. Several had community concerts events at which the proposals were explained and submissions gathered, others used social media – in particular a Facebook video to appeal to new demographics – and most had informal 'Have Your Say' events that were interactive. People could talk casually but directly to decision makers and also use stickers, Post-its and social media tools to indicate their views.

All of these non-traditional methods make it easier for everyone to engage, not least women. The family-friendly nature of such consultation events, where children were usually welcomed and catered for, also made it easier for those with caring responsibilities to attend. Some local boards continually operate these kinds of easy-to-access input opportunities, for example stalls at local events, monthly informal community forums and seeking feedback through Facebook.

The approachability of women local board members should not be underestimated. I often get messages from other women asking questions about local government through Twitter and Facebook, and I offer to assist when I can. One such example was in a small group of friends when someone I did not know personally shared her tale of a sexist bus driver. She asked if anyone knew how she could complain and I (virtually speaking) put up my hand. As a result, the driver's manager had a conversation with them and ascertained that the driver was unaware they were doing anything wrong by refusing to open the back door for a woman, meaning she would have to walk to the front of the bus and that he 'got to see the pretty girls twice'. Not only did the driver get a written warning but all those involved were reminded, or made aware if they didn't know, of the importance of treating everyone like a human being. The person who raised the issue, and all those reading about it on the Facebook group, could see the effectiveness of complaining, and that their local government valued inclusion. A woman's voice counted for something.

This subsidiarity model, both the decision-making happening at the local level and also the commitment of local boards to meaningful local engagement, provides positive chances for women to participate in ways they have not been able to in the past. I have seen new issues raised that impact women, such as the role of town-centre safety in the ability for women to use public transport options. Traditionally, public transport decision-making has focused on the concept of the male commuter doing a nine-to-five job in the city, and the riskiness of the first and last leg – getting to and from the bus stop or train station – has been minimised. Now instead we are seeing recognition of the importance of lighting to enable women's activity in our community (although that may give a false sense of security).

Similarly, with cycling infrastructure there has been, historically, an assumption that those wishing to get around by bicycle were largely men. Why would we need cycle racks at a supermarket when most people who go there are mums with kids and a station wagon? The work of groups of women such as Frocks on Bikes and Women in Urbanism needs to be acknowledged for challenging these stereotypes and pointing out the absence of women in the planning of the past. Slowly, some recognition is coming that we are not all the same, and sometimes have different needs that are equally valid. Women hold up half of Auckland's sky, but do not yet have a fair say in how the city develops and supports all its people. The local board model, innovations in engagement and consultation, particularly through social media, and the slowly increasing representation of women in Auckland Council give me hope.

Urbanism Is Pretty Damn Sexist – Emma McInnes

This section will unpack the following three themes. First, it will cover who Women in Urbanism is and what it's achieved over its first year. Second, it will outline the key issues for Women in Urbanism. And third, it will outline some of what we would like to see change.

The statistics are bleak. There's a serious lack of women in New Zealand's urban industries at all levels. Only 15 percent of Mayors and 20 percent of District Mayors in Aotearoa are women (The Department of Internal Affairs, 2016). In the profession of architecture (Diversity Agenda, 2018), women make up 29 percent of the industry, 17 percent in construction (NAWIC, 2018), and just 14 percent of engineers are women (Diversity Agenda, 2018). There are even fewer Māori, Pasifika and Asian women and men in these industries. Professions and disciplines such as planning are much younger in New Zealand than Europe (Sánchez de Madariaga and Roberts (eds), 2013). In 1961 there were only 55 members of the New Zealand Planning Institute (NZPI) and by 1976 this had risen to 339 (Miller, 2007). Whereas women had enrolled on the first planning programmes in Liverpool, United Kingdom in 1909, in New Zealand it was 1968 before the first woman, Helen Tobin, graduated.

This lack of representation impacts the lives and experiences of women in our communities. Historically, women have been left out of city building. This has delivered urban environments that neglect to design for the diverse needs of many of the people who use cities (Rustin, 2014; Hazelton, 2017). With such shameful representation of women in the urban industries, our cities in many cases are still planned, built and renewed without a woman's perspective (Hayden, 1980; Rustin, 2014).

Yet, one of Women in Urbanism's biggest problems is that a lot of city builders don't think that Women in Urbanism is needed. They believe they are practising inclusive design and that their designs could not be improved by women. They do not agree that a woman's perspective would provide valuable insight into their work. So why do we still have to put up with city designs that make us, as women, feel unsafe and unwelcome? Here's the thing: you cannot claim to value diversity and value it in your work if you don't value diversity around your decision-making table.

So, who is Women in Urbanism Aotearoa?

We're a group of women who aim to transform our towns and cities into more beautiful, inspiring and inclusive places for everyone by amplifying the voices and actions of all women. We're doing this through advocacy on transport, housing and urban issues.

We're non-partisan.

- We're all unpaid volunteers.
- Our purpose, first and foremost, is that we're here to start the conversation. We want more women in the urban industries at all levels. We want to encourage young people (particularly women) into our industry. And we want diversity in the industry to result in good urban outcomes for women in our communities.
- We operate with a core group of volunteers (under 30) and 1000s of supporters and members.
- Our volunteers are women from our urban industries and our communities. We have members in engineering, planning, urban design, local and central government, architecture, marketing, midwifery and nursing.
- We have branches in Wellington, Dunedin and Christchurch.
- We decided to keep the name, Women in Urbanism, broad because we don't think we will create meaningful change if the group is just industry-focused. Because the women in our urban industries are largely Pākehā (white) women, we can more accurately understand the diverse experiences and lives of all the women that make up our urban areas if we keep our focus broad. Opening the group to the wider community, we believe, will allow for a more intersectional approach to our work, and therefore better decision-making.
- We in Aotearoa like to congratulate ourselves for being the first country in the world to allow women to vote. Yet what we don't acknowledge is that freedom to vote was only extended to white Pākehā and Māori women. Chinese women in Aotearoa didn't get the vote until much later (Mellow Yellow, 2018). Our goal is to make sure we take an intersectional approach to our work. To give manaakitanga (kindness and support) to all women in the movement.

Our Work

We host speaking events where we invite, or are approached by, technical experts in urbanism who talk about what they do, with a specific lens focused on women's and urban issues. We've been approached to be on panels, to key-note at events and to take media interviews regularly. We blog about the issues of gender and cities, and we also run events that focus on giving young girls the confidence to freely use public spaces.

For example, in April 2018 we hosted a 'Pump Tracks are for Girls Too' event with Sarah Walker, New Zealand BMX Olympic medallist (McInnes, 2018). We used this event to have a conversation about how we deal with spaces that tend to be male-dominated.

The challenges we face include:

• Perceptions around why Women in Urbanism should exist.
• Ensuring we are an intersectional movement (women can only advance when all women are lifted from their oppression).
• Measuring outcomes of feminist spaces and streets.
• Lack of funding.

We started out with some initial 'networking' events and then let the group grow organically. This has helped us to assess if there was a mandate for Women in Urbanism. A lot of our events are exclusively for women. This is to create safe spaces for women in the industry, and the feedback we've had is that this is preferred. When hosting events for women and men, we've found that when we put 'Women' in the title of the events, fewer men attend.

The Issues for Wāhine in Our Cities

Safety from Everyday Sexism and Harassment

We know that the fear felt by women in public spaces leads to behavioural adjustments and precautions (Ceccato, 2017; Hazelton, 2017) such as: avoiding travel at some times of the day, avoiding certain modes, avoiding locations and adjusting appearances.

Women do feel unsafe, and *are* unsafe, on our transport networks and in our public spaces (Casey, 2018). In a recent survey conducted by Women in Urbanism Aotearoa, we found that 71.4 percent of women have experienced some form of harassment while using New Zealand's public spaces (this includes using public transport, walking and cycling). Women with disabilities (and there are different levels of vulnerabilities) are particularly the targets of harassment (Ceccato, 2017).

Urban Design

Especially in Auckland, there's a lack of well-designed public spaces. This means spaces and places where a diversity of people are comfortable relaxing and spending time, where there are toilets, quiet spaces, areas for mothers to change diapers and rest, seating, shade, lighting, good street frontage and natural surveillance.

We also have too many parking lots and parking garages, which are breeding grounds for harassment and violence due to few exits, lack of natural surveillance, spaces for perpetrators to 'hide' and the general darkness (Loftus, 2018).

Transport and Access

Women's trips tend to be shorter, more frequent, relate to multiple sites (trip chaining – not necessarily linear), involve care of others, are more influenced by cultural/safety considerations and add up to more time in transit (Hayden, 1980; Ministry of Transport, 2014). Women also walk more than men in Aotearoa whereas men drive more than women (Shaw et al., 2016). Although our motorway network is now developed, our walking network is not well-designed (Ministry of Transport, 2014).

In cities where there is quality infrastructure and a real emphasis on cycling as a viable choice, such as Amsterdam, more women cycle than men (Slavin, 2015). In Aotearoa, because the cycling infrastructure is in its infancy, women cycle much less than men (Auckland Transport, 2017).

Housing and Sprawl

When urban sprawl occurs, women (Hayden, 1980), those in the poorest communities, Māori and Pasifika in Aotearoa particularly, are disproportionately affected and find themselves being detached from job opportunities (Chant and Mcilwaine, 2013).

In conclusion, Women in Urbanism wants to see a safer and more reliable transport network, with more public toilets. Car-free Central Business Districts (CBDs) enable the repurposing of car-storage buildings or car parks into community facilities. An emphasis on the first and last mile of a trip would mean more of a focus on how far and how comfortable the first and last stage of a journey from home can be. In addition, Women in Urbanism would like to see harassment in our cities and towns addressed with a more effective way of reporting. Finally, the integration and mainstreaming of gender into all policy development and project design at local and national level can bring about a fundamental change in the way we plan and design our cities and towns.

Te Mana o te Wāhine

Māori Women in the Built-Environment Professions

At the root, at the core, I think, of that understanding of it, is the understanding of mana wāhine. Mana wāhine under the korowai of Māreikura. I think with colonisation we've gone away from that understanding. And when our wāhine suffer, then we all suffer, and it's simply because we've gone away from that understanding, of the mana that our wāhine carry. We've gone completely away from that .... we've torn ourselves and our umbilical cord is sliced, is cut. The pito connects with Rangi and Mother Earth ... The moment you stop suckling from the breast of your mother, you suckle at the breast of Papatūānuku. So we've got to get back into that psychology.

~ Te Warihi Hetaraka nō Ngāti Wai, Tohunga Whakairo
(Hetaraka, 2018)

As Māori, we hold clear beliefs about the status and sanctity of women. From this perspective, how might our cultural attitudes towards women inform and direct the relationships that we have with our environment? And what might be the role of wāhine Māori in shaping our built environment? Māori, and particularly Māori women, are hugely under-represented in the built-environment professions. So why does this matter, from both a diversity and Treaty perspective, and what can we do about it?

Current Picture

It wasn't until I started university that I saw how much the profession looked nothing like me. And in no way represented my life, where I came from, and where I – quite naively at the time but probably ambitiously – thought I was heading. And that was always to be more helpful to my community. But, I suppose on first glance the profession has never presented itself as that. I realised it just took me having to carve that out for myself.

~ Elisapeta Heta nō Ngāti Wai raua ko Tokelau ko Sāmoa, Architectural
Graduate, Former Co-Chair Architecture + Women NZ and Ngā
Aho representative to the New Zealand Institute of Architects Board
(Heta, 2018)

The low numbers of women in the architectural profession, and, particularly, issues of their retention and occupation of leadership roles, have been widely recognised by the built-environment professions in recent years. What is largely missing in Aotearoa New Zealand is where this intersects with ethnicity and other demographic data. Most professional registration boards in New Zealand don't keep detailed demographic data on ethnicity, and for Māori, tribal affiliations.

The makeup of our built-environment professions matters because we each bring with us a set of cultural assumptions, norms and relationships. The representation of Māori within the built-environment professions is particularly relevant in Aotearoa, given the existence of a Treaty that, at least theoretically and, increasingly, in practical reality, positions us as equal decision makers. Who makes decisions about the design of our cities? And for whom? These questions carry significant political importance.

The New Zealand Registered Architects Board (NZRAB) is not required to keep detailed demographic data, but on a recent check the number of

Māori women (or women openly identifying as Māori) on the register was as low as four (by the author's estimate) out of a total of 1,959 registered architects (NZRAB, 2018). The Registration Authority for Professional Chartered Engineers is similarly not required to maintain detailed demographic data.

Both the architecture and engineering professions are regulated by legislation (Public Act, 2002a, 2005), which dictates what standards must be met for registration, and which information must be entered into the register. The planning and landscape architecture industries don't have a separate registration board and are regulated by their professional bodies, the New Zealand Institute of Landscape Architects and the New Zealand Planners' Institute. Both maintain a directory of practices and individual practitioners, searchable by region and services offered.

Why are the numbers so low? Why is it important to increase diversity across our industry? How do we get there?

Use of Surveys/Data

> So we do have low numbers, and then the same, a lot of the similar issues around access, inclusivity, visibility, unconscious bias, all of those kinds of things, can be barriers towards long careers of Māori and Pasifika peoples in the industry. We already know when you look at stats around wāhine staying in the profession, for architecture we're really lucky, we have a good 50/50 kind of output of men and women, more or less. But we're still not necessarily retaining them in the ten years on position, and that's when the wage gap tends to appear.
>
> I haven't come across necessarily any good statistics that talk about the wage gap in relation to Māori within architecture. Partly because the numbers are probably so low that it would be fairly pointed I suppose. It's looking at stats in different ways, and there's all sorts of ways you can slice it. If you look at the general trajectory of average wage gaps or pay gaps amongst Māori and Pacific, and men and women, which are traditionally actually Pākehā men and Pākehā women in New Zealand as a whole, we already know that Māori women earn much less than Pākehā women, and Pasifika women earn less again.
>
> *(Heta, 2018)*

Surveys are one mechanism used to produce an accurate picture of the lack of (and impact of this lack of) diversity within the built-environment professions. Efforts have been made in recent years to understand the persistent lack of diversity within the architecture profession (despite huge improvements within university cohorts), including the 'Where do all the women go?' survey conducted through the website, Parlour: Women, Equity, Architecture (Clark et al.,

2012) and the survey about diversity in the architecture profession (American Institute of Architects, 2015, 2016).

Some lessons taken from these projects include the need to request detailed demographic data, but also to have mechanisms in place to ensure this data is secure and confidentiality is retained. There is a risk with such small sample sizes for the identity of anonymous respondents to become known, along with the accompanying release of personal details. It is also useful to ask questions about micro-aggressions, and experiences in the workplace and the wider profession, that are causing women and non-white architects to leave the profession.

There is currently a project underway that seeks to address some of these issues in Aotearoa New Zealand, and to produce better evidence based on individual experiences in the workplace within the built-environment professions.

Current Initiatives in Aotearoa New Zealand

I think we need to put our hands up more for being involved. What I mean by that, is getting on Boards, or speaking up in meetings, it can be that simple. Actually getting involved in your community. Kind of putting yourself out there to maybe be a judge on something, or to organise social events in your office, or speak on particular topics or issues. I guess what I mean by that is, create visibility of yourself and of other Māori Pacific practitioners. And why that's important is that it helps maybe the practitioners that are standing beside them or around them to recognise the value of them, to recognise the value that Māori and Pacific points of views have, and also really critically important for generations coming through. To actually be able to look to somebody, and that is really crucial.

And I suppose I have benefited from that through being involved in Architecture + Women, where our entire sort of philosophy has been built on the idea of visibility and inclusivity. And the visibility part is literally just kind of social media, and newsletters and all those things that kind of go hey, these are people doing good things. But that could only really happen because those good people doing good things are putting their hands up to do stuff. Not saying be a chronic overachiever … but there are ways of speaking up slightly beyond what may be comfortable, to just push a little bit. Because I think, in order for true change to happen we all need to pushing a little bit further.

(Heta, 2018)

There are a number of very active organisations across Aotearoa championing diversity in the built-environment professions in a variety of ways. Architecture + Women New Zealand focuses on increasing women's representation and visibility within the architecture profession. The National Association of Women in

Construction New Zealand supports women working in the construction industry to pursue and sustain careers in construction. Women in Urbanism is a grassroots movement led by women involved in cities and city-making, working to make our cities more just and inclusive.

Ngā Aho, the society of Māori design professionals, is the main organisation supporting Māori practitioners working across the built-environment professions, including architects, landscape architects and planners. In 2016, Ngā Aho and the New Zealand Institute of Architects [NZIA] formed a Kawenata (covenant) agreement (NZIA, 2017). The Kawenata, which was signed by both parties in early 2017, sets out a set of principles for a Treaty-based relationship between the two organisations. Initiatives progressed to date include the appointment of a co-opted Ngā Aho member to the New Zealand Institute of Architects board (Architecture + Women NZ, 2017). This is a permanent position.

Te Tau-a-Nuku, the Māori Landscape Architects Roopu, is a chapter of Ngā Aho, and since February 2018 it has had a non-voting voice on the New Zealand Institute of Landscape Architects Executive Committee (Challenger, 2018). Papa Pounamu has strong links with Ngā Aho and is the Māori roopu (group) within the New Zealand Planners' Institute [NZPI]. A Pasifika planners' group (which was previously bannered underneath Papa Pounamu) was formed in late 2017 (NZPI, 2017).

The Institute of Architects and Engineering New Zealand launched the Diversity Agenda in 2018 (Engineering New Zealand, 2018), a campaign designed to shift the gender balance within the architecture and engineering professions. Whilst the campaign has done a good job to highlight the lack of gender diversity within the professions, more could be done to work alongside organisations such as Ngā Aho to address other aspects of diversity.

Future Directions?

> I think there needs to be a serious, very serious recognition of unconscious bias and what that does. Both from the wāhine-tane perspective, so we get instances in which say, men don't realise that they have an unconscious bias to ask the male in the room a question over the female in the room. That's not necessarily something that they're doing out of malice, but it's actually something that they're doing unconsciously because it's a bias they have internally. That exists, that's one of those big barriers we see for women in a practice, that exists again as another layer for Māori [and] Pacific. So everybody needs to get better at understanding what their unconscious biases are, pushing their practices – I think – to get more savvy around that. And I really think that people who are running businesses, who are directors, who are principals, actually need to just front up and be honest with themselves about what it is they are and are not doing as practices.
>
> (Heta, 2018)

Surveys and other forms of engagement led by professional bodies could tell us a lot about why – despite increasing student and graduate numbers – Māori women (and indeed, other under-represented groups) are failing to progress to registration or remain within the profession. Many of the reasons would undoubtedly mirror those of other women. But likely these will also be compounded by the experiences of being Māori within what is still a fundamentally Eurocentric profession, plus other outside factors, including whānau and cultural obligations.

Registration boards, with the guidance of their associated professional institutes, could use this information to do more to support alternative pathways. The professional institutes could use this information to provide more critical, cultural and technical support to graduates and sole practitioners, particularly those working within isolated communities, and to support larger practices to engender a fundamental shift in culture within their organisations. Despite the numerous initiatives and active organisations working to address the issue of diversity, there remains a critical lack of intersectionality.

The solutions are necessarily collaborative, require a significant paradigm shift within the professions, and are by no means simple. Some potential solutions have been outlined in the paragraphs above as a starting point. By collecting data that more accurately represents our position as Māori women within the profession, and by using our already active networks to mobilise and communicate this information to professional bodies with which we have an enduring relationship, we have the opportunity to engender real change within our professions.

Gender and Planning Education in New Zealand – Dory Reeves

Planning education has a responsibility to ensure that it plays its role in bringing about gender equality. Research in the field of urban planning has demonstrated that there is a positive relationship between the spatial planning and design of cities and gender equality (UN-Habitat, 2009) and 'that sex and gender bias can be socially harmful and expensive' (Schiebinger et al., 2011).

An up-to-date, future-minded planning programme should include, as part of its core, an introduction to the importance of understanding planning from a gender perspective and an awareness of: (a) the limitations of the traditional history of planning; (b) gender planning as an approach to planning; (c) feminist theories and the feminist critique of planning; (d) the role of planning in delivering the sustainable development goals; and (e) the impact of planning decisions in a non-binary world. Building on the core, the role of a gender and planning specialism is then to enable students of planning to gain an understanding of gender and planning so that they can appreciate how to further develop their expertise and engage the services of an expert where appropriate. A specialism is one of many components of the overall curricula.

However, if gender bias and discrimination is not tackled throughout the curricula then the impact of a gender specialism will be limited. Initiatives, such as the UK's Athena SWAN charter, which have helped universities approach gender equality more holistically, are not widely used in New Zealand (ECU, 2016).

The New Zealand Planning Institute (NZPI) accredits planning courses in New Zealand and has a constitution and education guidelines. The former states that: 'A planner shall ensure that special attention is paid to the interrelatedness of decisions and the environment, social, cultural and economic consequences of planning actions' (NZPI, 2015). That is the closest you will get to a reference to gender. The Tertiary Education and Accreditation Procedures (NZPI, 2016) sets out what accredited planning programmes must address. 'Social equity' is used as a catch-all phrase. Gender equality is not mentioned, neither is age nor disability. Programmes need to demonstrate that they cover:

> analysing and managing the built and natural environment through techniques and tools for environmental evaluation, impact assessment and urban design; policy development and analysis; planning and monitoring systems; principles of sustainability; and planning for a multi-ethnic, multicultural society and social equity.
>
> *(NZPI, 2016: 8)*

Under contextual issues, graduates must have an 'understanding of a range of socio-economic and equity issues' (NZPI, 2016: 9). If we look at the five planning programmes delivered in New Zealand, we see that gender equality is not systematically addressed. None of the programmes have a specific gender specialism and there is no evidence that gender issues are consistently integrated into all aspects of the curricula. Two programme leaders contend that gender is integrated but find it difficult to present the evidence. At least one would argue that their focus is on difference and that this embraces gender. The evidence shows that the promotion of gender and planning is too reliant on individuals and when these individuals move on or retire these parts of the curricula are under threat. The most recent reviews of planning education by the accrediting bodies in New Zealand and Australia have reinforced the generic language of social equity, which means that gender is not explicit.

Planning programmes need to integrate gender in its broadest sense into the entire planning curricula. Gender needs to be integrated into the core curricula and specialisms should then be developed from the core. All planners need to understand how the decisions they will make in practice affect gender equality and women's empowerment. Acknowledging Petra Doan's comment that the 'Heterosexist bias runs deep within the field of planning and is interwoven in many of its basic assumptions' (Doan, 2011: 224), educators supported by professional institutes need to equip the next generation of professionals to work with grassroots groups effectively.

A consideration of gender should be mainstreamed and integrated into every aspect of planning education. The curricula need to acknowledge the non-binary gender world. Material needs to: (i) be introduced early in the programme; (ii) be integrated so that students see the connection between gender equality, theory and practice; (iii) involve links with locally based groups; and (iv) involve learning by doing. A gender specialism on its own is not sufficient.

Conclusion

Aotearoa New Zealand is at a potential tipping point when it comes to gendering cities. Women's activism, the work of mana wāhine, politics, research, education and practice are highlighting the importance of gender perspectives. Eva Zombori's investigation of the legislative framework and guidelines highlights the need for a more explicit reference to gender in design guidance. Julie Fairey concluded that women in Aotearoa New Zealand need a fair say in how cities and towns develop so that they can support all people. She is hopeful that the current trends can continue with support. Emma McInnes, writing on behalf of Women in Urbanism Aotearoa emphasises transport and the importance of advocacy groups. Finally, Jade Kake and Dory Reeves point to the need for built-environment professional institutes to ensure that professional programmes address gender equality as well as support and encourage women from all backgrounds. All want to see legislation, institutions and governance adapting to respond to the needs of all women. Gender-analysis tools need to be routinely used in all areas of public policy impacting on the planning and design of our cities.

References

American Institute of Architects. (2015). Diversity in the Profession of Architecture: Key Findings 2015. [Online]. Available: www.architecturalrecord.com/ext/resources/news/2016/03-Mar/AIA-Diversity-Survey/AIA-Diversity-Architecture-Survey-02.pdf [28 July 2018].

American Institute of Architects. (2016). Diversity in the Profession of Architecture: Executive Summary 2016. [Online]. Available: www.architects.org/sites/default/files/AIA_DiversitySurvey_2016.pdf [28 July 2018].

Architecture + Women NZ. (2017). NZIA Creates Ngā Aho Position on Board. [Online]. Available: www.architecturewomen.org.nz/archives/nzia-creates-nga-aho-position-board [28 July 2018].

Auckland Council. (undated). Auckland Design Manual. [Online]. Available: www.auck landdesignmanual.co.nz/ [6 August 2018].

Auckland Transport. (2017). The Auckland Cycling Account: A Snapshot of Cycling in Auckland in 2016. [Online]. Available: https://at.govt.nz/media/1973770/at-cycling-account-book-2017.pdf [8 August 2018].

Blue, J. (2014). Inspiring Change: International Women's Day. Wellington: Human Rights Commission.

Casey, A. (2018). What Is Being Done about Sexual Harassment on Public Transport? Spinoff, 11 May. [Online]. Available: https://thespinoff.co.nz/society/ 11-05-2018/what-is-being-done-about-sexual-harassment-on-public-transport/ [27 July 2018].

Ceccato, V. (2017). Women's Transit Safety: Making Connections and Defining Future Directions in Research and Practice, *Crime Prevention & Community Safety*, 19 (3–4): 276–287. [Online]. Available: https://doi.org/10.1057/s41300-017-0032-5 [6 August 2018].

CEDAW. (2018). Consideration of New Zealand – 1616th Meeting 70th Session Committee on the Elimination of Discrimination against Women. [Online]. Available: http:// webtv.un.org/watch/consideration-of-new-zealand-1616th-meeting-70th-session-com mittee-on-the-elimination-of-discrimination-against-women-/5808501542001/? lan=original [9 August 2018].

Challenger, N. (2018). Māori Voice Added to Executive Committee 28 February. [Online]. Available: https://nzila.co.nz/news/2018/02/news-from-te-tau-a-nuku-the-maori-landscape-archit [28 July 2018].

Chant, S. and Mcilwaine, C. (2013). Gender, Urban Development and the Politics of Space. [Online]. Available: www.e-ir.info/2013/06/04/gender-urban-development-and-the-politics-of-space/ [2 July 2018].

Clark, J., Roan, A., Stead, N., Burns, K., Whitehouse, G., Matthewson, G., Willis, J., and Kaji-O'Grady, S. (2012). Technical Report and Preliminary Statistics: Where Do All the Women Go? Survey Conducted through the Website: Parlour: Women, Equity, Architecture. [Online]. Available: http://archiparlour.org/ wp-content/uploads/2014/08/Technical-Report_Where-do-all-the-Women-go_Up load.pdf [28 July 2018].

Curtin, J. (2014). The Evolution of Gender Equality Policy in New Zealand, in M. Hill (ed.), *Studying Public Policy*, Bristol: Policy Press, 116–126.

Diversity Agenda. (2018). The Diversity Agenda. [Online]. Available: https://diversitya genda.org [24 July 2018].

Doan, P. (2011). Queerying Identity: Planning and the Tyranny of Gender, in P.L. Doan (ed.), *Queerying Planning: Challenging Heteronormative Assumptions and Reframing Planning Practice*, Farnham, GB: Routledge, 89–106.

ECU. (2016). ECU Athena Swan Charter. [Online]. Available: www.ecu.ac.uk/equality-charters/athena-swan/ [11 December 2016].

Engineering New Zealand. (2018). Engineers and Architects Confront Their Gender Problem [Press release]. [Online]. Available: www.scoop.co.nz/stories/BU1804/ S00232/engineers-and-architects-confront-their-gender-problem.htm. [28 July 2018].

Hayden, D. (1980). What Would a Non-Sexist City Be Like? Speculations on Housing, Urban Design, and Human Work, *Signs*, 5 (3): S170–S187. [Online]. Available: www. jstor.org/stable/3173814 [6 August 2018].

Hazelton, J. (2017). The Shocking Connection between Street Harassment and Street Lighting. [Online]. Available: https://medium.com/the-establishment/the-shocking-connection-between-street-harassment-and-street-lighting-5db8497ef653 [19 July 2018].

Heta, E. Architectural Graduate. (Personal communication, 15 June 2018).

Hetaraka, T.W. Tohunga Whakairo. (Personal communication, 8 May 2018).

Higgins, M. (2010). Urban Design and the Planning System in Aotearoa New Zealand: Disjuncture or Convergence, *Urban Design International*, 15 (1): 1–21. Available: www. mfe.govt.nz/publications/about/soi/2010/page6.html [6 August 2018].

Irwin, K. (1993). Māori Feminism, in W. Ihimaera (ed.), *Te Ao Marama 2: Regaining Aotearoa – Māori Writers Speak Out*, Auckland: Reed, 299–304.

Loftus, M.E. (2018). Parking Lot Safety. [Online]. Available: www.crime-safety-security.com/Parking-Lot-Safety.html [2 July 2018].

Logie, J. (2018). See CEDAW 2018.

Māori Women's Welfare League (MWWL). (2015). Māori Women's Welfare League. [Online]. Available: http://mwwl.org.nz [21 August 2018].

McInnes, E. (2018). Pump Tracks are for Girls, Too! [Online] Available: www.bikeauckland.org.nz/pump-tracks-girls/ [20 June 2018].

Mellow Yellow. (2018). Suffrage and Settler Colonialism: A Tauiwi Chinese Feminist Perspective. *Mellow Yellow* (blog). [Online] Available: https://mellowyellow-aotearoa.blogspot.com/2018/06/suffrage-and-settler-colonialism-tauiwi.html?m= [16 June 2018].

Miller, C. (2007). *The Unsung Profession. A History of the New Zealand Planning Institute 1946–2002*. Wellington: Dunmore Publishing.

Ministry for the Environment. (2005). *The Urban Design Protocol*. Wellington: The Ministry. [Online]. Available: www.mfe.govt.nz/more/towns-and-cities/urban-design-protocol [6 August 2018].

Ministry for the Environment. (undated). Statement of Intent 2010-2013. [Online]. Available: www.mfe.govt.nz/publications/data/ministry-environment-statement-intent-2016-2020 [6 August 2018].

Ministry of Transport. (2014). Household Travel Survey. [Online] Available: www.transport.govt.nz/resources/household-travel-survey/ [24 July 2018].

National Association of Women in Construction NAWIC. (2018). [Online]. Available: www.nawic.org.nz/news-construction [6 August 2018].

New Zealand Institute of Architects NZIA. (2017). New Zealand Institute of Architects and Ngā Aho Sign Te Kawenata O Rata. [Online]. Available: www.nzia.co.nz/explore/news/2017/new-zealand-institute-of-architects-and-ng%C4%81-aho-sign-te-kawenata-o-rata [6 August 2018].

New Zealand Planning Institute NZPI. (2017). Pacific Practitioners Special Interest Group. [Online]. Available: www.planning.org.nz/Story?Action=View&Story_id=2862 [28 July 2018].

New Zealand Registered Architects Board NZRAB. (2018). The New Zealand Architects Register. [Online]. Available: www.nzrab.nz/ [28 July 2018].

NZPI. (2015). Constitution, 8.1.4. [Online]. Available: www.planning.org.nz/Attachment?Action=Download&Attachment_id=3715 [20 August 2018].

NZPI. (2016). Learning for a Better Future: Tertiary Education Policy and Accreditation Procedures. [Online]. Available: www.planning.org.nz/Attachment?Action=Download&Attachment_id=1872 [20 August 2018].

Public Act. (1991). No 69. Resource Management Act. [Online]. Available: www.legislation.govt.nz/act/public/1991/0069/latest/DLM230265.html?search=qs_act_resource±management±act_resel_25_h&p=1&sr=1 [20 August 2018].

Public Act. (2002a). No 17 Chartered Professional Engineers of New Zealand Act. [Online]. Available: www.legislation.govt.nz/act/public/2002/0017/latest/DLM144381.html [28 July 2018].

Public Act. (2002b). No 84 Local Government Act. [Online]. Available: www.legislation.govt.nz/act/public/2002/0084/latest/DLM170873.html?search=qs_act_local±government±act_resel_25_h&p=1&sr=1 [20 August 2018].

Public Act. (2005). No 38. Registered Architects Act 2005. [Online]. Available: www.legis lation.govt.nz/act/public/2005/0038/latest/whole.html [28 July 2018].

Reeves, D. and Zombori, E. (2016). Engendering Cities: International Dimensions from Aoteoroa. *Town Planning Review*, 87 (5): 567–588.

Rustin, S. (2014). If Women Built Cities, What Would Our Urban Landscape Look Like? *The Guardian*, December 5, 2014. [Online]. Available: www.theguardian.com/cities/ 2014/dec/05/if-women-built-cities-what-would-our-urban-landscape-look-like [6 August 2018].

Salmond, A. (2015). Commentary following Kirstin Locke's "Female Professors in Denmark and New Zealand – Why the Inequality?" Seminar (seminar on the EU FP7 IRSES project 'University reform, globalisation and Europeanisation', Auckland, 20 August).

Sánchez de Madariaga, I. and Roberts, M. (eds.) (2013). *Fair Shared Cities. The Impact of Gender Planning in Europe*. Aldershot-New York: Ashgate.

Schiebinger, L., Klinge, I., Sanchez de Madariaga, I., and Schraudner, M., (eds.) (2011). *Gendered Innovations in Science, Health & Medicine, Engineering, and Environment*. Stanford University – Comisión Europea – US National Science Foundation. [Online]. Available: (genderedinnovations.stanford.edu). Translations: Chinese, German, Spanish, Korean https://searchworks.stanford.edu/view/9523784

Shaw, C., Russell, M., van Sparrentak, K., Merrett, A., and Clegg, H. (2016). *Benchmarking Cycling and Walking in Six New Zealand Cities: Pilot Study*. Wellington: New Zealand Centre for Sustainable Cities.

Simon-Kumar, R. (2011). Differences that Matter: From "Gender" to "Ethnicity" in Contemporary Aotearoa/New Zealand, *Women's Studies Journal*, 25: 74–90.

Slavin, T. (2015). If There Aren't as Many Women Cycling as Men … You Need Better Infrastructure. *The Guardian*, July 9, 2015. [Online]. Available: www.theguardian.com/ cities/2015/jul/09/women-cycling-infrastructure-cyclists-killed-female [6 August 2018].

Statistics NZ. (2013). Celebrating 120 Years of Women's Suffrage. [Online] Available: http://archive.stats.govt.nz/about_us/what-we-do/previous-initiatives/statistics2013/ 120-years-suffrage.aspx [20 August 2018].

The Department of Internal Affairs. (2016). Local Authority Election Statistics. [Online]. Available: www.dia.govt.nz/diawebsite.nsf/wpg_URL/Services-Local-Elections-Local-Authority-Election-Statistics-2016?OpenDocument [24 August 2018].

UN. (2015). (2030) Agenda for Sustainable Development, Sustainable Development Goals, UN. [Online]. Available: www.un.org/sustainabledevelopment/sustainable-develop ment-goals/ [6 August 2018].

UN. (2016). New Urban Agenda, United Nations Conference on Housing and Sustainable Urban Development (Habitat III) Quito, 17–20 October. [Online]. Available: www2. habitat3.org/bitcache/99d99fbd0824de50214e99f864459d8081a9be00?vid=591155&dis position=inline⊕view [6 August 2018].

UN (United Nations). (2014). CEDAW: Concluding Observations on the Seventh Periodic Report of New Zealand. [Online]. Available: http://women.govt.nz/sites/public_ files/CEDAW%20report%20follow-up%202014_0.pdf [20 August 2018].

UN-Habitat. (2009). Planning Sustainable Cities: Global Report on Human Settlements 2009. London: Earthscan. [Online]. Available: http://unhabitat.org/books/global-report-on-human-settlements-2009-planning-sustainable-cities [20 August 2018].

Vallance, S., Perkins, H., and Moore, K. (2005). The Results of Making a City More Compact: Neighbours' Interpretation of Urban Infill, *Environment and Planning B: Planning and Design*, 32: 715–733.

Glossary of te reo Māori terms

Aotearoa	North Island – now used as the Māori name for New Zealand
iwi	Extended kinship group, tribe, nation, people, nationality, race – often refers to a large group of people descended from a common ancestor and associated with a distinct territory
Kawenata	Covenant, testament, charter, contract, agreement, treaty – any undertaking that binds the parties in a permanent and morally irrevocable relationship
korowai	Cloak, protective garment
mana	Prestige, authority, control, power, influence, status, spiritual power, charisma
Māreikura	Supernatural goddesses occupying the twelfth heaven in Māori theology, the term is also used to denote women of high rank
Papatūānuku	Earth, ancestral Earth mother and wife of Ranginui – all living things originate from them
Rangi	Abbreviated form of Ranginui, the ancestral Sky father, atua of the sky and husband of Papatūānuku, from which union originate all living things
roopu	Group
tane	Men
tangata whenua	Local people, hosts, indigenous people – people born of the whenua, i.e. of the placenta and of the land where the people's ancestors have lived and where their placentas are buried
wāhine	Women
whānau	Extended family, family group, a familiar term of address to a number of people

15

GENDER IMPACT ASSESSMENTS, A TOOL FOR THE IMPLEMENTATION OF THE NEW URBAN AGENDA

The Case of Madrid Nuevo Norte

Inés Novella Abril

Introduction

Gender issues and women's specific needs in cities and human settlements are well integrated in the New Urban Agenda (NUA) that resulted from the Quito Declaration adopted by the United Nations at the Habitat III Conference (UN 2016). Of the 175 paragraphs that make up the agenda, up to 34 include references to either women or gender (Sánchez de Madariaga and Novella 2018). Cities and gender equality also play an important role in the achievement of the Sustainable Development Goals (SDGs) established by the Agenda 2030 for Sustainable Development, with two respective specific standalone objectives, numbers 11 and 5 respectively (UN 2015). Additionally, most of the remaining 15 SDGs do address urban and equality issues (Novella Abril 2017).

However, gender mainstreaming in spatial planning is demonstrating a certain difficulty when translated into practice. Two recent books (Sánchez de Madariaga and Roberts 2013; Zibell et al. 2018), in addition to the present collection, provide an overview of advances and experiences in Europe and beyond. In Europe, the integration of gender mainstreaming as a principle for public policy at all levels as enshrined in the Treaty of Amsterdam of 1998 has produced a significant degree of gender mainstreaming in different policy fields across the continent. In developing countries, policies addressing women and gender have been, rather, linked to criteria set up by international development organizations, agencies, and banks (UN Women 2014). These agencies have moved from an approach focusing on women's issues to a more encompassing outlook that integrates gender considerations (Campa 2018).

This chapter will look at one particular tool, the Gender Impact Assessment (GIA). GIAs are considered a relevant tool for promoting equality between men and women in spatial planning and urban policies by the First Quadrennial

Report for the Implementation of the New Urban Agenda (UN 2018). This First Report sets the criteria and topics for the future evaluation every four years of advances in the implementation of the NUA worldwide. As such, it is highly relevant that a tool for the integration of gender dimensions has been explicitly included among the recommended instruments. GIAs have also been introduced as tools for gender mainstreaming in different policy areas in Europe, as well as in some national legislations. However, specific applications in the field of planning are still scarce.

This chapter aims at discussing the possibilities and conditions for the effective application of GIAs in spatial planning. To that end it analyses how gender has been integrated into Madrid Nuevo Norte, one of the most important urban redevelopment projects in Europe. The way this project has integrated gender aspects while developing a GIA as part of its technical documents can provide useful insights on the relevance and usefulness of GIAs as tools for the effective mainstreaming of gender issues in planning agendas.

Gender Impact Assessments as a Planning Tool in Spain

GIAs or reports are mandatory in Spain, since 2003, for all legislation and regulations emanating from public bodies (Ley 30/2003). This mandate was originated by European policy, in particular by the Action Plan on Improving Legislation of 2002, which made it compulsory to elaborate such reports for all European legislation. This European Action Plan aimed at firstly improving the quality of the legislation and secondly enhancing gender mainstreaming in public policies (Macías Jara 2018).

Unlike in some other European countries, spatial plans at different scales in Spain are also pieces of legislation. Because urban development plans are in effect legislative instruments, some regional level courts in Madrid and Andalucía revoked, in 2016 and 2017, a number of Municipal Urban Comprehensive Development Plans (Planes Generales de Urbanismo) on the basis that they lacked the specific report addressing gender impacts. These court decisions would be following the national legislation of 2003 and its subsequent law of 2015 that regulates GIAs for all pieces of legislation (Ley del Gobierno, 40/2015; Real Decreto, 2009).

However, a more recent ruling by the national level Supreme Court in 2018 overrules the previous ones of 2016 and 2017 made by lower echelons of the judiciary. Briefly summarized, the current decision by the Supreme Court (Tribunal Supremo 2018) addresses an issue of procedure and competence between state and regional levels, while acknowledging that promoting gender equality should be an objective of urban plans, to which the national land-use legislation makes succinct reference (TRLSRU 2015). In short, it says that national legislation requiring elaboration of GIAs as a specific official document accompanying legislative instruments cannot be applied across the board as a suppletory legal formal requirement of urban development plans when the regional level planning legislation does not explicitly address gender requirements among its regulations (Sánchez de Madariaga & Novella Abril 2020).

While the Supreme Court recognizes that the national land-use law includes a brief mention of the equality of treatment and opportunities among the several aspects of sustainable development that planning needs to take into account, it stresses that planning legislation in Spain is the exclusive competence of the regions. The national land-use law in Spain has a very limited scope because planning legislative powers are exclusively attributed by the Constitution to the 17 regions in which the country is divided (comunidades autónomas). So, the Supreme Court states that the relevant issue is how the regional-planning legislations refer to gender as a substantive aspect to be addressed by urban plans.

Now, how do regions address the topic of gender in their planning and housing policies? While some regions have included significant sections on gender in planning law – Catalonia, Extremadura, Valencia – some have done it through regional legislation on gender equality – Basque Country for instance – and others do not make explicit reference to gender mainstreaming in the field of planning and housing policies (Sánchez de Madariaga 2018). However, many among this last group do have regional legislation on GIAs for regulations emanating from regional governments. This diverse panorama sets the stage for the emergence of GIAs as a relevant tool for gender planning in Spain, albeit in evolving and uneven ways in different parts of the country.

Background, Context and Description of Madrid Nuevo Norte

This chapter presents the case study of Madrid Nuevo Norte, whose GIA was completed as part of the process of design between 2017 and 2018. Madrid Nuevo Norte is one of the most important current urban regeneration projects in Europe. Its main objective is the reuse and filling-in of more than two million square meters of land located north of the city. The project also aims at solving the problems of accessibility, isolation, and discontinuity that currently afflict this area of the city. Much of the land on which Madrid Nuevo Norte will be developed are *brownfield* sites that are, or were, linked to railway infrastructure and small industrial areas that are now obsolete and surrounded by the consolidated urban fabric of different morphologies. The current state of this section of the city supposes an important urban void and a focus of urban degradation, but also an opportunity of the first order for Madrid.

Due to its location and size, the project involves the remodelling, expansion, and improvement of much urban infrastructure, mainly associated with mobility and the urban water cycle. This very significant engineering work involves the construction of bridges, the partial covering of the railway tracks, the extension of the subway, new subway and railway stations, as well as the intervention on various Canal de Isabel II facilities – the public company that manages the urban water cycle in the region of Madrid. The complexity of Madrid Nuevo Norte is maximal at both technical and management levels (see Figure 15.1). It requires strong economic investment and collaboration between the three administrative levels existing in Spain (local, regional and state), since a large proportion of the land belongs to one or more of the three administrations or affects infrastructures within their competence.

The complexity of the project and other variables of an economic, political, and legal nature are at the base of the long-running history of Madrid Nuevo Norte, which started being planned at the beginning of the 1990s. However, the current proposal for "Operación Chamartín", as this project is popularly known, has a more optimistic horizon than its predecessors, with a final official approval date in the near future. The current project, finally, is backed by all the political parties that have a say in its approval process, as well as a broad consensus among the citizens of Madrid.

Madrid Nuevo Norte is the first major urban regeneration project in Spain, and possibly in Europe, that incorporates the perspective of gender in a broad and technical manner.

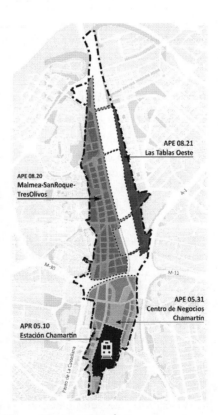

FIGURE 15.1 Madrid Nuevo Norte master plan

Source: Own elaboration.

The general approach of the project, and the city model proposed by Madrid Nuevo Norte, is a good basis for the application of the gender perspective, since its guiding principles point to a mixed and compact urban model from the start that prioritizes public transport and the quality of public space. More specifically, the project seeks to provide improvements beyond its own development site through urban regeneration, by considering its impact on different scales: from neighbourhood to territorial scale.

From the planning point of view, Madrid Nuevo Norte (MNN) constitutes a Specific Modification of the Land-Use Plan of Madrid (MPG)[1] of 1997 affecting two planning areas (APR 08.03 and APE 05.27). The project entails two scales of urban planning: the structural scale and the detailed one. The first scale defines the structural parameters of the whole site, such as land-use, major public infrastructure, or how the land is divided for urban development purposes. With respect to this last issue, MNN establishes four planning areas. Three of these areas (APEs)[2] are being developed through the detailed planning tools included in the documentation of Madrid Nuevo Norte. The fourth one, corresponding to the redevelopment of the Chamartín Station, is remitted to a later planning tool (APR).[3] The second scale of detailed planning specifically develops each area according to its internal and external characteristics, with the aim of generating coherent and autonomous urban units. In the case of Madrid Nuevo Norte, there are three articulating elements guaranteeing the integration and relationship of these planning areas: the public transport system, the streets and roads system and the network of local open spaces.

Before going on to describe how the gender perspective is integrated into this complex urban project, we will describe the general features of the urban proposal. The element that articulates the whole project is the Green Urban Axis[4] which runs longitudinally through the site from the north to the south. New transversal connections such as tunnels to redirect road traffic, bridges and foot-bridges play a key role in the planning proposal, connecting the existing neighbourhoods. The ring road M–30 stands out, dividing the site into two areas with a different planning approach. APE 8.21 and APE 8.20 are located north of the M–30 and their planning is residentially led while ensuring a mix of uses to avoid monofunctional areas. Approximately three-quarters of the residential floor of the project is located in these two planning units. South of M–30 there are APE 05.31 (an international business district) and APR 05.10 (the redevelopment of Chamartín Station). Both are approached as exceptional planning units due to their central location and maximum accessibility.

The public transport system is another of the strategic aspects of Madrid Nuevo Norte. It is designed on an intermodal basis all over the site and it has been planned in a coordinated manner with other aspects of the plan, especially regarding its interaction with the active mobility network, local-scale facilities, and the system of green areas. Another of the highlights of Madrid Nuevo Norte involves access to housing, which is a growing problem in and around Madrid. The plan envisages the construction of some 10,500 dwellings 20% of which will be subsidized, thereby doubling the percentage required by current legislation (10%). Additionally, in accordance with the agreements of the project, the City of Madrid will receive transfers of additional residential land during the development process. This means that the municipality will have the capacity to provide some additional 4,000 subsidized housing units.

One of the most important issues for Madrid Nuevo Norte is the redevelopment of the Chamartín Station so as to convert the current infrastructure in the main transport hub in Spain. The new station and its surrounding area will hold all transport modalities, including the connection to Madrid–Barajas Airport. The new station will transform the current isolated area of Chamartín into an accessible station, fully integrated at ground level into the surrounding urban space.

The new central business district (CBD) is aimed at creating prime office space that will enhance the international competitiveness of Madrid, exploiting the excellent connectivity of the site. The CBD model proposed by Madrid Nuevo Norte is based on public transportation, well integrated into the city and with a mix of uses that ensure 24/7 activity in the area.

Another iconic element of Madrid Nuevo Norte is the partial covering of the railway tracks. This entails complex civil engineering works but aims to reduce the gaping wound in the urban fabric of the city, providing spatial continuity in the area. The covering of the railway tracks also provides extra land upon which a huge green area is proposed (Parque Central).

Gender Mainstreaming in Madrid Nuevo Norte

In the case of Madrid Nuevo Norte, the way gender is mainstreamed into the project can be described in three blocks: planning and design; the Gender Impact Assessment as a stand out, independent official document that is part of the technical and administrative documentation of the project; exploratory safety walks with women in the neighbouring areas.

Planning and Design Solutions

The following paragraphs present the most relevant planning and design solutions in which gender is mainstreamed in coordination with other spatial planning variables and requirements. This selection has been made after a systematic analysis of the project using the categories, criteria and recommendations established in the literature, in particular the work of Sánchez de Madariaga (2004) and Damyanovic et al. (2013), which provide systematic checklists and detailed analyses covering the gender-relevant dimensions of all substantive areas of planning and design, including housing, office areas, facilities, public space, safety, and mobility.[5]

One relevant aspect of the project has to do with environmental issues. The general guideline was to balance sustainability, so that environmental issues did not conflict with the gender variable wherever this situation might occur – for example, regarding the perception of safety in public spaces. In this sense, the technical documentation aimed at the protection of the night-time environment[6] establishes that decisions about public lighting should take into account both the environmental and gender perspectives. This requirement is contained in the document at two levels: as an environmental indicator to assess the night-time environment, and as a specific criterion that must be taken into account during the design phase of the detailed planning of the MPG (Land-Use Plan of Madrid).

As an environmental indicator, gender requirements are included in the regulation of energy-saving measures for public lighting. The reduction of energy consumption must not lead to poorly lit public spaces. At the least, the design of public lighting should provide the necessary illumination to note the presence of a person at 25 m and his or her facial features at a distance of 4 m. Similarly, the particularities of women's perception of safety should be taken into account as a design criterion for public-space lighting, together with the other most common variables of this type of environmental consideration, such as biodiversity preservation, energy saving, or residents' night rest.

In the definition of the Madrid Nuevo Norte plan on a structural scale (*ordenación estructural*), dimensions of gender are considered among other aspects in the definition phase of the road structure of the project – particularly in the definition of the roads or streets that constitute an edge, either internal or external to the site. The gender dimension is taken into account in these roads to avoid areas of insecurity, defining and integrating the edge between the proposal and the adjoining neighbourhoods, and bringing to an urban scale existing roads that are currently a barrier within the urban fabric of this part of the city.

The blocks are defined with the purpose of limiting their dimensions and thus laying the basis for a good pedestrian mobility. They do not exceed 120 m per side as a general criterion for blocks. This is guaranteed either as a result of the structural organization of roads or by other regulations that are to be defined in subsequent planning tools that address issues at a more detailed level. The final proposal of Madrid Nuevo Norte picks up this criterion across practically the whole site through one of the three mechanisms mentioned above.

The gender dimension is also important when locating the different land uses, particularly in the case of public facilities and green areas. The most suitable type of public facility, from the point of view of gender, is assigned for each plot that is zoned for social infrastructure, taking into consideration the context of adjoining neighbourhoods as well as the area over which each plot could have an impact. These plots are preferably located at the edge of the scheme, so that public facilities included in Madrid Nuevo Norte are closer to and more accessible by adjoining neighbourhoods.

The type of facility proposed for each plot is responsive to gender-sensitive spatial planning criteria, particularly in terms of the mix of uses and support for caring activities but could also complement some of the social infrastructure deficiencies that were detected in the neighbouring areas. In the location and distribution of social infrastructure land and green areas, gender-relevant criteria are used, such as accessibility and proximity to pedestrian routes and public transportation, or strategic combinations of local facilities to support caring activities, work–life balance, and personal autonomy.

At the scale of detailed planning (*ordenación pormenorizada*), the gender perspective is included through the specific planning ordinances[7] of each APE, subdivided into two levels: development projects and building projects.[8] In the first level, the ordinance includes what is prescribed by the Strategic Environmental Report regarding lighting criteria (see note 6) – the documentation of these projects must ensure that the lighting of public spaces guarantees the perception of safety according to the perspective of gender. In addition, it is mandatory to include a specific annex analysing how the project responds to the everyday needs of the different life stages of users and the perspective of gender.

This annex should justify issues related to the perception of safety, such as public-space lighting or the existence of safe active mobility routes. The annex should also explain how the urban design in question supports the autonomy of all kinds of people, particularly those who are dependent, and how the public space is designed and equipped to support caring activities. Building projects must also include a specific annex similar to the one described above but adapted to the scale of the building and its plot.

For example, if plots are residential, in the specific annex mentioned above it will be necessary to include an account of how common spaces are designed (visibility, lighting, etc.), and what equipment or spaces are available in the building or its plot to support caring activities, especially those addressing the requirements of early childhood and the elderly. The ordinance also requires reserving spaces in residential buildings for the storage of bicycles, baby buggies, wheelchairs, or any other instrument to support the mobility and autonomy of people. These spaces must also respond to gender criteria regarding their location and design. For example, they should preferably be on the ground floor, have adequate lighting and allow visual control by allowing people inside buildings to keep an eye on what happens in the street.

In addition to the requirement of the annex, the detailed ordinance includes several sections covering other types of gender-relevant requirements, such as the prohibition of surrounding the plots with fences that prevent visual permeability, the prohibition of assigning residential use on the ground floor or, again, the need to provide enough lighting to avoid the perception of insecurity at certain conflicting points (entrances to transport infrastructure and buildings, public bicycle parking, etc.).

Through the Building Conditions[9] regulations, gender criteria are introduced at the detailed scale, regulating the disposition of volume of building within the plot. For instance, establishing mandatory alignments with the street for plots located in areas of the site that are seeking commercial activity on ground floors; or a strong relation between the building and public space in order to create safer and more active environments. As an example, this strategy is used in Madrid Nuevo Norte to support the creation of local centres throughout the whole site.[10]

In addition to the examples described above, a gender perspective is introduced or reinforced in other issues which are perhaps not so obvious or so easy to link to the rest of planning variables taken into account in the everyday work of a large urban redevelopment project. In addition to the examples described above, a gender perspective is introduced or reinforced in other issues, including issues of mobility, social infrastructure provisions, or the quality of public space.

Gender Impact Assessment

The GIA report[11] is divided into four different documents: one aimed at analysing the MPG for the whole site of Madrid Nuevo Norte regarding issues of structural planning, and three other documents that analyse each of the APEs at the level of detailed planning.

The main report is the one that addresses gender analysis of the whole site at a structural level. The document includes some complementary sections that put the issue in context and contribute to a better understanding of the whole report. The first section of this document provides the legal framework from the European to the local scale and explains how gender in spatial planning is approached in the most important international agendas such as the New Urban Agenda or Agenda 2030. The second section provides the conceptual framework on which the gender analysis is based. The report also includes a section about the gender analysis done on the neighbouring areas of the site. The gender analysis of the plan (both at a structural and detailed scale) goes through the issues discussed in the previous section of this chapter but also covers many others which are relevant from a gender perspective in spatial planning. Some of these issues include pedestrian routes, the public transport system, diversity and affordability of housing, or the design of the business district centre to support work–life balance and the integration of women into the workforce. The complementary sections included in the main gender analysis report of the MPG are not included in the three corresponding reports for the APEs. The gender analysis of each APE focuses on their detailed planning, developing the issues included in the main report and taking into account the particularities of the area and its relationship with the rest of the site.

The Gender Impact Assessment has a technical approach and is tailored to the specific scope of a Modification of a General Plan – that is, the planning tool involved – and the particular characteristics of an urban redevelopment plan such as Madrid Nuevo Norte. The report is itself a technical document, integrated with the rest of the documentation composing the administrative file of Madrid Nuevo Norte. It is built upon data, urban planning criteria, measurements, percentages, etc. and based on a solid theoretical framework and expert knowledge.

Exploratory Safety Audits with Women

The gender-related work at Madrid Nuevo Norte also entails work focused on engaging women's participation and on placing value in the gender-responsive approach of the plan. The main activity is the coordination and implementation of several participatory processes with women from three different areas surrounding the Madrid Nuevo Norte site. This used the methodology of exploratory safety walks, together with workshops and visits to the site. This experience has produced interesting results and lessons that deserve deeper analysis, including a report with specific recommendations and ideas for further technical developments of the project.

Conclusions from Madrid Nuevo Norte and Other European Experiences

The main conclusion drawn from the analysis of this case is that GIAs on spatial planning tools cannot involve a simple translation of existing methodologies or guidelines for GIAs, because most of these have been elaborated to be applied in other areas of public policy. The nature of spatial planning practice and documentation requires a technical approach tailored to truly respond to the competencies and scope of spatial planning. This leads to the need to involve professionals with knowledge in both areas: planning and gender studies. Unfortunately, people with this profile are not abundant, since gender perspectives are not substantially included in the education of professionals who usually participate in spatial planning fields. Also, educational programmes associated with gender studies or equal opportunities do not include training on spatial planning either – this is not the better option in any case because spatial planning is a complex technical field requiring years of education.

Another conclusion to be drawn is that there is not a clear and homogenous methodology on how to implement GIAs in spatial planning, their contents, or even right way to handle the document. This also has consequences for expectations about the impact of including gender perspectives in spatial planning, especially for women's and feminist groups. In general terms, there is a lack of understanding of how spatial variables affect gender equality and what is the scope of the actions and possibilities of each spatial planning tool and policy measures to address and to correct those inequalities. As a result, citizens, or even public administrations and professionals in charge of drafting the plans and policies, experience frustration about the limited examples where gender perspectives have been included in spatial planning, as is the case of Madrid Nuevo Norte.

Our conclusions match those drawn from other experiences in Europe. According to Dutch architect and planner Lidewij Tummers, GIAs have not been carried out in their full form in spatial planning policies. In the Netherlands, GIAs started to be applied in some plans and policy documents in the 1990s, but in a limited form: a sort of "quick scan" version (Tummers 2013). Tummers warns that a wrong approach in the implementation of GIAs might lead to negative effects, including the gradual disappearance of gender in spatial planning policies and practice. The reasons why GIAs have faced in the past and until now difficulties in being fully implemented in spatial planning are varied and include, among others, the following:

- Lack of understanding of what gender equality is in spatial terms, and what are its goals.
- Lack of a theoretical framework that could "translate" the regular GIA methodologies to make them applicable to spatial planning and territorial development.
- Misunderstanding gender as a "women's issue" and a static category.
- Lack of gender awareness in the spatial planning sector, and resistance of planners to acquiring such knowledge.
- Lack of intersectionality in the way gender perspectives have been introduced in those spatial planning projects or policies where GIAs have been implemented.
- The belief that gender is only relevant at local-scale planning, not at territorial or regional-planning scales.

Notes

1 "Modificación Puntual del Plan General de Ordenación Urbana" (MPG) in Spanish.
2 "Áreas de Planeamiento Específico" (APE) in Spanish. The APEs included in Madrid Nuevo Norte are APE 08.21 "Las Tablas Oeste", APE 08.20 "Malmea-San Roque-Tres Olivos" and APE 05.31 "Centro de Negocios Chamartín".
3 "Área de Planeamiento Remitido" (APR) in Spanish. The APR for the redevelopment of the Chamartín Station in APR 05.10 "Estación de Chamartín".
4 The Green Urban Axis constitutes the prolongation of the *Paseo de la Castellana*, the main artery of the city of Madrid, which is transformed into an "environmental axis" that connects the centre of the city with el Monte de El Pardo, a forested and protected area located to the north of the municipality.
5 Sánchez de Madariaga 2004 and Damyanovic et al. 2013 are respectively the two main reference books in Spanish and English that provide systematic approaches with clear and detailed guidance on how to integrate gender aspects into urban planning.

Additional references from which this text also draws include the following: Hayden 1977, 1981; Horelli, Booth and Gilroy 2000; Matrix 1984; RTPI 2007. Feinstein and Servon 2005 provide a wide overview widely illustrated with case studies covering an ample geographical area across continents. Not explicitly addressing gender topics, but the requirements of pedestrians and advocating for a city that takes better consideration of persons in public spaces, are the classics by Jacobs 1961 and Gehl 2010.

6 The protection of the night-time environment is part of the Environmental Strategy Report of the project, a document that accompanies the planning documentation and that is part of the same administrative dossier.

7 The Spanish term is "ordenanzas particulares".

8 The Spanish terms are "proyectos de urbanización" and "proyectos de edificación".

9 The Spanish term is "condiciones de la edificación".

10 Local centres were based on combining public transport hubs with areas of a more intensive presence of commercial floor, public facilities, services, offices and green areas.

11 The regulations of the Community of Madrid require four sectoral reports on issues related to gender. Two of them are addressed to the LGBTQ+community, covered by Laws 2/2016 of March 29, 2016 and Law 3/2016 of July 22, 2016 that seek to combat discrimination due to gender identity and expression and sexual orientation respectively. A third report is the impact report on childhood, adolescence and family, supported by different national laws. Finally, there is the gender impact report, with the aim of combating the inequality of opportunities between men and women, and which is supported by different laws of regional, state and European scale. In this chapter we refer to the gender impact report, which also includes considerations for childhood, adolescence and family, given the close connection that both issues have in urban planning. The reports addressed to the LGBTQ+community were merged into one that was addressed in a different way, based on the specialized bibliography, and are not the subject of this chapter.

References

Berlin Senate Department for Urban Development. (Ed.) (2011a). *Gender mainstreaming in urban development. Berlin handbook*. Berlin: Kulturbuch-Verlag. Available at: www.stad tentwicklung.berlin.de/soziale_stadt/gender_mainstreaming/download/gender_en glisch.pdf [Accessed 15 May 2019].

Campos Rubio, A. (2018). De los enfoques de género en el desarrollo al enfoque de género en el desarrollo. In: Ventura Franch, A. and García Campa, S. (dir.), *El Derecho a la Igualdad Efectiva de Mujeres y Hombres. Una Evaluación del Primer Decenio de la Ley Orgánica 3/2007*. Pamplona: Editorial Arandazi, 385–410.

Damyanovic, D., Reinwald, F. and Weikmann, A. (2013). *Gender mainstreaming in urban planning and urban development*. Werkstattbericht, Nr. 130A. [Online]. Vienna: Urban Development Vienna, Municipal Department 18 (MA 18) – Urban Development and Planning. Available at: www.wien.gv.at/stadtentwicklung/studien/pdf/b008358.pdf [Accessed 10 June 2019].

Fainstein, S. S. and Servon, L. (Eds.) (2005). *Gender and planning. A reader*. New Brunswick, NJ and London: Rutgers University Press.

Gehl, J. (2010). *Cities for people*. Washington, Covelo and London: Island Press.

Hayden, D. (1977). *Seven American utopias. The architecture of communitarian socialism 1790–1975*. Cambridge, MA: MIT Press.

Hayden, D. (1981). *The grand domestic revolution. A history of feminist approach for American homes, neighbourhoods and cities*. Cambridge, MA: MIT Press.

Horelli, L., Booth, C. and Gilroy, R. (2000). *The EuroFEM toolkit for mobilising women into local and regional development*. Revised version. Helsinki: Helsinki University of Technology.

Jacobs, J. (1961). *The death and life of great American cities*. New York: Random House.

Ley 30/2003. de 13 de octubre, sobre medidas para incorporar la valoración del impacto de género en las disposiciones normativas que elabore el Gobierno.

Ley del Gobierno 40/2015. introducida a través de la Disposición Final tercera de la Ley 40/2015, de Régimen Jurídico del Sector Público (LRJSP).

Macías Jara, M. (2018). Los informes de impacto de género en la producción normativa. In: Ventura Franch, A. and García Campa, S. (dir.), *El Derecho a la Igualdad Efectiva de Mujeres y Hombres. Una Evaluación del Primer Decenio de la Ley Orgánica 3/2007*. Pamplona: Editorial Arandazi, 385–410.

Matrix. (1984). *Making space. Women and the man-made environment*. London and Sydney: Pluto Press.

Novella Abril, I. (2017). Gender and urban planning in the construction of the international agenda for sustainable development. From Stockholm 1972 to Quito 2016. In: *Revista Kul-tur*, vol. 4, no. 8, pp. 93–114.

Real Decreto 1083/2009. de 3 de julio, por el que se regula la memoria del análisis del impacto normativo.

Real Decreto 7/2015 por el que se aprueba el Texto Refundido de la Ley de Suelo y Rehabilitación Urbana.

RTPI – Royal Town Planning Institute. (2007). *Gender and spatial planning. Good practice note 7*. London. Available at: http://rtpi.org.uk/media/1731629/gpn7-_gender_and_spatial_planning__2007_.pdf [Accessed 15 June 2019].

Sánchez de Madariaga, I. (2004). *Urbanismo con perspectiva de género*.

Sánchez de Madariaga, I. (2018). La igualdad efectiva en las políticas de vivienda y en el planeamiento urbanístico en España. en Ventura Franch, A., García Campá, S. (Eds.), *El derecho constitucional a la igualdad efectiva de mujeres y hombres. Una evaluación del primer decenio de aplicación de la Ley Orgánica 3/2007*. Thomson Reuters-Aranzadi.

Sánchez de Madariaga, I. and Novella, I. (2018). A new generation of gender mainstreaming policies in spatial development for the effective implementation of the international agendas on sustainable development. en Zibell, B., Damyanovic, D. y Sturm, U. (Eds.), *Gendered approaches to spatial development in Europe – perspectives, similarities and differences*. New York: Routledge, 181–203.

Sánchez de Madariaga, I. and Novella Abril, I. (2020). Género y Urbanismo en España: experiencias y perspectivas. en *Ciudad y Territorio Estudios Territoriales*, Vol. LII Cuarta época N° 203 primavera 2020.

Sánchez de Madariaga, I. and Roberts, M. (Eds.) (2013). *Fair share cities: The impact of gender planning in Europe*. Aldershot, UK and New York: Ashgate.

Tribunal Supremo. (2018) Sentencia de 10 de diciembre de 2018 Sobre el problema de la supletoriedad del Derecho estatal en procedimientos y elaboración de reglamentos por las Comunidades Autónomas.

Tummers, L. (2013). Gendered perspectives on spatial planning and housing in the Netherlands. In: Sánchez de Madariaga, I. and Roberts, M. (Eds.), *Fair shared cities: The impact of gender planning in Europe*. Farnham: Ashgate, 107–129.

UN Women. (2014). *Gender mainstreaming in development planning*. New York: UN Women.

United Nations. (2015). Transforming our world. The 2030 agenda for sustainable development. New York: UN General Assembly. Available at: https://sustainabledeve

lopment.un.org/content/documents/21252030%20Agenda%20for%20Sustainable%20Development%20web.pdf [Accessed 10 June 2019].

United Nations. (2016). New urban agenda. Quito declaration. New York: UN General Assembly. Available at: www2.habitat3.org/file/537306/view/591158 [Accessed 10 June 2019].

United Nations. (2018). Progress on the implementation of the New urban agenda report of the secretary-general. New York: General Assembly.

Zibell, B., Damyanovic, D. and Sturm, U. (2018). *Gendered approaches to spatial development in Europe – perspectives, similarities and differences*. New York: Routledge.

16

GENDER AND THE URBAN IN THE TWENTY-FIRST CENTURY

Paving the Way to 'Another' Gender Mainstreaming

Camilla Perrone

Gender and the Urban: in the Mainstreaming Post-millennium Era

A fundamental change in urbanization processes has been taking place over the past decades. It challenges the future life of the planet and the survival of living environments. These processes are becoming extended across regions and are also producing new conditions of connectivity between rural and urban domains, mainly due to the unprecedented blurring of the distinction between one another (Soja, 2011; Brenner, 2014). If, on the one hand, cities are places where most of the world's population is concentrated (Batty, 2011; OECD, 2014); on the other hand, territories, apparently far from being 'urban', increasingly interact with what we have been classifying as urban over the centuries (Soja, 2011; Keil, 2013; Brenner, 2014).

Measures to cope with the consequences of the post-millennium urban condition have been undertaken internationally by means of mainstream European Union and United Nations policies, declarations, global conferences, partnerships, and action-oriented recommendations for the betterment of planetary living conditions. These policies (detailed hereafter) aim to address the challenges deriving from new urban changes and to set new global standards for sustainable urban development (within a new global development approach). They thus provide a roadmap for building cities that can serve as engines of prosperity, cultural and social wellbeing, from a gender perspective as well, while protecting the environment.

Within the large range of policy priorities, critical issues, and challenges, including structural and policy constraints, which would serve as inputs to the New Urban Agenda, gender issues have also been included as important goals for the achievement of sustainable development. This relevant step forward in promoting gender has triggered a debate on the launch of a new season of 'gender mainstreaming' able to overcome the contradictions and challenges of the previous period (season), particularly with reference to spatial development and planning.

An abundant literature, recalled over the next paragraphs, shows the limitations of the EU's gender-mainstreaming strategy launched in 1996[1] to promote gender equality across the whole of the EU, and the failures of a selection of short-sighted international documents with regard to the gender issue.

Past experience shows a mainstream prevalence of the rhetorical use of the gender issue whenever mentioned, as shown below, which penalizes the effectiveness of policies, planning, and actions, except for a few exceptions that are limited to pilot cases and good practices. The fundamental goal of the first season of the gender-mainstreaming public policy – a process of assessing the implications for women and men of any planned action – has almost vanished, or at least it has not fully succeeded in strongly prioritizing gender equality de facto in implementing gendered politics and decision-making. The various measures adopted to combat inequality, social injustice, and poverty, as well as to promote gender equality, have often turned out to be only 'nominal' (limited to formulas written in public policy statements or agendas), rather than 'constitutive' (referring to the substance and effectiveness of the measures and their consequences in spatial development).

A similar fate, as demonstrated later on through the Mondeggi case, was left to spatial planning. Even in this case, gender issues have often remained in descriptions within general documents. They have not been effectively adopted at all stages and scales of planning processes and actions. Even when some planning practices proved to be effective, they were never incorporated into the planning system systematically, remaining in the group of one-off cases.

Past experience and debate have, in the opinion of the author, further highlighted the gap between *mainstreaming policies* at all stages, which are fundamental for the dissemination and promotion of a gender-mainstreaming strategy, but more exposed to the risk of being just nominal and rhetorical, without being properly implemented into practices. Indeed, many scholars agree on the fact that gender has been used in most cases as a label, rather than as a constitutive category of policies (Sánchez de Madariaga and Roberts, 2013; Cowman et al., 2014).

Accordingly, and on the basis of current investigations, this contribution highlights the urgent need for current policies to be fed by a reloaded gender theory and inspired by new urban practices that are changing our life environment in ways that are not often caught by the current official policies related to urban questions (Wekerle, 2004; Parker, 2012). And this can be seen as a way to inspire a more effective post-millennium gender mainstreaming, which apparently was initiated through documents and agendas (such as Sustainable Development Goals and the New Urban Agenda).

In this regard, many ideas may develop from the practices of twenty-first century urbanization that emerge in unexpected ways and places and demonstrate new challenges and implications for planetary living conditions. This chapter explores how these new urban conditions might be favourable to the emergence of living and producing practices – which, in certain cases, are explicitly gendered – that need to be recognized as specific policy subjects in order to implement urban policy agendas and, in particular, gendered urban agendas.

Given that the plural, diverse, variegated, transforming 'universe' of practices is always a pool of learning and innovation, and that some implementation of gender mainstreaming or other public policy strategies needs to feed on these ingredients, this chapter suggests – experimentally and illustratively – a new start from the observation of some types of practices that were at the origin of the questions of the gender issue and that concern women's ability to build relations between the urban environment, food, and agriculture (Buckingham, 2005). We can refer to certain types of practices that 'inhabit' the territories of extended urbanization, more often the green belts around/within metropolitan areas and others in general domains that are apparently non-urban. That is: new urban life practices that originated and developed in non-urban environments based on the connection between agriculture, economic innovation, urban transformation, knowledge sharing, and production processes.

These kinds of practices can be investigated as innovation vectors for effective policies 'in fact' rather than just 'in name'. In this chapter, for example, gender-sensitive policies, inspired by an analysis of an urban life experiment in Mondeggi, Italy, are suggested. This experiment can be considered a source of inspiration for new processes of engendering urbanization by practice. It was born of the changing nature of the new urbanization processes (described later), is located in the city-region of Florence – being a context of extended urbanization and the blurring of urban/rural borders – and is related to the question of women's food growing and agriculture.

A new theoretical work (here defined as a research agenda) at the intersection of urban and gender issues is strongly needed to distil inputs from practices and then address post-millennium gender mainstreaming in the domain of international policy. The concluding paragraphs of this chapter address a few lines of work in this direction.

Premises for a 'New Gender Mainstreaming' beyond the Actual Paradox of (Gendered) Urban and Spatial Planning Agendas

Milestones of the international policy on urban issues range from the post-2015 Development Agenda,[2] – launched with 17 Sustainable Development Goals (SDGs) that include the first global urban goal (SDG 11) to make cities safe, inclusive, resilient, and sustainable – to the Habitat III's New Urban Agenda

(NUA) announced in October 2016[3] that addresses how cities, still seen as one of many sites for sustainable development, can be located in relation to the SDGs.

In particular, the NUA, which has integrated all the SDGs as substantive topics for action at the urban level, details how urban issues are understood and acted upon by national and international bodies:

> cities may be framed as the absolute drivers of sustainable development in what amounts to an urban Anthropocene, an epoch in which human living in urban areas are considered as the dominant drivers of global environmental change, and in which cities, as the locus of humanity, create the tipping points of global sustainability.
>
> *(Short, 2017, 88)*

Development Agenda 2030 has recently become the most cited policy document and it certainly provides a reference point for most of the other international agendas (particularly the New Urban Agenda) for sustainable development and climate change that have been addressed worldwide 'with the aspiration to develop a new generation of more effective and systematic gender-based policies in urban planning and spatial development' (Sánchez de Madariaga and Novella, 2019, 182).[4]

Most of these agendas, and particular the two explicitly mentioned, can undoubtedly boast gender-sensitive objectives and policies as an achievement reached by women's groups and organizations representing civil society. As stated by Sánchez de Madariaga and Novella in the case of the NUA:

> undoubtedly, women have been key protagonists who have been the most successful advocates from among all representatives of civil society. They were able to make their voice heard in the process in the most articulate and decisive way. Judging by the high number of mentions of women and gender, the document finally adopted could be considered a success of women. [...] noteworthy mentions refer to: the representation of women on the public agenda and in urban decision-making processes; the economic empowerment of women; decent employment [...].
>
> *(Sánchez de Madariaga and Novella, 2019, 182)*

However, recent studies have pointed out how, despite this new (emerging) generation of gender-mainstreaming strategy, and the renewed attempt to link the urban and gender together, the chance – and the intensity with which it happens – for gender perspectives to be integrated into mainstream policy with effective planning implications (namely policy implementation into practice) is still too weakly supported and thus not guaranteed. And it still strongly depends on contingency: the period, spatial context, level of intervention, and project content (Parpart, 2000; Sánchez de Madariaga and Roberts, 2013; Zibell et al., 2019).

Despite the fact that Agenda 2030 for Sustainable Development and the New Urban Agenda have explicitly recognized the need to address issues of women and gender, the processes of contemporary planetary urbanization show how the question of gender, which is intertwined with spatial development and socio-spatial transformations, is only blandly embedded into the general interests of political and strategic measures. On the one hand it's becoming more and more evident, at least in the international documents, that gender is a fundamental feature of the urban question for the twenty-first century. On the other hand it's also recognized in the literature (Zibell et al., 2019), that gender mainstreaming in planning often happens at the very local scale and depends on contextual and contingent factors and causes (the people involved, types of funding, temporality of actions, local policies, etc.) much more than on global mainstreaming policies, which are often too universal and general. Moreover, gendered local practices and projects, although successful, seem not to change consistently and permanently the planning system at the various levels and scales. And this happens despite the fact that since 2000 planning has been theorized as a transformative process that includes the various gender variables.[5] The district or regional-scale interventions, when explicitly gender-addressed, are mostly dependent on promoters and stop working when the promoter steps down. As explained by Zibell, Damyanovic and Sturm:

> short-term local and neighbourhood projects may impact on the everyday use of space by adding user-specific qualities focusing on practical needs, but mostly do not change the planning system [...]. Regional or district projects which are conceived explicitly as gender projects and refer to gender concepts require strong political will and leadership figures with convincing personalities. The gender perspective in institutions is often lost when the key person leaves.
>
> *(Zibell et al., 2019, XXIV)*

Moreover, referring to the evidence provided on the state of the art (Reeves, 2012; Sánchez de Madariaga and Roberts, 2013) of actual practices at both the European and global level:

> the field of urban planning is emerging as one of the areas of public policy least permeable to the integration of gender-equality policies. Where gender equality is addressed experiences are often limited to pilot projects, one-off measures, specific approaches, or are restricted to a particular topic.[6]
>
> *(Sánchez de Madariaga and Novella, 2019, 190)*

As highlighted by Marion Roberts, a gendered approach – understood as a process and focused on the integration of gender at all stages of planning – has rarely been part of the mainstream planning theory and practice (Roberts, 2013). In fact, due to this lack of a general political strategic interest (whether it is completely absent or just nominal), the 'gender turn' seems to remain simply a way of envisioning future changes which are local, case-based, and particular, rather than becoming a general planning/policy framework for gender transformation projects which achieve societal change by transforming gender relations at all stages. At the same time, the impact of particular case-based gendered measures actioned within a local planning system in a specific economic situation still remains a crucial opportunity for this turn to become gender mainstreaming proper (Zibell et al., 2019).

So, an almost paradoxical dialectic emerges that still needs to be efficiently approached and that will constitute the main insight for future gendered urban and spatial planning agendas – working in a domain where particular and local gendered approaches can feed general strategic political interests and vice versa instead of such agendas ignoring each other. In fact, a gendered planning agenda needs planning measures at all stages to become mainstream. At the same time, gendered planning practices/actions need a mainstreaming policy strategy to be transformative and effective to a larger extent (beyond the local and the particular economic situation and planning system).[7]

An urgent question arises   one that is aware of the fact that the conditions of gendered sustainability in spatial development still remain vague and insufficient to reload a gender–urban question in the twenty-first century: to what extent does gender effectively matter in spatial development with regard to urban policy and spatial planning?

This chapter doesn't set itself the task of answering this evergreen question, but it certainly relaunches the issue and suggests ways to implement gendered measures/actions in both planning processes and institutional structures. It takes its lead from the variegated terrain of gender-mainstreaming strategy: the debate about a new generation of gender mainstreaming in spatial and urban planning, and the new international framework of policies for sustainable development (Sánchez de Madariaga and Novella, 2019).

According to the SDGs, many fields that connect gender and the urban are equally relevant. They include gender equality, gender mobility, sustainable cities and communities, climate actions, the life of lands, wellbeing, and many other factors. All of them can work ('in name' and 'in fact') as a frame for a new gendered and sustainable form of mainstreaming and are crucial horizons of reflection and research nowadays. However, a particular issue is highlighted, even if not explicitly detailed in the SDGs or the NUA: it is the question of women's food growing/agriculture. This question is highlighted for two reasons in particular. The first relates to the linkage between food, cities and planning at all stages (Ladner, 2011; Cockrall-King, 2012; Viljoen and Wiskerke, 2012; Calori and Magarini, 2015; Expo Milano, 2015). The second reason can be traced back to the role of women in food production, with reference to both the rural context (Dalla Costa, 2008; Hovorka et al., 2009) and the urban context (Buckingham, 2005; Counihan and Kaplan, 1998). Among other things, this question reveals gender differences in food choices (Wardle et al., 2004; Allen and Sachs, 2007). The emphasis is on women's inescapable responsibility for reproductive work, regarding producing food for their families and their relationship to food and eating. This reflects the significance of food-centred activities to gender relations and to the construction of gendered identities.

Therefore, as an example, this chapter will just refer to the topic of women's food growing/agriculture, which still remains central to a gender perspective. The case of Mondeggi Bene Comune/Fattoria Senza Padroni (Mondeggi Common Land/Ownerless Farm) in the metropolitan area of Florence (Italy), will serve this purpose.

Past Failures for Bringing Gender into Urban Policy Mainstreaming

International policymaking on the cusp of the twentieth and twenty-first centuries proved largely unsuccessful in embedding the gender issue as a constitutive ingredient in actual practice (Greed, 2013). It mostly failed in effectively promoting the gender issue as a key subject of a contemporary urban agenda and implementing it in practice, particularly with reference to EU mainstreaming and UN documents for a New Urban Agenda.

The decision to focus on these two UN and EU international policy documents (never deeply explored from a gender perspective) stems from the author's experience and conviction that problems regarding the implementation of gendered urban policies result from the breaking of the chain between official frameworks (international policy documents), planning policy at local and regional levels, and actual practices. The official framework of international policies seems to be weak at addressing gendered urban issues, in that the rhetoric is somewhat removed from reality.

In support of this argument, this chapter proposes a selective review of the following: (1) the controversial debate on the implementation of the 'gender mainstreaming strategy' policy into practice (Moser and Moser, 2005; Sánchez de Madariaga and Roberts, 2013; Moser, 2014); (2) the EU reports and the European Commission's communications – with particular reference to the EU New Urban Agenda mentioned because of the long-term European Community commitment to social issues, which include gender; (3) the Milan Charter for Expo 2015 (Feeding the Planet, Energy for Life) considered because it refers to a recent international event that involved a large number of institutions, countries, people, and issues.

The gender-mainstreaming EU strategy has been addressed through inter-national manifestos, events and legal documents (such as the Treaty of Amster-dam in 1999 and the Women's World Conferences in Nairobi and Peking in 1985 and 1994) and launched in Europe in 1996 to promote gender equality across all EU policies. This strategy has been questioned regarding the effective-ness of its implementation (Sánchez de Madariaga and Roberts, 2013). Critiques highlighted how it has consolidated the nominal use of the word 'gender', which nonetheless has lost some of its constitutive meaning over time. This occurred, despite its positive impact on theory, by raising a 'debate that is simul-taneously normative philosophical, theoretical, substantive, empirical, and policy-relevant' (Walby, 2005, 326).

The panorama of 'exceptionality' depicted by the literature on gendered urban planning offers single-issue stories, mostly related to housing and mobility (Parker, 2012, 618).[8] More generally the literature expresses critiques of gender policies in Western cities, while addressing the debate on the rhetoric of the gender-mainstreaming approach.

Since the Treaty of Amsterdam was signed on 2 October 1997 and came into force on 1 May 1999, a greater stress on citizenship and the rights of individuals, as well as emphasis on equality polices, has been embodied in a range of other EU legislative measures, such as the Equal Treatment Directives. European pol-icymaking has welcomed many initiatives, such as employment strategies, gender-equality policies, the reconciliation of work and family, and so forth (Stratigaki, 2004, 2005; Greed, 2006).

What emerges as a common feature of EU gender policy is a very weak link-age to spatial gender-mainstreaming implementation and implications. This is seen in ambiguous, sometimes blurred, or even absent considerations regarding how to address urban policy and spatial planning while constructing a gendered urban agenda. Despite the conspicuous number of official urban policymaking tools and the dissemination of experiences across Europe, an official European Urban Agenda was still missing until recently. It is within this frame that the recent attempt to shape an EU Urban Agenda for Cities of Tomorrow took place. The debate was reignited by the report *Cities of Tomorrow – Challenges, Visions and Ways Forward* and the documents delivered by the URBACT II pro-gramme. The 'Cities of Tomorrow: Investing in Europe Forum', organized by the Directorate-General Regional and Urban Policy in 2014, put the urban agenda back at the heart of EU policymaking.

What is relevant is that the first document presented by the European Com-mission, published on 18 July 2014 (COM (2014)) and entitled *The Urban Dimension of EU Policies – Key Features of an EU Urban Agenda* (EU, 2014), does not even mention the issue of gender. Based on consultations with EU stake-holders, it fixes priorities in terms of major European societal challenges (i.e. CO_2 reduction, climate adaptation, inclusion or demographic change, and urban poverty). Although the document asserts that an 'EU urban agenda cannot be formulated in a vacuum but should be fully in line with the EU's overall object-ives and strategy, particularly the revised Europe 2020 strategy' (EU, 2014, 9), it seems to leave out the 'gender mainstreaming' approach and the enormous debate surrounding it.

Not even the Declaration of Ministers towards the EU Urban Agenda in Riga on 10 June 2015, from the Informal Meeting of EU Ministers Responsible for Territorial Cohesion and Urban Matters, provides for any objective or policy addresses in the field of gender. Indeed, the very word 'gender' is missing. This seems like a gaping absence in a period when the meaning of the 'urban', which is strictly related to gender, is very much under debate (Brenner, 2014).

References to gender issues appear only later in the list of priority themes and cross-cutting issues in the last version of the Urban Agenda (European Commission, 2016), as follows: '12.6 Impact on societal change, including behavioural change, promoting, among other things, equal access to information, gender equality and women empowerment'.[9]

The Milan Charter for Expo 2015 (Exposition 2015, *Feeding the Planet, Energy for Life*) (Expo Milano, 2015) shares a similar fate. The Charter is the result of an international event that belongs to a family with historical echoes: the world's fairs. Since the first world fair, which was held in the Crystal Palace in London, 1851, through to the Paris Exposition of 1889 (with the construction of the Tour Eiffel) and up until the last Expo 2015, held in Milan, the world fairs have been an occasion for discussing major economic, technological, and sometimes urban and social issues. In many cases, they have dealt with a specific issue of great importance, as, indeed, was the case for the Milan Expo. The res-onance of such an event and the relevance of the issue submitted to the atten-tion of a wide audience, also considering the media impact, has driven the attention towards the potentially strong role of the Charter in policy terms.

The Charter discusses food as a key issue for the survival of the planet and the organization of cities and the living environment. Also, it focuses on the role of inhabitants, especially women, which is emphasized through building a chain to link food, the environment, and the resources required for production and protection together. The Charter was conceived through meetings with stakeholders and similar well-established interactive practices and includes a series of principles, policy lines, and responsibilities that cross through many relevant facets of life. Nevertheless, the fundamental relational domain between women, food and 'the urban' is not mentioned, even in the contribution by the WE – Women for Expo project, thanks to which the Expo puts women and women's rights at the centre for the first time, 25 years after the Beijing Plat-form for Action. From the 96 contributors – associations, ministries, partner-ships, European Commissions, roundtables open to citizens and stakeholders, etc. – there was no input in this direction.

The Charter emphasizes the role played by women within the food system, which spans from their primary role in food provision (as farmers) to their active role throughout the food value chain (as food workers) and the educational role played by women as nutrition providers and sharers for the whole family and their inner circle. The Charter also includes concepts such as resources, land, food, and innovation in agriculture, rights, water, territory, cultural heritage, sustainable production, and consumption strategies and so forth. But it fails to mention the realm of connections between food, agriculture, the city as urban environment, and the question of gender. There is no explicit or constitutive reference to women's ability to build relations between the urban environment, food, and agriculture.

Indeed, the lessons learned from this review, albeit short and partial, highlight the need for a reconceptualization of gender under a relational rationale, which could help to focus on the very meaning of gender through practice in the urban realm. The argument that follows focuses on how to start changing this trend, from the field of practices.

Reloading Gendered Urban Policy: Lessons from New Practices Emerging in Extended Urbanization – The Case of Mondeggi Common Land/Ownerless Farm in Florence, Italy

As indicated above, the question of change in urbanization processes towards extended urbanization (Brenner, 2014) has a strong impact in redefining urban/rural and (inter)urban connectivity (Brenner and Keil, 2014), as well as the domain of urban policy. The argument here is that the widening of the urban domain opens up a new challenge, not only for urban policies in general, but also for gendered urban policies (Moser, 2014), particularly the ones based on practice.

Within the emerging extended urban domain, new kinds of practices emerge that can inspire urban policy. These are spreading throughout a region, regardless of city boundaries. Yet they can be classed as urban in terms of interconnectivity, exchanges, and lifestyles.

This argument is put forward with reference to the relationship between food production at the regional scale and the city, and the role that women can play in reconnecting these processes and bettering the place they live in. The question of women's food growing/agriculture as an urban challenge is, however, a long-term urban challenge (Buckingham, 2005; Dalla Costa, 2008; Viljoen and Bohn, 2014). At the present historical moment, this topic specifically concerns the practices – including entrepreneurial agricultural activities – in which the contribution of women is visible. These practices represent alternative models of food-chain management at a regional level which could provide solutions to the socio-economic and environmental problems associated with contemporary food production and consumption (Kneafsey, 2010). The intent here is to widen the domain of gendered urban policies so as to include urban/regional agriculture and urban food strategies (Magnaghi, 2014).

Mondeggi Bene Comune/Fattoria Senza Padroni (Mondeggi Common Land/ Ownerless Farm) in Bagno a Ripoli, a municipality adjacent to the city of Florence, is an exemplary case of what a new gendered practice of 'food growing' and a model of food-chain management in the (inter)urban domain means. This is due to these practices evincing a strong connection to the regional urbanization processes in a domain where the urban/rural borders are blurring. Detailed descriptions of this case have been published elsewhere (Canale and Ceriani, 2013; Angiolini, 2015; Perrone, 2016). Here, this case is briefly introduced to highlight some lessons and findings that this kind of practice can offer to a new season of gendered urban policy.

There are three specific reasons to present this case.[10] First, Mondeggi is considered a leading case in Tuscany and, indeed, throughout Italy, as regards its processes and results in terms of social innovation, social agriculture, and women's contributions in the field of agricultural experiments and community building. Second, Mondeggi intersects with at least three contemporary issues that are very much under debate in the international literature and might be relevant to the question of constructing a new gendered urban agenda. These issues include gender, food and agriculture, and the question concerning what 'urban' means with regard to the changing nature of regional urbanization processes. Third, since 2013 Mondeggi has also been a groundbreaking case of rural squatting that is strongly supported by local inhabitants, who refer to Mondeggi as a community with unique social capital. It is also an example of reactivating agriculture and food-chain processes, since most of the Florentine rural estates have been abandoned.

Mondeggi is a typical example of a large estate within a traditional *mezzadria* (crop-sharing) system located in the rural landscape of Tuscany in the southeastern periphery of Florence's urban area. Mondeggi was an uninhabited Renaissance villa with parkland it and forms one of the most inspiring landscapes in the surroundings of Florence and includes valleys, hills, streams and forests.[11]

Mondeggi has been public property since 1964, when it was purchased by the Province of Florence. In 2001, the provincial administration set up a society to manage the farm and the land: the Mondeggi Lappeggi Srl Agricultural Society. Due to severe financial difficulties which bankrupted the society itself, this society and its assets were put up for sale in 2009.

Because the property was not sold, in 2013 a social movement called Terra Bene Comune (Land as a Common Good) – a local group belonging to the nationally active movement called Genuino Clandestino (Genuine Clandestine) – became interested and, together with other people in the area, including students, farmers, and activists, produced some proposals on how to reuse the Mondeggi farmland. They also disseminated these proposals through a *Charter of Principles and Intentions*.[12]

Most of the people involved are women, with leading roles in promoting social, agricultural, educational, and commercial activities managed by their own communities as well as in coordination with a network of similar communities. This forms part of a larger urban/regional organic farm and market network. It is self-organized by local farmers and young agricultural entrepreneurs who work outside the mainstream market, with no mediators. They autonomously and directly sell packaged food from their agricultural activities. Most of the activities organized at Mondeggi combine agricultural product management with respect for old traditions, yet with a sustainable, organic, and technology-driven contemporary approach.

Mondeggi is, therefore, an innovative 'laboratory' that works on agriculture, food, traditions, and long-term local knowledge, resulting in an experimental model of production.

The Mondeggi case highlights questions that help to clarify why the reference to women's food growing/agriculture in a city-region context is relevant in addressing new fields of work for a gendered policy.

The first finding concerns women's strategic roles.[13] According to related interviews, women have a key role in organizing connections between land, agriculture, food, environment, heritage, energy, water, waste, community, the city, and the world. This role is fully described in Susan Buckingham's consideration of the 'regen(d)eration of urban food growing' as a process, with social, educational and environmental implications (Buckingham, 2005, 2013). The same intertwined mix of activities is condensed in the case of Mondeggi, where the contribution of women has generated an experiment that is unique. Although there is no scientific evidence that it would have been worse or even better without a recognizably strong contribution by women, there is practical evidence that women have taken the lead and are managing and interconnecting some of the most relevant activities at Mondeggi. The gendered practice of Mondeggi has made evident a different way to be urban while living in rural areas, including in the manner of self-sustainment and building networks between land, food, and local knowledge. Of course, more research is needed in this area to implement a gendered urban agenda. According to Buckingham: 'the urban environment we need to be aiming for is one which is simultaneously gender-just and seeks to minimise environmental damage (or maximise gender – and other – equality and social and environmental wellbeing)' (2013, 29).

The second finding underlines two trends. One, as indicated above, is the interconnection between the rural and the urban within a regional domain. This in turn opens up new perspectives about where practices can inform urban policy and how to address policy so that it becomes more gender-sensitive. The other trend suggests, jointly with the first one, that urban/regional food strategies are becoming increasingly central to urban policy. The Mondeggi case provides an experiment that also highlights women's roles as promoters and guides in this fields.

The third key finding, which also becomes a direct input for a gendered urban policy agenda, relates to the nature of a new generation of gendered practices. They stem from the entrepreneurial combination of interconnected activities, thus becoming substantial and significant by being synergistically intertwined. They deal with not just housing, urban farming, feeding, or training; rather, they include all of these dimensions in a new way of urban life that has emerged in a heretofore rural area.

The remarkable intermingling quality of these experiences provides fertile conditions for a constitutive (and not just nominal) transfer of the substantial gender contribution to an urban policy that addresses gender more effectively.

Concluding Remarks and Inputs for a Research Agenda on 'Another' Gendered Mainstreaming

This paper introduces a new experimental terrain into the discourse in order to contribute to a new gendered mainstreaming and avoid the trap of rhetoric embedded so far into gender mainstreaming and international policy. It is an explicit invitation to start afresh from the substance of gendered practices to define an effective way of implementing gendered policies. The main problem deals, in fact, with the rhetorical/nominal use of gender as a label rather than as a constitutive approach to policy. This leads to failures of implementing gender mainstreaming into planning systems and spatial development agendas at all stages and actions. While recalling the controversial debate on the implementation of a 'gender-mainstreaming strategy towards a new gender mainstreaming' (Sánchez de Madariaga and Novella, 2019), the chapter reflects on the need to reconceptualize gender as a constitutive versus nominal essence to advance the debate and to give new input to the new emerging form of gender mainstreaming.

Defining a new post-millennium gender-mainstreaming strategy is complex, particularly at this time of great change in planetary urbanization processes. Certainly, the associated topics could be huge in number, and the chapters of the current volume as whole can be considered a fundamental input to this effort.

This chapter does not intend to fulfil this whole challenge. It is instead meant to suggest some hints for a research agenda aimed at addressing 'another' gender mainstreaming that are inspired by new emerging gendered practices. It might more usefully be understood to highlight possible directions of research. In this sense, inputs for a research agenda on a 'new gender mainstreaming' could include the following.

The first input is associating research on the new urban question with research on gender in the post-millennium era. Changes in urbanization processes may actually affect living practices with implications for sustainable development, gender equality, climate change, responsible consumption, and so forth. Consequently, gender practices can change and become more and more inspirational for a new generation of gender-sensitive urban policy. In this regard, practices like Mondeggi's provide an example of the kind of practices (what, how, and where) that are gendered, but also related to post-millennium changes, which include urbanization processes and food challenges for the future. Such practices emerge in non-central places, such as suburban areas, agricultural parks, and other areas surrounding the city. They include the active involvement of women in urban/regional agricultural experiments, educational activities related to the place and its history, interconnections among the community, the city, the region, and the economy. These practices show a different kind of urban life in rural areas being closely connected to the traditionally understood urban life in cities. They are relevant to gender-sensitive policies to the extent that they show, de facto, the role of women in the construction of new living environments that are 'urban', even though located in a wider regional domain that cannot be considered rural anymore. To pursue reflection in this direction, all in all, this chapter highlights grounds for reloading gender and the urban in the post-millennium era, paving the way to a possible mainstreaming gendered agenda in a new climate-change regime (Perrone, 2016; Scheller, 2018; Buckingham and Lada, 2019).[14]

The second input relates the mutual exchange of innovation and knowledge between particular and local gendered approaches and general strategic political interest. Paradoxically, the survey on international gender mainstreaming and the other EU and UN documents, particularly the post-millennium ones such as SDGs and the NUA, shows how, despite the number of gender-sensitive measures, addresses, and principles, planning systems at different stages and local actions are gendered only in exceptional cases. When it happens, it is not due to mainstreaming, or systematic change, it is just a particular case. This question has a lot to do with the controversial debate on the implementation of gender-mainstreaming strategy into practice that goes back many decades. By reviewing a selection of official international policy documents, this chapter brings attention to the fact that there is not enough transfer of innovation from practice to policy and vice versa. The evidence suggests that to adopt a successful policy, policymaking needs to reconnect the official institutions more closely with gendered practices on the ground, so as to avoid rhetorical drift and a (merely) nominal use of the word 'gender'. On the other hand, practices on the ground without a proper political and strategic framework risk remaining as single cases, pilot projects, or exceptional results. Thus, a constructive dialectic between the two directions of innovation is needed to reconstruct a successful chain between official policy documents, lower levels of government and planning (i.e. regional, provincial, municipal, local) and the level of practice.

Finally, the third input relates to the need to reconceptualize gender for a new, effective gender mainstreaming, not so much in the official policy and documents but rather in practice where the reality challenges the theoretical issues and gives substantial inputs about how to address policy.

Theory on gender over the last few decades has flourished among scholars (geographers, urban planners, sociologists, anthropologists and advocates of social justice and equity such as Butler, 1993; Duden, 1994; Nussbaum, 2000; Bridge, 2005; Jarvis et al., 2009; Buckingham, 2013; Damyanovic, Zibell, 2019). Gender has served as a normative goal in city planning for over a generation (Moser, 1993; Fincher and Jacobs, 1998; Fenster, 2004; Fainstein and Servon, 2005). Furthermore, theory has reinvigorated gender and shown its potential in building socio-spatial urban environments that are more inclusive and respectful of diversity. These theories specifically refer to contemporary practices of urban life that are enriched by the contribution of gendered actions – in particular those practices where the gender contribution is visible and produces appreciable results.

The existing literature shows a long-standing lack of coherence in the approach to gender when shifting from a general strategic interest to particular actions (Walby, 2005; Poggio, 2006; Jarvis et al., 2009; Parker, 2012; Cohen and Reynolds, 2014). Further steps might delve into the renewed role of gender with regard to new, global, urban challenges and see how these practices can support the betterment of policymaking and also guarantee the implementation of gender mainstreaming in practice.

These inputs do not claim to be all-embracing. They emerge from the incomplete survey (on gender mainstreaming and selected international docu-ments about the urban agenda) presented in this chapter and from some of the evidence from the literature discussed. However, it could be said that they are paving the way towards strong reflection on a future research agenda about gender mainstreaming in spatial planning. All in all, the message from this chap-ter is that a strong post-millennium research agenda is needed for promoting another variety of gender mainstreaming.

Notes

1 The gender mainstreaming strategy was first proposed at the 1985 Third World Con-ference on Women in Nairobi, Kenya. The idea was pushed in the United Nations development community and formally featured in 1995 at the Fourth World Confer-ence on Women in Beijing, China and subsequently adopted by the European Com-mission in 1996.

2 The Sustainable Development Goals have been built on the lessons of the Millen-nium Development Goals (MDGs) established in 2000 following the United Nations Millennium Summit that committed the nations of the world to achieving certain goals across eight priority areas of social and economic development by 2015. For an in-depth insight into gender, space and development nexus see Huning et al. (2019).

3 The Habitat III's New Urban Agenda has been built on its predecessors Habitat I and II (see Sánchez de Madariaga and Novella, 2019): 'Within the framework of Habitat III, the Third Conference on Housing and Sustainable Urban Development, in October 2016 the UN member states adopted a New Urban Agenda entitled the "Declaration of Quito on Sustainable Cities and Towns for All", which lists a number of shared guidelines for urbanisation processes on the planet over the coming decades (United Nations, 2016). The NUA will guide the actions of a broad

range of players in cities over the next 20 years and fully take on board the principles
and objectives of the 2030 Agenda for Sustainable Development' (186).
4 See this contribution for a gendered survey on the international mainstreaming
agendas.
5 See Damyanovic and B. Zibell (2019) for an in-depth analysis of the societal and political framework for gendered perspectives in spatial development. In the same chapter, the authors stress the shift from women-centred approaches to gender as
a difference category and its planning implications, as well as gender approaches in
the context of spatial planning theory (25–36).
6 The quotation continues as follows: 'In other cases, they lack efficient means of implementation, or the involvement of planning departments [...]. On other occasions they
have been of limited duration, their existence depending on the presence of specific individuals in decision-making positions' (Sánchez de Madariaga and Novella, 2019, 190).
7 In this context, the political strategy of gender mainstreaming is also crucial for the
concept of gender planning as 'gender mainstreaming in spatial planning' (Huning
et al., 2019, 2) as well as sustainable development stands a critical concept, which
allows the nexus of gender, space and spatial development.
8 An exceptional example of successful gender mainstreaming has occurred in
Vienna, with both its policy and action in the areas of housing, urban mobility
and parks. These have been documented in the pilot gender-mainstreaming process
in the Mariahilf district of Vienna (Kail, 2005; Irschik and Kail, 2013; Sturm
et al., 2019). While Vienna is an exception, the most frequent attributes of acts of
gendered urban policy are their singularity (they happen just once), exceptionality
(deviation from the mainstream), episodic nature and their focus on a single issue
(Cortesi et al., 2006).
9 https://ec.europa.eu/futurium/en/system/files/ged/pact-of-amsterdam_en.pdf, down-
loaded 7 May 2019.
10 The methodology used to study this case is based on an ethnographic field survey, in
addition to five in-depth interviews with the people living there, 15 short interviews
with people belonging to the wider community involved in this experience, scientific
articles (Canale and Ceriani, 2013; Angiolini, 2015) and some workshops with members of the local academic community engaged in the project, where the author has
played a key role as co-organiser and informed observer.
11 The Mondeggi estate has been historically owned by a number of families of the
Florentine aristocracy (such as Bardi, Portinai, Della Gherardesca, etc.) and consists,
besides the villa, of six farmhouses and other farm buildings spread over a total area
of 200 hectares. The villa is also surrounded by a nineteenth-century landscaped
park. The lands hold about 12,000 olive trees, as well as vineyards (now abandoned),
and it comprises orchards, arable extents, forests and pastures. The Mondeggi estate
portion worked by squatters extends about 20 hectares.
12 Soon after, the social movement 'Mondeggi Bene Comune' (Mondeggi as
a Common) was created. By this action, the local community opposed privatisation
of the area, while with other stakeholders proposed to manage the farm as
a 'common asset' (with an explicit reference to Ostrom's theory on 'Governing the
Commons') (Ostrom, 1990). The municipality of Bagno a Ripoli accepted this proposal for negotiation and forwarded it to the Province of Florence, which subsequently rejected it. In response, the Province of Florence published a new call for
tenders to substitute the bankrupted 'Mondeggi Lappeggi Srl Agricultural Society'. In
June 2014, a small community of about 40 people, comprising new farmers, artists,
students, technicians, professionals, graduates and unemployed people, occupied one
of the buildings of the estate as squatters, beginning an important process of innovation and experimentation of 'governing the commons'.
13 Interviews (eight of 20) and the ethnographic fieldwork support this finding. According to the interviews, the women stressed their contribution in making this

experience a better one. They described how they are practicing a different lifestyle, which is based on self-organisation, self-sustainment, local knowledge sharing and experiments in community building. From interviews it also emerged that women are active in research through promoting experimental crops in connection with some Italian and Spanish universities. The many activities organised with local inhabitants (youngsters, children and elderly people) and promoted by women of the Mondeggi community provide evidence of how women are able to build up a community by connecting different generations, offering training courses in agriculture and food-growing for children and therefore transferring traditional local knowledge to others living in the same municipality and in the urban region of Florence.

14 Particularly with reference to sustainable development understood as transformative project with its new and old ingredients (women's food growing, gendered mobility, spatial justice for example).

References

Allen, P. and Sachs, C. (2007). 'Women and food chains. The gendered politics of food', *International Journal of Sociology of Food and Agriculture*, 15, 1–23.

Angiolini, C. (2015). 'Collettività e governo dei beni comuni. Il caso di Mondeggi', *Rivista di Diritto Agrario*, 1, 143–57.

Batty, M. (2011). 'Commentary. When all the world's a city', *Environment and Planning A*, 43, 765–72.

Brenner, N. (ed.) (2014). *Implosions/Explosions: Towards a Study of Planetary Urbanisation*, Berlin, Jovis.

Brenner, N. and Keil, R. (2014). 'Study of planetary urbanisation', *Glocalism: Journal of Culture, Politics and Innovation*, 3, 1–17.

Bridge, G. (2005). *Reason in the City of Difference: Pragmatism, Communicative Action and Contemporary Urbanism*, London, Routledge.

Buckingham, S. (2005). 'Women (re)construct the plot: the regen(d)eration of urban food', *Area*, 2, 171–79. 604.

Buckingham, S. (2013). 'Gender, sustainability and urban environment', in I. Sánchez de Madariaga and M. Roberts (eds), *Fair Shared Cities: The Impact of Gender Planning in Europe*, Aldershot, Ashgate, 21–32.

Buckingham, S. and Lada, A. S. (2019). 'Contemporary challenges in spatial development', in B. Zibell, D. Damyanovic and U. Sturm (eds), *Gender Approaches to Spatial Development in Europe: Perspectives, Similarities, Differences*, London and New York, Routledge, 204–26.

Butler, J. (1993). *Bodies that Matter*, London, Routledge.

Calori, A. and Magarini, A. (2015). *Food and the Cities: Politiche del cibo per città sostenibili*, Milano, Edizioni Ambiente.

Canale, G. and Ceriani, M. (2013). 'Contadini per scelta. Esperienze e racconti di nuova agricoltura', *Scienze del Territorio*, 1, 195–200.

Cockrall-King, J. (2012). *Food and the City: Urban Agriculture and the New Food Revolution*, New York, Prometheus Books.

Cohen, N. and Reynolds, K. (2014). 'Urban agriculture policy making in New York's "new political spaces". Strategizing for a participatory and representative system', *Journal of Planning Education and Research*, 34, 221–34.

Cortesi, F., Cristaldi, F. and Fortuijn, J. D. (eds) (2006). *La Città delle Donne*, Bologna, Pàtron.

Counihan, C. M. and Kaplan, S. L. (1998). *Food and Gender: Identity and Power*, Amsterdam, Harwood Academic Publisher.

Cowman, K., Javette Koefoed, N. and Karlsson Sjögren, A. (eds) (2014). *Gender in Urban Europe: Sites of Political Activity and Citizenship, 1750–1900*, London, Routledge.

Dalla Costa, M. R. (2008). 'Sovranità alimentare, contadini e donne', *Foedus*, 21, 75–89.

Damyanovic, D. and Zibell, B. (2019). 'Brief historical review of gendered approaches in spatial development and planning', in B. Zibell, D. Damyanovic and U. Sturm (eds), *Gender Approaches to Spatial Development in Europe: Perspectives, Similarities, Differences*, London and New York, Routledge, 25–36.

Duden, B. (1994). *Der Frauenleib als öffentlicher*, München, Ort. Vom Missbrauch des Begriffs Leben, dtv.

European Commission. (2016). *Urban Agenda for the EU*, Brussels, European Commission https://ec.europa.eu/futurium/en/urban-agenda-eu/what-urban-agenda-eu (accessed 23 February 2020).

EU (European Union). (2014). 'The urban dimension of EU policies – key feature of an EU urban agenda', http://ec.europa.eu/regional_policy/sources/consultation/urb_a genda/pdf/comm_act_urb_agenda_en.pdf (accessed 30 July 2015).

Expo Milano. (2015). The Milan Charter, http://carta.milano.it/en/ (accessed 30 July 2015).

Fainstein, S. and Servon, L. J. (eds) (2005). *Gender Planning: A Reader*, New Brunswick, Rutgers University Press.

Fenster, T. (2004). *The Global City and the Holy City: Narratives on Planning, Knowledge and Diversity*, London, Pearson.

Fincher, R. and Jacobs, J. (eds) (1998). *Cities of Difference*, New York, Guilford University Press.

Greed, C. (2006). 'Institutional and conceptual barriers to the adoption of gender main-streaming within spatial planning departments in England', *Planning Theory & Practice*, 2, 179–97.

Greed, C. (2013). 'A feminist perspective on planning cultures: tacit gendered assumptions in a taciturn profession', in G. Young and D. Stevenson (eds), *The Ashgate Research Companion to Planning and Culture*, Burlington, Ashgate, 89–104.

Hovorka, A., de Zeeuw, H. and Njenga, M. (2009). *Women Feeding Cities: Gender in Urban Agriculture and Food Security*, Rugby, Practical Action Publisher.

Irschik, E. and Kail, E. (2013). 'Vienna: progress towards a fair shared city', in I. Sánchez de Madariaga and M. Roberts (eds) *Fair Shared Cities. The Impact of Gender Planning in Europe*, Aldershot, Ashgate, 193–230.

Jarvis, H., Kantor, P. and Cloke, J. (2009). *Cities and Gender*, London, Routledge.

Kail, E. (2005), 'Leitstelle für Alltagsgerechtes Bauen und wohnen: Stadt Fair Teilen. Gender Mainstreaming in Mariahilf. Wien', (report), Vienna, City of Vienna.

Keil, R. (2013). *Suburban Planet: Making the World from the Outside*, Cambridge, UK and Medford, MA, Wiley Polity Press.

Kneafsey, M. (2010). 'The region in food – important or irrelevant?', *Cambridge Journal of Regions, Economy and Society*, 3, 177–90.

Ladner, P. (2011). *The Urban Food Revolution: Changing the Way We Feed Cities*, Gabriola Island, New Society Publisher.

Magnaghi, A. (2014). *La Bioregion Urbaine: Petit Traité sur le Territore Bien Commun*, Paris, Eterotopia, France, Rhizome, Routledge.

Moser, C. (1993). *Gender Planning and Development: Theory, Practice and Training*, New York and London, Routledge.

Moser, C. (2014). 'Gender planning and development: revisiting, deconstructing and reflecting', (DPU60 Working Paper Series: Reflections NO. 165/60), Development Planning Unit, London, The Bartlett, University College.

Moser, C. and Moser, A. (2005). 'Gender mainstreaming since Beijing: a review of success and limitations in international institutions', *Gender and Development*, 2, 11–22.

Nussbaum, M. C. (2000). *Women and Human Development: The Capability Approach*, Cambridge, Cambridge University Press.

OECD (Organisation for Economic Co-Operation and Development). (2014). *OECD Regional Outlook 2014: Regions and Cities: Where Policies and People Meet*, Paris, OECD Publishing.

Ostrom, E. (1990). *Governing the Commons: The Evolution of Institutions for Collective Action*, Cambridge, Cambridge University Press.

Parker, B. (2012). 'Gender, cities, and planning', in R. Weber and R. Crane (eds), *The Oxford Handbook of Urban Planning*, Oxford, Oxford University Press, 609–33.

Perrone, C. (2016). 'Grounds for future gendered urban agendas: policy patterns and practice implications', *Town Planning Review*, 87 (5), 589–606.

Poggio, B. (2006). 'Editorial: outline of a theory of gender practices', *Gender, Work and Organization*, 13, 225–33.

Reeves, D. (2012). UN Habitat (2012) Gender and Urban Planning, authored by Dory Reeves, Bonnie Parfitt and Carol Archer.

Roberts, M. (2013). 'Introduction. Concepts, themes and issues in a gendered approach to planning', in I. Sánchez de Madariaga and M. Roberts (eds), *Fair Shared Cities: The Impact of Gender Planning in Europe*, Farnham, Ashgate, 1–18.

Sánchez de Madariaga, I. and Novella, I. (2019). 'A new generation of gender mainstreaming in spatial and urban planning and the new international framework of policies for sustainable development', in B. Zibell, D. Damyanovic and U. Sturm (eds), *Gender Approaches to Spatial Development in Europe: Perspectives, Similarities, Differences*, London and New York, Routledge, 181–203.

Sánchez de Madariaga, I. and Roberts, M. (eds) (2013). *Fair Shared Cities: The Impact of Gender Planning in Europe*, Farnham, Ashgate.

Scheller, M. (2018). *Mobility Justice: The Politics of Movement in an Age of Extremes*, London, Verso Books.

Short, J. R. (2017). *A Research Agenda for Cities*, Cheltenham, Elgar.

Soja, E. (2011). 'Regional urbanisation and the end of the metropolis era', in G. Bridge and S. Watson (eds), *New Companion to the City*, Chichester, Wiley-Blackwell, 679–89.

Stratigaki, M. (2004). 'The co-optation of gender concepts in EU policies: the case of reconciliation of work and family', *Social Politics: International Studies in Gender, State & Society*, 1, 30–56.

Stratigaki, M. (2005). 'Gender mainstreaming vs positive action. An ongoing conflict in EU gender equality policy', *European Journal of Women's Studies*, 2, 165–86.

Sturm, U., Tuggener, S., Damyanovic, D. and Kail, E. (2019). 'Gender sensitivity in neighborhood planning. The example of case studies from Vienna and Zurich', in B. Zibell, D. Damyanovic and U. Sturm (eds), *Gender Approaches to Spatial Development in Europe: Perspectives, Similarities, Differences*, London and New York, Routledge, 124–56.

Viljoen, A. and Bohn, K. (2014). *Second Nature Urban Agriculture: Designing Productive Cities*, London, Routledge.

Viljoen, A. and Wiskerke, J. (2012). *Sustainable Food Planning: Evolving Theory and Practice*, The Netherlands, Wageningen Academic Publisher.

Walby, S. (2005). 'Gender mainstreaming: productive tensions in theory and practice', *Social Politics*, 3, 321–43.

Wardle, J., Haase, A. M., Steptoe, A., Nillapun, M., Jonwutiwes, K. and Bellisle, F. (2004). 'Gender differences in food choice: the contribution of health beliefs and dieting', *Annals of Behavioural Medicine*, 27, 107–16.

Wekerle, G. R. (2004). 'Food justice movements, policy, planning, and networks', *Journal of Planning Education and Research*, 23, 378–86.

Zibell, B., Damyanovic, D. and Sturm, U. (2019). *Gender Approaches to Spatial Development in Europe: Perspectives, Similarities, Differences*, London and New York, Routledge.

17

EPILOGUE

Unifying Difference and Equality Concepts to Buttress Policy

Inés Sánchez de Madariaga

In the introductory chapter of this book, we made an argument stressing how some traditionally feminine values that were historically and culturally developed in the domestic sphere of private life have the potential to transform the public sphere as they become more widely embraced by all, irrespective of gender. We also argued how and why many traditional feminine values are not to be considered as stereotyping or as essentializing women but, instead, as values on their own that anybody can and should uphold.

Because of historical, cultural, and biological reasons, women have been and still are the main providers of care. We wrote in the introduction that the values necessary and inherent to protect, support and care for the life of those who cannot take care of themselves, are the values that could underlie a global shift to a world less predatory with nature, more voluntarily frugal, and more sensitive to the needs of all human beings irrespective of age, gender, race, ethnicity, physical ability, or any other individual or group characteristic that sets persons in positions of vulnerability.

Here, one cautious note on extreme positions needs to be recognized. We should not attribute these capacities only to women, thereby essentializing caring values as intrinsically women's virtues, which would be nothing more than a specific type of double standard and a form of gender bias too commonly found, even among researchers.

Double standards occur when a human attribute or trait is assigned in a prescriptive way to individuals of one sex, while at the same time the attribute is given ontological status and considered to be more important for those of that particular sex. Arguments of this kind were used to criticize the so-called second wave of feminism, or the feminism of difference, some decades ago. They are also being used today by those who, eager to demonstrate that women are equally capable in professional fields, often label as an essentializing stereotype any evidence – even statistical evidence – that women tend to assume tasks that imply caring for others more often than do men.

It is important not to fall into extreme, simplifying, and essentializing interpretations at any point on the spectrum. While attributing caring values as a double standard only to women does reinforce gender stereotypes, it is also important not to fall into opposing arguments which fail to recognize that differences on issues related to the care of others do exists between men and women. The point being that valuing traditional feminine roles and bringing them to the public sphere could help transform political and planning agendas into more sustainable patterns that also bring in greater consideration to the needs of all.

In this postscript I will argue that we need to rebalance current debates between supporters of a feminism of difference that stresses women's issues, with supporters of a feminism of equality that stresses equality between men and women in the workplace.

Rather than looking at the issue from the extremes of each side, which leads to a framework that sets up the problem as an issue of equality *versus* difference, a more nuanced outlook should allow us to set the conceptual discussion in terms of complementarity; that is equality *and* difference as two interrelated, equally important, and inextricable sides of the same coin.

In today's landscape of feminist debates, this might imply a certain reevaluation of feminisms of difference which, in my personal perception, has lost ground with respect to feminisms of equality, both in theoretical discussions and in their practical applications through policy.

Difference vs. Equality as Conceptual Approaches for Gender Policy

Debates addressing gender issues in a number of policy areas including planning oscillate between those who, focusing primarily on issues of difference, stress the specific needs of women, and those who, prioritizing issues of equality, put the main focus on equality in the workplace and the public sphere. In many formulations and many solutions proposed, these two approaches are often contradictory and supporters of each are often in disagreement.

Concepts underlying policy options are important because the shape and impact of the latter often derive from the former, even when these are not made explicit. Approaches based on theories of difference and of equality, although not always made explicit, shape contemporary gender policies in many ways. The divide between those privileging feminisms of difference approaches and those who privilege feminisms of equality is becoming particularly visible as the impact of the #MeToo movement and other political events has created unprecedented public support for gender equality policies in some countries.

One key contribution of gender studies has been the conceptualization of care as an important human activity that needs to be recognized, studied, valued, made visible, and taken into account in policymaking. Care refers to the activities needed for the reproduction of life, including the necessary tasks for the upkeep of the home and for the caring of dependent people: the sick, the young, and the old.

Policy debates on the scope and objectives of recently approved parental permits in Spain and Europe illustrate current discussion between policy approaches based on feminisms of difference and feminisms of equality. In Spain, a recently approved non-transferable, equal maternity and paternity permit grants 100% 16 weeks' paid allowance for each parent, of which the first six are compulsory for both the mother and the father, and the remaining ten are voluntary, but non-transferable to the other parent. This new policy has been adopted by a socialist government, under the initiative of the leftist party Podemos, but with support from parties across the political spectrum including the conservative party, Partido Popular.

Over the years, women's demands to increase, up to 6 months, the length of maternity permits – from 16 weeks; scant if compared with most European countries – were systematically denied on the grounds of lack of funds. By contrast, the current policy has put Spanish fathers at the head of Europe with costly, longer permits than those existing in several much richer Scandinavian countries, including some from among those with the most established and well-funded welfare systems in the continent, like Sweden.

The new policy is mostly based on arguments of equality. The main argument explicitly stated in the regulation is that it will help remove obstacles in women's careers related to maternity, and will additionally incentivize the co-responsibility of fathers in care tasks. By making it compulsory for fathers to take the permit during the first 6 weeks, it is argued, the measure will produce greater involvement of men in care tasks later in life.

Detractors of the policy from within the feminist movement have mainly argued that insistence on non-transferability puts employment center stage rather than maternity and the care of dependents, which are considered primarily a burden for women's careers instead of being valued as key elements of social and individual welfare. They stress that the specific and differential aspects of motherhood, from physical issues of the mother to the physical and emotional ties of mother–child in early life, are substantially different to those of father–child, and are not properly taken into consideration or given their full value and recognition.

In the field of planning, the main debate focuses on the issue of to what extent the daily needs of women in urban space, in their role as "carers" of others (a current fact demonstrated statistically), is or should be the key aspect on which to build gendered approaches to planning. This being the reality of the daily lives of most women, looking at women's needs is de facto looking at gender issues. And responding to these needs will provide better conditions for the realization of care tasks in the city, *regardless* of who *in fact* accomplishes them, whether this is individual men or women who undertake these tasks.

Alternative views stress that planning should instead propose other types of more structural objectives, aiming at transforming gender relations. Some argue that urban planning and design should go beyond looking to the needs and realities of women and contribute to building spaces that can help support wider structural changes in gender relations among men and women. Planning and design should aim at creating physical spaces that are structurally different from what we know today, contributing to a future in which current relationships between the care economy and the formal economy would be transformed.

These two alternative views are discussed by several contributors to three recent reference books on gender, transportation and planning in Europe which illustrate these points (Sánchez de Madariaga and Roberts, 2013; Scholten and Joelsson, 2018; Zibell, Damyanovic and Sturm, 2018).

This debate in some ways mirrors and updates the concepts proposed by Molyneux several decades ago (1985). Molyneux spoke of practical versus strategic needs as underlying options for policy measures in the field of development programs and plans. She did so within a Latin American context but with a theoretical conceptualization that can be appropriately translated for use also in First-World countries and in the specific domain of city planning.

The concept I coined in 2009 as "mobility of care" (Sánchez de Madariaga, 2009, 2013), for instance, was grounded on conceptual approaches to planning that can be considered as primarily based on feminisms of difference—although secondarily, because they also address issues of equality in the workplace. The concept *mobility of care* represents an attempt to provide a tool for a better understanding of the mobility of those persons who have care responsibilities in their everyday life most often compounded with work in paid employment. The mobility of care includes all travel resulting from home and caring responsibilities: escorting others; shopping for daily living, with the exclusion of leisure shopping; household maintenance, organization, and administrative errands, all being different from personal trips for recreation.

These tasks may be realized in the home or in other places and facilities around the city, and they imply the use of transport systems. As societies become richer, the type and number of activities required for the reproduction of life increases, as does the number of locations around the city where they take place, and the need for using transport systems to get to those places.

The concept mobility of care allows one to quantify, qualify, recognize, and make visible all the trips that people make for the upkeep of the home and the care of those who cannot move autonomously in the city. That is, it allows one to better understand the needs of those who take care of others, which are, statistically, the mobility needs of women in the city. By better understanding these mobility needs, it provides the scientific and knowledge base necessary to redefine the priorities of the policy agendas and their means of implementation.

Looking at the specific needs of women has also been the main approach adopted by the city of Vienna, as documented by Elisabeth Irschik and Eva Kail (2013) and Franziska Ullmann (2013) in many publications. Vienna has developed, within a span of slightly more than two decades, a quite significant number of projects, plans and policies that address in practical ways the specific needs in public space, transportation, and housing of those – mainly women – who are responsible for the upkeep of the home and the care of those who cannot move autonomously around the city, being the young, the elderly, the sick.

This approach has been criticized by some as essentializing women and reinforcing gender roles and stereotypes, rather than aiming at transforming gender relations. A main criticism is that by focusing on the specific needs of women arising mostly from maternity, it reinforces the gender roles of women rather than contributing to increasing shared responsibilities of care tasks between men and women, hence supporting a structural transformation of gender relations that would eventually shake the current status quo between the care economy and the formal economy.

Building a Common Conceptual Ground for Equality and Difference

These divergent approaches within the feminist movement and among planning practitioners and academics point to an underlying disagreement on issues related to motherhood and femininity/masculinity. Is stressing the specificity of women particularly through their role as mothers, necessarily an essentializing intent which reinforces stereotypes, gender roles of women and men, and sexual divisions of labor, as critics of the feminism of difference often argue? Or is motherhood a really core experience for women and substantially different from fatherhood, so it needs some kind of specific attention? Does stressing equality in the workplace and the public sphere necessarily imply an insufficient consideration of the realities and values of motherhood and of feminine traditional roles?

Arguments supporting gender mainstreaming in planning need to be based on conceptualizations that support radical equality of women in the workplace and the public sphere, promoting full participation of women, and that also consider, in central ways, the specificity of women's lives, which for most involves motherhood as a core experience.

This postscript does not allow me to fully develop such a conceptual program. However, I will just suggest what could be one among surely many other possible theoretical avenues from which to develop this constructive framework. The writings of philosopher Edith Stein (1996, 2015) are one possible source from which to build deeper levels of understanding that could integrate relevant elements of both perspectives into one coherent argument that takes account of the main problems relevant to both approaches that have implications for planning and transportation.

While it is not possible to summarize her thought in a few paragraphs, key aspects of it are as follows. Stein's discussion of women's professional vocations supports full professionalization of women in any and in all fields of endeavor. This was certainly a radical and even revolutionary assertion for her time, the early 20th century. At the same time, she affirms the existence of a specific feminine professional vocational *ethos*. Both assertions are built into one single intellectual argument which uses concepts with specific meanings.

Important sections of this discussion are particularly relevant for contemporary policies specifically designed to attract women into male-dominated STEM areas in which efforts to attract women students and to keep women professionals have not always yielded significant results. For her, the specific feminine professional vocational *ethos* can manifest through motherhood, through traditionally feminine professions, and through traditionally male professions.

How and in what ways this happens – the specific implications of each of these three paths for women, and, in wider terms, for the work done, the workplace, the professions, the public sphere, and society in general – are some of the issues to look at. Work needs to be done in order to build sound intellectual conceptualizations that can support policy measures addressing both issues of difference and of equality as complementary parts rather than opposing views.

References

Irschik, E. and Kail, E. 2013. "Vienna: Progress towards a Fair Shared City", in I. Sánchez de Madariaga and M. Roberts (Eds.), *Fair Shared Cities. The Impact of Gender Planning in Europe*. Farnham: Ashgate, 193–230.

Molyneux, M. 1985. "Mobilisation without Emancipation? Women's Interests, States and Revolution in Nicaragua", *Feminist Studies* 11(2), 227–254.

Sánchez de Madariaga, I. 2009. "Vivienda, movilidad y urbanismo para la igualdad en la diversidad: ciudades, género y dependencia", *Ciudad y Territorio* XLI(161–162), 581–598.

Sánchez de Madariaga, I. 2013a. "From Women in Transport to Gender in Transport. Challenging Conceptual Frameworks for Improved Policy Making", in *The Gender Issue: Beyond Exclusion*, special issue, *Journal of International Affairs* 67(1), Columbia University, NY, 43–66.

Sánchez de Madariaga, I. 2013b. "The Mobility of Care. Introducing New Concepts in Urban Transportation", in I. Sánchez de Madariaga and M. Roberts (Eds.), *Fair Shared Cities. The Impact of Gender Planning in Europe*. Farnham and Burlington, VT: Ashgate, 33–48.

Sánchez de Madariaga, I. and Roberts, M. (Eds.) 2013. *Fair Shared Cities. The Impact of Gender Planning in Europe*. Farnham and Burlington, VT: Ashgate.

Sánchez de Madariaga, I. and Zucchini, E. 2018. "Measuring Mobilities of Care, a Challenge for Transport Agendas", in C. L. Scholten and T. Joelsson (Eds.), *Integrating Gender into Transport Planning*. New York and London: Springer, 145–173.

Scholten, C. L. and Joelsson, T. (Eds.) 2018. *Integrating Gender into Transport Planning.* New York and London: Springer.

Stein, E. 1996. *Essays on Woman.* Washington, DC: ICS Publications.

Stein, E. 2015. *Obras Completas. The Complete Works of Edith Stein.* 5 vols. Madrid: Editorial Monte Carmelo.

Ullmann, F. 2013. "Choreography of Life", in I. Sánchez de Madariaga and M. Roberts (Eds.), *Fair Shared Cities. The Impact of Gender Planning in Europe.* London and New York: Ashgate, 297–324.

Zibell, B., Damyanovic, D., and Sturm, U. (Eds.) 2018. *Gendered Approaches to Spatial Development in Europe – Perspectives, Similarities and Differences.* New York: Routledge.

INDEX

Page numbers in *italics* and **bold** type refer to information in figures and tables respectively. Those followed by 'n' refer to notes.